Fodor's

LOS ANGELES

Welcome to Los Angeles

Drive for miles between towering palm trees, bodega-lined streets, and Downtown's skyscrapers, and you'll still never discover all of L.A.'s hidden gems. Scratch the surface to find people-watching on Rodeo Drive, historic bars on the Sunset Strip, and the glitz and grime of Hollywood Boulevard. From the trendy Eastside to beachy Santa Monica, experience everything in the city's year-round idyllic weather. As you plan your upcoming travels to Los Angeles, please confirm that places are still open and let us know when we need to make updates by writing to us at editors@fodors.com.

TOP REASONS TO GO

★ **Seeing Stars:** Both through the telescope atop Griffith Park and among the residents of Beverly Hills.

★ **Eating:** From food trucks to fine dining, an unparalleled meal awaits your palate.

★ **Beaches and Boardwalks:** The dream of '80s Venice is alive in California.

★ **Shopping:** Peruse eclectic boutiques or window-shop on Rodeo Drive.

★ **Architecture:** Art deco wonders to Frank Gehry masterpieces abound.

★ **Scenic Drives:** You haven't seen the sunset until you've seen it from a winding L.A. road.

Contents

Fodor's Features

MAPS

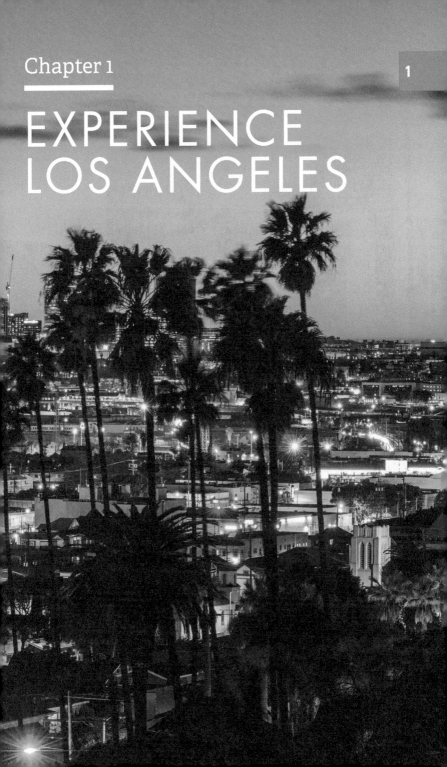

Chapter 1

EXPERIENCE
LOS ANGELES

20 ULTIMATE EXPERIENCES

Los Angeles offers terrific experiences that should be on every traveler's list. Here are Fodor's top picks for a memorable trip.

1 Walt Disney Concert Hall

Designed by Frank Gehry, the curves of this stainless steel-clad masterpiece are a signature of the modern metropolis. The 2,265-seat Disney Hall is home to the Los Angeles Philharmonic. *(Ch. 10)*

2 Disneyland

"The Happiest Place on Earth" continues to delight children and all but the most cynical adults. *(Ch. 14)*

3 Santa Monica Pier

Spend a sunny day beside the Pacific Ocean riding the Ferris wheel and playing dozens of games for prizes at this popular family destination. *(Ch. 4)*

4 Universal Studios Hollywood

Universal is more of a theme park with lots of roller coasters and thrill rides than a backstage pass, though its tour provides a good firsthand look at familiar TV and movie sets. *(Ch. 9)*

5 Los Angeles County Museum of Art

LACMA is the focal point of the museum district along Wilshire Boulevard. Chris Burden's *Urban Light* sculpture, with more than 220 cast-iron street lamps, marks the location. *(Ch. 7)*

6 Venice Beach Boardwalk

The bohemian vibe of this famous boardwalk is constantly threatened by gentrification. Still, the magicians, fortune tellers, and Muscle Beach weight lifters survive. *(Ch. 5)*

7 Grand Central Market

In continuous operation since 1917, this market is a hub for fresh produce, deli staples, and dozens of restaurant vendors that attracts hungry lunch crowds. *(Ch. 10)*

8 Pacific Coast Highway

Nothing epitomizes L.A. more than a drive down the scenic PCH. After taking in the sweeping views, stop at a seafood shack for ahi burgers or fish-and-chips. *(Ch. 3)*

9 The Broad Museum

Philanthropists Eli and Edythe Broad built this striking museum to house their stunning art collection, which features work from Jean-Michel Basquiat and Kara Walker. *(Ch. 10)*

10 TCL Chinese Theatre and the Walk of Fame

When this theater opened in 1927, the tradition of stars imprinting their hands or feet into the cement began. Today, the Walk of Fame runs a mile along Hollywood Boulevard. *(Ch. 8)*

11 Mexican Food

Whether you're searching for authentic Oaxacan mole, fresh ceviche, cheap tacos, or bottomless margaritas, L.A. has unbeatable choices for every type of Mexican food experience. *(Ch. 3–11)*

12 Sunset Boulevard

This avenue began humbly in the 18th century as a route from El Pueblo de Los Angeles to the Pacific. Today, as it passes through West Hollywood, it becomes the sexy and seductive Sunset Strip. *(Ch. 7)*

13 Rodeo Drive

Dominated by exclusive fashion brands, Rodeo Drive is a shoppers' paradise. Along the cobblestoned Via Rodeo, you can drop $1,000 on python pumps or splurge on a $500 sushi dinner. *(Ch. 6)*

14 The Hollywood Sign

It's actually illegal to get up close to one of the city's most iconic images, but there are multiple hiking trails in and around Griffith Park to help you get the perfect pic. *(Ch. 8)*

15 Malibu

The white-sand beaches of Malibu are magnets for surfers, sunbathers, swimmers, and whale-watchers. Spots like Point Dume and Zuma Beach also beckon. *(Ch. 3)*

16 Hollywood Bowl

Nothing compares to spending a summer evening at the Hollywood Bowl. For a true local experience, pack a picnic and don't be afraid to share with your neighbors. *(Ch. 8)*

17 Paramount Pictures

This is the only surviving major studio from Hollywood's golden age. Paramount offers probably the most authentic studio tour, giving you a real sense of the film industry's history. *(Ch. 8)*

18 Koreatown

As the biggest (and many claim best) Koreatown in the country, this L.A. neighborhood wows with its collection of authentic and delicious restaurants, many focusing on Korean BBQ. *(Ch. 10)*

19 Getty Center

On a hillside above Brentwood, the Getty Center houses airy galleries filled with impressionist canvases, Greek antiquities, and French decorative arts. *(Ch. 4)*

20 Griffith Park and Observatory

The country's largest municipal park has plenty of hiking and biking trails, along with its famed observatory offering breathtaking city views. *(Ch. 11)*

WHAT'S WHERE

1 Malibu. Drive up the Pacific Coast Highway to Malibu, where the rich and famous reside, or plop down on the white-sand beaches along the way to spy on sunbathing sea lions and migrating whales deep in the Pacific.

2 Santa Monica, Pacific Palisades, and Brentwood. In Santa Monica, a lively beach scene plays out daily while Brentwood and the Palisades provide a bevy of bougie dining and shopping options.

3 Westside. The Westside is an amorphous part of the city that roughly translates to west of the 405 Freeway. Head to the Venice Boardwalk for the wild and crazy, the Marina for a laid-back boating vibe, Sawtelle for its bustling Japantown, and Culver for Sony Studios, new restaurants, and a great bar scene.

4 Beverly Hills. Go for the glamour, the restaurants, and the scene. Rodeo Drive is particularly good for a look at wretched or ravishing excess.

5 West Hollywood, Fairfax, Mid-Wilshire. West Hollywood is an area for urban indulgences—shopping, restaurants, nightlife—rather than sightseeing.

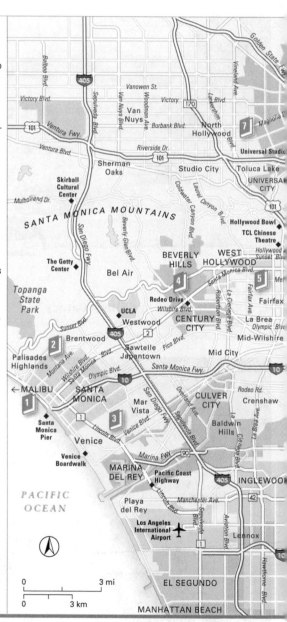

The Fairfax District within WeHo offers loads of shopping options and a wide array of restaurants. Mid-Wilshire is a glorious hodgepodge of manicured lawns and art deco highrises. Here you can also peruse art along Museum Row.

6 Hollywood. Glitzy and tarnished, good and bad—Hollywood is just like the entertainment business itself. The Walk of Fame, TCL Chinese Theatre, Paramount Pictures studio, and the Hollywood Bowl keep the romantic past alive.

7 The Valley. It's a (VERY) large valley that encompasses Burbank, Studio City, North Hollywood, and Universal City. Within that are the Warner Bros. and Universal Studios, the NoHo Arts District, and literally thousands of restaurants. For family fun, go here.

8 Downtown and Koreatown. One of the oldest parts of the city, DTLA shows off spectacular modern architecture. The MOCA and the Broad anchor a world-class art scene, while El Pueblo de Los Angeles, Chinatown, and Little Tokyo reflect the city's diversity. To the west is Koreatown, which boasts some of the best bars and restaurants in the city.

WHAT'S WHERE

9 Los Feliz, Silver Lake, and the Eastside. If you've come to L.A. in search of everything young, cool, and hip, then head east. This is a land of good eats and better booze.

10 Pasadena. Parts of Pasadena are even older than Downtown. It's a quiet, genteel area to visit, with an outstanding arts scene, beautiful craftsman homes, and a pair of exceptional museums.

11 The Beaches. L.A.'s beach spine is littered with surf spots, board-walks, sunset cafés, aquariums, historic sites, and so much more. Driving down the famous Highway 1 will take you through El Segundo, Manhattan Beach, Hermosa Beach, Redondo Beach, San Pedro, and Long Beach.

12 Orange County and Catalina Island. For decades, Orange County was equated with Disneyland, but these days, the OC's beach communities are getting just as much attention, even if they aren't quite as glamor-ous as seen on TV. Coastal spots like Huntington Beach, Newport Harbor, and Laguna Beach (which offers arts festivals and

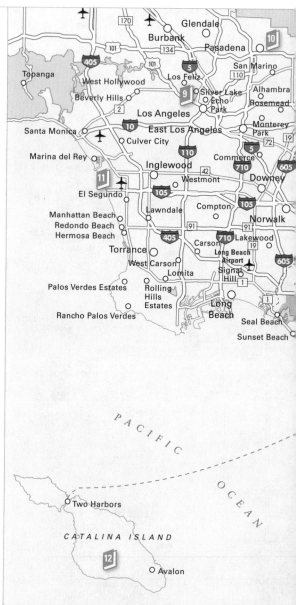

nature preserves) are perfect for chilling out in a beachfront hotel. A short boat ride away is Catalina Island, with its pocket-size town and large nature preserve.Of course, for many, the main attraction in this part of California is Walt Disney's first theme park, Disneyland. The park is a fraction of the size of Florida's Disney World and beloved by fans for its nostalgia factor. You'll want at least a full day to visit, preferably two to comfortably take in all the rides and sights of both Disneyland and Disney California Adventure.

Los Angeles Today

Starstruck. Excessive. Smoggy. Superficial? There's a modicum of truth to each of the adjectives regularly applied to L.A., but the locals dismiss their prevalence as envy from those who aren't as blessed with year-round sunshine. Pop culture does permeate life here, its massive economy employing millions of Southern Californians, but the city where dreams are made accommodates those from all avenues of life.

POLITICS

L.A.'s political scene is completely dominated by Democrats; so much so, that 15 of the county's 18 congressional seats are typically held by the Democratic Party. Locally, the biggest hotbed issue the city faces surrounds housing, or a lack thereof. The latest homeless numbers in Los Angeles have reached apocalyptic levels with close to 70,000 people sleeping on the streets. The city is constantly trying to solve the issue with new shelters, tax hikes, and ordinances, but it's a problem that has only gotten worse throughout the past decade.

DEMOGRAPHICS

Officially, Los Angeles is home to more than 10 million people. Unofficial estimates put the number somewhere between 12 and 15 million. Regardless of the count, the city is one of the most diverse in the country. Nearly half the population is Hispanic or Latinx, the Asian population is more than 15%, and 9% of residents are Black or African American.

WILDFIRES

Every year, wildfires rip through California causing people to lose their lives and their homes. Stories of harrowing escapes are becoming more common than ever. Fortunately, the city of Los Angeles has mostly been spared from massive fire damage (air quality aside), though the dried foliage in Griffith Park and the Santa Monica Mountains keep residents on high alert. Make sure to check local news reports when hiking on hot summer days.

HOLLYWOOD

Hollywood may disappoint tourists looking to overdose on glitz; after all, most of its moviemakers departed for the San Fernando Valley decades ago, leaving the area to languish. Even after the much-hyped debut of the Hollywood & Highland Center, the area remains more gritty than glamorous, but that's part of its charm.

Tourists continue to flock to the region, trodding over the stars on the Hollywood Walk of Fame or seeing how the size of their hand compares to celebrities both living and dead at the TCL Chinese Theatre. It's truly the Times Square of the city, but it's still a must for any first-time visitor to experience.

SCOOTERS AND AIRBNBS

It's no secret that L.A. is a hard town to maneuver without a car, but competing scooter companies—Bird, Lime, and Uber—have popped up throughout the city, especially in tourist-heavy areas on the Westside and in Hollywood. The scooter invasion may have some residents griping that they're discarded on sidewalks like trash, but it's heavenly for the out-of-towner who doesn't want to hoof it along the long stretches between Metro stops.

Meanwhile, another tech solution for tourists is being heavily limited: the Los Angeles City Council has restricted Airbnb rentals. Since 2019, property owners have only been able to list their primary residence (as opposed to one owner renting out multiple properties through the website) and only homes that are not under rent control.

HIP HOODS

First, it was Los Feliz. Then it was Silver Lake. Then it was Echo Park. Now it's Highland Park, Glassell Park, Cypress Park. The cool kids keep going farther and farther northeast. So, if you want to find the best bars in town, you'll have to keep venturing farther afield.

THE FOOD SCENE

Star chefs continue to make their mark in every pocket of Los Angeles. You can head to Chinatown for David Chang's eclectic spot Majordomo or dine in style at Wolfgang Puck's überfamous Beverly Hills hub, Spago. Get carnivorous at chef Curtis Stone's meat-lovers' den Gwen in Hollywood. Or slurp up spaghetti at *Top Chef* alum Antonia Lofaso's Scopa Italian Roots in Venice.

Eating in L.A. remains relatively egalitarian. Even posh places seldom require jackets, so the dress code is casual. Ditto for the menu. (In the city that invented fast food, it's no coincidence that Govind Armstrong flips gourmet burgers at LAX or that Nancy Silverton built her reputation on pizza.) If you want to go budget, you can easily justify chowing down at McDonald's, Carl's Jr., and In-N-Out Burger since they qualify as true local cuisine; they all originated in the Five-County Area.

WHAT'S NEW

After a few delays, the Academy Museum of Motion Pictures finally opened and has slowly become one of the city's leading attractions. The 300,000-square-foot Renzo Piano–designed museum houses stunning cinematic exhibits that tell the stories of movies past, present, and future. The newest installment is the *The Oscars® Experience,* where you can accept an actual Oscar statue and send yourself a video of your excitement on stage. Just next door is the Los Angeles County Museum of Art, which is going through a massive $750 million renovation that is set to be completed in late 2024.

For more cinematic (and gaming) wonders, in 2023 the new *Super Nintendo World* inside Universal Studios opened, and here you can race in *Mario Kart: Bowser's Challenge* and meet your favorite Mario characters face to face. Coming in 2025, however, is the eagerly anticipated Lucas Museum of Narrative Art dedicated to film, video, sculpture, comics, and more. Star Wars fans will have a lot to love here.

On the sports front, Inglewood is slowly becoming the epicenter for L.A. football and basketball fans. SoFi stadium opened for business in 2021 and hosts the Chargers and Rams. Meanwhile, the Clippers are moving into the new Intuit Dome in 2024 (also a new concert venue), helping to reinvigorate the surrounding area with more restaurants, bars, and coffee shops.

Helping to ferry people to Inglewood is the newly opened Crenshaw/LAX line of the Metro, which connects the Expo Line in the north to the Green Line in the south. Commuters can now access Leimert Park and Hyde Park, and eventually, LAX. In 2023, the Purple Line expanded into Mid-City, connecting it with Downtown and beyond. The LA Metro project is gearing for completion in 2028 when the city hosts the Summer Olympic Games. Fingers crossed.

The city has experienced a hotel boom in the past few years. Downtown has seen the addition of The Conrad, The Proper, and Moxy; West Hollywood added The Edition, Hotel Ziggy, and the Pendry; and on the west side boutiques popped up like the Venice V and Found Hotel in Santa Monica.

What to Eat and Drink in Los Angeles

VEGAN FARE
Los Angeles is one of the best places in the country to eat healthy, and for anyone trying to eat less meat, it's overflowing with restaurants catering to vegans. Places like Café Gratitude and Pura Vita are excellent plant-based dining stops.

L.A. HOTDOGS
While every major city in the country has their own take on street hot dogs, L.A.'s Mexican-inspired version is arguably the best. They're wrapped in bacon and topped with grilled onions, bell peppers, ketchup, mustard, mayo, and jalapeños. Look for street carts in areas with a lot of bars—Spring Street and Staples Center in Downtown, Sunset Boulevard in Echo Park, and Normandie Avenue in Koreatown. Historic hot dogs are also a thing, and you can find classics at Tail O' the Pup (from 1946) in West Hollywood or at Pink's Hot Dogs (from 1939) on Melrose Ave.

KOREAN BBQ
Los Angeles claims to have the biggest (and best) Koreatown in the world. So if there's one place you should feast on Korean BBQ—outside of South Korea, that is—it's here. There are so many Korean BBQ joints in the city, in fact, that it's hard to pick the best ones, though Park's BBQ and Magal certainly have our votes. If you like Korean BBQ and you enjoyed those street tacos, then you might be ready for Korean BBQ tacos, which is one of the few culinary creations that originated in La La Land. They're exactly what it sounds like—tacos but with Korean BBQ meats, and the best place to get them is from one of Roy Choi's legendary Kogi food trucks. To find a location, go to ⊕ *kogibbq.com.*

ORGANIC JUICE AND SMOOTHIES
Make fun of L.A.'s healthy juice obsession all you want, but they're actually surprisingly delicious, not to mention nutritious. Don't knock it until you try it. Naturewell and Erewhon Market are good, popular spots to sample them.

STREET TACOS
This is a beautifully simple dish: grilled meat (*al pastor*, chorizo, or carne asada) with chopped cilantro and onion, wrapped in corn or flour tortillas, drizzled with lime and salsa. They're not only delicious, but cheap at $1 to $3 apiece. Every Angeleno has their own go-to spot, usually a stand or a truck, so ask your favorite local for recommendations. Mariscos Jalisco is always a good choice with multiple locations, including Boyle Heights, Downtown, Mid-City, and Pomona.

ELOTE
This Mexican corn concoction is essentially just grilled corn smothered with butter, *crema fresca* (or mayo), cotija, chili powder, and lime then served on a cob or in a cup. But it's a delightful assault on your taste buds and a favorite Los Angelenos snack. Keep an eye out for street carts that tout it or take a chance at one of L.A.'s many farmers' markets.

Korean BBQ

FILIPINO FOOD

The city is teeming with Filipino food joints that either champion traditional Filipino dishes like pork adobo, kare-kare, and pinakbet, or boast modern takes. For a traditional take, go to Max's in Glendale. For a soulful version, Big Boi in Sawtelle Japantown is a good spot. Regardless of your choice, leave room for dessert, as they're to die for.

IN-N-OUT

No L.A. food list is complete without the legendary In-N-Out. "Where's the closest In-N-Out" is asked by just about every tourist the moment they arrive. Not that we blame them—In-N-Out burgers and fries are made fresh and made to order, which is why they're so good in the first place. But which location should you go to? Any of them! Whether it's the one near LAX as soon as you leave the airport or in Hollywood, which gets a lot of traffic.

FRENCH DIP SANDWICH

There's an ever-present debate about where the legendary French Dip sandwich was created. But whether you're a fan of Cole's French Dip in the middle of Downtown or Philippe the Original in Chinatown, know that both have over 100 years of history and create savory versions that make the debate moot.

CHICKEN AND WAFFLES

Angelenos are in love with the magical combo of chicken and waffles. The craze really took off in the 1970s when Roscoe's House of Chicken and Waffles opened in Hollywood. Today, you can find the tasty mix at multiple restaurants like the Broad-adjacent Otium in Downtown or at A.O.C. in West Hollywood, which makes a Spanish version with cornmeal waffles.

SUSHI

People understandably think of L.A. as a Mexican-food city, but the sushi here is also world-class. There are hundreds and hundreds of options to choose from, such as counter spots Hide or Sushi Gen, the omakase magicians at Sushi|Bar or Sushi Ginza Onodera, or sceney joints like Katsuya.

CRAFT BEER

As one of the most creative cities in the world, it shouldn't be shocking that L.A. artisans have been doling out incredibly unique craft beers. There are respectable spots all over the city—check out Highland Park Brewery, Monkish Brewing Co., and Brouwerij West for some of the tastiest.

The Best Beaches in Los Angeles

EL MATADOR BEACH

Throngs of people flock to Malibu's worst-kept secret, from selfie-taking tourists to locals hoping for quiet spots to call their own. But don't worry about the crowds. El Matador's sweeping, sea-meets-land panoramas make up for it.

HERMOSA BEACH

Blazing orange sunsets draw sunning crowds and shutterbugs, but this is, without a doubt, a surfing beach. Even its famous landmark—the statue of Tim Kelly riding a swell—is a declaration of this fact.

SURFRIDER BEACH

There are two sets of people who frequent the sandy Malibu outpost—the surf nuts (hence the name) and the anglers.

WILL ROGERS STATE BEACH

This stretch in Pacific Palisades is known for its epic sunsets. Out of L.A.'s top beaches, Will Rogers is also probably the quietest.

ZUMA BEACH

On summer weekends, you'll be hard-pressed to find a good place to lay your blanket, but this popular Malibu beach is 2 miles of gorgeous zigzagging shore.

VENICE BEACH

Even though Venice is now shockingly expensive, a colorful, artistic past still lingers. Along the boardwalk, vibrant street art adorns the modern retail and gastronomic spaces. Watch out for the tech bros that have taken over the neighborhood.

POINT DUME

Walk along the trail that meanders through this state beach and nature reserve, and you'll often see waves crashing against the wind-carved bluff, tide pools, the occasional migrating whale, and one of the most epic panoramas in Southern California.

Manhattan Beach

LEO CARRILLO STATE PARK

This is a tale of two beaches. When the tide is in, it's a serene spot to gaze at the sea. When out, it's for those seeking exploration—that's when the tide pools and caves are unveiled. Camping is allowed, so pitch a tent and stay awhile.

MANHATTAN BEACH

A day at this beach might involve taking your cruiser for a spin along the bike trail, a bit of retail therapy, and a nosh at a restaurant serving freshly caught seafood.

DOCKWEILER STATE BEACH

Is there a dreamier way of topping off your day at the beach than a bonfire at twilight? Beach bonfires are largely illegal in L.A., but at Dockweiler's 3.7-mile stretch, lighting up isn't just permitted, it's practically encouraged. It's for this reason that the beach is almost always a scene where twenty- and thirty-somethings roast marshmallows and guzzle beer.

The Best Famous Film Locations in Los Angeles

GRIFFITH PARK OBSERVATORY
Movie buffs will recognize this building in countless films like *Rebel Without a Cause* with James Dean (there's even a James Dean bust outside), *Charlie's Angels: Full Throttle,* and recent (almost) best picture Oscar winner, *La La Land.*

MILLENNIUM BILTMORE HOTEL
A grande dame of L.A.'s Downtown hospitality scene, the hotel was opened in 1923 and was once the home of the Academy Awards ceremony. It's also made appearances in movies like *Ghostbusters, Beverly Hills Cop,* and *Cruel Intentions.*

CIRCUS LIQUOR
If you happen to be hanging out in Burbank after a tour at the Warner Bros. lot, head over to Circus Liquor, which is known for its 32-foot clown sign. More famously, however, it's the parking lot where Cher Horowitz was mugged in *Clueless.* "It's an Alaïa!"

BEVERLY WILSHIRE HOTEL
This iconic hotel was built in 1928 and has hosted the likes of Elvis, John Lennon, and Barack Obama. But it's mostly known as the setting for *Pretty Woman,* starring Julia Roberts. Fans of the movie can book the "Pretty Woman for a Day" experience at the hotel.

POINT DUME
Point Dume and Westward Beach are constantly in the movies. There's a good chance on any given weekday that you may spot a film crew here. It's been used in *The Big Lebowski* and *Iron Man.* But its most famous claim to fame: the iconic ending of the original *Planet of the Apes.*

THE WESTIN BONAVEN-TURE HOTEL
Another behemoth Downtown hotel, the Bonaventure is actually the biggest in L.A. with more than 1,300 rooms. Its unique cylindrical towers have starred in a bevy of films. California's former governor, Arnold Schwarzenegger, rode a horse into the glass elevator in *True Lies.*

GAMBLE HOUSE
Head up to Pasadena and check out Doc Brown's house, a stunning example of American Craftsman style. Close your eyes, and you can picture Michael J. Fox wearing an orange windbreaker vest as he runs up to the front door in *Back to the Future.*

USC CAMPUS
The University of Southern California is a private school known for its football team and stunning campus that also houses one of the best film schools in the country. So it shouldn't come as a surprise that a number of its graduates and wannabe attendees have taken time to film here in movies like *Legally Blonde* and *The Graduate.*

BRADBURY BUILDING
Built in 1893, this DTLA architectural marvel is like an M.C. Escher painting come to life. With a series of interlocking wrought-iron stairs and caged elevators, the Bradbury Building has been featured in *500 Days of Summer, Double Indemnity, D.O.A.,* and most famously, *Blade Runner.*

10 Best Celebrity Hangouts in Los Angeles

CAFÉ GRATITUDE LARCHMONT

Round out your L.A. vacation with a plant-based meal at local chain Café Gratitude. For a celeb sighting, head to their Larchmont Boulevard location where Jake Gyllenhaal and Beyoncé obligingly declare what they're grateful for before digging in.

THE HOLLYWOOD ROOSEVELT

The Hollywood Roosevelt is one of L.A.'s oldest hotels, and has hosted numerous celebrities and dignitaries in its Spanish Colonial Revival rooms. Set in the heart of Hollywood, it offers a convenient location as well as a number of watering holes, including Tropicana Bar next to the pool.

PINZ BOWLING CENTER

For a bit of family-friendly fun, head to Pinz in Studio City, where bowling is more than just a game, it's also a neon- and black-light party. Celebrities often pop in here for bowling night, from A-listers like Vin Diesel and Jessica Alba to performers like Bruno Mars and Missy Elliott.

THE GROVE

L.A. may be strewn with outdoor malls, but it's The Grove that gets the highest billing, not just for its collection of mid- to high-end shops and restaurants, but also for its next-door neighbor, the Farmers Market. It's also one of the best places to see stars like Lena Headey, Zendaya, and Mario Lopez.

NOBU MALIBU

Nobu is a known A-list hot spot that's hosted everyone from Keanu Reeves to Kaia Gerber. Even if you don't spot a star, it's still worth the trip for its impeccable sushi and sashimi. Be warned, though: mingling with A-listers doesn't come cheap.

TOSCANA

Upscale Brentwood is home to many celebrities, and rustic trattoria Toscana is one of their neighborhood haunts. It may not be L.A.'s best Italian restaurant—for that, check out Osteria Mozza—but for star sightings, it's your best bet.

CHATEAU MARMONT

The Chateau Marmont is possibly L.A.'s best-known celebrity haunt. Come for brunch in the garden terrace or drop in at night for the Hollywood-inspired cocktails. Photos are not allowed.

Catch

CRAIG'S

A West Hollywood dining staple, Craig's plain facade provides a safe haven for the movie industry's most important names and well-known faces like John Legend and Chrissy Teigen. Just keep in mind this joint is always busy, so you might not even get a table. It's a good thing the food is worth the effort.

CATCH

Secure a table at the flora-cluttered Catch in West Hollywood and rub elbows with the likes of David Beckham and the Jenner-Kardashian clan. This eatery is as L.A. as you can get, with its alfresco setting, vegan and gluten-free offerings, and locally and sustainably grown ingredients.

RUNYON CANYON

Out of L.A.'s numerous beautiful hiking spots, Runyon Canyon gets the biggest share of celebrity regulars, probably because it's strategically tucked between the Hollywood Hills, where many stars live, and the Sunset Strip. It's also a great venue for getting some fresh air, not to mention an ideal spot to take panoramic sunset photos.

Best Historic Restaurants in Los Angeles

The Musso & Frank Grill

COLE'S

There's a fight in Los Angeles over who created the French Dip sandwich. The first contender is Cole's, whose sign on the door says they're the originator of the salty, juicy, melt-in-your-mouth meats. The restaurant opened in 1908 and today is still going strong with dark lighting, delicious sandwiches, and a secret speakeasy called the Varnish hidden in the back.

PHILLIPE'S

Also opened in 1908, Phillipe's is the second restaurant to claim ownership of the French Dip. Owner Philippe Mathieu claimed that the sandwich was invented in 1918 when he accidentally dropped the roll into a vat of hot jus and the customer said he didn't care. It was so good, he came back the next day for more. The French Dip sandwich was coined because of the dipping into the jus and because of Mathieu's French heritage or possibly because the customer was French. No one actually knows, but their sandwiches are incredible.

THE MUSSO & FRANK GRILL

This classic steak house opened in 1919 by Frank Toulet, Joseph Musso, and French chef Jean Rue. The

eatery quickly became a hot spot for A-list guests like Charlie Chaplin, Gary Cooper, Marilyn Monroe, Elizabeth Taylor, and even F. Scott Fitzgerald who allegedly proofread his novels in the booths. Today the restaurant is known for perfect martinis, red tux–wearing waiters, leather booths, and sizzling steaks.

ORIGINAL PANTRY CAFÉ
Opened in 1924 by Dewey Logan, this classic diner claims to have never closed in the entirety of its run and is currently owned by former L.A. mayor Richard Riordan. Today, it closes on Mondays and Tuesdays and has more limited hours, but the diner still serves American food for breakfast, lunch, and dinner, and is known for cakes, pies, steaks, and chops. The classic establishment is also a Los Angeles historic cultural monument.

BAY CITIES
Considered the best sandwich shop in L.A., this Italian deli has been open since 1925 and is home to the famous Godmother, a signature sandwich made with prosciutto, ham, capicola, mortadella, Genoa salami, and provolone cheese. The restaurant doubles as an Italian market where you can get everything from meats and cheeses to wine and beer.

CANTER'S
Opened in 1931, Canter's is your classic Jewish deli, through and through. In front you can buy freshly baked breads and pastries, while the enormous restaurant offers everything from giant sandwiches to matzo ball soup 24 hours a day. In addition to the food, there's also the Kibbitz Room, which features live music and comedy throughout the week.

EL COYOTE
Blanche and George March opened El Coyote in 1931 and they chose the name because the word is the same in English and Spanish. The family-friendly Mexican restaurant is one of the oldest in town and offers up all the standard nachos, burritos, and enchiladas. If it's on the menu, make sure you get the ostrich tacos—they're one of a kind.

PINK'S HOT DOGS
Since it opened in 1939 by Paul and Betty Pink, this ultrafamous hot dog stand has had lines around the block filled with Angelenos and tourists alike. Pink's is best known for its chili dogs as well as being open until 2 am on weekends.

Under the Radar
Los Angeles

THE LAST BOOKSTORE

Built inside an abandoned bank, this Instagram-worthy book paradise is a two-floor behemoth with more than 250,000 books, old and new, including rare first editions. As you wind through the maze of shelves, you'll be surprised to find tucked-away shops with curios, art, and even yarn.

WATTS TOWERS

It's probably not on most tourists' top lists, but that's a mistake considering the Watts Towers is on the U.S. National Register of Historic Places, a U.S. National Historic Landmark, a California Historical Landmark, and a Los Angeles Historic-Cultural Monument. The towers were built over 33 years ago by Italian immigrant Simon Rodia between 1921 and 1954 and consist of 17 interlaced iron spirals with mosaics and other architectural features.

BRONSON CAVES

Located in the southwest section of Griffith Park, the Bronson Caves are the remnants of an old quarry that was used in the early 1900s. Fans of the original '60s *Batman* TV show might recognize this spot as the Batcave.

THE MAGIC CASTLE

Up on a hill, just north of Hollywood Boulevard is a Victorian mansion that is home to the Academy of Magical Arts. Inside this secret spot is a magician's Shangri-La filled with multiple bars and stages. In order to get in, you need to be invited by a member, but there is a work-around. If you stay at the Magic Castle Hotel next door, they can get you inside without any hocus-pocus.

THE CECIL HOTEL

Fans of the macabre will find lots to love when they learn about the history of Downtown L.A.'s most notorious hotel. Originally built in 1924, the hotel was once home to multiple serial killers, including the Night Stalker, and the spot of many mysterious deaths, including suicides and unsolved murders. The most recent occurred only a few years ago when they found the remains of a tourist inside the hotel's water tower. The hotel was converted to low-income housing so be respectful of residents and keep your picture-taking to the outside.

MARILYN MONROE'S GRAVE

The world's fascination with Marilyn Monroe, the most famous blonde bombshell in Hollywood history, continues decades after her death. That fascination even carries over to Monroe's final resting place, which is in a hallway of aboveground crypts at the Pierce Brothers Westwood Village Memorial Park and Mortuary. While you're there, you can also find other luminaries like Truman Capote, Billy Wilder, Rodney Dangerfield, Jack Lemmon, and many others.

BINOCULARS BUILDING

Frank Gehry is known around the world for his architectural master-pieces. In L.A. alone he's

responsible for multiple houses and buildings like the Gehry Residence, Loyola Law School, and Walt Disney Hall. But one of his most interesting creations is the Binoculars Building, a quirky Venice spot that is exactly as advertised: a giant set of binoculars. The project was originally designed for the Chiat/Day advertising agency and today is home to Google's main L.A. office.

BARNSDALL ART PARK
In East Hollywood is a hidden-away park that happens to be a Los Angeles Historic-Cultural Monument and National Historic Landmark that features the Hollyhock House, a Frank Lloyd Wright masterpiece. Named after Aline Barnsdall, an oil heiress who commissioned the Wright work in 1915, the park today is a destination for art, architecture, and a city getaway. During summer months, the park hosts a Friday night wine tasting event where Angeleno's can picnic on the lawn with glasses of Chardonnay while watching the setting sun.

PETERSEN AUTOMOTIVE MUSEUM
Car lovers will salivate over the insane collection at this museum set right on Museum Row in the Miracle Mile section of L.A. But what tourists may not know is that beyond the standard museum exhibitions, there's a secret vault that has more than 250 additional vehicles that are some of the coolest and most-rare automotive treasures in the world.

HOLLYWOOD FOREVER CEMETERY
The most famous celebrity burial ground around is without question the Hollywood Forever Cemetery. Built in 1899, the cemetery is home to Judy Garland, Bugsy Siegel, Cecil B. DeMille, and many others. There are tours of the space that last around two hours where you can discover lots of history and a few mysteries. The cemetery is also known for movie screenings and concerts.

SPADENA HOUSE
Otherwise known as the Witch's House in Beverly Hills, the Spadena House has an interesting history. First built on the Willat Studios lot in 1920, the house was physically moved to its current ritzy location in 1924. The house is not open for tourists, but the fairy tale–like appearance is viewable from the street for onlookers to snap pics. Movie buffs will also recognize it from a background shot in the film *Clueless*.

Los Angeles with Kids

With seemingly endless sunny days, Angeleno kids almost never have to play indoors. There are a few things to keep in mind, however, when navigating the city with little ones: if possible, avoid the freeways by exploring no more than one neighborhood each day, and remember that you can never have too much sunscreen—L.A. parents don't leave home without the stuff.

Of course, the top reason many families come to the L.A. area is to visit Disneyland. Experience all the classic attractions that you may recall from your own childhood visit, such as the "It's a Small World" ride, a meet-and-greet with Tinkerbell, or a Mickey Mouse home tour, who, unlike less amenable celebrities, makes a daily appearance for fans. But there's plenty more to see and do.

HEAD UNDER THE SEA

Head down to the **Aquarium of the Pacific** in Long Beach to learn tons of interesting facts about the Pacific Ocean. On display are shimmering schools of fish, a swaying kelp forest, a shark lagoon featuring more than 150 varieties, and a tropical reef habitat filled with zebra sharks, porcupine puffers, and a large blue Napoleon wrasse.

COMMUNE WITH NATURE

Catch a film at the seven-story IMAX theater or an ever-changing array of science exhibits at the **California Science Center.** Just down the road is the **Natural History Museum,** where kids can explore everything from diamonds to the vast dinosaur hall. In spring, there's the outdoor butterfly habitat, fittingly named the Butterfly Pavilion, which makes way for the Spider Pavilion come fall.

WALK IN THE PARK

Griffith Park is the largest municipal park and urban wilderness area in the United States, and the kids will go wild for the pony rides and the classic 1926 merry-go-round (often closed so check ahead). But the pièce de résistance is the Griffith Park and Southern Railroad, a circa-1940s miniature train that travels through an old Western town and a Native American village. Other highlights are the Los Angeles Zoo and the Griffith Observatory, an L.A. icon in its own right.

LEARN BY DOING

Little ones can pan for gold in a small creek, play Spider-Man on a weblike climber, or race around a trike track at the **Kidspace Children's Museum.** Indoor activities include a walk-through kaleidoscope, two climbing towers—one mimicking raindrops, the other modeled after a wisteria vine, a bug diner (think banana worm bread and roasted cricket pizza), and a contraption that lets kids generate their very own earthquake.

HIT THE BEACH

The best way to check out **Santa Monica Beach** is by renting bikes or roller skates at any one of the shacks on the Strand (a stretch of concrete boardwalk that snakes along the beach toward Venice). Some must-sees along the way: the roller dancers of Venice Beach, the bodybuilders of Muscle Beach, and the Santa Monica Pier, a 100-year-old structure that's home to a vintage 1920s carousel, an oversize Ferris wheel, and old-time amusement park games. After hitting the beach, drive over to the pedestrian-only Third Street Promenade to grab a bite and do some shopping.

Sports in Los Angeles

BASEBALL

Los Angeles Angels of Anaheim. The Angels often contend for the top slot in the Western Division of pro baseball's American League. ⊠ *Angel Stadium of Anaheim, 2000 E. Gene Autry Way, Anaheim* ☎ *714/940–2000* ⊕ *www.angelsbaseball. com.*

Los Angeles Dodgers. The Dodgers take on their National League rivals at one of major league baseball's most comfortable ballparks, Dodger Stadium. ⊠ *Dodger Stadium, 1000 Elysian Park Ave., Echo Park* ✛ *Exit off I–110, Pasadena Fwy.* ☎ *323/224–1507* ⊕ *www.dodgers.com.*

BASKETBALL

Los Angeles Clippers. L.A.'s "other" pro basketball team, the Clippers, was formerly an easy ticket, but these days the club routinely sells out its home games. The team is planning to move to a new home in Inglewood, the Intuit Dome, in time for the 2024-2025 season. ⊠ *Crypto.com Arena, 1111 S. Figueroa St., Downtown* ☎ *213/742–7100* ⊕ *www. nba.com/clippers* Ⓜ *Pico.*

Los Angeles Lakers. The team of pro-basketball champions Magic, Kareem, Shaq, and Kobe had slipped in recent years, but thanks to LeBron's arrival, excitement has been renewed, championships restored, and seats are packed. ⊠ *Crypto.com Arena, 1111 S. Figueroa St., Downtown* ☎ *310/426–6000* ⊕ *www.nba.com/lakers* Ⓜ *Pico.*

Los Angeles Sparks. The women's pro basketball team has made it to the WNBA playoffs more than a dozen times in the past two decades. ⊠ *Crypto.com Arena, 1111 S. Figueroa St., Downtown* ☎ *310/426–6031* ⊕ *www.wnba.com/ sparks* Ⓜ *Pico.*

University of California at Los Angeles. The University of California at Los Angeles Bruins play at Pauley Pavilion on the UCLA campus. ⊠ *Pauley Pavilion, 301 Westwood Plaza, Westwood* ☎ *310/825– 2101* ⊕ *www.uclabruins.com.*

University of Southern California. The Trojans of the University of Southern California play at the Galen Center. ⊠ *Galen Center, 3400 S. Figueroa St., Downtown* ☎ *213/740–4672* ⊕ *www.usctrojans.com.*

FOOTBALL

The Los Angeles Rams began playing home games at the L.A. Memorial Coliseum in 2016, and the Los Angeles Chargers joined them in town in 2018, although they claimed the Dignity Health Sports Park as their home field. Since 2021, both call the brand-new SoFi Stadium in Inglewood home sweet home.

UCLA Bruins. The UCLA Bruins pack 'em in at the Rose Bowl. ⊠ *Rose Bowl, 1001 Rose Bowl Dr., Pasadena* ☎ *626/577– 3100* ⊕ *www.uclabruins.com.*

USC Trojans. The USC Trojans play at the L.A. Memorial Coliseum, both a state and federal historic landmark. ⊠ *L.A. Memorial Coliseum, 3911 S. Figueroa St., Downtown* ☎ *213/740–4672* ⊕ *wwwl. usctrojans.com* Ⓜ *Expo/Vermont.*

HOCKEY

Anaheim Ducks. The Anaheim Ducks push the puck at Honda Center. They became the first Southern California team to win the Stanley Cup, in 2007. ⊠ *Honda Center, 2695 E. Katella Ave., Anaheim* ☎ *877/945–3946* ⊕ *www.nhl.com/ducks.*

L.A. Kings. The National Hockey League's L.A. Kings clinched the Stanley Cup for the first time in 2012, and in 2014 they won it again against the New York Rangers. ⊠ *Crypto.com Arena, 1111 S. Figueroa St., Downtown* ☎ *213/742–7100* ⊕ *www.lakings.com* Ⓜ *Pico.*

What to Watch and Read Before You Go

AMERICAN CRIME STORY: THE PEOPLE VERSUS O.J. SIMPSON

With the backdrop of race relations and police brutality in L.A. in the 1990s, *American Crime Story: The People Versus OJ Simpson* retells the cultural phenomenon that was the trial of OJ Simpson for the murder of his wife Nicole Brown Simpson and her friend Ron Goldman. The series won multiple Emmy awards, including Outstanding Lead Actress for Sarah Paulson's portrayal of Marcia Clark and Outstanding Lead Actor for Courtney B. Vance's portrayal of Johnnie Cochran.

BEVERLY HILLS 90210

For the more glamorous side of L.A. life, this 1990s teen drama is the reason everyone knows at least one Los Angeles zip code. It centers around a group of high school friends as they grow up, grow apart, and come back together.

THE BIG LEBOWSKI

A Coen Brothers masterpiece, *The Big Lebowski* is a tale of mistaken identity. The Dude (Jeff Bridges) is an L.A. slacker who gets mixed up in a tale of murder, pornography, nihilists, and more when people think he's a millionaire. The tale winds through Los Angeles and into Malibu, where The Dude is no longer welcome.

BOJACK HORSEMAN

This Netflix animated show is about a washed-up TV star from the '80s and '90s suffering from depression and addiction in Hollywood. The surreal animation imagines humans and animals living and working together (Bojack is actually a horse), and yet the show does a fantastic job tackling myriad social issues like depression, anxiety, and addiction, while also critiquing L.A. culture and the entertainment industry as a whole.

BOYZ N THE HOOD

A striking look at South Central Los Angeles, *Boyz n the Hood* follows the exploits of a group of high schoolers as they deal with the temptations of sex and drugs, gang violence, and family dynamics. The movie, starring Cuba Gooding Jr., Ice Cube, Angela Bassett, and Lawrence Fishburne shows another side of L.A. rarely seen in movies before.

CHINATOWN

In this classic film noir, a young private eye (Jack Nicholson) in Depression-era Los Angeles gets in over his head with a client's case involving her husband's death and the city's sketchy water rights dealings. Incorporating fictionalized details of L.A.'s historic water wars, it's a tale of corruption and mystery.

THE FRESH PRINCE OF BEL-AIR

The ultimate fish-out-of-water comedy, *The Fresh Prince of Bel-Air* is about Will (Will Smith) who moves from the rough streets of Philadelphia to the stunning confines of Bel-Air. The classic comedy deals with issues of family dynamics, class warfare, racism, and more in a very light-hearted yet warm-hearted way (and with one of the best sitcom theme songs of all time).

GENTEFIED

This L.A.-based TV show is about three Latino cousins who run their grandfather's taco shop in Boyle Heights as the neighborhood goes through rapid gentrification. The show's satire focuses on how L.A. neighborhoods can change on a dime while also exploring the Latinx experience in the city.

INSECURE

Starring stand-out performer Issa Rae, *Insecure* follows the life of Issa and Molly, two Black, single women trying o navigate their careers and love lives in Los Angeles. The biting comedy tackles ssue of race, class, and more through the eyes of young women in the biggest city in America.

LA LA LAND

An ode to classic Hollywood tales like Singin' in the Rain, La La Land idealizes the entertainment industry and reveals the Faustian bargains many actors are forced to make in order to succeed. The film centers around a love story of two up-and-comers: Ryan Gosling playing a jazz musician, and Emma Stone as a wannabe movie star, both of whom are forced to grapple with the ultimate question of "What if?"

MULHOLLAND DRIVE

Surreal, psychotic, and artsy, David Lynch's Mulholland Drive paints L.A. as a city of scary fun house turns that blur the lines between reality and cuts from a movie. Such dichotomies exist as well in the two main characters: Betty (Naomi Watts), the blond Midwesterner fresh to L.A. and full of dreams, and Rita, an amnesiac whose life seems to be shrouded in violence and mystery.

ONCE UPON A TIME IN HOLLYWOOD

Quentin Tarantino writes and directs this retelling of the Charles Manson murders through the eyes of a washed-up movie star played by Leonardo DiCaprio and his stunt double played by Brad Pitt. Like in other films by Tarantino, it's a reimagining of history that lets viewers ponder what would have happened if certain events during the end of Hollywood's golden age took place in a slightly different way.

SINGIN' IN THE RAIN

In this classic film, two stars of the silent film era, Don Lockwood (Gene Kelly) and Lina Lamont (Jean Hagen), have to confront the advent of talkies. Through the help of his friend Cosmo (Donald O'Connor) and love interest Kathy Selden (Debbie Reynolds), Lockwood embraces the new format and sings and dances his way into the future, with Selden along for the ride. It's the perfect film to capture Hollywood's golden age.

SUNSET BOULEVARD

This 1950s Billy Wilder classic is a wild ride and entertaining glimpse into the film business and its eccentric characters. A has-been star and a young screenwriter hope to use each other in some way, while things get more complicated—proving that what happens behind the scenes in Hollywood isn't the same as what appears on the big screen.

TANGERINE

Shot entirely with an iPhone camera, this indie film explores the streets of Hollywood with a close lens on a few characters. Recently out of prison, a transgender sex worker tries to track down her pimp and his new girlfriend with the help of a friend. It's hard to explain just how much light, humor, and beauty fills this film—you just have to see it for yourself.

THE BIG SLEEP BY RAYMOND CHANDLER

In this classic noir crime novel, L.A.-based detective Philip Marlowe is hired to solve a blackmail case, but gets entwined with double-crosses, surprises, and disappearances. The book has been adapted for film and TV multiple times including the 1946 version starring Humphrey Bogart and a 1978 version starring Robert Mitchum.

What to Watch and Read Before You Go

HELTER SKELTER BY VINCENT BUGLIOSI

Vincent Bugliosi was the prosecutor in the trial of Charles Manson and this book is his firsthand account of the entire story. The Manson murders took place in 1969 in Los Angeles and have been recounted by multiple books and movies, but Bugliosi's is the most chilling and best-selling of any true crime book in history.

IF HE HOLLERS LET HIM GO BY CHESTER HIMES

Considered to be a protest novel, the book follows an African American shipyard worker in L.A. during World War II. The novel delves into issues of racism, classism, and even communism.

INHERENT VICE BY THOMAS PYNCHON

Taking place in Los Angeles in the 1970s, this detective novel follows the exploits of Larry "Doc" Sportello with the backdrop of the Manson family trials. The story follows Doc as he tries to find his missing former girlfriend in the midst of drugs, gambling, and the city's counterculture. The book was turned into a movie starring Joaquin Phoenix and directed by Paul Thomas Anderson.

PLAY IT AS IT LAYS BY JOAN DIDION

This terse novel by author Joan Didion delves into the mental breakdown of an actress and the dichotomy of the glitz and glamour of Hollywood with the grittier side of the city in the 1960s. The book was turned into a 1972 movie starring Anthony Perkins.

THE REVOLT OF THE COCKROACH PEOPLE BY OSCAR ZETA ACOSTA

This story about Chicano radicalization in East Los Angeles is based on real events. The protagonist lawyer is based on Oscar Zeta Acosta himself, an author, activist, and lawyer/politician with his own fascinating life (and mysterious disappearance), and a key player in the Chicano movement.

THE RIOT WITHIN: MY JOURNEY FROM REBELLION TO REDEMPTION BY RODNEY KING AND LAWRENCE J. SPAGNOLA

In Los Angeles in 1992, the world was appalled by the video of police officers beating Rodney King on the side of the road. The beating was followed by the infamous L.A. riots that ravaged the city, but also brought media attention to the realities of police violence against Black men and women. Rodney King's autobiography not only recounts the incident, but also his life leading up to that pivotal moment and his role as a civil rights figure afterward.

SHANGHAI GIRLS BY LISA SEE

Two sisters from Shanghai begin the novel as young women celebrated for their beauty in a sophisticated, international city—but all this works against them when they are forced into marriage by their father and must leave a now war-torn Shanghai for a new life in L.A. Set in the late 1930s, at the brink of change and revolution, this novel mixes historical events, revolution, and culture clashes with themes about womanhood and friendship.

THE WHITE BOY SHUFFLE BY PAUL BEATTY

Dealing with issues of race, identity, and sexuality, The White Boy Shuffle is a coming-of-age novel about an African American poet who recounts his personal history, taking place in Santa Monica. The satirical novel focuses on the idea of the Black Messiah and Black representation.

Chapter 2

TRAVEL SMART

Updated by
Paul Feinstein

POPULATION:
4 million in the city;
10 million countywide

LANGUAGE:
English

$ CURRENCY:
U.S. dollar

AREA CODES:
310, 323, 213, 424

⚠ EMERGENCIES:
911

DRIVING:
On the right

⚡ ELECTRICITY:
120–240 v/60 cycles;
plugs have two or three
rectangular prongs

⏱ TIME:
Three hours behind New York

⊕ WEB RESOURCES:
www.discoverlosangeles.com
www.lacity.org

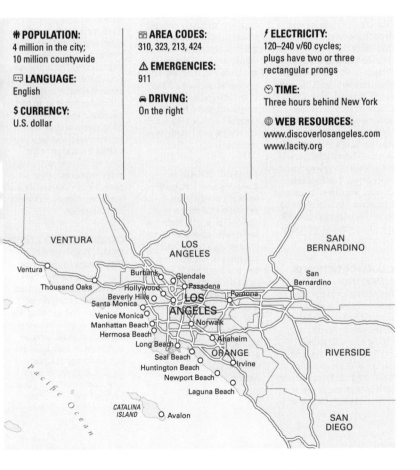

Know Before You Go

As one of the country's most visited cities, Los Angeles has dozens of notable attractions and can even be a little overwhelming for a first-time visitor. Here are some key tips to help you navigate your trip, whether it's your first time visiting or your twentieth.

THIS CITY IS BIG.

Oh, you wanted to do Malibu and Disneyland on the same day? That's cute. Here's some perspective—that drive is 77 miles and, depending on traffic, can take more than three hours from end to end. It's best to picture L.A. in pieces, and to think about visiting one neighborhood or a collection of nearby neighborhoods a day. There's the Westside, consisting of Malibu, Santa Monica, and Venice. The middle: Beverly Hills, West Hollywood, and Hollywood. The Eastside: Downtown, Silver Lake, and Pasadena. Stick to these on individual days or else risk spending most of your day in traffic.

TRANSPORTATION IS ANNOYING.

You have a lot of options, so choose wisely. You can rent a car, ride a bus, take the Metro, use a ride-sharing app, or scoot. Lesson 1: The bus lines can be challenging to navigate, even for locals, and traffic still exists for buses; chances are as a tourist, taking the bus will be more trouble than it's worth. Lesson 2: The Metro doesn't go everywhere, so pick your routes carefully. Lesson 3: Ride-sharing apps are infinitely cheaper than taxis. Lesson 4: If you must, scooter. The newest transpo kids on the block are Lime and Bird, electric scooters that make it easy to get around individual neighborhoods. Just be careful because bike lanes are scarce and L.A. drivers don't look.

TRAFFIC IS BAD.

Knowing how L.A. traffic works is the difference between a sweet vacation and hell on earth. Here are some rules to live by: first, only get in a car before 7 am, after 10 am, before 3 pm, or after 7 pm. If you must drive at any other times, find routes that don't involve L.A.'s maze of freeways. Side streets are your friends and give you lots of alternatives. If you get stuck on the 405 at 5:30, you will miss your dinner reservation.

PARKING IS COMPLICATED AND EXPENSIVE.

If you've seen L.A.'s draconian signage, you know how confusing things can be. But to avoid a ticket, stick to the meters (which take credit cards). If they're blinking red/green, you'll generally know you're in a place that works. If you rent a car, hotel parking can be obnoxiously expensive. We're talking $50–$60 per night. To avoid all these pitfalls, use ride-sharing apps and save yourself the hassle.

THE HOUSING CRISIS IS REAL.

This is probably the most shocking thing that newcomers to L.A. will experience. The homeless population has exploded in the last decade and rough estimates put it at 70,000 people on the streets. It's a big problem that the government is struggling to find a solution to fix. Just don't be surprised and, most important, don't be rude. People are people, and everyone deserves respect and kindness.

CELEBRITIES LIVE HERE, TOO.

If you want to see celebs, you need to know where to find them. But this isn't a safari and they're not animals—so be cool. If you want some guarantees, go to lunch at the Chateau Marmont or Polo Lounge. Hit up dinner at Craig's or Catch LA. If you're more into movie stuff than movie people, head over to the Warner Bros. and Universal

tudios lots, where you can
ur soundstages and movie
ets and maybe, just maybe,
e an A-lister eating lunch
the commissary—again,
e cool.

MARIJUANA IS LEGAL.

K, stoners, this is what
ou've been waiting for. L.A.
as legalized marijuana and
ou want to know where to
et high. First off, think of
he marijuana rules like the
lcohol rules. You need to
e 21. You can't consume in
ublic. You can't smoke and
rive (and you absolutely
houldn't). Fines can be as
igh (not a pun) as $250 just
or driving with an open
ontainer. So, if you need
pick-me-up or take-me-
own, look for the green
rosses on storefronts.

HERE ARE A LOT OF
EACHES.

o trip to L.A. would be
omplete without lounging
n one of the city's many
eaches. Whether you're a
urfer, skater, or volleyball
layer, there's a beach for
ou. Malibu is worth hitting
or the drive alone along
he Pacific Coast Highway,
ut it is far away. Santa
Ionica and Venice are
loser, though less serene.
Iead a little farther south
nd you'll get your top surf
pots: Manhattan, Hermosa,
nd Redondo.

THIS IS A FOODIE'S
ARADISE.

lew Yorkers can disagree
ll they want—L.A. is one
f the best food cities in
America. The food truck
as practically invented

here, and you'll find a
rolling restaurant for any
cuisine imaginable. Beyond
the trucks, L.A. has dozens
of farmers' markets and
near-weekly food festivals
celebrating the melting
pot that is this city. Lastly,
you'll find more celebrity
chefs in L.A. than just
about any other metropolis
as cheap(er) rents have
ushered in an experimen-
tal wave of food not seen
elsewhere. Whether it's
tacos, Italian, Ethiopian,
Korean, or burgers, L.A. is a
primo place for any traveling foodie.

YOU CAN LEAVE THE
UMBRELLA AT HOME.

Los Angeles's weather is so
ideal that most locals shrug
off the high cost of living as
a "sunshine tax." But it does
get chilly (read: highs in the
50s). January and February
tend to be the coldest and
rainiest months; however,
occasionally the rain begins
in December and ends in
March.

Springtime in Los Angeles
is typically from mid-March
to May, when the tempera-
tures fluctuate between
the low 70s and mid-80s.
Nights tend to be in the
50s. Jacaranda trees bloom
across the city and purple
flowers litter the sidewalks.
It's no cherry blossoms in
Japan, but it's still pretty.
September is usually the
hottest and driest month.
It's also when the Santa Ana
winds begin—the hot "devil
winds" that usher in fire
season and fray everyone's
nerves. They usually blow
on out of here in December.

The peak season runs from
June through August.
Beaches are packed every
weekend, so plan to go
early and expect traffic,
especially en route to
Malibu. June is usually
cooler, especially in the
mornings and evenings
when the fog rolls in—they
don't call it "June gloom" for
nothing. But temperatures
in July and August hover
in the 80s and can spike
to triple digits. The coasts
are usually between 5 and
10 degrees cooler than
Downtown.

THERE IS SUCH A THING
AS AWARDS SEASON.

Awards Season in Los
Angeles can be mildly
annoying. From January
through February, L.A.
hosts the Golden Globes,
the Academy Awards, the
Grammys (sometimes), and
a slew of other ceremonies.
This creates two problems:
hotel prices tend to go up
on the weekends of events,
especially in Beverly Hills,
West Hollywood, and
Downtown; and traffic is
even worse—Hollywood
Boulevard is closed around
Hollywood & Highland, the
Oscars venue, for a week.

Getting Here and Around

The Los Angeles metro area has more than 13 million residents, so be prepared to rent a car and fight for space on the freeway (especially at rush hour) to make your way along the array of destinations that span from the carefree beaches of the coastline to the glitz and glamour of Beverly Hills shops, the nightlife of Hollywood, and the film studio action of the Valley. It's worth it. Nowhere else in the country can you spot celebrities over breakfast or sunbathe on the beach and head to the slopes for skiing on the same day.

Air

Nonstop flights from New York to Los Angeles take about six hours; with the three-hour time change, you can leave JFK by 8 am and be in L.A. by 11 am. Some flights may require a midway stop, making the total excursion between 7½ and 8½ hours. Flight times are three hours from Dallas, four hours from Chicago, and 11½ hours from London.

AIRPORTS

The fourth-largest airport in the world in terms of passenger traffic, Los Angeles International Airport (LAX) is served by more than 65 major airlines. Because of heavy traffic around the airport (not to mention the city's extended rush hours), you should allow yourself plenty of extra time. All departures are from the upper level, while arrivals are on the lower level. There's no Metro in or out of the airport, but it's coming in the not-too-distant-future.

Several secondary airports serve the city. Hollywood Burbank Airport in Burbank is close to Downtown L.A., so it's definitely worth checking out. Long Beach Airport is equally convenient. Flights to Orange

County's John Wayne Airport are often more expensive than those to the other secondary airports. Also check out L.A./ Ontario International Airport.

Driving times from LAX to different parts of the city vary considerably: it will take you 20 minutes to get to Santa Monica, 30 minutes to Beverly Hills, and at least 45 minutes to Downtown L.A. In heavy traffic it can take much longer. From Burbank Airport, it's 30 minutes to Hollywood and Downtown. Plan on at least 45 minutes for the drive from Long Beach Airport, and an hour from John Wayne Airport or L.A./Ontario International Airport.

GROUND TRANSPORTATION

If you're not renting a car, a taxi is the most convenient way to get to and from the airport. There's a flat rate between LAX and Downtown for $50.50. Getting Downtown from Hollywood Burbank Airport costs $50 to $60. Taxis to and from L.A./Ontario International Airport run on meter and cost more than $100, depending on traffic. From Long Beach Airport, trips to Downtown L.A. are metered and cost roughly $77.

For two or three passengers, shuttles can be an economical option at $17 to $35. These big vans typically circle the airport, departing when they're full. Your travel time depends on how many other travelers are dropped off before you. At LAX, Kamel Shuttle Service and Prime Time shuttles are great options but call at least 24 hours in advance.

Operated by Los Angeles World Airports FlyAway buses travel between LAX and Van Nuys and Union Station in Downtown L.A. The cost is $9.75 and is payable only by credit or debit card. With departure at least every hour, buses run 24 hours a day.

Most Angelenos use ride-share apps like Lyft, which you can download to your smartphone. The app will estimate the cost before you accept the ride. A ride from the airport (drivers pick you up at a dedicated lot) to the Eastside could cost as much as $50 or less if you pick up another passenger along the way. But double-check because surge pricing during busy times can make it much more costly.

LAX-it is a free shuttle that drives you from the airport to the rideshare and taxi lots that are just outside the airport.

FLIGHTS
Delta, United, Southwest, and American have the most nonstop flights to LAX. JetBlue and Alaska also have numerous daily flights to airports in and around Los Angeles.

 # Bus

Inadequate public transportation has plagued L.A. for decades. That said, many local trips can be made, with time and patience, by buses run by the Los Angeles County Metropolitan Transit Authority. In certain cases—visiting the Getty Center, for instance, or Universal Studios—buses may be your best option. There's a special Dodger Stadium Express that shuttles passengers between Union Station and the world-famous ballpark for home games.

Metro Buses cost $1.75, which includes two hours of unlimited transfers to another bus or to the subway. A one-day pass costs $3.50, and a weekly pass is $12.50 for unlimited travel on all buses and trains. Passes are valid from Sunday through Saturday. For the fastest service, look for the red-and-white Metro Rapid buses; these stop less frequently and are able to extend green lights. There are 25 Bus Rapid Transit (BRT) routes, including along Wilshire and Vermont Boulevards.

Other bus services make it possible to explore the entire metropolitan area. DASH minibuses cover six different circular routes in Hollywood, Mid-Wilshire, and Downtown. You pay 50¢ every time you get on. The Santa Monica Municipal Bus Line, also known as the Big Blue Bus, is a pleasant and inexpensive way to move around the Westside. Trips cost $1.10.

You can pay your fare in cash on MTA, Santa Monica, and Culver City buses, but you must have exact change. You can buy MTA TAP cards at Metro Rail stations, customer centers throughout the city, and some convenience and grocery stores.

 # Car

If you're used to urban driving, you shouldn't have too much trouble navigating the streets of Los Angeles. If not, L.A. can be unnerving. However, the city has evolved with drivers in mind. Streets are wide and parking garages abound, so it's more car-friendly than many older big cities.

If you get discombobulated while on the freeway, remember this rule of thumb: even-numbered freeways run east and west, odd-numbered freeways run north and south.

GASOLINE
As of this writing, gasoline costs around $4.50 a gallon. Most stations are self-service; the few remaining full-service stations are mostly in and around the Westside. There are plenty of stations everywhere. Most stay open late, and many are open 24 hours.

Getting Here and Around

GETTING AROUND

There are plenty of identical or similarly named streets in L.A. (Beverly Boulevard and Beverly Drive, for example), so be as specific as you can when asking directions or inputting into a map app. Expect sudden changes in addresses as streets pass through neighborhoods, then incorporated cities, then back into neighborhoods. This can be most bewildering on Robertson Boulevard, an otherwise useful north–south artery that, by crossing through L.A., West Hollywood, and Beverly Hills, dips in and out of several such numbering shifts in a matter of miles.

PARKING

Parking rules are strictly enforced in Los Angeles, so make sure you check for signs and read them carefully. Illegally parked cars are ticketed or towed quickly. Parking prices vary from 25¢ (in public lots and at meters) to $2 per 15-minutes (in private lots). Downtown and Century City rates may be as high as $25 an hour.

Parking in Downtown L.A. can be tough, especially on weekdays. Try the garage at the FIG at 7th retail complex which is spacious, reasonably priced, and visitor-friendly. ⊠ *725 S. Figueroa St.*

In Hollywood, the underground facility at the Hollywood & Highland shopping complex charges $3 for the first two hours with validation. ⊠ *6801 Hollywood Blvd.*

In Beverly Hills, the first two hours are free at several lots on or around Rodeo Drive. The Westside Pavilion offers three hours of free parking at its garage. ⊠ *10800 Pico Blvd.*

At some shops, most restaurants, and hotels in Los Angeles, valet parking is virtually assumed. The cost is usually $6 to $16 for restaurants, but can be as high as $70 for hotels. Keep small bills on hand to tip the valets.

ROAD CONDITIONS

Beware of weekday rush-hour traffic, which is heaviest from 8 to 10 am and 3 to 7 pm. Go511.com and the Waze app offer real-time traffic information, and the California Highway Patrol has a road-conditions hotline. To encourage carpooling, some crowded freeways reserve an express lane for cars carrying more than one passenger.

Parallel streets can often provide viable alternatives to jam-packed freeways, notably Sepulveda Boulevard for I-405; Venice and Washington Boulevards for I-10 from Mid-Wilshire west to the beach; and Ventura Boulevard, Moorpark Street, or Riverside Drive for U.S. 101 through the San Fernando Valley.

ROADSIDE EMERGENCIES

For minor problems faced by motorists (running out of gas, blowing a tire, needing a tow to the nearest phone), California's Department of Transportation has a Metro Freeway Service Patrol. More than 145 tow trucks patrol the freeways offering free aid to stranded drivers. Reach them on your cell phone by calling 511.

If your car breaks down on an interstate, pull over onto the shoulder and call the state police from your cell phone or walk to the nearest emergency roadside phone. When calling for help, note your location according to the small green mileage markers posted along the highway.

RULES OF THE ROAD

Seat belts are required for all passengers in California, as is the use of federally approved car seats for children under nine or less than 4 feet, 9 inches tall.

California law requires that drivers use hands-free devices when talking on cell phones. Texting and driving is illegal and results in a hefty fine.

The speed limit is 25 to 35 mph on city streets and 65 mph on freeways unless otherwise posted. Some towns, including Beverly Hills and Culver City, use cameras at traffic lights to reduce speeding. Speeding can earn you fines starting at $266. It is illegal to drive in California with a blood alcohol content of 0.08% or above (0.01% if you're under 21). There are strict penalties for first offenders. Checkpoints are set up on weekends and holidays across the county.

Parking infractions can result in penalties starting at $65. Having your vehicle towed and impounded will cost nearly $300 even if you pay up immediately, and more if you don't. LAX is notorious for handing out tickets to drivers circling its busy terminals; avoid the no-parking zones and keep loading or unloading to a minimum.

Turning right on red after a complete stop is legal unless otherwise posted. Many streets in Downtown L.A. are one-way, and a left turn from one one-way street onto another is allowed. On some major arteries, left turns are illegal during rush hour. Certain carpool lanes, designated by signage and a white diamond, are reserved for cars with more than one passenger. Freeway on-ramps often have stop-and-go signals to regulate the flow of traffic, but cars in high-occupancy-ve-hicle (HOV) lanes can pass the signal without stopping.

Keep in mind that pedestrians always have the right of way in California; not yielding to them, even if they're jaywalk-ers, may result in a $238 ticket.

RENTALS

In Los Angeles, a car is a necessity. Keep in mind that you'll likely be spending a lot of time in it, and options like a plug for your cell phone could make a significant difference in your day-to-day comfort.

Major-chain rates in L.A. begin at $60 a day and $400 a week, plus sales tax and concession fees. Luxury vehicles start at $100 a day. Open-top convertibles are a popular choice for visitors wanting to make the most of the sun. Note that the major agencies offer services for travelers with disabilities, such as hand controls, for little or no extra cost.

In California you must be 21 and have a valid credit card to rent a car. Some agencies won't rent to those under 25, and those that do may charge extra.

Ⓜ Metro/Public Transport

Metro Rail covers only a small part of L.A.'s vast expanse, but it's convenient, frequent, and inexpensive. Most popular with visitors is the underground Red Line, which runs from Downtown's Union Station through Mid-Wilshire, Hollywood, and Universal City on its way to North Hollywood, stopping at the most popular tourist destinations along the way.

The light-rail Green Line stretches from Redondo Beach to Norwalk, while the partially underground Blue Line travels from Downtown to the South Bay. The monorail-like Gold Line extends from Union Station to Pasadena and out to the deep San Gabriel Valley and Azusa. The Orange Line, a 14-mile bus corridor, connects the North Hollywood subway station with the western San Fernando Valley.

Getting Here and Around

Most recently extended was the Expo Line, which connects Downtown to the Westside, and terminates in Santa Monica, two blocks from the Pacific Ocean.

Daily service is offered from about 4:30 am to 1:30 am, with departures every 5 to 15 minutes. On weekends trains run until 2 am. Buy tickets from station vending machines; fares are $1.75, or $3.50 for an all-day pass. Bicycles are allowed on Metro Rail trains at all times.

Ride-Sharing

Request a ride using apps like Lyft or Uber, and a driver will usually arrive within minutes. Fares increase during busy times, but it's often the most affordable option, especially for the convenience.

Taxi

Instead of trying to hail a taxi on the street, phone one of the many taxi companies. The Curb Taxi app allows for online hailing of L.A. taxis. The metered rate is $2.97 per mile, plus a $3.10 per-fare charge and an additional $2 curb fee. Taxi rides from LAX have an additional $4 surcharge. Be aware that distances are greater than they might appear on the map so fares add up quickly.

On the other end of the price spectrum, limousines come equipped with everything from full bars to night-club-style sound-and-light systems. Most charge by the hour, minimum hours sometimes required.

Train

Downtown's Union Station is one of the great American railroad terminals. The interior includes comfortable seating, restaurants, and several bars. As the city's rail hub, it's the place to catch an Amtrak, Metrolink commuter train, or the Red, Gold, or Purple lines. Among Amtrak's Southern California routes are 13 daily trips to San Diego and 5 to Santa Barbara. Amtrak's luxury *Coast Starlight* travels along the spectacular coastline from Seattle to Los Angeles in just a day and a half (though it's often a little late). The *Sunset Limited* arrives from New Orleans, and the *Southwest Chief* comes from Chicago.

Essentials

🍴 Dining

Los Angeles may be known for its beach living and celebrity-infused backdrop, but it was once a farm town. The hillsides were covered in citrus orchards and dairy farms, and agriculture was a major industry. Today, even as L.A. is urbanized, the city's culinary landscape has reembraced a local, sustainable, and seasonal philosophy at many levels—from fine dining to street snacks.

With a growing interest in farm-to-fork, the city's farmers' market scene has exploded, becoming popular at big-name restaurants and small eateries alike. In Hollywood and Santa Monica you can often find high-profile chefs scouring farm stands for fresh produce.

The status of the celebrity chef carries weight around this town. People follow the culinary zeitgeist with the same fervor as celebrity gossip. You can queue up with the hungry hordes at Nancy Silverton's **Mozza,** or try and snag a reservation at Ludo Lefebvre's ever-popular **Petit Trois** or David Chang's L.A. outpost, **Majordomo.**

International eats continue to be a backbone of the L.A. dining scene. People head to Koreatown for epic Korean cooking and late-night coffeehouses and to West L.A. for phenomenal sushi. Latin food is well represented in the city, making it tough to choose between Guatemalan eateries, Peruvian restaurants, nouveau Mexican bistros, and Tijuana-style taco trucks. With so many dining options, sometimes the best strategy is simply to drive and explore.

CHILDREN
Although it's unusual to see children in the dining rooms of L.A.'s most elite restaurants, dining with youngsters here does not have to mean culinary exile.

SMOKING
Smokers should keep in mind that California law forbids smoking in all enclosed areas, including bars.

RESERVATIONS
You'll be happy to hear it's getting easier to snag a desired reservation, but it's still a good idea to plan ahead. Some renowned restaurants are booked weeks or even months in advance. If that's the case, you can get lucky at the last minute if you're flexible—and friendly. Most restaurants keep a few tables open for walk-ins and VIPs. Show up for dinner early (6 pm) or late (after 9 pm) and politely inquire about any last-minute vacancies or cancellations. Try booking apps like Open Table and Resy. Most places, except small mom-and-pop establishments, provide valet parking at dinner for semi-reasonable rates (often around $10, plus tip).

DINING HOURS
Despite its veneer of decadence, L.A. is not a particularly late-night city for eating. (The reenergized Hollywood dining scene is emerging as a notable exception.) The peak dinner times are from 7 to 9, and most restaurants won't take reservations after 10. Unless otherwise noted, the restaurants listed in this guide are open daily for lunch and dinner. Generally speaking, restaurants are closed either Sunday or Monday; a few are shuttered both days. Most places—even the upscale spots—are open for lunch on weekdays, since many Hollywood megadeals are conceived at that time.

Essentials

WHAT TO WEAR

Dining out in Los Angeles tends to be a casual affair, and even at some of the most expensive restaurants you're likely to see customers in jeans (albeit expensive jeans). It's extremely rare for L.A. restaurants to actually require a jacket and tie or formal cocktail dresses, but L.A. is a fashionable city, so it never hurts to dress up a little.

TIPPING AND TAXES

In most restaurants, tip the waiter 16%–20%. (To figure out a 20% tip quickly, just move the decimal point one place to the left on your total and double that amount.) Note that checks for parties of six or more sometimes include the tip already. Tip at least $1 per drink at the bar, and $1 for each coat checked. Never tip the maître d' unless you're out to impress your guests or expect to pay another visit soon. Also, be prepared for a sales tax of around 9.5% to appear on your bill.

PRICES

If you're watching your budget, be sure to ask the price of daily specials recited by the waiter. The charge for specials at some restaurants is noticeably out of line with the other prices on the menu. Beware of the $10 bottle of water; ask for tap water instead.

If you eat early or late, you may be able to take advantage of a prix-fixe deal not offered at peak hours. Most upscale restaurants are offering great lunch deals with special menus at cut-rate prices designed to give customers a true taste of the place.

Credit cards are accepted unless otherwise noted in the review. While many restaurants do accept credit cards, some smaller places accept only cash. If you plan to use a credit card it's a good idea

to double-check its acceptability when making reservations or before sitting down to eat.

⇨ *Restaurant reviews have been shortened. For full information, visit Fodors. com. Prices in the restaurant reviews are the average cost of a main course at dinner or, if dinner is not served, at lunch.*

What It Costs in U.S. Dollars

	$	$$	$$$	$$$$
RESTAURANTS				
	under $20	$20–$30	$31–$40	over $40

✚ Health

The air pollution in L.A. may affect sensitive people in different ways. When pollution levels are high, it's a good idea to plan a day indoors or on a windy beach. The sun can burn even on overcast days, and the dry heat can dehydrate, so wear hats, sunglasses, and sunblock, and carry water with you.

🛏 Lodging

When it comes to finding a place to stay, travelers have never been more spoiled for choice than in today's Los Angeles. From luxurious digs in Beverly Hills and along the coast to budget boutiques in Hollywood, hotels are stepping up service, upgrading amenities, and trying all-new concepts, like upscale hostels and retro-chic motels. Hotels in Los Angeles today are more than just a place to rest your head; they're a key part of the experience.

RESERVATIONS

Hotel reservations are an absolute necessity when planning your trip to Los Angeles—although rooms are easier to come by these days. Competition for clients also means properties undergo frequent improvements, so when booking ask about any renovations, lest you get a room within earshot of construction. In this ever-changing city, travelers can find themselves without amenities like room service or spa access if their hotel is upgrading.

SERVICES

Most hotels have air-conditioning and flat-screen cable TV. Those in the moderate and expensive price ranges often have coffeemakers, bathrobes, and hair dryers. Most also have high-speed Internet access in guest rooms, with a 24-hour use fee (though at a number of hotels, it's free). Wi-Fi is common even at budget properties. Southern California's emphasis on being in shape means most hotels have fitness facilities; if the one on-site is not to your liking, ask for a reference to a nearby sports club or gym.

STAYING WITH KIDS

From Disneyland to the beach cities, laid-back Los Angeles definitely has a reputation as a family-friendly destination. Resorts and hotels along the coast, in particular, attract plenty of beach-going family vacationers looking for sun and sand castles. Some properties provide such diversions as in-room movies, toys, and video games; others have suites with kitchenettes and fold-out sofa beds. Hotels often provide cribs, rollaway beds, and references for babysitting services, but make arrangements when booking the room, not when you arrive.

⇨ *Properties that are especially kid-friendly are marked FAMILY throughout the chapters.*

PARKING

Exploring Los Angeles, a sprawling city of wide boulevards and five-lane freeways, requires a car. Though you might stroll Rodeo Drive on foot or amble along the Hollywood Walk of Fame, to get from one part of town to another, you'll need wheels. Thankfully, there's street parking in most areas (read signs carefully as some neighborhoods are by permit only), and many public parking lots are free for the first hour or two. Though a few hotels have free parking, most charge for the privilege, and some resorts only have valet parking, with fees as high as $70 per night.

PRICES

Tax rates for the area will add 10%–14% to your bill depending on where in Los Angeles County you stay; some hoteliers tack on energy, service, or occupancy surcharges—ask about customary charges when you book your room.

When looking for a hotel, don't write off the pricier establishments immediately. Price categories here are determined by "rack rates"—the list price of a hotel room—which are often higher than those you'll find online or by calling the hotel directly. Specials abound, particularly in Downtown on the weekends. Many hotels have packages that include breakfast, theater tickets, spa services, or luxury rental cars. Pricing is competitive, so always check with the hotel for current special offers.

When making reservations, don't forget to check the hotel's website for exclusive online specials.

⇨ *Hotel reviews have been shortened. For full information, visit Fodors.com. Prices in the hotel reviews are the lowest cost of a standard double room in high season.*

Essentials

What It Costs in U.S. Dollars			
$	$$	$$$	$$$$
HOTELS			
under $200	$201–$350	$351–$500	over $500

Nightlife

Los Angeles is not the city that never sleeps—instead it parties until 2 am (save for the secret after-hours parties at private clubs, Hollywood Hills mansions, and warehouses) and wakes up to imbibe green juices and breakfast burritos as hangover cures or to sweat it out in a yoga class. Whether you plan to test your limit at historic establishments Downtown or take advantage of a cheap happy hour at a Hollywood dive, this city's nightlife has something for you.

A night out in Los Angeles can simultaneously surprise and impress. Seeing an unscheduled set by an A-list comedian at a comedy club, being talked into singing karaoke at the diviest place you've ever seen, dancing at a bar with no dance floor because, well, the DJ is just too good at his job—going out isn't always what you expect, but it certainly is never boring.

The focus of nightlife once centered on the Sunset Strip, with its multitude of bars, rock clubs, and dance spots, but more neighborhoods are competing with each other and forcing the nightlife scene to evolve. Although the Strip can be a worthwhile trip, other areas of the city are catching people's attention. Downtown Los Angeles, for instance, is a destination in its own right. Other areas foster more of a neighborhood vibe. Silver Lake and Los Feliz have both cultivated a relaxed environment.

So if you find yourself disappointed with a rude bouncer, or drinks that are too watery, or a cover charge that just isn't worth it, try again. Eventually you'll find that perfect place where each time is the best time. If not, at least you'll walk away with a good story.

Performing Arts

The arts scene in Los Angeles extends beyond the screen and onto the stage. A place of artistic innovation and history, one can discover new and challenging theatrical works across L.A. stages, while the city still maintains a respect for tradition with its restored theaters and classic plays. See live music at impeccably designed amphitheaters like the Hollywood Bowl or listen in on captivating lectures by authors and directors at various intimate spaces. In homage to the city's roots as a filmmaking mecca, there are also retrospectives and rare screenings in movie theaters all over the city, often followed by Q&As with the cast.

L.A.'s arts scene is varied and caters to all budgets and tastes. East West Players at the David Henry Hwang Theatre focuses on Asian American–themed plays, and if an opera at the Dorothy Chandler Pavilion seems out of your price range, The Actors' Gang in Culver City offers a free Shakespeare play in Media Park in the summer. The Independent Shakespeare Co. hosts a free Shakespeare festival in Griffith Park, also during summer.

Temperate weather allows for an extended season of outdoor events. Enjoy a classic summer picnic listening to the L.A. Philharmonic at the Hollywood Bowl or watching a play outdoors at The Ford Amphitheater.

American Cinematheque, showing classic and independent films, operates out of the Aero Theatre in Santa Monica, as well as the historic Egyptian Theatre on Hollywood Boulevard.

⊕ Safety

Very minor earthquakes occur frequently in Southern California; most of the time they're so slight that you won't notice them. If you feel a stronger tremor, follow basic safety precautions. If you're indoors, take cover in a doorway or under a table or desk—whichever is closest. Protect your head with your arms. Stay clear of windows, mirrors, or anything that might fall from the walls. Do not use elevators. If you're in an open space, move away from buildings, trees, and power lines. If you're outdoors near buildings, duck into a doorway. If you're driving, pull over to the side of the road, avoiding overpasses, bridges, and power lines, and stay inside the car. Expect aftershocks, and take cover again if they are strong.

Of the Metro lines, the Red, Green, and Expo lines are the safest and are more regularly patrolled. The Blue Line can be sketchy after dark. Avoid riding in empty cars, and move with the crowd when going from the station to the street.

ⓢ Taxes

The sales tax in L.A. is 9.5%, one of the highest in California. There's none on most groceries, but there is on newspapers and magazines. The tax on hotel rooms ranges from 13% to 15.5%. Food tax varies, but expect to pay around 9.5%.

💵 Tipping

The customary tip rate is 15%–20% for waiters, taxi drivers, hairdressers, and barbers. Bellhops and baggage handlers receive $1–$2 per bag; parking valets and hotel housekeepers are usually tipped $2–$3. Bartenders get about $1 per drink, but tip your mixologists like you would a waiter.

⊙ Visitor Information

Discover Los Angeles, the official tourism site, has an annually updated general information packet that includes suggestions for entertainment, lodging, and dining and a list of special events. There are two visitor information centers, both accessible to Metro stops: the Hollywood & Highland Center and Union Station.

Great Itineraries

The Perfect Week in Los Angeles

The trick to having a decent quality of life in Los Angeles, claims one longtime Angeleno, is to live near where you work. The same adage holds true for visitors in that staying put in a single area of the city—being in a car for as short a time as possible—is a good rule of thumb. The best way to explore is one neighborhood at a time. Here's how to spend the perfect week in L.A. doing just that.

DAY 1: DOWNTOWN LOS ANGELES

Formerly an unwelcoming neighborhood dominated by the glass-and-steel office buildings of Bunker Hill on one side and the poverty and despair of Skid Row on the other, Downtown Los Angeles has staged a major comeback.

Start your first day with some culture on Grand Avenue: the Walt Disney Concert Hall, the Broad Museum, and the Museum of Contemporary Art are all next to each other and are home to priceless works of art and stunning architecture. At the concert hall, be sure to take the hour-long self-guided audio tour. It can be tough, but not impossible to see all three in one morning/afternoon trip.

After feasting on culture, grab lunch at one of the many stalls of Grand Central Market. Then Uber over to the art deco icon, Union Station, to admire the heavy wood-beam ceilings, leather-upholstered chairs, and inlaid marble floors. You can also stay for a happy hour drink or snack at one of the many restaurant and bar options now open inside.

For more L.A. history, walk across Alameda Street to stroll past the shops and restaurants of historic Olvera Street,

where you'll find traditional Mexican fare. For dinner, venture into Little Tokyo for a wide variety of Japanese cuisine or head to Chinatown for authentic eats. With a full belly, head back into the historic core of Downtown, where you'll find a large concentration of bars on Spring Street between 5th and 7th Streets, and on 6th between Main and Los Angeles Streets.

DAY 2: HOLLYWOOD

On your second day, you can join the tourists who flock to Hollywood Boulevard to see old movie palaces such as TCL Chinese Theatre, where movie stars have left their mark, literally, in the concrete courtyard of the theater since 1927. These days the theater's entrance is also graced by dozens of impersonators—from Marilyn Monroe to Spiderman—who are more than happy to pose for photos with visitors (they do expect to be paid, however).

To avoid the heaviest crowds, go to Hollywood & Highland Center in the morning, followed by a tour of the Dolby Theatre, which hosts the annual Academy Awards ceremony.

Wander the Walk of Fame, a 1.3-mile stretch of bronze stars embedded in pink terrazzo that lines Hollywood Boulevard, to pay homage to your favorite movie stars. For lunch, head into the famous Roosevelt Hotel and grab a spot by the pool. Look up and you'll see the Marilyn Monroe suite hovering over the sunbathers.

Pre-dinner, you should take part in a Hollywood rite of passage and see a movie in the town that made them famous. Some of the historic movie palaces, including TCL, still show films.

Post-dinner, check out Hollywood's famous food scene and then make the night truly epic at one of the neighborhood's clubs, music venues, or dive bars.

DAY 3: WEST HOLLYWOOD

Thanks to its central location, West Hollywood is the ideal place to spend a couple of hours without committing an entire day—not that there isn't a day's worth of things to do in this neighborhood.

Like most things in L.A., the early bird gets the worm. For shoppers, that means going to stores when they open and are less crowded. A shopping hub in its own right, West Hollywood has multiple indoor and outdoor shopping options like The Grove and the mammoth indoor Beverly Center. There are also countless small boutiques and specialty shops lining Beverly Boulevard, 3rd Street, and Melrose Avenue.

For lunch, grab a corned beef sandwich or some matzo ball soup at Canter's Delicatessen, a Los Angeles landmark since 1931, or head to the Farmers Market for a collection of ethnic food stalls and local products.

If you haven't had your shopping fill, tack Robertson Boulevard onto your agenda to find boutiques ranging from Chanel to Kitson. Swing by the picket-fenced Ivy, a restaurant which had its celebrity heyday in the mid-aughts, but you still may see a star or two.

Finally, West Hollywood is known for its buzzing nightlife, so afterward choose from hundreds of small restaurants for dinner, then follow up with a drink from one of the area's many bars.

DAY 4: BEVERLY HILLS AND MID-WILSHIRE

Depending on how hard-core of a shopper you are, you can easily check out the boutiques of Beverly Hills in a couple of hours. In fact, with all of the designer flagships and tony department stores, it might be dangerous to spend too much time (translation: too much money) in this ritzy neighborhood.

Hit Rodeo Drive in the morning for all the runway names, such as Chanel, Christian Dior, Dolce & Gabbana, Fendi, Gucci, Prada, Valentino, and Versace.

Of course, not all the action is on Rodeo; don't forget to wander the side streets for more high fashion. The department stores—Neiman Marcus and Saks Fifth Avenue—are located nearby on Wilshire Boulevard. After you finish shopping, refuel with a dose of sugar at local dessert favorite Sprinkles Cupcakes.

After all that shopping, jump in the car to get some culture by heading east to the Miracle Mile in Mid-Wilshire, a stretch of Wilshire Boulevard that's home to the mammoth Los Angeles County Museum of Art, the Petersen Automotive Museum, and the Academy Museum of Motion Pictures. Depending on your preference of cuisine, have dinner in either Little Ethiopia or at the buzzy Fanny's restaurant and bar at the Academy Museum.

DAY 5: SANTA MONICA AND VENICE

With a couple of hours on your hands, it's a quick trip (if there's no traffic) to the beaches of Santa Monica or Venice. While they may not offer quite as much in the natural beauty department as their Malibu counterparts, they have plenty of sights of a different variety.

Start the day at Santa Monica Pier, where you can enjoy the old-school amusement park. Then walk (or bike ride) down the Strand, which eventually takes you to Venice Beach. Take your time browsing (and stopping for lunch) at the many

Great Itineraries

beachside restaurants and quirky shops; you can even enjoy a few hours on the beach itself if you like.

Then end the day with a walk over the Venice Canals and a meal at any of the increasingly hip restaurants in Venice; don't miss sunset over the beach.

DAY 6: MALIBU

The ideal way to see Los Angeles's most beautiful beaches is to set aside an entire day for Malibu. Driving up the scenic Pacific Coast Highway is a treat in and of itself with sheer cliffs on one side of the road and ocean views on the other.

Stop at the Malibu Country Mart along the way for a seafood-laden lunch and gawk at the high-end shoppers and possible celebrity or two.

As you drive, you'll hit Topanga State Beach, Malibu Lagoon State Beach, and Malibu Surfrider Beach, which are all beautiful and popular spots to pass the day, but it's worth the extra drive time to see Point Dume State Beach, which is nestled away from the hustle and bustle of the highway.

Be sure to seek out the single-track trail that winds its way up a nearby coastal bluff revealing breathtaking views of Santa Monica Bay, the Malibu Coast, and Catalina Island. Stop for dinner at any of the seafood shacks that line PCH and catch an epic California sunset.

DAY 7: ORANGE COUNTY AND CATALINA ISLAND

If you want the California coastline all to yourself, head out in the early morning to one of the seemingly endless strings of beaches along this stretch of shoreline, extending from Long Beach to San Juan Capistrano. There's plenty to do besides sit in the sand: check out one of the fascinating aquariums, explore a nature preserve, or take in some impressive art at the area's surprisingly good museums.

Finding somewhere to eat lunch won't be a problem, as this area is a major foodie destination. There are also plenty of reasonably priced family eateries.

If you're traveling with kids, you're going to end up at one of the classic theme parks, either Disneyland or Knott's Berry Farm (plan an entire day around Disneyland). Grown-ups, though, will be drawn to the natural beauty of Catalina Island, and it's worth spending a whole day exploring. There's a tiny town with its fair share of attractions, but make sure you see the unspoiled coastline.

On the Calendar

Spring

Knotts's Boysenberry Festival. Known as the birthplace of the boysenberry, the Knotts's festival celebrates all things purple with live shows, plenty of boysenberry-inspired food, and no shortage of wine for adults.

Los Angeles Marathon. Starting at Dodger Stadium and ending in Santa Monica, the L.A. Marathon is the biggest running event in the city, and various streets are shut down to give runners free reign on a Sunday morning in March.

***Los Angeles Times* Festival of Books.** Taking place on the USC campus in April, the *L.A. Times* Festival of Books celebrates authors and readers alike with new releases, lectures, celebrity signings, and food trucks.

Summer

Los Angeles Pride Festival and Parade. West Hollywood is home to the largest LGBTQ+ population in the city and hosts one of the biggest Pride festivals and parades in America. The festivities usually happen in June.

Nisei Week Japanese Festival. Over eight days in August in the Little Tokyo neighborhood of Downtown Los Angeles, Japanese culture is on full display with tea ceremonies, food stalls, parades, and the coronation of the Nisei Week Queen.

U.S. Open of Surfing. Every late July/early August, the best surfers on the planet (and their thousands of fans) congregate on Huntington Beach for the most prestigious surf competition in the country.

Fall

Abbot Kinney Festival. Every September/October, the entire stretch of the city's famous Venice street Abbot Kinney is turned into a free community festival with food trucks, concerts, art booths, and all the weird and wonderful quirks of the neighborhood.

Día de los Muertos (Day of the Dead). Head down to Olvera Street on November 1 for food, dancing, and more to celebrate the Day of the Dead and remember loved ones we've lost.

West Hollywood Halloween Carnaval. One of the craziest, flashiest, and most fun parties in L.A., the WeHo Halloween Carnaval is a costumed extravaganza in the heart of the city's LGBTQ+ neighborhood.

Winter

Chinese New Year. Head down to Chinatown for the annual Golden Dragon Parade along Hill and Temple streets. The festivities include fireworks, a lantern procession, food stalls, and more.

Hollywood Christmas Parade. More than a million people flock to Hollywood and Sunset boulevards to watch celebrities, floats, antique cars, and marching bands roll through Hollywood in this annual holiday celebration.

Tournament of Roses Parade. Since 1890, every New Year's Day in Pasadena is filled with the spectacular Tournament of Roses Parade. Elaborate floats roll through the streets and draw in millions of spectators. Following the parade is always the big Rose Bowl college football game inside Rose Bowl Stadium.

The Best Tours in Los Angeles

Bus Tours

Guideline Tours. This company offers sightseeing trips all around L.A., including Downtown and Hollywood. ⊠ *Los Angeles* ☎ *323/465–3004, 213/385–3004* ⊕ *www.tourslosangeles.com* ✉ *From $83* ☞ *2-ticket minimum purchase.*

Starline Tours. Operating double-decker and open-roof-van tours, Starline Tours offers hop-on/off tours around town. Passengers are picked up from the TCL Chinese Theatre and in Santa Monica. ⊠ *6801 Hollywood Blvd., Hollywood* ☎ *323/463–3333* ⊕ *www.starlinetours. com* ✉ *From $39* Ⓜ *Hollywood/Highland.*

TMZ Celebrity Tour. If you want to feel like a paparazzi for a day, then check out the slightly tawdry TMZ Celebrity Tour of reputed celebrity hot spots that leaves from in front of the Hard Rock in Hollywood. ⊠ *Los Angeles* ☎ *844/869–8687* ⊕ *www.tmztour.com* ✉ *From $44.*

Special-Interest Tours

Access Hollywood Celebrity Homes Tours. This company takes groups in an open-air van through the glitzy streets of Beverly Hills where you can see homes belonging to the likes of A-listers like Mick Jagger, Tom Cruise, Katy Perry, and many more. ⊠ *Los Angeles* ☎ *323/472–7938* ⊕ *www.accesshollywoodtours.com* ✉ *From $39* ☞ *2-person minimum for tickets.*

Architecture Tours L.A. With Architecture Tours L.A., you can zip all over the city in a comfortable minivan on a private tour with a historian. See famous buildings and homes designed by luminaries like Frank Lloyd Wright, Frank Gehry, and more. ⊠ *Los Angeles* ☎ *323/464–7868* ⊕ *www.architecturetoursla.com* ✉ *From $80.*

Beverly Hills Trolley Tours. Beverly Hills operates year-round trolley tours focused on art and architecture. They last 40 minutes and depart from 11 am to 4 pm every weekend throughout the year. ⊠ *Dayton Way and Rodeo Dr., Beverly Hills* ☎ *310/285–2467* ⊕ *www.beverly-hills.org/departments/publicworks/trans-portation/transit* ✉ *Free.*

Esotouric. With an innovative take on the city, Esotouric's varied weekend bus tours explore historic architecture along Route 66 and the darker side of L.A. that Raymond Chandler revealed in books like *The Big Sleep* and *The Long Goodbye.* ⊠ *Los Angeles* ☎ *213/373–1947* ⊕ *www. esotouric.com* ✉ *From $64.*

My Valley Pass Tours. This company serves as an excellent guide to the San Fernando Valley and runs one-of-a-kind tours. The San Fernando Valley Film Tour is one of their best and takes tourists on a three-hour trip to the Valley's most iconic film locations. ⊠ *Los Angeles* ☎ *818/850–3836* ⊕ *www.myvalleypass. com/tours* ✉ *From $22.*

Neon Cruise. Soak up the glow of classic neon signs around L.A. from an open double-decker bus on tours offered by the Museum of Neon Art. There are also walking tours through different neighborhoods like Chinatown, the Broadway Theatre District, Hollywood, and more. ✉ *Los Angeles* ☎ *818/696–2149* ⊕ *www. neonmona.org/neon-cruise* ✆ *$65.*

Sidewalk Food Tours. For food lovers, the Sidewalk Food Tours are unique walking tours around Los Angeles that let you explore this incredible city through its many cuisines. Tours are broken up between West Hollywood and Downtown L.A., run for 2½ hours, and hit five to seven different food outlets along the way. ✉ *1933 Bronson Ave., Los Angeles* ☎ *877/568–6877* ⊕ *www.sidewalkfood-tours.com/los-angeles* ✆ *$75.*

Take My Mother Please. Take My Mother Please will arrange lively, thematic combination walking and driving tours; for instance, you could explore sights associated with the film *L.A. Confidential.* ✉ *Los Angeles* ☎ *323/737–2200* ⊕ *www. takemymotherplease.com* ✆ *From $450 for up to three people for a half day.*

Walking Tours

Los Angeles Conservancy. The Los Angeles Conservancy's 2½-hour-long walking tours ($15) cover the Downtown area. ✉ *Los Angeles* ☎ *213/623–2489* ⊕ *www. laconservancy.org/tours.*

Red Line Tours. This company offers daily walking tours of behind-the-scenes Hollywood. Tours are led by docents and include headsets to block out street noise. ✉ *6708 Hollywood Blvd., Hollywood* ⊕ *www.redlinetours.com* ✆ *From $15* ☞ *Groups only. Booking only through website.*

Universal Studio Tour. For one hour, you can get a unique look behind the scenes of one of the biggest film studios in the world. The tour covers 13 blocks as Jimmy Fallon virtually guides you through a close encounter with *Jaws*, the wreckage of a 747 from *War of the Worlds*, and much more. ✉ *100 Universal City Plaza, Universal City* ☎ *800/864–8377* ⊕ *www. universalstudioshollywood.com/web/en/ us/things-to-do/rides-and-attractions/the-world-famous-studio-tour* ✆ *From $109* Ⓜ *Universal City/Studio City.*

Contacts

Air

AIRPORTS Hollywood Burbank Airport. (*BUR*). ⊠ *2627 N. Hollywood Way, near I–5 and U.S. 101, Burbank* ☎ *818/840–8840* ⊕ *www.hollywood-burbankairport.com.* **John Wayne Airport.** (*SNA*). ⊠ *18601 Airport Way, Santa Ana* ☎ *949/252–5200* ⊕ *www.ocair.com.* **L.A./Ontario International Airport.** (*ONT*). ⊠ *2500 E. Airport Dr., off I–10, Ontario* ☎ *909/544–5300* ⊕ *www.flyontario. com.* **Long Beach Airport.** (*LGB*). ⊠ *4100 Donald Douglas Dr., Long Beach* ☎ *562/570–2600* ⊕ *www. lgb.org.* **Los Angeles International Airport.** (*LAX*). ⊠ *1 World Way, off Hwy. 1, Los Angeles* ☎ *855/463–5252* ⊕ *www.flylax.com.*

AIRPORT TRANSPORT FlyAway. ⊠ *Los Angeles* ☎ *714/507–1170* ⊕ *www. flylax.com/en/flyaway-bus.* **SuperShuttle.** ⊠ *Los Angeles* ☎ *800/258–3826* ⊕ *www.supershuttle.com.*

Bus

Culver CityBus. ⊠ *Los Angeles* ☎ *310/253–6510* ⊕ *www.culvercitybus. com.* **DASH.** ⊠ *Los Angeles* ☎ *310/808–2273* ⊕ *www. ladottransit.com.* **Los Angeles County Metropolitan Transit Authority.** ⊠ *Los Angeles* ☎ *323/466–3876* ⊕ *www.metro.net.* **Santa Monica Big Blue Bus.** ⊠ *Los Angeles* ☎ *310/451–5444* ⊕ *www.bigbluebus.com.*

Metro/Public Transport

Los Angeles County Metropolitan Transit Authority. ⊠ *Los Angeles* ☎ *323/466–3876* ⊕ *www. metro.net.*

🚕 Taxi

LIMO COMPANIES Apex Limo. ⊠ *Los Angeles* ☎ *818/788–5466, 877/427–1777 for 24-hr pickup* ⊕ *www.apexlimola. com.* **Empire CLS.** ⊠ *Los Angeles* ☎ *800/451-5466* ⊕ *www.empirecls.com.* **First Class Limousine Service.** ⊠ *Los Angeles* ☎ *800/400–9771* ⊕ *www. first-classlimo.com.*

TAXI COMPANIES Beverly Hills Cab Co. ⊠ *Los Angeles* ☎ *800/273–6611* ⊕ *www.beverlyhills-cabco.com.* **Independent Cab Co.** ⊠ *Los Angeles* ☎ *800/521–8294* ⊕ *www. lataxi.com/new.* **United Checker Cab.** ⊠ *Los Angeles* ☎ *877/201-8294* ⊕ *www.unitedcheckercab. com/taxi-los-angeles. html.* **Yellow Cab Los Angeles.** ⊠ *Los Angeles* ☎ *424/222–2222* ⊕ *www. layellowcab.com.*

Train

Amtrak. ⊠ *Los Angeles* ☎ *800/872–7245* ⊕ *www.amtrak.com.* **Metrolink.** ⊠ *Los Angeles* ☎ *800/371–5465* ⊕ *www. metrolinktrains.com.* **Union Station.** ⊠ *800 N. Alameda St., Downtown* ☎ *213/683–6979* ⊕ *www. unionstationla.com* Ⓜ *Union Station.*

📍 Visitor Information

Beverly Hills Conference and Visitors Bureau. ☎ *310/248–1015, 800/345–2210* ⊕ *www. lovebeverlyhills.com.* **Discover Los Angeles.** ⊠ *Los Angeles* ☎ *213/624–7300* ⊕ *www.discoverlosange-les.com.* **Hollywood Chamber of Commerce.** ☎ *323/469–8311* ⊕ *www. hollywoodchamber.net.* **Long Beach Area Convention and Visitors Bureau.** ☎ *562/436–3645* ⊕ *www. visitlongbeach.com.* **Pasadena Convention and Visitor Bureau.** ☎ *800/307–7977* ⊕ *www.visitpasadena. com.* **Santa Monica Travel and Tourism.** ⊠ *Los Angeles* ☎ *800/544–5319* ⊕ *www.santamonica.com.* **Visit California.** ☎ *916/444–4429, 800/862–2543* ⊕ *www.visitcalifornia. com.*

Chapter 3

MALIBU

Updated by
Candice Yacono

◉ Sights	🍴 Restaurants	🛏 Hotels	💼 Shopping	🍸 Nightlife
★★★★☆	★★★★☆	★★☆☆☆	★★☆☆☆	★☆☆☆☆

NEIGHBORHOOD SNAPSHOT

TOP EXPERIENCES

■ **Watch the sunset over the Pacific:** Whether you enjoy it cliff-side or parked on a beach blanket, the view will stay fixed in your mind as a trip highlight.

■ **Sunbathe the day away at Zuma Beach:** When people picture California beaches, odds are they're picturing a place like Zuma. Miles long with easy access, this strip of sand attracts everyone from teenagers to seniors all intent on the perfect day out.

■ **Enjoy a world-class Japanese meal and drinks at Nobu:** This beachfront fixture perched along the Pacific is where movie moguls and other Malibu royalty go to see and be seen, all while enjoying Iron Chef Nobu Matsuhisa's heavenly sushi, Wagyu beef, and the beloved bento box dessert.

■ **Take in a performance at Will Geer's Theatricum Botanicum:** Want something different? This tucked-away amphitheater is a true locals' secret, with Malibu's famous weather accompanying outstanding outdoor shows. It boasts the opportunity for everyone in the family to watch or learn about theater, from Shakespeare to kids' acting workshops.

GETTING HERE

From Downtown, the easiest way to get to Malibu is by taking the Santa Monica Freeway (I–10) due west. Once you reach the end of the freeway, I–10 runs into Pacific Coast Highway. Head north on PCH to pass through Pacific Palisades into Malibu. Driving along the coast is a quintessential L.A. experience—but so is sitting in beach traffic, especially on weekends and in ideal weather conditions. Also avoid driving to Malibu during rush hour, when traffic along PCH moves at a snail's pace. Infrequent public transportation options are not recommended for Malibu, unless you only want to visit one location and can afford to wait.

PLANNING YOUR TIME

■ A visit to Malibu can easily be done in half a day to a day, including stops at select beaches, taking in a couple of restaurants, and savoring the sunset at your perch of choice. A partially cloudy day can yield the best sunsets. Plan your timing carefully: Arrive an hour beforehand to take advantage of "golden hour," especially if your plans include a photo shoot. Nightlife options, with the exception of a few restaurants and chic bars, are limited.

VIEWFINDER

■ **Point Dume Overlook:** For the ultimate Malibu photo op, work a yoga pose or make your best heart hands toward that dazzlingly deep blue Pacific while perched atop this dramatic cliff. Unsurprisingly, sunset amplifies the beauty here with a dizzying array of colors. ✉ 29377 *Cliffside Dr.*

■ **Malibu Beach Swings:** Influencers are drawn to the old-fashioned wooden swings set on the sand and facing the crystal clear water like moths to the Insta-flame. To find them, look for the beach access sign; from there, turn left and walk along the coast for about 10 minutes. ✉ 22133 *Pacific Coast Hwy.*

When people imagine the quintessential beach experience, they envision Malibu—a dream destination for nature lovers, celebrity followers, and beachgoers alike. Known for its iconic surf breaks and expansive sandy shores, Malibu is tucked away north of Santa Monica and is home to blockbuster names like Spielberg, Hanks, and Streisand. If you can tear yourself away from the beach, you'll find spectacular hiking opportunities with trails winding through the Santa Monica Mountains.

This ecologically fragile, 23-mile stretch of coastline is a world of its own, with its slopes slipping dramatically into the ocean. But like some of its more tempestuous celebrity residents, Malibu can be fickle when it comes to its looks. Whether it's natural disasters or architectural trends, Malibu is constantly reinventing itself.

With its luxurious beachfront villas, top-notch dining options, and breathtaking views of the Pacific, Malibu is the perfect place to escape and indulge in the California lifestyle.

Sights

Adamson House and Malibu Lagoon Museum

HISTORIC HOME | With spectacular views of Surfrider Beach and lush garden grounds, this Moorish Spanish–style house epitomizes all the reasons to live in Malibu. It was built in 1929 by the Rindge family, who owned much of the Malibu area in the early part of the 20th century. The Rindges had an enviable Malibu lifestyle, decades before the area was trendy. In the 1920s, Malibu was quite isolated; in fact, all visitors and some of the supplies arrived by boat at the nearby Malibu Pier. (The town becomes isolated today whenever rockslides close the highway.) The house, covered with magnificent tile work in rich blues, greens, yellows, and oranges from the now-defunct Malibu Potteries, is right on the beach—high chain-link fences keep out curious beachgoers. Even an outside dog bathtub near the servants' door is a tiled gem. Docent-led tours provide insights on family life here as well as the history of Malibu and its real estate. Signs posted around the grounds outside direct you on a self-guided tour, but you can't go inside the house without a guide. Guided tours take place on Thursdays, Fridays, and Saturdays from 11 am to 2 pm on the hour. There's paid parking in the adjacent county lot or in the lot at PCH and Cross Creek Road. ⊠ *23200 Pacific Coast Hwy., Malibu* ☎ *310/456–8432* ⊕ *www.adamsonhouse.org* ⚏ *$7* ☉ *Grounds close at sunset daily.*

Malibu Pier

MARINA/PIER | **FAMILY** | This rustically chic, 780-foot fishing dock is a great place to drink in the sunset, take in some coastal views, or watch local fishermen reel up a catch. Some tours also leave from here. A pier has jutted out on this spot since the early 1900s; storms destroyed the last one in 1995, and it was rebuilt in 2001. Over the years, private developers have worked with the state to refurbish the pier, which now yields a gift shop, water-sport and beach rentals, a jeweler housed in a vintage Airstream trailer, and a wonderful farm-to-table restaurant with stunning views and locations at both ends of the pier. ⊠ *Pacific Coast Hwy. at Cross Creek Rd., Malibu* ⊕ *www.malibupier.com.*

Topanga State Park

STATE/PROVINCIAL PARK | Boasting more than 14,000 acres of open space and 36 miles of celebrity-studded trails, Topanga State Park is many Malibu residents' extended backyard. The Trippet Ranch entrance gives you several trail options including a ½-mile nature loop, a 7-mile round-trip excursion to the Parker Mesa Overlook—breathtaking on a clear day—or a 10-mile trek to the Will Rogers park. (Exit U.S. 101 onto Topanga Canyon Boulevard in Woodland Hills and head south until you can turn left onto Entrada; if going north on PCH, turn onto Topanga Canyon Boulevard—a bit past Sunset Boulevard—and go north until you can turn right onto Entrada.) ⊠ *20829 Entrada Rd., Malibu* ☎ *310/574–2488* ⊕ *www.parks.ca.gov/?page_id=629* ⚏ *Parking $15.*

 Beaches

Dan Blocker Beach (*Corral Beach*)

BEACH | The narrow stretch of fine sand and rocks here make this little beach great for walking, light swimming, kayaking, and scuba diving rather than large gatherings. Clustered boulders create cozy spots for couples and picnickers, and because of the limited parking available along the PCH and the short hike necessary to reach the beach, it's rarely crowded. Originally owned by the star of the *Bonanza* TV series, the beach was donated to the state after Dan Blocker (who played Hoss) died in 1972. Locals still know this as Corral Beach. From the parking lot, walk a short distance up PCH in either direction to access the beach. **Amenities:** lifeguards; toilets. **Best for:** solitude; walking; swimming; snorkeling. ⊠ *26000 Pacific Coast Hwy., at Corral Canyon Rd., Malibu* ☎ *310/305–9503* ⊕ *beaches.lacounty.gov. dan-blocker-beach.*

Las Tunas Beach

BEACH | This small, rarely crowded beach, the southernmost in Malibu, is known for its groins (metal gates constructed in 1929 to protect against erosion) and has good swimming, diving, and fishing conditions and a rocky coastline that wraps elegantly around Pacific Coast Highway. Watch out for high tides and parking along PCH. **Amenities:** lifeguards; food and drink. **Best for:** solitude; swimming. ⊠ *19444 Pacific Coast Hwy., Malibu* ☎ *310/305–9545* ⊕ *beaches.lacounty.gov. las-tunas-beach.*

Leo Carrillo State Park

BEACH | **FAMILY** | On the very edge of Ventura County, this narrow beach is better for exploring than for sunning or swimming (watch that strong undertow!). If you do plan to swim, stay north of lifeguard towers 2, 4, and 5, but be sure to ask lifeguards about water conditions when you arrive. On your own or with a ranger, venture down at low tide to

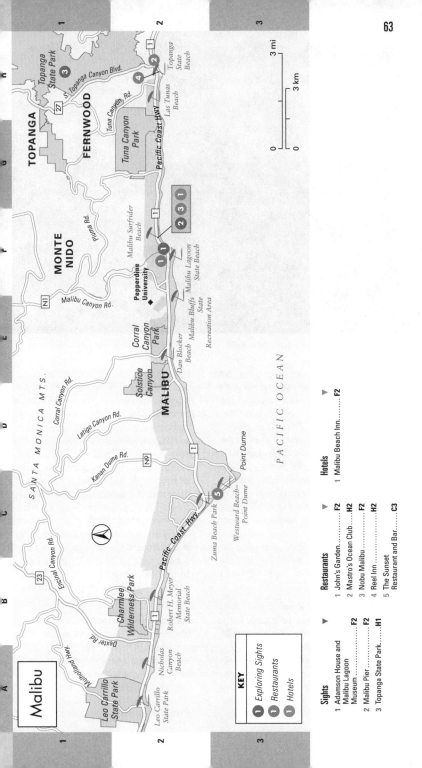

KEY

1 Exploring Sights

1 Restaurants

1 Hotels

Sights
▶
1 Adamson House and
Malibu Lagoon
Museum **F2**
2 Malibu Pier.................**F2**
3 Topanga State Park.......**H1**

Restaurants
▶
1 John's Garden............**F2**
2 Mastro's Ocean Club....**H2**
3 Nobu Malibu **F2**
4 Reel Inn **H2**
5 The Sunset
Restaurant and Bar.......**C3**

Hotels
▶
1 Malibu Beach Inn.........**F2**

Malibu is surrounded by the ocean on one side, and the Santa Monica Mountains on the other.

examine the tide pools among the rocks. Sequit Point, a promontory dividing the northwest and southeast halves of the beach, creates secret coves, sea tunnels, and boulders on which you can perch and fish. Generally, anglers stick to the northwest end of the beach; experienced surfers brave the rocks to the southeast. Campgrounds are set back from the beach; campsites must be reserved well in advance. Tide pools make this a great place for exploration. **Amenities**: parking; lifeguards (seasonally); toilets; showers. **Best for:** sunset; surfing; swimming; walking; windsurfing. ⊠ *35000 Pacific Coast Hwy., Malibu* ☎ *310/457–8144* ⊕ *parks. ca.gov/?page_id=616.*

Malibu Lagoon State Beach

BEACH | Bird-watchers, take note: in this 5-acre marshy area near Malibu Beach Inn you can spot egrets, blue herons, avocets, and gulls. (You need to stay on the boardwalks so as not to disturb their habitats.) The path leads out to a rocky stretch of Surfrider Beach and makes for a pleasant stroll. The sand is soft,

clean, and white, and you're also likely to spot a variety of marine life. Look for the signs to help identify these sometimes exotic-looking creatures. The lagoon is particularly enjoyable in the early morning and at sunset—and even more so now, thanks to a restoration effort that improved the lagoon's scent. The parking lot has limited hours, but street-side parking is usually available at off-peak times. The on-site Malibu Lagoon Museum reveals local history, and close by are shops and a theater. **Amenities:** parking (fee); lifeguards; toilets; showers. **Best for:** sunset; walking. ⊠ *23200 Pacific Coast Hwy., Malibu* ☎ *310/457–8143* ⊕ *www. parks.ca.gov/?page_id=835* 🅿 *Parking $12.*

Malibu Surfrider Beach

BEACH | Steady 3- to 5-foot waves make this beach, just west of Malibu Pier, a surfing paradise. Water runoff from Malibu Canyon forms a natural lagoon that's a sanctuary for 250 species of birds. Bird-watch, play volleyball, or take a walk on one of the nature trails, which are perfect for romantic sunset strolls. Guided tours of the surrounding wetlands are available seasonally. **Amenities:** parking (fee); lifeguards; toilets; food and drink; showers. **Best for:** sunset; surfing; swimming; windsurfing. ⊠ 23050 Pacific Coast Hwy., Malibu ☎ 310/457–8143 ⊕ www.beaches.lacounty.gov/malibu-surfrider-beach ☑ $12 parking.

Nicholas Canyon County Beach

BEACH | FAMILY | Sandier and less private than most of the rocky beaches surrounding it, this little beach is great for picnics. You can sit at a picnic table high up on a bluff overlooking the ocean and cast out a fishing line. Surfers call it Zero Beach because the waves take the shape of a hollow tube when winter swells peel off the reef. Peak weather attracts local food trucks. This site also hosts a 4-acre traditional Chumash village, which replicates a day in the life of the indigenous Chumash people, including their homes, canoes, handicrafts, and ceremonies. Request a guided tour in advance. **Amenities:** parking (fee); lifeguards; toilets; showers. **Best for:** solitude; surfing; walking; windsurfing. ⊠ 33805 Pacific Coast Hwy., Malibu ☎ 310/305–9503 ⊕ www.beaches.lacounty.gov/nicholas-canyon-beach.

★ Robert H. Meyer Memorial State Beach

BEACH | Part of Malibu's most beautiful coastal area, this beach is made up of three minibeaches—El Pescador, La Piedra, and El Matador—each with the same spectacular view. Scramble down the steps to the rocky coves via steep, steep stairways; all food and water needs to be toted in, as there are no services. Portable toilets at the trailhead are the only restrooms. "El Mat" has a series of caves, Piedra some nifty rock formations, and Pescador a secluded feel, but they're all picturesque and fairly private. **Amenities:** parking (fee); toilets. **Best for:** snorkeling; solitude; sunsets; surfing; walking; windsurfing.

⚠ **Keep track of the incoming tide so you won't get trapped between those otherwise scenic boulders.** ⊠ 32350, 32700, and 32900 Pacific Coast Hwy., Malibu ☎ 818/880–0363 ⊕ www.parks.ca.gov/?page_id=633.

Topanga State Beach

BEACH | The beginning of miles of public beach, Topanga has good surfing at the western end, at the mouth of the canyon, but is not an ideal swimming spot. Close to a busy section of PCH and rather narrow, the beach here is more lively, as groups of teenagers often zip over Topanga Canyon Boulevard from the Valley. There are swing sets on-site, as well as spots for fishing. **Amenities:** parking (fee); lifeguards; toilets; food and drink; showers. **Best for:** surfing. ⊠ 18700 block of Pacific Coast Hwy., Malibu ☎ 310/305–9503 ⊕ beaches.lacounty.gov/topanga-beach.

Westward Beach–Point Dume State Beach

BEACH | This famed promontory is a Malibu pilgrimage for any visitor to the area. Go tide pooling, fishing, snorkeling, or bird-watching (prime time is late winter to early spring). Hike to the top of the sandstone cliffs at Point Dume to whale-watch—their migrations can be seen between December and April—and take in dramatic coastal views. Westward is a favorite surfing beach, but the steep surf isn't for novices. The Sunset restaurant is between Westward and Point Dume (at 6800 Westward Beach Road). Otherwise, bring your own food, since the nearest concession is a long hike away. **Amenities:** parking (fee); lifeguards; toilets; food and drink; showers. **Best for:** surfing; walking. ⊠ 71030 Westward Beach Rd., Malibu ☎ 310/305–9503 ⊕ www.parks.ca.gov/?page_id=623 ☑ Parking $15.

Zuma Beach Park

BEACH | This 2-mile stretch of white sand, usually dotted with tanning teenagers, has it all, from fishing and kitesurfing to swings and volleyball courts. Beachgoers looking for quiet or privacy should

Around Point Dume, you'll find beautiful sandy coves.

head elsewhere. Stay alert in the water: the surf is rough and inconsistent, and riptides can surprise even experienced swimmers. A new metered parking program limits visits to 90 minutes at a time. **Amenities:** parking; lifeguards; toilets; food and drink; showers. **Best for:** partiers; sunset; swimming; walking. ✉ *30000 Pacific Coast Hwy., Malibu* ☎ *310/305–9522* 🌐 *beaches.lacounty.gov/zuma-beach* 🎫 *Metered parking: $0.50 per 15 mins (90-min max).*

🍴 Restaurants

John's Garden

$ | **SANDWICHES** | Assemble a beach picnic like a Malibu local at this humble, health-conscious spot where sandwiches include the Surfer Princess (turkey and avocado) and the salads include the Quinoa Queen. You can also choose from smoothies and juices, salads, açaí bowls, snacks, drinks, and more. John's has served locals for more than four decades; you'll find yourself mingling with them in the sunny outdoor dining area. **Known for:** ever-changing weekly specials; killer juices and smoothies; popular post-surf or beach-snacks spot. [$] *Average main: $16* ✉ *3835 Cross Creek Rd., Malibu* ☎ *310/456–8377* 🌐 *www.johnsgardenmalibu.com.*

Mastro's Ocean Club

$$$$ | **STEAKHOUSE** | This steak house doesn't just feature the best views of the beach; it's also a great place to scope out A-listers. You may be paying for the ambience, but mouthwatering Wagyu steaks, Dungeness crab, and lobster mashed potatoes just seem to taste better when the ocean is nipping at your feet. **Known for:** lively weekend brunch; live jazz nightly; reservations needed in advance. [$] *Average main: $60* ✉ *18412 Pacific Coast Hwy., Malibu* ☎ *310/454–4357* 🌐 *www.mastrosrestaurants.com.*

★ **Nobu Malibu**

$$$$ | **JAPANESE** | At famous chef-restaurateur Nobu Matsuhisa's coastal outpost, superchic clientele sails in for morsels of the world's finest fish. It's hard not to be seduced by the oceanfront

property; stellar sushi and ingenious specialties match the upscale setting. **Known for:** exotic fish; A-list celebrity chef; exceptional views. $ *Average main: $46* ✉ *22706 Pacific Coast Hwy., Malibu* ☎ *310/317–9140* ⊕ *www.noburestaurants.com.*

Reel Inn

$ | SEAFOOD | FAMILY | Escape the glitz and glamour at this decades-old, down-home Malibu institution. Long wooden tables and booths are often filled with fish-loving families chowing down on mahimahi sandwiches and freshly caught swordfish. **Known for:** easy-to-miss spot on PCH; fresh catches; dog-friendly patio. $ *Average main: $19* ✉ *18661 Pacific Coast Hwy., Malibu* ☎ *310/456–8221* ⊕ *www.reelinnmalibu.com.*

★ The Sunset Restaurant and Bar

$$$ | AMERICAN | This local secret is as close to the beach—Zuma Beach, in this case—as you can get for a meal without getting sand in your drink. Stop in at this friendly spot for a cocktail, selections from the raw bar, a meal from the extensive menu, or one of the unique salads. **Known for:** close to the beach; off-the-beaten path location; beautiful views; good happy hour. $ *Average main: $34* ✉ *Off Pacific Coast Hwy., just north of Zuma Beach, 6800 Westward Beach Rd., Malibu* ☎ *310/589–1007* ⊕ *www.thesunsetrestaurant.com.*

Hotels

★ Malibu Beach Inn

$$$$ | B&B/INN | Set right on exclusive Carbon Beach in a stretch known as Billionaire's Beach, Malibu's hideaway for the superrich remains the room to nab along the coast, with an ultrachic look thanks to designer Waldo Fernandez and an upscale restaurant and wine bar perched over the Pacific. **Pros:** views of the ocean from your private balcony; walking distance to the pier; epitome of beachside luxury. **Cons:** added fee for

the health club across the way; some in-room noise from PCH; no pool, gym, or hot tub. $ *Rooms from: $749* ✉ *22878 Pacific Coast Hwy., Malibu* ☎ *310/456–6444* ⊕ *www.malibubeachinn.com* ⤳ *47 rooms* ❍ *No Meals.*

Nightlife

Duke's Barefoot Bar

BARS | With a clear view of the horizon from almost everywhere, a sunset drink at Duke's Barefoot Bar inside Duke's Restaurant is how many beachgoers like to end their day. The entertainment is in keeping with the bar's theme, with Hawaiian dancers as well as live music by Hawaiian artists on Aloha Friday nights. The menu features island favorites like poke tacos, macadamia-crusted fish, and kalua pork. Indulge in a Sunday brunch buffet from 10 to 2. Just don't expect beach-bum prices, unless you stop by the happy hour weekday events like Taco Tuesday (bargain-priced fish, kalua pork, or grilled chicken tacos and beers). ✉ *21150 Pacific Coast Hwy., Malibu* ☎ *310/317–0777* ⊕ *www.dukesmalibu.com.*

Moonshadows

COCKTAIL LOUNGES | This indoor-outdoor lounge attracts customers with its modern look and views of the ocean. Think dark woods, cabana-style draperies, and ambient lighting in the Blue Lounge, open late on weekends. DJs are constantly spinning in the background, and there's never a cover charge. Sunday afternoons perfectly blend the laid-back ambience with good vibes. There's also a full-service restaurant on-site; try a sunset dinner or the lobster roll and dessert lineup to go with your cocktails. ✉ *20356 Pacific Coast Hwy., Malibu* ☎ *310/456–3010* ⊕ *www.moonshadowsmalibu.com.*

Performing Arts

Will Geer Theatricum Botanicum

THEATER | FAMILY | This open-air theater has put on classics like Shakespeare as well as new and relevant plays for five decades. You'll also find improv, performances of rare works, special events like Elizabethan and holiday fairs, classes, and Family Fundays in this bucolic space. The gardens have sitting areas for picnics before the show. You're encouraged to "Play and Stay" in the Topanga area by pairing your theater experience with a hike in the local hills or a trip to one of the area's unique restaurants beforehand; the company also hosts dinner (and a show) on certain nights.

■ **TIP→ Select weekends are great for families, with special shows performed with children in mind.** ⊠ *1419 N. Topanga Canyon Blvd., Topanga* ☎ *310/455–3723* ⊕ *www.theatricum.com.*

Shopping

Malibu Country Mart

SHOPPING CENTER | Stop by this outdoor outpost for the ultimate Malibu lifestyle experience, complete with browsing on-trend clothing (Nati, Ron Herman, or Madison) and eclectic California housewares and gifts (Malibu Colony Co.), picking up body-boosting wellness goodies (SunLife Organics), and finishing the day off with dinner at long-standing eatery Tra di Noi, reputed to be a favorite of Barbra Streisand. If you can squeeze in a workout, there are multiple studios to choose from, plus tarot readings at metaphysical outpost Malibu Shaman. Then reward yourself for your good health habits by stopping at K Chocolatier by Diane Krön for some of her famed truffles, derived from a Hungarian family recipe. ⊠ *3835 Cross Creek Rd., Malibu* ☎ *310/456–7300* ⊕ *www.malibucountrymart.com.*

Malibu Lumber Yard

SHOPPING CENTER | This shopping complex is your entrée into California beachfront living. Emblematic Malibu lifestyle stores in this shopping complex just down the street from the Malibu Country Mart include James Perse and Maxfield. The playground, with a large aquarium and alfresco dining area, makes this an ideal weekend destination for families. Try out the latest vintages at Strange Family Vineyards. Café Habana, a fresh import from NoLiTa and Brooklyn, brings pan-Cuban cuisine and a Shepard Fairey patio mural to the mix. ⊠ *3939 Cross Creek Rd., Malibu* ⊕ *www.themalibulumberyard.com.*

Activities

Solstice Canyon

HIKING & WALKING | Popular with local hikers and dog walkers, the 3-mile Solstice Canyon trail above Dan Blocker Beach is a scrub-filled hillside with wildflowers, a waterfall, and the ruins of old buildings. There are options for easy, moderate, or strenuous hikes. Bring a picnic and enjoy the dazzling ocean views. When you reach the top of the trail, return the same way you came for an easy hike. For a tougher option, detour onto the Rising Sun Trail on your way back to make a loop. The Solstice waterfall is a popular destination. On your way there you will pass the Keller House, a stone hunting cabin built over one hundred years ago and damaged in wildfires. If you're going on a sunny weekend, arrive early for parking. ⊠ *Intersection of Corral Canyon Rd. and Solstice Canyon Rd., Malibu* ⊕ *www.nps.gov/samo/planyourvisit/solsticecanyon.htm.*

Chapter 4

SANTA MONICA WITH PACIFIC PALISADES AND BRENTWOOD

4

Updated by
Candice Yacono

 Sights
★★★★☆

 Restaurants
★★★★☆

 Hotels
★★★★☆

 Shopping
★★★★☆

 Nightlife
★★★☆☆

NEIGHBORHOOD SNAPSHOT

TOP EXPERIENCES

■ **Bike along the Strand:** Spend the day on this 22-mile paved path, also known as the South Bay Bike Trail, which stretches from Santa Monica to Redondo Beach.

■ **Explore the Getty Villa:** Pretend you're a Roman patrician at this sprawling museum and garden complex in Pacific Palisades, designed to replicate an authentic villa unearthed near Pompeii.

■ **Spend the day at Santa Monica Pier:** See concerts here in the summer, or bring your family for a stroll during the day and enjoy classic fair food and carnival attractions; you can even try your hand at aerial trapeze work.

■ **Dine at a Michelin-starred eatery:** Santa Monica is the happy home to multiple Michelin-honored restaurants; one, Mélisse, even has two coveted stars. Act quick to get a reservation, then prepare your taste buds for paradise.

■ **View world-class art in a world-class place:** Rise up into the hills of Brentwood, where the architecturally striking Getty Center towers over the city and houses priceless works of art.

PLANNING YOUR TIME

The best way to tour Santa Monica is to park your car and walk, cycle, or skate along the area's famed bike path, known as the Strand. Short jaunts from there will take you to noncoastal main thoroughfares like Third Street Promenade or Abbot Kinney, though some of the top Santa Monica restaurants lie a bit farther east. Pedal (if you're hardy) or drive north from the pier to reach Pacific Palisades, or head inland on San Vicente Blvd. or Montana Avenue to reach the tony environs of Brentwood.

VIEWFINDER

■ **Santa Monica Pier:** The most coveted shots from any Santa Monica trip can be taken on or around the pier. Try a wide shot from the beach on either side, with the boardwalk visible in the background. For the perfect couples or group shot, perch yourself along the pier's railing with the carousel in the background. For a selfie you won't see every day, position yourself so the carousel radiates like a halo around your head. ⊠ *Colorado Ave.*

■ **The Getty Villa:** You can pose in the mosaic fountain in the East Garden or the grape arbor, find interesting architectural angles, or mimic the pose of one of the statues. But for the ultimate shot, stand at the far end of the reflecting pool by the satyr statue, with the colonnades and villa in the background. ⊠ *17985 Pacific Coast Hwy.*

■ **Inspiration Point:** This setting on a short, easy loop trail in Pacific Palisades is accessible from Will Rogers State Park. It comes with a heavenly panoramic view of the Pacific Ocean and the surrounding hills. Start your hike an hour before sunset for the perfect golden hour light. ⊠ *1525 Casale Rd.*

Santa Monica is one of the region's most iconic destinations. Silicon Beach, Southern California's tech hub, is centered in the Santa Monica area, which means employees from hundreds of companies like Activision, Hulu, and Snap (of Snapchat fame) flood the area and influence the flavor of its shops, restaurants, and nightlife. (Silicon Beach's influence also impacts many hotel amenity lists, to your benefit.)

Though its eyes are firmly on the future, Santa Monica nonetheless knows how to honor its past. The Santa Monica Pier, with its Ferris wheel and roller coaster, is the scene of a thousand movie and television show filmings, from *Forrest Gump* to *Iron Man*. And echoes of the area's heady, Hollywood-adjacent past are everywhere, from art deco former speakeasies to dive bars that still stand the test of time.

Nestled along the coast between Malibu and Santa Monica, Pacific Palisades is a hidden gem. This exclusive neighborhood boasts beautiful homes, stunning natural scenery, and a relaxed atmosphere. Enjoy a day at the beach, explore nearby parks and canyons, or indulge in some retail therapy at the Palisades Village. But the area's highlight is the historic Getty Villa, home to an impressive collection of ancient art and artifacts. To spend the day like an A-lister, head to Brentwood, a chic and upscale neighborhood. Known for its luxury estates, high-end shopping, and fine dining, this enclave is home to the trendy Brentwood Country Mart, where Gwyneth Paltrow's Goop store is joined by other designer names. Afterward, dine at acclaimed restaurants or explore the nearby Getty Center museum complex.

Santa Monica

This pedestrian-friendly little city, about 8.3 square miles, has a dynamic population of artists and writers, entertainment folks, educators, and retired people; its left-wing politics have earned it the nickname of the People's Republic of Santa Monica (just like Berkeley in Northern California). Mature trees, Mediterranean-style architecture, and strict zoning have helped create a sense of place often missing from L.A.'s residential neighborhoods, and its cooler, sometimes-foggy climate is another draw. Since it's a desirable neighborhood, real estate here isn't cheap.

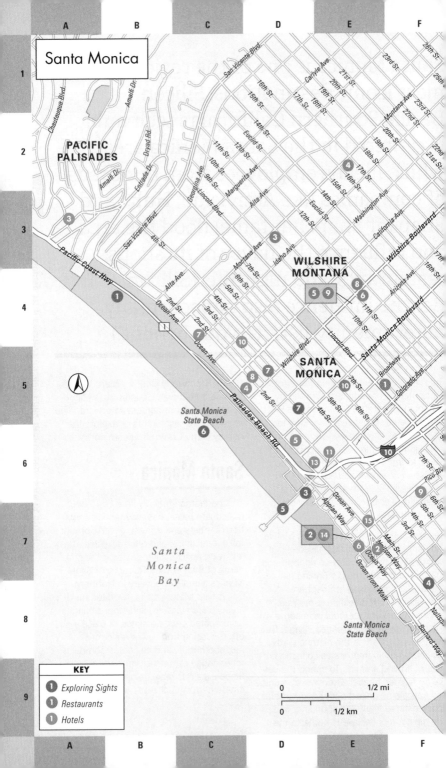

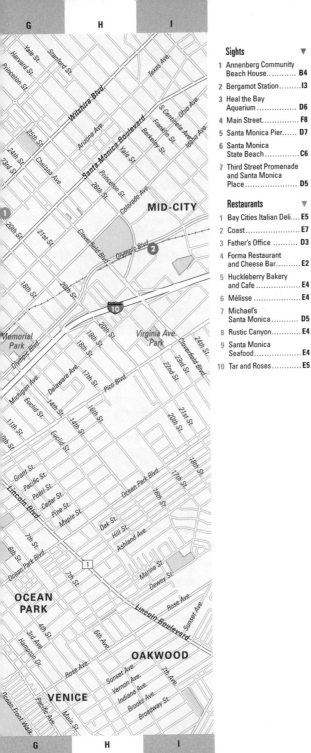

Sights ▼

1 Annenberg Community
  Beach House............ **B4**
2 Bergamot Station.........**I3**
3 Heal the Bay
  Aquarium **D6**
4 Main Street............... **F8**
5 Santa Monica Pier...... **D7**
6 Santa Monica
  State Beach.............. **C6**
7 Third Street Promenade
  and Santa Monica
  Place **D5**

Restaurants ▼

1 Bay Cities Italian Deli.... **E5**
2 Coast...................... **E7**
3 Father's Office **D3**
4 Forma Restaurant
  and Cheese Bar.......... **E2**
5 Huckleberry Bakery
  and Cafe **E4**
6 Mélisse **E4**
7 Michael's
  Santa Monica **D5**
8 Rustic Canyon............ **E4**
9 Santa Monica
  Seafood................... **E4**
10 Tar and Roses............ **E5**

Hotels ▼

1 The Ambrose............ **G3**
2 Bayside Hotel **E7**
3 Channel Road Inn....... **A3**
4 Fairmont Miramar Hotel
  and Bungalows
  Santa Monica **D5**
5 The Georgian Hotel..... **D6**
6 Hotel Casa del Mar...... **E7**
7 Hotel Oceana............ **C4**
8 Huntley Santa Monica
  Beach **D5**
9 Le Meridien Delfina
  Santa Monica **F6**
10 Palihouse
  Santa Monica............ **C4**
11 The Pierside.............. **E6**
12 Sea Shore Motel......... **F8**
13 Shore Hotel.............. **D6**
14 Shutters on
  the Beach................. **E7**
15 Viceroy
  Santa Monica **E7**

Santa Monica Pier has several classic amusement park rides, including the Looff Carousel, built in 1922.

Sights

Annenberg Community Beach House

OTHER ATTRACTION | This beachfront property was originally developed in the 1920s by William Randolph Hearst as a palatial private residence and a gathering spot for Hollywood's megastars. In 1947 it was converted into a members-only beach club; the state of California bought and renamed the club in 1959, but it took the earthquake of 2004 for the state to reconceive the property as a public place. With the help of the Annenberg Foundation, it reopened as a community beach house in 2009. Feel like a millionaire lounging by the pool on one of the beachside chairs, or lunch at the café while enjoying uninterrupted ocean views. The house's Beach=Culture event series includes a variety of classes (yoga, beach volleyball), readings, and exhibits; check the website for the calendar. Hours are subject to change, so call to confirm hours and book in advance. Book a pool reservation online in advance if possible. ⊠ 415 Pacific Coast Hwy., Santa Monica ☎ 310/458–4904 ⊕ www.annenberg-beachhouse.com ⊠ Free; pool $10.

Bergamot Station

ART GALLERY | Named after a stop on the Air Line trolley that once shuttled between Downtown and the Santa Monica Pier, Bergamot Station is now a depot for intriguing art. The industrial facades house more than 30 art galleries, shops, a café, a theater, and a museum. The galleries cover many kinds of media: photography, jewelry, and paintings from somber to lurid. Leashed, tame dogs are welcome and admission is free. ⊠ 2525 Michigan Ave., Santa Monica ☎ 310/453–7535 ⊕ www.bergamotstation.com ☉ Closed Sun. and Mon.

Heal the Bay Aquarium

AQUARIUM | **FAMILY** | Run by beach conservation group Heal the Bay, this live marine-life menagerie contains more than 100 species of marine animals and plants, all found in Santa Monica Bay. The Dorothy Green Room features live and interactive exhibits about local watersheds and short educational films on the weekends. The Kid's Corner provides books, games, and a puppet show. Don't miss this chance to learn about the area's ecology and staggering evidence of how pollution is affecting ocean life. The aquarium can be tricky to find—look for it tucked under the eastern end of the Santa Monica Pier bridge along Ocean Front Walk. Follow the colorful seascape murals that cover the outside walls.

■ TIP➜ Kids ages 12 and under receive free admission. ⊠ *1600 Ocean Front Walk, Santa Monica* ☎ *310/393–6149* ⊕ *www. healthebay.org/aquarium* ➲ *$10* ⊗ *Closed Mon. and Tues. seasonally.*

Main Street
BUSINESS DISTRICT | FAMILY | This thoroughfare is a great spot for star sightings or for strolling among the laid-back California crowd. Streets are lined with old-fashioned, colorful, and cozy boutiques that stock everything from high-end garments to bohemian favorites. There's also a standard crop of shopping mall outposts plus a good selection of casual restaurants and cafés. If you're in town on the last Saturday of the month, check out the sidewalk sale. ⊠ *Between Pacific St. and Rose Ave., and Santa Monica and Venice Blvds., Santa Monica* ⊕ *www. mainstreetsm.com.*

★ Santa Monica Pier
AMUSEMENT PARK/CARNIVAL | FAMILY | Souvenir shops, carnival games, arcades, eateries, an outdoor trapeze school, a small amusement park, and an aquarium all contribute to the festive atmosphere of this truncated pier at the foot of Colorado Boulevard below Palisades Park. The pier's trademark 46-horse Looff Carousel, built in 1922, has appeared in several films, including *The Sting.* The Soda Jerks ice-cream fountain (named for the motion the attendant makes when pulling the machine's arm) inside the carousel building is a pier staple, and the MariaSol restaurant at the end of the pier serves great fajitas. Free concerts are held on the pier in the summer. ⊠ *Colorado Ave.,*

Santa Monica ☎ *310/458–8901* ⊕ *www. santamonicapier.org.*

Santa Monica State Beach
BEACH | FAMILY | The first beach you'll hit after the Santa Monica Freeway (Interstate 10) runs into the Pacific Coast Highway, wide and sandy Santa Monica is *the* place for sunning and socializing. The Strand, which runs across the beach and for 22 miles in total, is popular among walkers, joggers, and bicyclists. Be prepared for a mob scene on summer weekends, when parking becomes an expensive ordeal. Swimming is fine (with the usual poststorm-pollution caveat); for surfing, go elsewhere. For a memorable view, climb up the stairway over PCH to Palisades Park, at the top of the bluffs. Free summer concerts are held on the pier on Thursday evenings. **Amenities:** parking; lifeguards; toilets; food and drink; showers; water sports. **Best for:** partiers; sunset; surfing; swimming; walking. ⊠ *1642 Promenade, PCH at California Incline, Santa Monica* ☎ *310/458– 8573* ⊕ *www.smgov.net/portals/beach* ➲ *Parking from $7 winter/$15 summer.*

Third Street Promenade and Santa Monica Place
BUSINESS DISTRICT | Stretch your legs along this pedestrian-only, three-block stretch of 3rd Street, close to the Pacific, lined with jacaranda trees, ivy-topiary dinosaur fountains, strings of lights, and branches of many major U.S. retail chains; indeed, it always seems to house the most-coveted brands for each generation of teens. Outdoor cafés, street vendors, movie theaters, and a rich nightlife make this a main gathering spot for locals, visitors, street artists and musicians, and performance artists, though it has yet to return to its pre-2020 level of bustle. Plan a night just to take it all in or take an afternoon for a long people-watching stroll. There's plenty of parking in city structures on the streets flanking the promenade. Santa Monica Place, at the south end of the

promenade, is a sleek outdoor mall and foodie haven. Its three stories are home to Nordstrom, Louis Vuitton, Coach, and other upscale retailers. Don't miss the ocean views from the rooftop food court. ✉ *3rd St., between Colorado and Wilshire Blvds., Santa Monica* 🌐 *www.downtownsm.com.*

🍴 Restaurants

This idyllic seaside town is a hotbed of culinary activity, with a dynamic farmers' market that attracts chefs from all over Los Angeles and local restaurants that celebrate farm-to-table, seasonal dining.

★ Bay Cities Italian Deli

$ | **SANDWICHES** | Part deli, part market, Bay Cities has been home to incredible Italian subs since 1925. This renowned counter-service spot is always crowded (best to order ahead), but monster subs run the gamut from the mighty meatball to the signature Godmother, made with prosciutto, ham, capicola, mortadella, Genoa salami, and provolone. **Known for:** market with rare imports; old-school, deli-style service; huge sandwiches. [$] *Average main: $10* ✉ *1517 Lincoln Blvd., Santa Monica* ☎ *310/395–8279* 🌐 *www.baycitiesitaliandeli.com* 🕘 *Closed Mon. and Tues.*

Coast

$$ | **AMERICAN** | Escape busy Santa Monica State Beach to dine at this casual café and bar within the unfussy oceanfront hotel Shutters on the Beach. Head here at sunset for sophisticated, fruity cocktails and fresh seafood, like oysters, Dungeness crab, or a lobster roll, just one block from Santa Monica Pier. **Known for:** great sunset drinks and dining; casual beachside atmosphere; California-inspired cuisine. [$] *Average main: $25* ✉ *Shutters on the Beach, 1 Pico Blvd., Santa Monica* ☎ *310/458–0030* 🌐 *www.shuttersonthebeach.com.*

Father's Office

$ | **AMERICAN** | Distinguished by its vintage neon sign, this gastropub is famous for handcrafted beers and a brilliant signature burger (along with a substantial and excellent menu). Topped with Gruyère and Maytag blue cheeses, arugula, caramelized onions, and applewood-smoked bacon compote, the Office Burger is a guilty pleasure worth waiting in line for, which is usually required. **Known for:** addictive sweet potato fries; strict no-substitutions policy; 36 craft beers on tap. [$] *Average main: $15* ✉ *1018 Montana Ave., Santa Monica* ☎ *310/736–2224* 🌐 *www.fathersoffice.com* 🕘 *Closed Mon. No lunch weekdays.*

Forma Restaurant and Cheese Bar

$$ | **ITALIAN** | Pasta is served here *dalla forma,* meaning it's cooked, then dipped into a cheese wheel and stirred up until it's coated with melted cheese before serving. Catering to a higher-end crowd, Forma specializes in cheeses, pastas, and pizzas. **Known for:** amazing pasta stirred in a cheese wheel; fresh mozzarella knots; Roman-style crispy artichokes. [$] *Average main: $28* ✉ *1610 Montana Ave., Santa Monica* ☎ *424/231–2868* 🌐 *www.formarestaurant.com.*

Huckleberry Bakery and Cafe

$ | **AMERICAN** | **FAMILY** | Founded by Santa Monica natives, Huckleberry brings together the best ingredients from local farmers and growers to craft diner-style comfort food with a chic twist. Nearly everything is made on-site, even the hot sauce and almond milk. **Known for:** from-scratch diner-style breakfast options; delectable pastries; house-made cold brew. [$] *Average main: $14* ✉ *1014 Wilshire Blvd., Santa Monica* ☎ *310/451–2311* 🌐 *www.huckleberrycafe.com.*

★ Mélisse

$$$$ | **FRENCH** | It's a gem tucked within a treasure box: hidden within Citrin, a one-Michelin-star restaurant, is Mélisse, a two-Michelin-star restaurant. Chef-owner Josiah Citrin entrusts chef de cuisine Ian

Scaramuzza to blend his modern French cooking with seasonal California produce at this Santa Monica institution. **Known for:** only 14 seats; the epitome of freshness and inventiveness; contemporary and elegant decor. $ *Average main: $399* ⊠ *1104 Wilshire Blvd., Santa Monica* ☎ *310/395–0881* ⊕ *www.melisse.com* ⊗ *Closed Sun.–Tues. No lunch.*

Michael's Santa Monica

$$$ | MODERN AMERICAN | Michael's, a Santa Monica institution, was one of the first to introduce "California cuisine" to a then-skeptical public more than four decades ago. Its rotating menu runs the gamut from 30-day dry-aged Wagyu bolognese with pappardelle to Japanese amberjack crudo with sweety drop peppers. **Known for:** stunning patio; storied history; happy hour marvels. $ *Average main: $35* ⊠ *1147 3rd St., Santa Monica* ☎ *310/451–0843* ⊕ *www.michaelssantamonica.com* ⊗ *Closed Sun., Mon. No lunch.*

Rustic Canyon

$$$ | MODERN AMERICAN | A Santa Monica mainstay, the seasonally changing menu at this farm-to-table restaurant consistently upends norms and has even earned a Michelin nod. The homey, minimalist space offers sweeping views of Wilshire Boulevard. **Known for:** never-ending wine list; knowledgeable staff; everything is made in-house. $ *Average main: $40* ⊠ *1119 Wilshire Blvd., Santa Monica* ☎ *310/393–7050* ⊕ *www.rusticcanyonrestaurant.com.*

Santa Monica Seafood

$$ | SEAFOOD | FAMILY | A Southern California favorite that seems like a tourist trap at first blush but decidedly isn't, this Italian seafood haven has been serving up fresh fish since 1939. This freshness comes from its pedigree as the largest seafood distributor in the Southwest. **Known for:** deliciously seasoned fresh entrées; oyster bar; historic fish market. $ *Average main: $20* ⊠ *1000 Wilshire Blvd., Santa Monica* ☎ *310/393–5244* ⊕ *www.santamonicaseafood.com.*

★ Tar and Roses

$$$ | MODERN AMERICAN | This small and dimly lit, romantic spot in Santa Monica is full of adventurously global options, like Singaporean chili crab cake or black cod with a fermented black bean marinade. The new American cuisine, which is centered on the restaurant's wood-fired oven, also features standouts like braised lamb shank with sweet potato, pomegranate, *labneh, zhough,* and flatbread. **Known for:** phenomenal oxtail dumplings; global inspirations; ever-changing menu. $ *Average main: $36* ⊠ *602 Santa Monica Blvd., Santa Monica* ☎ *310/587–0700* ⊕ *www.tarandroses.com.*

 Hotels

The Ambrose

$$$ | HOTEL | Tranquility pervades the airy, California Craftsman–style, four-story Ambrose, which blends right into its mostly residential Santa Monica neighborhood. **Pros:** "green" practices like nontoxic cleaners and recycling bins; partial ocean views; nice amenities (like car service and wine reception) for a $25 extra fee. **Cons:** quiet, residential area of Santa Monica; parking fee ($39); not walking distance to beach. $ *Rooms from: $389* ⊠ *1255 20th St., Santa Monica* ☎ *310/315–1555, 877/262–7673* ⊕ *www.ambrosehotel.com* ⤴ *77 rooms* ⦿ *No Meals.*

Bayside Hotel

$$$ | HOTEL | Tucked snugly into a narrow corner lot, the supremely casual Bayside's greatest asset is its prime spot directly across from the beach, within walkable blocks from the Third Street Promenade and Santa Monica Pier. **Pros:** cheaper weeknight stays; beach access and views; some rooms with kitchens and balconies. **Cons:** no lobby and expensive parking; basic bedding; thin walls and street noise. $ *Rooms from:*

$359 ✉ 2001 Ocean Ave., Santa Monica ☎ 310/396–6000, 800/525–4447 🌐 baysidehotel.com 🛏 45 rooms 🍴 No Meals.

★ Channel Road Inn

$$$ | B&B/INN | A quaint surprise in Southern California, the Channel Road Inn is every bit the country retreat bed-and-breakfast lovers adore, with four-poster beds, fluffy duvets, and a cozy living room with a fireplace. **Pros:** free wine-and-cheese hour each afternoon; home-cooked breakfast included; meditative rose garden on-site. **Cons:** no pool; need a car (or Uber) to get around; decidedly non-L.A. decor is not for everyone. [$] *Rooms from: $365 ✉ 219 W. Channel Rd., Santa Monica ☎ 310/459–1920 🌐 www.channelroadinn.com 🛏 15 rooms 🍴 Free Breakfast.*

Fairmont Miramar Hotel and Bungalows Santa Monica

$$$$ | HOTEL | A mammoth Moreton Bay fig tree dwarfs the main entrance of the 5-acre, beach-adjacent Santa Monica wellness retreat and lends its name to the inviting on-site Mediterranean-inspired restaurant, FIG, which focuses on local ingredients and frequently refreshes its menu. **Pros:** coveted central location with a private club feel; swanky open-air cocktail spot, the Bungalow, on-site; retrofitted '20s and '40s bungalows. **Cons:** all this luxury comes at a big price; standard rooms are on the small side; breakfast not included. [$] *Rooms from: $599 ✉ 101 Wilshire Blvd., Santa Monica ☎ 310/576–7777, 866/540–4470 🌐 www.fairmont.com/santamonica 🛏 297 rooms 🍴 No Meals.*

The Georgian Hotel

$$$$ | HOTEL | Driving by, you can't miss the Georgian, built in 1933: its art deco exterior is aqua, with ornate bronze grillwork and a charming oceanfront veranda. **Pros:** many ocean-view rooms; front terrace is a great people-watching spot; lively bar and restaurant. **Cons:** pricey parking and daily amenity fee; some rooms have unremarkable views; decor a bit tired in places. [$] *Rooms from: $875 ✉ 1415 Ocean Ave., Santa Monica ☎ 310/395–9945, 800/538–8147 🌐 www.georgianhotel.com 🛏 84 rooms 🍴 No Meals.*

Hotel Casa del Mar

$$$$ | HOTEL | In the 1920s, it was a posh beach club catering to the city's elite; now the Casa del Mar is one of SoCal's most luxurious and pricey beachfront hotels with a heavenly lobby, three extravagant two-story penthouses, a raised deck and pool, an indulgent spa, and an elegant ballroom facing the sand. **Pros:** excellent dining at Catch; modern amenities; gorgeous beachfront rooms. **Cons:** no room balconies; without a doubt, one of L.A.'s priciest beach stays; atmosphere can be a bit stuffy. [$] *Rooms from: $700 ✉ 1910 Ocean Way, Santa Monica ☎ 310/581–5533, 800/898–6999 🌐 www.hotelcasadelmar.com 🛏 129 rooms 🍴 No Meals.*

Hotel Oceana

$$$$ | HOTEL | Following an ultraswank refresh, the suites-only Oceana manages to achieve a low-key vibe while still dripping in luxury. **Pros:** walk to prime shopping districts; gorgeous guests-only restaurant with stunning ocean views; bubbly at check-in. **Cons:** small pool; breakfast not included; no coffeemakers in rooms. [$] *Rooms from: $925 ✉ 849 Ocean Ave., Santa Monica ☎ 310/393–0486, 800/777–0758 🌐 www.hoteloceanasantamonica.com 🛏 70 suites 🍴 No Meals.*

Huntley Santa Monica Beach

$$$$ | HOTEL | This sleek, tech-savvy property keeps the Silicon Beach business traveler in mind. **Pros:** great ocean views; fun social scene; great views (and drinks) at the Penthouse, the hotel's top-floor restaurant. **Cons:** no pool; noise from the restaurant and bar; tech bro vibe not for everyone. [$] *Rooms from: $549 ✉ 1111 2nd St., Santa Monica ☎ 310/394–5454 🌐 www.thehuntleyhotel.com 🛏 220 rooms 🍴 No Meals.*

Le Meridien Delfina Santa Monica

$$$ | **HOTEL** | **FAMILY** | Not far from I–10 and four blocks from the Expo Line, this hotel appeals to business travelers and leisure travelers who fancy the sleek interiors and close proximity to beaches and restaurants. **Pros:** solid dining on property; retro designer touches; cabanas and pool on ground floor. **Cons:** not as centrally located as some Santa Monica hotels; not all rooms have balconies; $52 daily parking. $ *Rooms from: $369 ⊠ 530 Pico Blvd., Santa Monica* ☎ *310/399–9344, 888/627–8532* ⊕ *www.lemeridiendelfina. com* ⤳ *310 rooms* ⦿ *No Meals.*

Palihouse Santa Monica

$$$ | **HOTEL** | Tucked in a posh residential area three blocks from the sea and lively Third Street Promenade, Palihouse Santa Monica caters to design-minded world travelers, with spacious rooms and suites decked out in whimsical antiques. **Pros:** Apple TV in rooms; walking distance to Santa Monica attractions; fully equipped kitchens. **Cons:** no pool; decor might not appeal to more traditional travelers; parking fee ($45). $ *Rooms from: $450 ⊠ 1001 3rd St., Santa Monica* ☎ *310/394–1279* ⊕ *www.palihousesantamonica.com* ⤳ *38 rooms* ⦿ *No Meals.*

★ **The Pierside**

$$$ | **HOTEL** | The closest hotel to the Santa Monica Pier (it's just across PCH, with easy pedestrian bridge access), the breezy, surf-inspired Pierside, opened in early 2023, is the epitome of Southern California cool. **Pros:** heated saltwater pool; elegant seaside aesthetic and atmosphere; proximity to the beach. **Cons:** some hallway noise; open showers in some rooms not for everyone; $55 parking fee. $ *Rooms from: $495 ⊠ 120 Colorado Ave., Santa Monica* ☎ *310/451–0676* ⊕ *www.thepiersidehotel.com* ⤳ *132 rooms* ⦿ *No Meals.*

Sea Shore Motel

$$ | **HOTEL** | On Santa Monica's busy Main Street, the Sea Shore (family-owned for five decades) is a charming throwback

to Route 66 and to '60s-style roadside motels, nestled in an ultratrendy neighborhood. **Pros:** close to beach and restaurants; free Wi-Fi, parking, and use of beach equipment; popular rooftop deck. **Cons:** street noise; motel-style decor and beds; not the Santa Monica style a lot of people are looking for. $ *Rooms from: $200 ⊠ 2637 Main St., Santa Monica* ☎ *310/392–2787* ⊕ *www.seashoremotel. com* ⤳ *25 rooms* ⦿ *No Meals.*

Shore Hotel

$$$ | **HOTEL** | With views of the Santa Monica Pier, this hotel with a friendly staff offers eco-minded travelers stylish rooms with a modern design, just steps from the sand and sea. **Pros:** near beach and Third Street Promenade; rainfall showerheads; solar-heated pool and hot tub. **Cons:** expensive rooms and parking fees; fronting busy Ocean Avenue; some sharing a room may be wary of the see-through shower. $ *Rooms from: $399 ⊠ 1515 Ocean Ave., Santa Monica* ☎ *310/458–1515* ⊕ *shorehotel.com* ⤳ *164 rooms* ⦿ *No Meals.*

★ **Shutters on the Beach**

$$$$ | **HOTEL** | **FAMILY** | Set right on the sand, this Cape Cod–inspired inn has become synonymous with staycations, with the beachfront location and showhouse decor making it one of SoCal's most popular luxury hotels. **Pros:** built-in cabinets filled with art books and curios; restaurants you'll never tire of dining in; bathrooms come with whirlpool tubs. **Cons:** have to pay for extras like beach chairs; very expensive; breakfast not included. $ *Rooms from: $675 ⊠ 1 Pico Blvd., Santa Monica* ☎ *310/458–0030, 800/334–9000* ⊕ *www.shuttersonthe-beach.com* ⤳ *198 rooms* ⦿ *No Meals.*

Viceroy Santa Monica

$$$$ | **HOTEL** | Tropical casual meets urbane at this stylized, airy seaside escape, where the cozy rooms, which all have French balconies, draw quite the upscale clientele. **Pros:** hip lobby and restaurant–lounge; chic lounge and

poolside socializing; pedestrian-friendly area. **Cons:** superpricey bar and dining; pool for dipping, not laps; sometimes snooty ambience. [$] *Rooms from: $499* ✉ *1819 Ocean Ave., Santa Monica* ☎ *310/260–7500, 800/622–8711* 🌐 *www.viceroysantamonica.com* 🛏 *162 rooms* 🍴 *No Meals.*

Nightlife

In Santa Monica, the focus of nightlife shifts toward live music, historic dives, and any space that has a view of the ocean.

★ Chez Jay

BARS | Around since 1959, this dive bar and steak joint continues to be a well-loved place in Santa Monica. Everyone from the young to the old (including families) frequents this historical landmark, where Marilyn Monroe is said to have once canoodled with JFK. It's a charming place, from the well-worn booths with their red-checkered tablecloths to the ship's wheel near the door. Photographs are discouraged, but if you ask politely, you can learn how one of the restaurant's famous free peanuts ended up on a trip to the Moon. The backyard lounge is perfect for warm, low-key days; the grub's solid, with a more contemporary menu, and the happy hour is popular amongst locals and tourists alike. ✉ *1657 Ocean Ave., Santa Monica* ☎ *310/395–1741* 🌐 *www.chezjays.com.*

The Galley

BARS | Nostalgia reigns at this true neighborhood fixture, which opened in 1934 and has had the same owner for more than 30 years. As Santa Monica's oldest restaurant and bar, the Galley has a consistent nautical theme inside and out: the boatlike exterior features wavy blue neon lights and porthole windows. Inside, fishing nets and anchors adorn the walls, and the whole place is aglow with colorful string lights. Most patrons tend to crowd the center bar, with the more dinner-oriented folks frequenting the booths. The back patio is also a solid choice in good weather, especially for weekend brunch. And strangely enough, the secret-recipe salad dressing is justifiably famous. ✉ *2442 Main St., Santa Monica* ☎ *310/452–1934* 🌐 *www.thegalleyrestaurant.net.*

Harvelle's

LIVE MUSIC | The focus of this bar and music club is on live jazz, blues, and soul, though it also serves up rock and roll and even live, band-accompanied karaoke on some nights. The club is small, with an even smaller checkerboard dance floor. Reserve tables in advance at this Westside establishment; order a martini off the Deadly Sins menu, and catch a Toledo burlesque show on Sunday night. ✉ *1432 4th St., Santa Monica* ☎ *310/395–1676* 🌐 *www.harvelles.com.*

Performing Arts

Aero Theatre

FILM | Look like a local and attend an event at this Santa Monica–based American Cinematheque theater first opened in 1940. The name refers to its roots: this Streamline Moderne-style theater was built by the Douglas Aircraft Company to entertain its armies of workers during the war effort. Newly renovated, it offers new projection equipment, improved sound, and cushier facilities. In addition to now-standard digital films, the theater is equipped to show 35mm and 70mm reels. American Cinematheque also hosts industry events like filmmaker discussions and revivals. ✉ *1328 Montana Ave., Santa Monica* ☎ *323/466–3456* 🌐 *www.aerotheatre.com.*

Santa Monica Playhouse

THEATER | **FAMILY** | Housing three theaters and boasting the same artistic direction for 50 years, this venue brings a number of original plays, touring companies, poetry readings, spoken-word events, and revival shows to the stage. The Family

The three-block Third Street Promenade is great for shopping and is for pedestrians only.

Theatre Musical Matinee Series features family-friendly reworked classic plays. Educational programs and workshops are available for all ages. ✉ *1211 4th St., Santa Monica* ☎ *310/394–9779* ⊕ *www. santamonicaplayhouse.com.*

 # Shopping

The breezy beachside communities of Santa Monica and Venice are ideal for leisurely shopping. Scores of tourists (and many locals) gravitate to the Third Street Promenade, a popular pedestrian-only shopping area that's within walking range of the beach and historic Santa Monica Pier. But there's more to the area than trendy chain stores; there's also a treasure trove of vintage goods and antiques to be found on Main Street and Ocean Park Boulevard, and Montana Avenue is home to retailers specializing in indie and artisanal wares.

In Venice, Abbot Kinney Boulevard is abuzz with spots to shop for chic clothing, accessories, and housewares—including plenty of upscale outposts. The strip also has some of the city's best eateries, so it's easy to kill two birds with one stone. Nearby Lincoln and Rose Avenues have also gained retail momentum in recent years, with many emerging brands choosing the area to open their first-ever storefronts. For those looking for the next big thing, this just might be the place to find it.

The Acorn Store

TOYS | FAMILY | Remember when toys didn't require batteries or apps? This old-fashioned shop (for ages 10 and under) sparks children's imaginations with dress-up clothes, science-oriented gifts, picture books, and hand-painted wooden toys by brands like Poan and Haba. ✉ *1220 5th St., near Wilshire Blvd., Santa Monica* ☎ *310/451–5845* ⊕ *www. theacornstore.com.*

Brat

MIXED CLOTHING | If your trip to La La Land has you itching to upgrade your wardrobe with a little attitude, look no further than Brat. No matter what your proclivity—be it rockabilly, Goth, punk, or cottagecore—Brat has that unique item you didn't even know you needed. It's also a perfect place to find something "L.A. cool" for folks back home. ✉ *1938 14th St., Santa Monica* ☎ *310/452–2480* ⊕ *www.bratstore.com.*

Kathmandu Boutique

OTHER SPECIALTY STORE | Founded by a Nepali owner, this shop instantly whisks you away to the Himalayas, with its wide-ranging selection of clothing, accessories, housewares, incense, and more. Sip on some chai tea and indulge your inner hippie, or find all the spiritual products you've been craving. ✉ *1844 Lincoln Blvd., Santa Monica* ☎ *310/396–4036* ⊕ *www.kathmanduboutique.com.*

Quinnie and B

TOYS | FAMILY | This self-described "tiny toy shop" fails to mention that it is also a beautifully curated jewel box of a tiny toy shop. Along with traditional toys like L.O.L. Surprise, this sunny, well-organized space offers a wide range of kids' books, plushies, accessories, musical instruments, science and craft kits, puzzles, art, holiday cookie kits and seasonal decorations, and more. ✉ *1632 Ocean Park Blvd., Santa Monica* ☎ *310/398–8814* ⊕ *www.quinnieb.com.*

Third Street Promenade

NEIGHBORHOODS | There is no shortage of spots to shop everything from sporting goods to trendy fashions on this pedestrian-friendly strip. Outposts here are mainly of the chain variety, and in between splurging on books, clothing, sneakers, and more, shoppers can pop into one of the many eateries, watch street performers and artists do their thing, or even catch a movie at one of the theaters. Additionally, the chef-approved Farmers Market takes over twice a week (Wednesday and Saturday), and with the beach just a few steps away, the destination is a quintessential California stop. ✉ *3rd St., between Broadway and Wilshire Blvd., Santa Monica.*

Parking Tip

Parking in Santa Monica can be next to impossible on Wednesdays, when some streets are blocked off for the Farmers Market, but there are several parking structures with free one- to two-hour parking.

Activities

Legends Beach Bike Tours

BEACH | FAMILY | Those who like a little history with their vacations should take a guided tour with Legends, part of Perry's Café and Rentals. A tour takes you through the unique enclaves of Santa Monica and Venice Beach, as you learn their role in the history of surf and skate in Southern California. Bike tours are offered daily at 11 am, last two hours (plus one hour of free riding), and cost $69 per adult, $35 for kids under 12, and $60 for students with ID and seniors. ✉ *930 Palisades Beach Rd., Santa Monica* ☎ *310/939–0000* ⊕ *www.perryscafe.com.*

Trapeze School New York

AMUSEMENT PARK/CARNIVAL | Get a different view of the energetic scene by taking a trapeze class right on the Santa Monica Pier. Launch off from a platform 23 feet high and sail above the crowds and waves. Beginners are welcome. Classes are held daily, but times vary, so check the website and make reservations in advance. ✉ *370 Santa Monica Pier, Santa Monica* ☎ *310/394–5800* ⊕ *www.losangeles.trapezeschool.com.*

Pacific Palisades

Stunning ocean views, glamorous homes, and dusty canyons define this affluent area snug between Santa

The Getty Villa is a gorgeous setting for a spectacular collection of ancient art.

Monica and Malibu. Although there is a downtown village of sorts south of Sunset Boulevard, natural terrain is a main draw here, luring visitors to hiking trails or the Palisades' winding roads. They also flock to the jaw-dropping Getty Villa, a residence-turned-museum designed to re-create a Roman residence of ancient times.

 Sights

★ **Getty Villa Museum**

ART MUSEUM | Feeding off the cultures of ancient Rome, Greece, and Etruria, the Getty Villa exhibits astounding antiquities, though on a first visit even they take a back seat to their environment. This megamansion sits on some of the most valuable coastal property in the world. Modeled after the Villa dei Papiri in Herculaneum, a Roman estate owned by Julius Caesar's father-in-law that was covered in ash when Mt. Vesuvius erupted, the Getty Villa includes beautifully manicured gardens, reflecting pools, and statuary. The structures blend thoughtfully into the rolling terrain and significantly improve the public spaces, such as the outdoor amphitheater, gift store, café, and entry arcade. Talks, concerts, and educational programs are offered at an indoor theater.

■**TIP**→ **An advance timed entry ticket is required for admission. Tickets are free and may be ordered from the museum's website or by phone.** ⊠ *17985 Pacific Coast Hwy., Pacific Palisades* ☎ *310/440–7300* ⊕ *www.getty.edu* ✉ *Free, tickets required; parking $20* ⊘ *Closed Tues.*

Self-Realization Fellowship Lake Shrine

GARDEN | A quintessential (and free) L.A. experience, the nondenominational Lake Shrine temple and meditation garden was founded by guru Paramahansa Yogananda's Self-Realization Fellowship, a nonprofit spiritual organization headquartered in Los Angeles that promotes traditional yoga and meditation. The gardens, lakes, trails, windmill, and other structures are enjoyed by practitioners, locals, celebrities, and office workers alike as a place to step out of the rat race

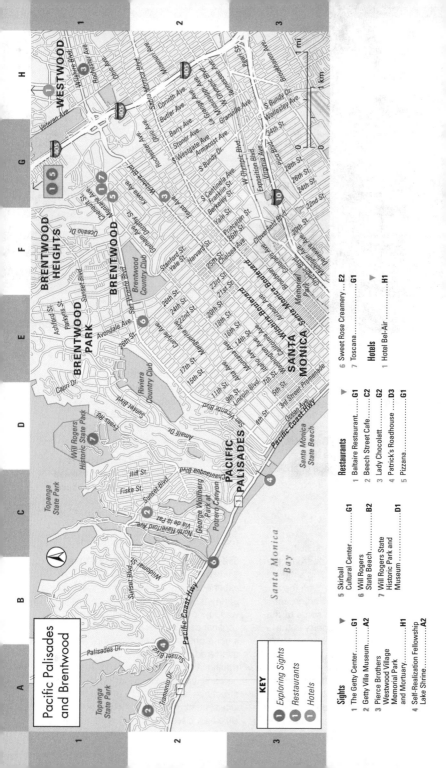

Pacific Palisades and Brentwood

KEY

1 Exploring Sights

1 Restaurants

1 Hotels

Sights ▶

1 The Getty Center **G1**

2 Getty Villa Museum **A2**

3 Pierce Brothers
Westwood Village
Memorial Park
and Mortuary **H1**

4 Self-Realization Fellowship
Lake Shrine **A2**

5 Skirball
Cultural Center **G1**

6 Will Rogers
State Beach **B2**

7 Will Rogers State
Historic Park and
Museum **D1**

Restaurants ▶

1 Baltaire Restaurant **G1**

2 Beech Street Cafe **C2**

3 Lady Chocolatt **G2**

4 Patrick's Roadhouse **D3**

5 Pizzana **G1**

6 Sweet Rose Creamery **E2**

7 Toscana **G1**

Hotels ▶

1 Hotel Bel-Air **H1**

and into tranquility for a few minutes. Free reservations are mandatory and can be made online. ✉ *17190 Sunset Blvd., Pacific Palisades* ☎ *310/454–4114* 🌐 *www.lakeshrine.org* ⏲ *Closed Mon. and Tues.* ✍ *Reservations are mandatory.*

Will Rogers State Beach

BEACH | FAMILY | This clean, sandy, 3-mile beach, with a dozen volleyball nets, gymnastics equipment, and a playground for kids, is an all-around favorite. The surf is gentle, perfect for swimmers and beginning surfers, and crowds are frequently smaller than in other spots along the shore. However, it's best to avoid the beach after a storm, when untreated water flows from storm drains into the sea. **Amenities:** parking; lifeguards; toilets; food and drink; showers. **Best for:** sunset; swimming; walking. ✉ *17700 PCH, 2 miles north of Santa Monica Pier, Pacific Palisades* ☎ *310/305–9503* 🌐 *www.parks.ca.gov* 🎟 *Parking from $5.*

Will Rogers State Historic Park and Museum

HISTORIC HOME | A humorist, actor, and rambling cowboy, Will Rogers lived on this site in the 1920s and 1930s. His ranch house, a folksy blend of Navajo rugs and Mission-style furniture, has become a museum of Rogers memorabilia. A short film shown in the visitor center highlights Rogers's roping technique and homey words of wisdom. Open for docent-led tours Thursday through Sunday, the ranch house features Rogers's stuffed practice calf and the high ceiling he raised so he could practice his famed roping style indoors.

Rogers was a polo enthusiast, and in the 1930s his front-yard polo field attracted such friends as Douglas Fairbanks Sr. for weekend games. Today the park's broad lawns are excellent for picnicking, and there are miles of eucalyptus-lined trails for hiking, as well as a horseback riding concession. Free non-holiday weekend games are scheduled from May through October, weather permitting.

Also part of the park is Inspiration Point Trail. Who knows how many of Will Rogers's famed witticisms came to him while he and his wife hiked or rode horses along this trail from their ranch? The point is on a detour off the lovely 2-mile loop, which you can join near the riding stables beyond the parking lot. The panorama is one of L.A.'s widest and most wow-inducing, from the peaks of the San Gabriel Mountains in the east and the Oz-like cluster of Downtown skyscrapers to Catalina Island looming off the coast to the southwest. If you're looking for a longer trip, the top of the loop meets up with the 65-mile Backbone Trail, which connects to Topanga State Park. ✉ *1501 Will Rogers State Park Rd., Pacific Palisades* ☎ *310/454–8212* 🌐 *www.parks.ca.gov/?page_id=626* 🎟 *Free; parking $12.*

🍴 Restaurants

Beech Street Cafe

$ | ITALIAN | This reliably quick and easy bistro serves up fresh, classic pastas and pizzas in the Palisades Village. Savor baked goat cheese on the romantic, breezy patio as you watch the glitterati go by, or enjoy a more substantial dish like linguine and clams inside under old-world wooden beams. **Known for:** charming patio area; quick service; delectable lobster ravioli. [$] *Average main: $18* ✉ *863 N. Swarthmore Ave., Pacific Palisades* 🌐 *www.beechstreetcafe.com.*

Patrick's Roadhouse

$ | AMERICAN | FAMILY | As the rooftop dinosaur and Lady Liberty statues suggest, this leprechaun-green roadhouse, tucked into the hillside of Pacific Palisades, is a maximalist ode to the past crammed with memorabilia ranging from British railway signs to cheeky bronze statuettes. An Old World portrait of a young Arnold Schwarzenegger in epaulets lords over the proceedings, along with Arnold's throne, which you can request to be seated in. **Known for:**

endless kitsch; solid diner fare; California's best roadside diner. $ *Average main: $19* ✉ *106 Entrada Dr., Pacific Palisades* ☎ *310/459–4544* ⊕ *patricks-roadhouse.info* ⊗ *No dinner Mon.*

Brentwood

This wealthy residential enclave north of Santa Monica is home to the world-class Getty Center.

Sights

★ The Getty Center

ART MUSEUM | FAMILY | With its curving walls and isolated hilltop perch, the Getty Center resembles a pristine fortified city of its own. You may have been lured there by the beautiful views of Los Angeles—on a clear day stretching all the way to the Pacific Ocean—but the amazing architecture, uncommon gardens, and fascinating art collections will be more than enough to capture and hold your attention. When the sun is out, the complex's rough-cut travertine marble skin seems to soak up the light.

Getting to the center involves a bit of anticipatory lead-up. At the base of the hill lies the underground parking structure. From there you either walk or take a smooth, computer-driven tram up the steep slope, checking out the Bel Air estates across the humming 405 freeway. The six pavilions that house the museum surround a central courtyard and are bridged by walkways. From the courtyard, plazas, and walkways, you can survey the city from the San Gabriel Mountains to the ocean.

In a ravine separating the museum and the Getty Research Institute, conceptual artist Robert Irwin created the playful Central Garden in stark contrast to Richard Meier's mathematical architectural geometry. The garden's design is what Hollywood feuds are made of: Meier couldn't control Irwin's vision, and the two men sniped at each other during construction, with Irwin stirring the pot with every loose twist his garden path took. The result is a refreshing garden walk whose focal point is an azalea maze (some insist the Mickey Mouse shape is on purpose) in a reflecting pool.

Inside the pavilions are the galleries for the permanent collections of European paintings, drawings, sculpture, illuminated manuscripts, and decorative arts, as well as world-class temporary exhibitions and photographs gathered internationally. The Getty's collection of French furniture and decorative arts, especially from the early years of Louis XIV (1643–1715) to the end of the reign of Louis XVI (1774–92), is renowned for its quality and condition; you can even see a pair of completely reconstructed salons. In the paintings galleries, a computerized system of louvered skylights allows natural light to filter in, creating a closer approximation of the conditions in which the artists painted. Notable among the paintings are Rembrandt's *The Abduction of Europa*, Van Gogh's *Irises*, Monet's *Wheatstacks, Snow Effects*, and *Morning*, and James Ensor's *Christ's Entry into Brussels*.

If you want to start with a quick overview, pick up the brochure in the entrance hall that guides you to collection highlights. There's also an instructive audio tour with commentaries by art historians and other experts. The Getty also presents lectures, films, concerts, art workshops, and special programs for kids, families, and all-around culture lovers. The complex includes an upscale restaurant and downstairs cafeteria with panoramic window views. There are also outdoor coffee carts.

■ TIP ➡ **On-site parking is subject to availability and can fill up by midday on holidays and in the summer, so try to come early in the day or after lunch.**

The Getty Center has stunning architecture, world-class art collections, and gorgeous views of the city.

A tram takes you from the street-level entrance to the top of the hill. Public buses (Metro Rapid Line 734) also serve the center and link to the Expo Rail extension. ✉ *1200 Getty Center Dr., Brentwood* ☎ *310/440–7300* 🌐 *www.getty.edu* 🎟 *Free; parking $15* 🕒 *Closed Mon.*

Pierce Brothers Westwood Village Memorial Park and Mortuary

CEMETERY | The who's who of the dearly departed can all be found at this peaceful, though unremarkable, cemetery. Notable residents include Marilyn Monroe and Joe DiMaggio; authors Truman Capote, Ray Bradbury, and Jackie Collins; actors Natalie Wood, Rodney Dangerfield, Farrah Fawcett, Jack Lemmon, and Dean Martin; and directors Billy Wilder and John Cassavetes. ✉ *1218 Glendon Ave., Westwood* ☎ *310/474–1579* 🌐 *www.dignitymemorial.com* 🕒 *Open 24 hrs.*

Skirball Cultural Center

ART MUSEUM | The mission of this Jewish cultural institution in the beautiful Santa Monica Mountains is to explore the connections "between 4,000 years of Jewish heritage and the vitality of American democratic ideals." The extraordinary museum, featuring exhibits like *Visions and Values: Jewish Life from Antiquity to America*, has a massive collection of Judaica—the third largest in the world. A big family draw is the Noah's Ark interactive exhibition, where children are invited to re-create the famous tale using their own imagination. ✉ *2701 N. Sepulveda Blvd., north of Brentwood, Los Angeles* ☎ *310/440–4500* 🌐 *www.skirball.org* 🎟 *$12; free Thurs.* 🕒 *Closed Mon.*

🍴 Restaurants

★ Baltaire Restaurant

$$$$ | **STEAKHOUSE** | The chicest and buzziest nighttime spot in the neighborhood, Baltaire attracts both well-heeled Brentwood denizens on dressed-up dates and single sippers looking for late-night rendezvous. The meat-heavy menu features giant slabs of porterhouse steaks as well as special A5 Wagyu straight from Japan. **Known for:** sizzling steaks; buzzing bar scene; classic cocktails. [$] *Average main:*

Did You Know?

With its palm trees and wide avenues, Brentwood is one of the most upscale neighborhoods in Los Angeles.

$50 ✉ 11647 San Vicente Blvd., Brentwood ☎ 424/273–1660 🌐 www.baltaire.com 🕒 No lunch weekends.

Lady Chocolatt

$ | BELGIAN | The purveyor of the finest Belgian chocolate in all of Los Angeles, Lady Chocolatt is the perfect answer to the age-old question of what to gift on any special occasion. The ornate display case is filled with dark chocolate truffles, hazelnut pralines, Grand Marnier ganaches, and so much more, all handcrafted by a Master Chocolatier in Belgium. **Known for:** Belgian chocolate; Italian espresso; tasty sandwiches. [$] *Average main: $5 ✉ 12008 Wilshire Blvd., Brentwood ☎ 310/442–2245 🕒 Closed Sun.*

★ Pizzana

$ | PIZZA | Certainly (and deservedly) on any short list for the best pizzaiolo in Los Angeles, chef Daniele Uditi's secret is his family's 65-plus-year-old sourdough starter, which he transported from Italy and still keeps alive. The sizzling pies here will remind you of Naples, with their crackling crusts and inventive toppings. **Known for:** excellent Neapolitan pizza; sandwich specials; laid-back atmosphere. [$] *Average main: $18 ✉ 11712 San Vicente Blvd., Brentwood ☎ 310/481–7108 🌐 www.pizzana.com.*

Sweet Rose Creamery

$ | ICE CREAM | Sweet Rose Creamery is the next-best thing you'll find to homemade ice cream—only with a much posher atmosphere in the Brentwood Country Mart. From-scratch offerings feature local farmers' fare and are all-natural. **Known for:** everything made in-house; all-natural ingredients; celeb spotting. [$] *Average main: $7 ✉ Brentwood Country Mart, 225 26th St., Suite 51, Brentwood ☎ 310/260–2663 🌐 www.sweetrosecreamery.com.*

Toscana

$$$ | ITALIAN | This rustic trattoria along San Vicente has been a favorite celebrity haunt for decades. Expect elevated sensory offerings, from its cozy atmosphere to its mouthwatering Tuscan and Italian fare (including carpaccio and gnocchi primavera) and excellent wine list. **Known for:** excellent wine list; seasonal menu; great celeb-spotting. [$] *Average main: $35 ✉ 11633 San Vicente Blvd., Brentwood ☎ 310/820–2448 🌐 www.toscanabrentwood.com.*

Hotels

★ Hotel Bel-Air

$$$$ | HOTEL | This Spanish Mission–style icon has been a discreet hillside retreat for celebrities and society types since 1946 and was given a face-lift by star designers Alexandra Champalimaud and David Rockwell. **Pros:** shuttle available within 3-mile radius of hotel; perfect for the privacy-minded; alfresco dining at Wolfgang Puck restaurant. **Cons:** not walking distance to restaurants or shops; hefty price tag; controversial ownership by the Sultan of Brunei. [$] *Rooms from: $1175 ✉ 701 Stone Canyon Rd., Bel Air ☎ 310/472–1211 🌐 www.dorchestercollection.com/en/los-angeles/hotel-bel-air 🛏 103 rooms 🍴 No Meals.*

Performing Arts

Nuart

FILM | Foreign, indie, documentaries, classics, recent releases, Oscar short-film screenings—there's not much the Nuart doesn't show. Midnight showings, like the long-running *Rocky Horror Picture Show* with a live "shadow cast" on Saturday nights, continue to bring in locals. Q&A sessions with directors and actors also happen here frequently. *✉ 11272 Santa Monica Blvd., West L.A. ☎ 310/473–8530 🌐 www.landmarktheatres.com/los-angeles/nuart-theatre.*

Shopping

Brentwood Country Mart

SHOPPING CENTER | This family-friendly faux country market was first built in the postwar boom of the 1940s and remains a staple of the community. Among the dozens of stores are Goop (Gwyneth Paltrow's lifestyle brand's gorgeous first brick-and-mortar store), Turpan (for luxury home goods), James Perse (for laid-back cotton knits), Jenni Kayne (for a curated mix of modern clothing, housewares, and gifts), and Malia Mills (for American-made swimwear separates). Grab a chicken basket at Reddi Chick and chow down on the open-air patio. ✉ *225 26th St., at San Vicente Blvd., Brentwood* ☎ *310/458–6682* ⊕ *www.brentwoodcountrymart.com.*

WESTSIDE

VENICE, MARINA DEL REY, SAWTELLE
JAPANTOWN, AND CULVER CITY

Updated by
Candice Yacono

⊙ **Sights**
★★★☆☆

🍴 **Restaurants**
★★★★☆

🛏 **Hotels**
★★★☆☆

🛍 **Shopping**
★★★★☆

🍸 **Nightlife**
★★☆☆☆

NEIGHBORHOOD SNAPSHOT

TOP EXPERIENCES

■ **Catch the mellow vibes in Venice Beach:** Walk along the canals, shop, and watch tanned locals in tie-dye toting longboards.

■ **Shop and dine on Abbot Kinney Boulevard:** Browse trendy boho boutiques and enjoy an all-organic lunch on this lively street.

■ **Visit the Museum of Jurassic Technology:** This quirky and fascinating museum of oddities and curiosities will delight even the most urbane museumgoer.

■ **Bike the Strand:** Take in the beach scenery on any stretch of this 22-mile bike path from Pacific Palisades to Torrance.

■ **Ogle at the varieties of beefcake at Muscle Beach:** See the famous outdoor gym and watch bodybuilders work out.

PLANNING YOUR TIME

No matter your interest, there's something on the Westside for you. If your priority is to discover the quintessential SoCal beach town, plan to spend a day in Venice, with its lively boardwalk scene and beautiful beach. Take a stroll through the Venice Canals or Muscle Beach, then shop and dine in the infinitely Instagrammable Abbot Kinney.

If you have stars in your eyes, make a quick stop in Culver City and listen for the whispers of its film history. Try any of the hip restaurants and historic cocktail bars in downtown Culver City, then take a peek at the historic Sony Pictures Studios, formerly Metro-Goldwyn-Mayer. If your friends know you as the biggest foodie in your group, book reservations for an evening in Sawtelle, Los Angeles's Japantown. This gastronomic feast is also a feast for the eyes. Or for a classic coastal experience at a slower pace, Marina del Rey is a good stop for a half-day excursion. Hop on a boat cruise or find a restaurant with a coveted harbor view.

GETTING HERE

Getting to the Westside of Los Angeles is easy and convenient, with several transportation options available. From Downtown, the Westside can be reached by car via the Santa Monica Freeway (I-10). For those coming from north or south of the area, the San Diego Freeway (I-405), or Pacific Coast Highway (CA-1) will get you here. However, traffic can be heavy and parking can be difficult during peak hours, so allow extra time for travel.

Though nobody walks in L.A., public transportation is also an option, with several bus lines serving the Westside. The Culver CityBus provides convenient access to Culver City and surrounding areas, while the Santa Monica Big Blue Bus connects visitors to Santa Monica and beyond. The Metro Expo Line provides light-rail service to Culver City and Santa Monica, and expansion plans are actively underway.

Once on the Westside, visitors can explore the various neighborhoods by foot, bike, scooter, or car. Many attractions are within walking distance of each other, while bike rentals and scooter-sharing services are also readily available.

The Westside, with its unique blend of beachside charm, trendy neighborhoods, and cultural hot spots, is where Angelenos come to play. Though its boundaries are a little loose, it comprises much of the Los Angeles area west of the 405 Freeway and south of the San Gabriel Mountains, including areas like Venice, Culver City, Sawtelle, and Marina del Rey.

Venice, just south of Santa Monica, has conjured images of greased-up body-builders, boho hippies, and boardwalk palm readers for generations. Venice is the quintessential SoCal beach town. In addition to sun, sand, and surf, it also offers a vibrant arts scene, with street performers, galleries, and the famous Venice Beach Skate Park.

Culver City is a hub of creativity, with film studios, art galleries, museums, and a vibrant nightlife scene. Don't miss the chance to visit the historic Sony Pictures Studios or take a stroll through the scenic Culver City Park.

Sawtelle, also known as Little Osaka, is a must-visit destination for foodies. This Japanese-American enclave boasts a variety of authentic eateries, from tiny sushi bars to hopping ramen joints. Afterward, grab a boba drink and check out some of the quirky shops and boutiques that line the street.

Marina del Rey is a boater's paradise, with its picturesque harbor filled with sailboats and yachts. Take a relaxing cruise through the marina or hit the bike path for some scenic exercise. The marina itself also boasts a variety of waterfront dining options, from seafood to sushi.

Venice

From the resident musicians and roving hippies of the boardwalk to the boho boutiques and farm-to-table cafés of Abbot Kinney Boulevard, Venice is not easily defined—which is what makes this creative-minded neighborhood so fun to explore.

Considering all of the dreamers who flock here today, it makes sense that Venice was a turn-of-the-20th-century fantasy that never quite came to be. Abbot Kinney, a wealthy Los Angeles business-man, envisioned this little piece of real estate as a romantic replica of Venice, Italy. He developed an incredible 16 miles of canals, floated gondolas on them, and built scaled-down versions of the Doge's Palace and other Venetian landmarks.

Ever since Kinney first planned his project, it was plagued by ongoing engineering problems and drifted into disrepair. Today, only a few small canals

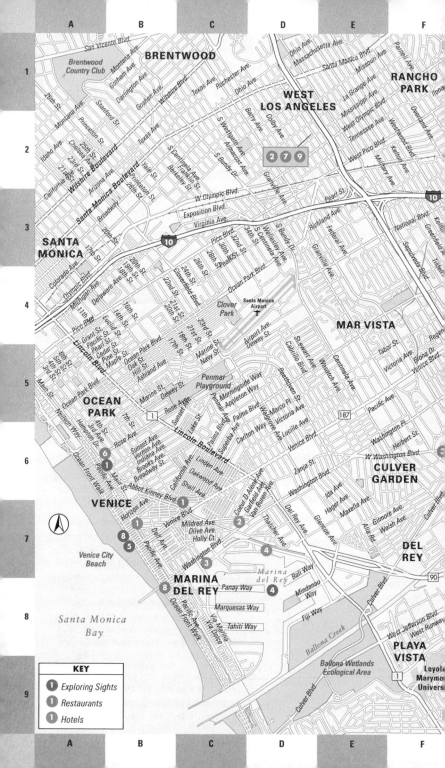

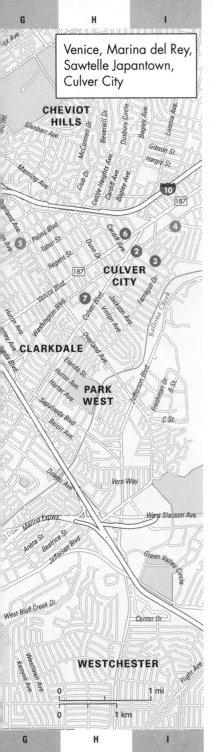

Venice, Marina del Rey, Sawtelle Japantown, Culver City

The boardwalk of Venice Beach offers some of Los Angeles's best people-watching.

and bridges remain. Some canals were rebuilt in 1996, but they don't reflect the old-world connection quite as well as they could (although they are still fun to wander around). On nearby **Abbot Kinney Boulevard,** there's a wealth of fashion, design, and home decor shops and chic cafés—plus great people-watching.

Sights

Binoculars Building

NOTABLE BUILDING | Frank Gehry is known around the world for his architectural masterpieces. In L.A. alone he's responsible for multiple houses and buildings like the Gehry Residence, Loyola Law School, and Walt Disney Hall. But one of his most interesting creations, completed in 1991, is the Binoculars Building, a quirky Venice spot that is exactly as advertised: a giant set of binoculars standing on their end. The project was originally designed for the Chiat/Day advertising agency and today is home to one of Google's Silicon Beach offices. While you can't tour the building, you can

take a clever Instagram shot out front. ✉ *340 Main St., Venice.*

Muscle Beach

OTHER ATTRACTION | Bronzed young men bench-pressing five girls at once, weightlifters doing tricks on the sand— the Muscle Beach facility fired up the country's imagination from the get-go. There are actually two spots known as Muscle Beach. The original Muscle Beach, just south of the Santa Monica Pier, is where bodybuilders Jack LaLanne and Vic and Armand Tanny used to work out in the 1950s. When it was closed in 1959, the bodybuilders moved south along the beach to Venice, to a city-run facility known as "the Pen," and the Venice Beach spot inherited the Muscle Beach moniker. The spot is probably best known now as a place where a young Arnold Schwarzenegger first came to flex his muscles in the late '60s and began his rise to fame. The area now hosts a variety of sports and gymnastics events, along with occasional "beach babe" beauty contests that always draw crowd. But stop by any time during aylight for an eye-popping array of beef-akes (and would-be beefcakes). ✉ *1800)cean Front Walk, Venice* 🌐 *www.\nusclebeach.net.*

★ Venice Beach Boardwalk

ROMENADE | The surf and sand of Venice re fine, but the main attraction here is ne boardwalk scene, which is a cosmos ll its own. Go on weekend afternoons or the best people-watching experience; ou'll see everything from Baywatch vannabes to breakdancers to TikTok nfluencers to would-be messiahs. You an also swim, fish, surf, and skateboard, r have a go at racquetball, handball, huffleboard, and basketball (the board-valk is the site of hotly contested pickup ames). Or you can rent a bike or in-line kates and hit the Strand bike path, then oke around the gloriously tacky tourist nd souvenir shops before pulling up a eat at a sidewalk café and watching the ction unfold. ✉ *1800 Ocean Front Walk, vest of Pacific Ave., Venice* ☎ *310/392-1687* 🌐 *www.venicebeach.com.*

🍴 Restaurants

bit rough around the edges, this urban each town is home to many of L.A.'s rtists, skaters, and surfers. The dining cene continues to grow but remains rue to its cool and casual roots.

★ Gjelina

$ | AMERICAN | Walk through the rustic vooden door and into a softly lit dining oom with long communal tables and a vely crowd; come later in the night and he place heats up with an enthusiastic ost-pub crowd lured by the seasonal nenu and outstanding small plates, harcuterie, pastas, and pizza. Begin with pizza made with house-made chorizo, rilled pear with burrata and prosciutto, r Snow Island oysters. **Known for:** lively rowd on the patio; late-night menu; Michelin-recommended restaurant. [$] *Av-erage main: $22* ✉ *1429 Abbot Kinney Blvd., Venice* ☎ *310/450-1429* 🌐 *www.gjelina.com.*

Rose Cafe

$$ | MODERN AMERICAN | FAMILY | This indoor–outdoor restaurant has served Venice for more than four decades but constantly reinvents itself, serving mouthwatering California cuisines and offering multiple patios, a full bar, and a bakery. Creative types sip espressos and tap on keyboards under the macramé chandeliers, while young families gather out back to snack on smoked radiatore carbonara and crispy brussels sprouts. **Known for:** sophisticated but unpreten-tious vibe; location in the heart of Venice; lively patio seating. [$] *Average main: $25* ✉ *220 Rose Ave., Venice* ☎ *310/399-0711* 🌐 *www.rosecafevenice.com.*

Venice Whaler

$ | AMERICAN | This beachfront bar has been the local watering hole for musi-cians like the Beatles, the Doors, and the Beach Boys since 1944. It boasts an amazing view and serves tasty Califor-nia pub food like fish tacos, pulled-pork sliders, and avocado toast with a basic selection of beers. **Known for:** rock and roll history; great pub food; fun brunch. [$] *Average main: $15* ✉ *10 W. Wash-ington Blvd., Venice* ☎ *310/821-8737* 🌐 *www.venicewhaler.com.*

🛏 Hotels

Hotel Erwin

$$$ | HOTEL | A boutique hotel a block off the Venice Beach Boardwalk, the Erwin will make you feel like a hipper version of yourself. **Pros:** dining emphasizing fresh ingredients; playful design in guest rooms; free Wi-Fi and use of hotel bikes and beach equipment. **Cons:** some rooms face a noisy alley; no pool; $49 valet parking. [$] *Rooms from: $395* ✉ *1697 Pacific Ave., Venice* ☎ *310/452-1111, 800/786-7789* 🌐 *www.hotelerwin.com* 🛏 *119 rooms* 🍴 *No Meals.*

Continued on page 101

ALONG
THE STRAND
L.A.'S COASTAL
BIKE PATH

Cycling along the Strand

Venice Beach

Venice Beach graffiti

Venice Beach Waterfront Café

When L.A. wants to get out and play by the water, people hit the Strand for the afternoon. This paved 22-mile path hugs the coastline and loops through tourist-packed stretches and sleepy beach towns. Quirky cafés, loads of souvenir stands, a family-packed amusement park on a pier, and spots for gazing at the Pacific are just a few things to see along the way.

The path extends from Santa Monica's Will Rogers State Beach to Torrance County Beach in South Redondo. It's primarily flat—aside from a few hills you encounter as you head toward Playa del Rey—and it's a terrific way for people of all fitness levels to experience L.A.'s beaches not far from Hollywood or Beverly Hills. You can explore at your own pace.

The hardest part of the journey isn't tackling the path itself—it's trying to get through it all without being distracted by the surrounding activity. With colorful graffitied murals, surfers and sailboats, weightlifters and tattoo parlors, local characters in carnivalesque costumes, volleyball games and skateboarders, there are almost too many things to busy youself with.

Santa Monica amusement park

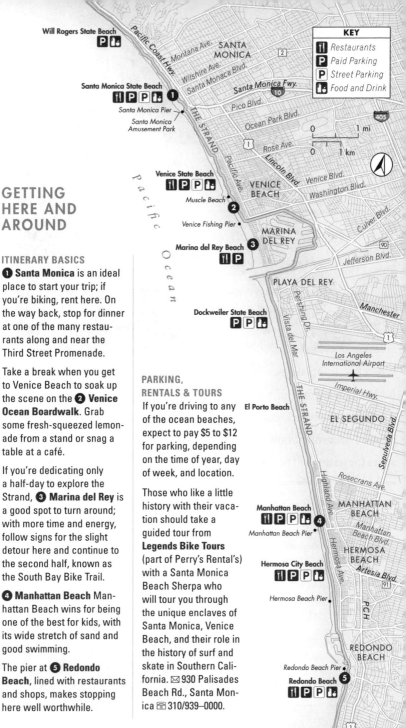

KEY

🍴 Restaurants
Ⓟ Paid Parking
Ⓟ Street Parking
🍹 Food and Drink

Will Rogers State Beach Ⓟ 🍹

Pacific Coast Hwy.

Montana Ave.

SANTA MONICA

Wilshire Ave.

Santa Monica Blvd.

Santa Monica State Beach 🍴 Ⓟ Ⓟ 🍹 ❶

Santa Monica Pier

Santa Monica Amusement Park

Santa Monica Fwy.

Pico Blvd.

Ocean Park Blvd.

THE STRAND

Rose Ave.

Lincoln Blvd.

Pacific Ave.

Pacific Ocean

Venice State Beach 🍴 Ⓟ Ⓟ 🍹

Muscle Beach

VENICE BEACH

Venice Blvd.

Washington Blvd.

Venice Fishing Pier ❷

Marina del Rey Beach 🍴 Ⓟ ❸

MARINA DEL REY

Culver Blvd.

Jefferson Blvd.

PLAYA DEL REY

Dockweiler State Beach Ⓟ Ⓟ 🍹

Pershing Dr.

Vista del Mar

Los Angeles International Airport

Imperial Hwy.

El Porto Beach

THE STRAND

EL SEGUNDO

Sepulveda Blvd.

Rosecrans Ave.

Highland Ave.

Manhattan Beach 🍴 Ⓟ Ⓟ 🍹 ❹

Manhattan Beach Pier

MANHATTAN BEACH

Manhattan Beach Blvd.

Hermosa City Beach 🍴 Ⓟ Ⓟ 🍹

HERMOSA BEACH

Hermosa Ave.

Artesia Blvd.

Hermosa Beach Pier

PCH

REDONDO BEACH

Redondo Beach Pier

Redondo Beach 🍴 Ⓟ Ⓟ 🍹 ❺

0   1 mi
0   1 km

GETTING HERE AND AROUND

ITINERARY BASICS

❶ **Santa Monica** is an ideal place to start your trip; if you're biking, rent here. On the way back, stop for dinner at one of the many restaurants along and near the Third Street Promenade.

Take a break when you get to Venice Beach to soak up the scene on the ❷ **Venice Ocean Boardwalk**. Grab some fresh-squeezed lemonade from a stand or snag a table at a café.

If you're dedicating only a half-day to explore the Strand, ❸ **Marina del Rey** is a good spot to turn around; with more time and energy, follow signs for the slight detour here and continue to the second half, known as the South Bay Bike Trail.

❹ **Manhattan Beach** Manhattan Beach wins for being one of the best for kids, with its wide stretch of sand and good swimming.

The pier at ❺ **Redondo Beach**, lined with restaurants and shops, makes stopping here well worthwhile.

PARKING, RENTALS & TOURS

If you're driving to any of the ocean beaches, expect to pay $5 to $12 for parking, depending on the time of year, day of week, and location.

Those who like a little history with their vacation should take a guided tour from **Legends Bike Tours** (part of Perry's Rental's) with a Santa Monica Beach Sherpa who will tour you through the unique enclaves of Santa Monica, Venice Beach, and their role in the history of surf and skate in Southern California. ✉ 930 Palisades Beach Rd., Santa Monica ☎ 310/939–0000.

⭐ The Kinney

$$ | HOTEL | Walking distance to Venice Beach and Abbot Kinney's artsy commercial strip, this playful hotel announces itself boldly with wall murals by Melissa Scrivner before you even enter the lobby. **Pros:** affordable, artistic rooms; Ping-Pong area; Jacuzzi bar. **Cons:** valet parking is a must ($15); hotel can get loud; some hipper-than-thou vibes. $ *Rooms from: $239* ✉ *737 Washington Blvd., Venice* ☎ *310/821–4455* ⊕ *www.thekinneyvenicebeach.com* 🛏 *68 rooms* ⏺ *No Meals.*

Nightlife

The Brig

BARS | This 70-plus-year-old, charming bar continually reinvents itself. The Brig has its pluses (interesting drinks, talented DJs, and some live music) and minuses (ugh, parking), but is worth a look if you're in the area. There's always a food truck around, and the bar's fine with you bringing in outside food. ✉ *1515 Abbot Kinney Blvd., Venice* ☎ *310/399–7537* ⊕ *www.thebrig.com.*

Shopping

Coutula

WOMEN'S CLOTHING | Owner Carrie Hauman of Coutula (a portmanteau of "Couture L.A.") travels around the globe to hand-select the clothing, accessories, jewelry, and home furnishings sold in her light-filled, airy Abbot Kinney 1930s cottage. Nab anything from a $10 bracelet to a $6,000 necklace here, along with floaty sundresses that look much more expensive than they are, handmade Cut n Paste leather handbags, and bliss-inducing Tyler candles. ✉ *1204 Abbot Kinney Blvd., Venice* ☎ *310/581–8010* ⊕ *www.coutula.com.*

General Store

GENERAL STORE | Right at home in the beachy, bohemian neighborhood, this well-curated shop is a decidedly contemporary take on the concept of general stores. The very definition of "California cool," General Store offers beauty and bath products loaded with organic natural ingredients, handmade ceramics, linen tea towels, and a spot-on selection of art books. Featuring an impressive number of local makers and designers, the boutique also sells modern, minimalist clothing and has a kids' section that will wow even the hippest moms and dads. ✉ *1801 Lincoln Blvd., Venice* ☎ *310/751–6393* ⊕ *www.shop-generalstore.com.*

Heist

WOMEN'S CLOTHING | Owner Nilou Ghodsi has admitted that she stocks her Westside shop like an extension of her own closet, which in her case means keeping the focus on floaty, modern-yet-classic pieces as opposed to trendy ones. The airy boutique offers elegantly edgy separates from American designers like Nili Lotan and Ulla Johnson, as well as from hard-to-find French and Italian designers like Faliero Sarti. ✉ *1100 Abbot Kinney Blvd., Venice* ☎ *310/450–6531* ⊕ *www.shopheist.com.*

LCD

WOMEN'S CLOTHING | Anyone who's looking to get a leg up on the hottest new designers will want to make this Lincoln Boulevard boutique a stop on their Venice shopping spree. The clean, modern space features cool, contemporary clothing by the likes of Ryan Roche, Sandy Liang, and Assembly New York, plus beauty loot from Verso, bags and eyewear from beloved local labels, and so much more for fashion followers to fawn over. The owner has a background in the music industry, and it shows. ✉ *1121 Abbot Kinney Blvd., Suite 2, Venice* ☎ *424/280–4132* ⊕ *www.shoplcd.co.*

Strange Invisible Perfumes

PERFUME | Finding your signature fragrance at this sleek Abbot Kinney boutique won't come cheap, but perfumer Alexandra Balahoutis takes creating her scents as seriously as a seasoned winemaker—and they're just as nuanced as a

The Venice Skatepark brings skateboarders, roller skaters, and drum circles.

well-balanced glass of vino. Essences for the perfumes are organic, wild crafted, biodynamic, and bottled locally. Highlights from SI's core collection include the cacao-spiked Dimanche and leathery Black Rosette. ✉ *1138 Abbot Kinney Blvd., Venice* ☎ *310/314–1505* ⊕ *www.siperfumes.com.*

Activities

Venice Skatepark

CITY PARK | Ride the concrete waves or watch others display a wide range of ability levels as they careen around this universally beloved skatepark, situated between the beach and the boardwalk in Venice. There's also an impressive crew of disco roller skaters, and drum circles that gravitate toward the middle of the boardwalk. Lessons are offered frequently, and there is an abundance of skate shops nearby if you are infected with the sudden need to hit the half pipe. ✉ *1800 Ocean Front Walk, off E. Market St., Venice* ⊕ *www.veniceskatepark.com.*

Marina del Rey

Home to thousands of boats, Marina del Rey is a scenic coastal neighborhood located just south of Venice. This beautiful area boasts stunning views and is a quieter option for families and businesspeople than its more rambunctious neighbor to the north. With a large range of activities, it's the perfect spot for outdoors enthusiasts, beachgoers, and foodies alike. Enjoy sailing, kayaking, or stand-up paddleboarding in the calm waters of the marina, or simply soak up the sun on the beach or your resort's pool deck. Look past the chain establishments to find an array of locally owned restaurants, cafés, and bars.

Sights

Marina del Rey

MARINA/PIER | Just south of Venice, this condo-laden, chain restaurant–lined development is a good place to grab brunch (but watch for price gougers), walk, or ride bikes along the waterfront. A number of places, such as **Hornblower Cruises and Events** in Fisherman's Village, rent boats for romantic dinner or party cruises around the marina. There are a few man-made beaches, but you're better off hitting the larger (and cleaner) beaches up the coast. ✉ *Fisherman's Village, 13755 Fiji Way, Marina del Rey* ☎ *888/467–6256* 🌐 *www.hornblower.com/port/category/mdr+diningcruises.*

Hotels

Marina del Rey Marriott
$$ | **HOTEL** | **FAMILY** | Just across from the protected waters of the marina and a short jaunt to Venice, this hotel has across-the-board appeal for families, business travelers, couples, and more. **Pros:** outdoor lounge for nighttime socializing; quiet beach across the street; 15 minutes to LAX. **Cons:** traffic and noise from busy Admiralty Way; predominantly corporate aesthetic; valet parking is $49. [$] *Rooms from: $329* ✉ *4100 Admiralty Way, Marina del Ray* ☎ *310/301–3000, 800/228–9290* 🌐 *www.marriott.com/hotels/travel/laxmb-marina-del-rey-marriott/* 🛏 *370 rooms* 🍴 *No Meals.*

★ **The Ritz-Carlton Marina del Rey**
$$$$ | **HOTEL** | **FAMILY** | You might have a sense of déjà vu here—this resort, overlooking L.A.'s largest marina's boats, is a favorite location of dozens of TV and film productions. Traditionally styled rooms are decked out in warm, gold tones with French doors, marble baths, and feather beds. **Pros:** sparkling gym and large, kid-friendly, chlorine-free pool; chic restaurant Cast and Plow on-site; feather beds and marble baths in rooms. **Cons:** formal dining only when seasonal poolside bar and grill isn't open; $42 valet parking; quite pricey. [$] *Rooms from: $500* ✉ *4375 Admiralty Way, Marina del Ray* ☎ *310/823–1700, 800/241–3333* 🌐 *www.ritzcarlton.com* 🛏 *304 rooms* 🍴 *No Meals.*

Sawtelle Japantown

The three blocks on Sawtelle Boulevard between Olympic Boulevard and Missouri Avenue are filled with predominantly Japanese specialty stores, restaurants, and plant nurseries. A trip here makes for an interesting, out-of-the-ordinary jaunt from Santa Monica.

In the 1920s, after a wave of Japanese immigrants arrived in L.A., Sawtelle began to resemble an authentic Japanese main street rather than a touristy Little Tokyo. Although most establishments remain Japanese, the area also encompasses Chinese, Taiwanese, and Malaysian businesses.

Restaurants

Hide Sushi
$ | **JAPANESE** | Some of the best sushi spots in Los Angeles are the most hidden and most discreet and come with zero fanfare, and the decades-old, no-reservations Hide (pronounced hee-day) is one of those restaurants. Walking through a curtained entryway, diners will find a smattering of tables and a sushi counter (which is where you should sit) where master sushi chefs slice raw cuts of the freshest fish in town. **Known for:** counter sushi; quiet atmosphere; cash-only policy. [$] *Average main: $13* ✉ *2040 Sawtelle Blvd., West L.A.* ☎ *310/477–7242* 🌐 *www.hidesushi.com* 💳 *No credit cards* 🕒 *Closed Mon. and Tues.*

★ **Tsujita L.A. Artisan Noodles**
$ | **JAPANESE** | Ramen lovers have no shortage of choices across Los Angeles, but if you want the best, head over to this Sawtelle Japantown hot spot. Lines typically bend around the corner as hungry Angelenos drive from far and wide to have Tsujita's signature *tsukemen* (a type of ramen where the noodles are served to the side of the broth and you dip each bite individually). **Known for:** signature

tsukemen ramen; lots of ramen options, including vegan ramen; long lines. $ *Average main: $12* ✉ *2057 Sawtelle Blvd., West L.A.* ☎ *310/231–7373* ⊕ *www. tsujita-la.com.*

Volcano Tea House

$ | ASIAN | Join the UCLA students in line at the venerable Volcano Tea House, where you can sample from a huge range of delectable bubble drinks. Stick with the house milk tea or brown sugar latte, or get adventurous with sakura jelly or matcha. **Known for:** cult-favorite house milk tea; massive menu of flavors and customizations; addicting popcorn chicken. $ *Average main: $6* ✉ *2111 Sawtelle Blvd., West L.A.* ☎ *310/445–5326.*

Shopping

Nijiya Market

MARKET | If you're looking for an authentic Japanese supermarket, you'll find everything you could ever want at Nijiya. Inside, you'll discover fresh fish for make-it-at-home sushi, baked Japanese delicacies, daily-made takeaway bento boxes, and every Japanese candy treat imaginable. On weekends, you'll find a giant skillet set up outside the entrance where employees fry up sizzling and savory *okonomiyaki* (Japanese pancake). ✉ *2130 Sawtelle Blvd., #105, West L.A.* ☎ *310/575–3300* ⊕ *www.nijiya.com.*

Culver City

Located about halfway between Hollywood and the coast, Culver City has a glamorous history of its own. The area boasts two film studios, Sony (formerly MGM) Studios and the Culver Studios. Culver City itself has seen revitalization in recent years as visitors discover the charming district of the area's "downtown." The Metro's new Expo Line has a Culver City Station stop, making it an easy subway and light rail trip from Hollywood or Downtown Los Angeles. The Culver Hotel is in the heart of Culver City, and the surrounding area is loaded with shops, cafés, the art deco–style ArcLight Cinemas, and a vibrant art gallery scene. It's a place for adventurous eaters, where you can also find cuisines spanning the globe.

Sights

Culver Hotel

HOTEL | In the heart of Culver City is the Culver Hotel, built in 1924 and now preserved as a historical landmark. It will catch your eye with its old-world glory and lobby entrance, which has sweeping dark wood and a high ceiling. It's as seductive as the many classic film stars that took up residency here over the years, including Greta Garbo, Joan Crawford, John Wayne, Clark Gable, Buster Keaton, Ronald Reagan, and cast members from *The Wizard of Oz* and *Gone with the Wind* as they filmed in the nearby studio. ✉ *9400 Culver Blvd., Culver City* ☎ *310/558–9400* ⊕ *www. culverhotel.com* Ⓜ *Culver City.*

Culver Studios

FILM/TV STUDIO | The Culver Studios are best known as the location where *Gone with the Wind* was filmed in addition to classics including *Citizen Kane* and the Desilu Productions TV hits of the '50s and '60s, including *The Andy Griffith Show, Lassie,* and *Batman.* Amazon Studios currently occupies the space and is further developing it. This studio currently does not offer tours to the public, but the view of historic buildings from the front gate is still Insta-worthy. ✉ *9336 W. Washington Blvd., Culver City* ☎ *310/202–1234* ⊕ *www.theculverstudios.com* Ⓜ *Culver City.*

★ Museum of Jurassic Technology

OTHER MUSEUM | If ever a museum had its own unique spin, it's the Museum of Jurassic Technology, with an oddball assortment of natural (and partly fictional)

In addition to movies and television shows, Sony Picture Studios is also where game shows like *Jeopardy!* are filmed.

"art" pieces such as fruit stone carvings, theater models, string figures, and finds from mobile home parks, and a tribute room filled with paintings of dogs from the Soviet Space Program. All are housed in a low-lighted, haunted house–style atmosphere that makes you feel as if the *Addams Family* butler will come to greet you at any moment. Go upstairs after your visit to enjoy complimentary tea and cookies in the Tula Tea Room, and short films in the Borzoi Kabinet Theater. ⚠ **The museum is home to multiple dogs and birds, so be advised if you have allergies.** ✉ *9341 Venice Blvd., Culver City* ☎ *310/836–6131* ⊕ *www.mjt.org* 🎟 *$12* 🕑 *Closed Mon.– Wed.* ⛅ *Advance online reservation required* Ⓜ *Culver City.*

Sony Pictures Studios

FILM/TV STUDIO | Sony Pictures Studios (former the MGM Studios), where movie magic from *The Wizard of Oz* to *Spider-Man* was made, offers two-hour weekday walking tours ($50, reservation required) to dive into their rich TV and blockbuster film history. If game shows are your thing, you can also be a part of the studio audience for *Jeopardy!* or *Wheel of Fortune.* ✉ *10202 W. Washington, Culver City* ☎ *310/244–8687* ⊕ *www. sonypicturesstudios.com* 🎟 *Tours $50* Ⓜ *Culver City.*

🍴 Restaurants

Lodge Bread Company

$ | **BAKERY** | Part restaurant, part bakery, and part learning annex, Lodge Bread Company beckons customers with freshly baked sourdough—the aroma of which wafts over the entire neighborhood. Inside, guests can enjoy fermented pizzas, savory sandwiches, and crisp morning toasts. **Known for:** incredible sourdough bread; fluffy pizzas; bakery items and bread-making classes. 💲 *Average main: $15* ✉ *11918 W. Washington Blvd., Culver City* ☎ *424/384–5097* ⊕ *www.lodgebread.com.*

Margot

$$ | **MEDITERRANEAN** | Boasting one of the most stunning rooftops in L.A., Margot is a fresh face and hopping hot spot for the Culver City dining and drinking scene. The expansive space gives off a Moroccan Casbah vibe, with just as many hints of Southern California for good measure. **Known for:** fresh fish and lots of shared plates; epic views; fun happy hour. [$] *Average main: $25* ✉ *8820 Washington Blvd., #301, Culver City* ☎ *310/643–5853* 🌐 *www.margot.la* 🕒 *No lunch weekdays* [M] *Culver City.*

★ n/naka

$$$$ | **JAPANESE** | *Chef's Table* star Niki Nakayama helms this two-Michelin-starred omakase (chef-selected) fine-dining establishment. Small and intimate, any given night will feature sashimi with *kanpachi*, sea bass with *uni* butter, or Myazaki Wagyu beef. **Known for:** decadent three-hour meal; excellent sake pairings; romantic atmosphere. [$] *Average main: $185* ✉ *3455 Overland Ave., Culver City* ☎ *310/836–6252* 🌐 *www.n-naka.com* 🕒 *Closed Sun.–Tues.*

Shopping

Platform

SHOPPING CENTER | **FAMILY** | Culver City's revitalization has created hot spots like Platform, a design-forward space filled with independent restaurants, boutiques, coffee shops, and spas. Standouts include Italian bakery Bianca, New York pizza transplant Roberta's, tech-bro chic from The Optimist, and a Blue Bottle Coffee shop with amphitheater seating. Weekly events include food and fashion pop-ups in addition to outdoor fitness classes. ✉ *8850 Washington Blvd., Culver City* ☎ *310/558–0415* 🌐 *www.platformlosangeles.com* [M] *Culver City.*

Urbanic Paper Boutique

STATIONERY | Founder Audrey Woollen brings her long experience as a leader in the stationery industry to her store, bringing in beloved brands and designs, many unique to Urbanic. You'll find cute cards and stationery to send those wish-you-were-here wishes as well as gifts and office and home decor. The store also holds occasional crafty special events; check online if you'll be in the area for a while. ✉ *11720 Washington Pl., Culver City* ☎ *310/401–0427* 🌐 *www.urbanicpaper.com.*

Chapter 6

BEVERLY HILLS

6

Updated by
Paul Feinstein

 Sights
★★☆☆☆

 Restaurants
★★★★☆

 Hotels
★★★★☆

 Shopping
★★★★★

 Nightlife
★☆☆☆☆

NEIGHBORHOOD SNAPSHOT

TOP EXPERIENCES

■ **Shop on Rodeo Drive:** Even if it's window-shopping, it's a one-of-a-kind experience to watch the parade of diamonds, couture gowns, and Ferraris being fetishized.

■ **Watch a concert:** Every summer, the Beverly Canon Gardens near the Maybourne Beverly Hills Hotel features a free concert series.

■ **See the stars:** Celeb spotting is practically an art form in this city, and the streets of Beverly Hills hide them in plain sight. Head to the area's many five-star hotel bars and swanky eateries to catch glimpses of your A-list favorites.

VIEWFINDER

Rodeo Drive Steps: The Beverly Hills version of Rome's Spanish Steps, this photogenic spot caps the world's most expensive street. For unobstructed snaps, visit early on a weekend morning. ⊠ *9800 Wilshire Blvd.*

Union 76 Gas Station: This Googie-designed station was completed in 1965 and is meant to be reminiscent of a parabolic spaceship. Come at night for fewer cars. ⊠ *427 N. Crescent Dr.*

Beverly Hills Sculptures: Designed by renowned street artist Mr. Brainwash, the bright pink *Beverly Hills is Beautiful* sculpture is located in Beverly Canon Gardens. You can also find a *Life is Beautiful* and *Beverly Hills is Life* sculpture on Rodeo Drive and South Santa Monica Boulevard if you want a trio of art-related photos. ⊠ *241 N. Canon Dr.*

Beverly Wilshire Hotel: For your *Pretty Woman* moment, grab the biggest shopping bags you can find and pose in front of the Beverly Wilshire Hotel. ⊠ *9500 Wilshire Blvd.*

The Beverly Gardens Park: One of the most famous Beverly Hills signs is in the middle of Beverly Gardens Park that hugs Santa Monica Boulevard. Your photographer may need to cross the street to capture you with the full sign. ⊠ *9439 Santa Monica Blvd.*

GETTING HERE

All main west–east roads in the city will get you toward Beverly Hills; Wilshire Boulevard is the easiest. It starts in Santa Monica, heads into Brentwood and continues east right into the heart of Beverly Hills. But traffic can be a nightmare, as it can be for L.A.'s other main artery, Santa Monica Boulevard, which also hits Beverly Hills and runs just south of Brentwood. For a smoother ride, try Pico or Olympic Boulevard, which both run roughly parallel a bit farther south.

In Beverly Hills, you can park your car in one of several municipal lots (often free for the first hour or two), and spend as long as you like strolling along Rodeo Drive. For street parking, bring quarters for the meter, or pay with a credit card. Parking on residential streets is often by permit only.

PLANNING YOUR TIME

Let's be honest—in Beverly Hills, you're probably here to shop and do lunch, and this can easily take a whole day. Once you're all shopped out, you'll find a lively nightlife scene in the bars of the high-end hotels that are peppered throughout the neighborhood.

The rumors are true: Beverly Hills delivers on a dramatic, cinematic scale of wealth and excess. A known celebrity haunt, come here to daydream or to live like the rich and famous for a day. Window-shop or splurge at tony stores, and keep an eye out for filming locales; just walking around here will make you feel like you're on a movie set—especially when you casually bump into the famous locales for *Pretty Woman*, *Beverly Hills Cop*, and *Clueless*.

When visiting Beverly Hills for the first time, many people head for the boutiques and restaurants that line the palm tree–fringed sidewalks of **Rodeo Drive.** People tend to stroll, not rush. Shopping ranges from the accessible and familiar (Pottery Barn) to the unique, expensive, and architecturally stunning (Prada).

 ## Sights

Fox Plaza
NOTABLE BUILDING | Towering over the 20th Century Fox studio lot in Century City is Fox Plaza, a 34-story skyscraper where former president Ronald Reagan once had an office. Savvy screen watchers will undoubtedly know it by its more famous name—Nakatomi Plaza. Starring in the blockbusting juggernaut *Die Hard*, the building is shot at, blown apart, and set on fire as Bruce Willis takes down a German terrorist cell. It can be fun to see if you're a fan of the movie, but be aware this is just an office building, so there's not a whole lot to do but look at it. ⊠ *2121 Ave. of the Stars, Century City.*

Gagosian Gallery
ART MUSEUM | This contemporary art gallery, owned and directed by the legendary Larry Gagosian, features cutting-edge artists in a minimalist-styled space. It's free to enter, exhibits rotate every six weeks, and the gallery has displayed everyone from Richard Avedon and Takashi Murakami to Frank Gehry and Jeff Koons. During Oscar season the gallery is known for its celeb-filled openings. ⊠ *456 N. Camden Dr., Beverly Hills* ☎ *310/271–9400* ⊕ *www.gagosian.com.*

Greystone Mansion
HISTORIC HOME | Built in 1928, this stunning mansion resides in a discreet residential part of Beverly Hills, surrounded by 18 acres of manicured grounds that are open to the public. The historic house was built by oil magnate Ned Doheny

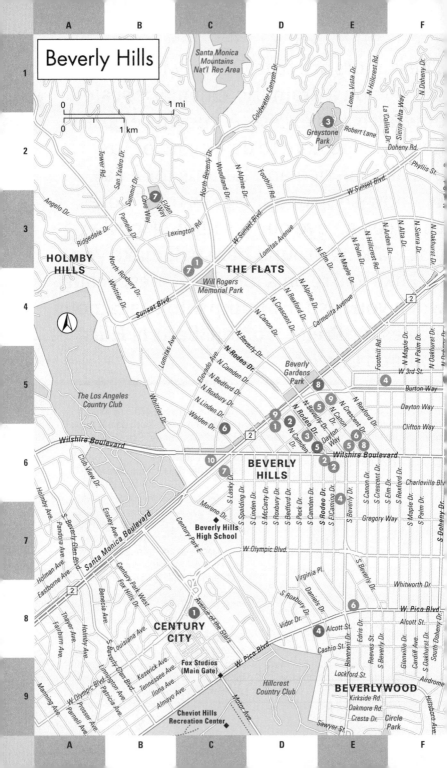

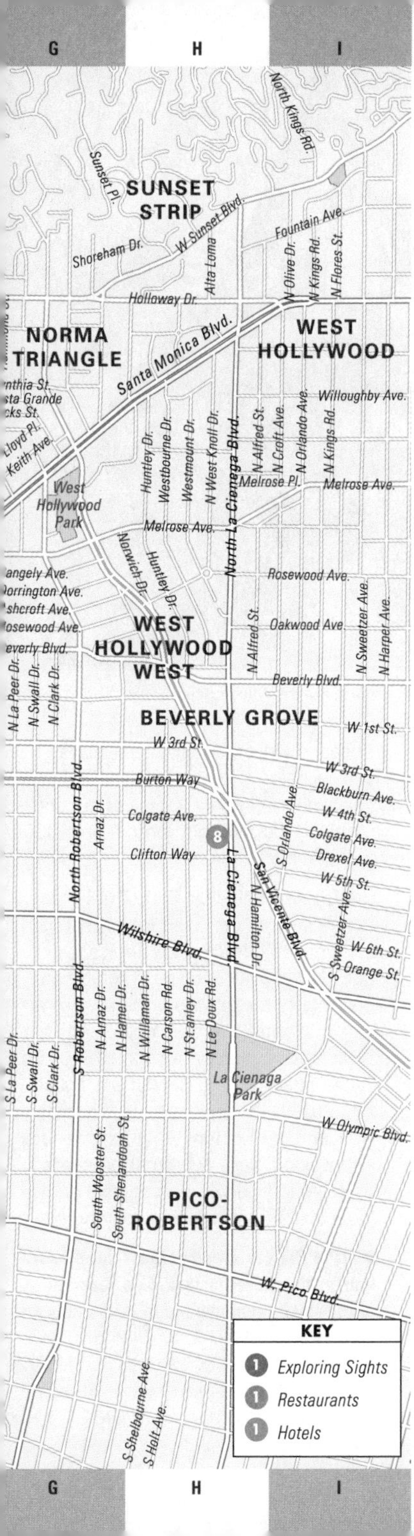

Sights ▼

1 Fox Plaza.................**C8**
2 Gagosian Gallery **D5**
3 Greystone Mansion **E2**
4 Museum of Tolerance..**D8**
5 Rodeo Drive **D6**
6 Spadena House..........**C6**
7 Virginia Robinson
   Gardens..................**B3**
8 Wallis Annenberg
   Center for the
   Performing Arts.........**D5**

Restaurants ▼

1 Crustacean **D6**
2 CUT.......................**E6**
3 Gucci Osteria da
   Massimo Bottura **D6**
4 Matū......................**E6**
5 Nate 'n' Al's.............**D5**
6 Nozawa Bar..............**E6**
7 Polo Lounge **C4**
8 Spago Beverly Hills......**E6**
9 Sprinkles Cupcakes **D5**

Hotels ▼

1 Beverly Hills Hotel.......**C3**
2 Beverly Wilshire,
   a Four Seasons Hotel ...**E6**
3 Four Seasons Hotel,
   Los Angeles at
   Beverly Hills..............**F5**
4 L'Ermitage
   Beverly Hills..............**E5**
5 The Maybourne
   Beverly Hills..............**E6**
6 Mr. C Beverly Hills.......**E8**
7 Peninsula
   Beverly Hills..............**C6**
8 SLS Hotel
   Beverly Hills.............**H5**
9 Sonder The Crescent
   Beverly Hills..............**E5**
10 Waldorf Astoria
   Beverly Hills..............**C6**

KEY

1 Exploring Sights
1 Restaurants
1 Hotels

One of L.A.'s most photographed homes is the Spadena House aka the Witch's House.

(inspiration for the Daniel Day-Lewis character in *There Will Be Blood*) and has been featured in a number of films like *The Big Lebowski*, *Spider-Man*, *The Social Network*, and *X-Men*. Park rangers offer tours for $20 where you can gawk at the 46,000-square-foot estate with a bowling alley, secret panels for liquor, and even a screening room. ✉ *905 Loma Vista Dr., Beverly Hills* ☎ *310/286–0119* ⊕ *www.greystonemansion.org.*

Museum of Tolerance

HISTORY MUSEUM | FAMILY | A museum that unflinchingly confronts bigotry and racism, one of its most affecting sections covers the Holocaust, with film footage of deportations and concentration camps. Upon entering, you are issued a "passport" bearing the name of a child whose life was dramatically changed by the Nazis; as you go through the exhibit, you learn the fate of that child. Another exhibit called *Anne: The Life and Legacy of Anne Frank* brings her story to life through immersive environments, multimedia presentations, and interesting artifacts, while Simon Wiesenthal's Vienna office is set exactly as the famous "Nazi hunter" had it while conducting his research that brought more than 1,000 war criminals to justice.

Interactive exhibits include The Forum where visitors can examine and debate solutions to controversial topics facing our nation today such as immigration, policing, homelessness, the pandemic, and bigotry; We the People, which looks at U.S. history from the 1600s up to the attack on the Capitol on January 6th, 2021, with an immense interactive wall; and the Point of View Experience, a four-sided glass cube that presents a different individual's perspective on a particular situation facing society.

■ **TIP→ Plan to spend at least three hours touring the museum; making a reservation is especially recommended for Sunday and holiday visits.** ✉ *9786 W. Pico Blvd., south of Beverly Hills, Beverly Hills* ☎ *310/772-2505 for reservations* ⊕ *www.museumoftolerance.com* 🎟 *From $16* ⊙ *Closed Fri. and Sat.*

★ Rodeo Drive

STREET | The ultimate shopping indulgence, Rodeo Drive is one of L.A.'s bona fide tourist attractions. The art of window-shopping (and reenacting your *Pretty Woman* fantasies) is prime among the retail elite: Tiffany & Co., Gucci, Jimmy Choo, Valentino, Harry Winston, Prada—you get the picture. Near the southern end of Rodeo Drive is Via Rodeo, a curvy cobblestone street designed to resemble a European shopping area and the perfect backdrop to pose for your Instagram feed. To give your feet a rest, free trolley tours depart from the southeast corner of Rodeo Drive and Dayton Way from 11:30 to 4:30. They're a terrific way to get an overview of the neighborhood. ✉ *Rodeo Dr., Beverly Hills* 🌐 *www.rodeodrive-bh.com.*

★ Spadena House

NOTABLE BUILDING | Otherwise known as the Witch's House in Beverly Hills, the Spadena House has an interesting history. First built on the Willat Studios lot in 1920, the house was physically moved to its current ritzy location in 1924. The house is not open for tourists, but the fairy-tale-like appearance is viewable from the street for onlookers to snap pics. Movie buffs will also recognize it from a background shot in the film *Clueless.* ✉ *516 Walden Dr., Beverly Hills.*

Virginia Robinson Gardens

GARDEN | As an heiress to the Robinson department store dynasty, Virginia Robinson lived on what is the oldest intact estate in Beverly Hills, dating back to 1911. The house and gardens cover 6½ acres of immaculately landscaped flora with a distinct Italian-villa vibe right out of Tuscany. The beaux arts–style house includes a tennis court, pool house, and five separate gardens including a rose garden, Italian terrace, palm tree forest, and more. ✉ *1008 Elden Way, Beverly Hills* ☎ *310/550–2087* 🌐 *www.robinson-gardens.org* 🕓 *Closed Sun.*

Wallis Annenberg Center for the Performing Arts

THEATER | Located in the heart of Beverly Hills, the Wallis Annenberg Center for the Performing Arts is a cultural hub for a wide variety of artistic performances. A breath of fresh air, the complex is centered on the 1934 Italianate-style Beverly Hills Post Office. The interior is gorgeous, with eight Depression-era murals painted by California artist Charles Kassler depicting laborers and artisans. The building includes the 500-seat Bram Goldsmith Theater and the 150-seat Lovelace Studio Theater. Affordable parking is available underneath the space. ✉ *9390 N. Santa Monica Blvd., Beverly Hills* ☎ *310/746–4000* 🌐 *www.thewallis.org.*

🍴 Restaurants

Dining in the 90210 is always an elegant experience, especially when you're leaving your car with the valet at one of the hot new restaurants along Rodeo Drive. But meals here don't always break the bank; there are plenty of casual and affordable eateries here worth a visit.

Crustacean

$$$ | VIETNAMESE | A Euro–Vietnamese fusion gem in the heart of Beverly Hills, Crustacean allows you to walk on water above exotic fish and see the kitchen preparing your perfect garlic noodles through a glass window. Standouts (besides the noodles) include Dungeness crab, A5 Wagyu beef, tuna cigars, and hearts-of-palm crab cakes. **Known for:** sake-simmered dishes; no-grease garlic noodles; unique cocktails like artichoke old-fashioneds. [$] *Average main: $36* ✉ *468 N. Bedford Dr., Beverly Hills* ☎ *310/205–8990* 🌐 *crustaceanbh.com* 🕓 *Closed Mon.*

CUT

$$$$ | STEAKHOUSE | In a true collision of artistic titans, celebrity chef Wolfgang Puck presents his take on steak houses in a space designed by Getty Center

Did You Know?

Beverly Hills became a haven for the stars during the Roaring '20s, when Charlie Chaplin, Rudolph Valentino, and dozens of other film luminaries built mansions here. Today it remains one of Southern California's most coveted addresses.

architect Richard Meier. Playful dishes like bone-marrow flan take center stage, while dry-aged and seared hunks of Nebraskan sirloin prove the Austrian-born chef understands America's love affair with beef. **Known for:** decadent dark chocolate soufflé; fantastic crab and shrimp cocktail; perfect cuts of beef. $ *Average main: $55* ⊠ *Beverly Wilshire (a Four Seasons Hotel), 9500 Wilshire Blvd., Beverly Hills* ☎ *310/275–5200* ⊕ *www. wolfgangpuck.com/dining/cut-beverly-hills* ⊗ *Closed Sun. No lunch.*

★ Gucci Osteria da Massimo Bottura

$$$$ | **ITALIAN** | Legendary Italian chef Massimo Bottura opened this spot, his first L.A. eatery, to loads of fanfare and celebrity sightings. The restaurant mirrors the Florence, Italy, location of the same name with a menu filled with favorites like a mouthwatering tortellini with Parmigiano Reggiano crema. **Known for:** excellent pastas; great people-watching; avant-garde design. $ *Average main: $80* ⊠ *347 N. Rodeo Dr., Beverly Hills* ☎ *424/600–7490* ⊕ *www.gucci.com/us/ en/st/capsule/gucci-osteria-beverly-hills.*

Matū

$$$$ | **STEAKHOUSE** | Matū is a steak restaurant that features 100% grass-fed Wagyu beef from New Zealand. Diners here are treated to a cavalcade of meaty options, but you should opt for the (surprisingly) affordable Matū dinner that comes with five courses and includes everything from steak tartare to eight-hour braised beef cheek. **Known for:** outstanding service; grass-fed New Zealand Wagyu; five-course prix-fixe menu. $ *Average main: $60* ⊠ *239 S. Beverly Dr., Beverly Hills* ⊕ *www.matusteak.com* ⊗ *No lunch Mon. and Tues.*

Nate 'n' Al's

$ | **SANDWICHES** | A longtime refuge from California's lean cuisine, Nate 'n' Al's serves up steaming pastrami, matzo ball soup, and potato latkes. Big-time media and entertainment insiders are often seen kibbitzing at this old-time

East Coast–style establishment. **Known for:** matzo ball soup; killer pastrami; long waits. $ *Average main: $18* ⊠ *414 N. Beverly Dr., Beverly Hills* ☎ *310/274–0101* ⊕ *www.natenals.com.*

Nozawa Bar

$$$$ | **JAPANESE** | Tucked into the back of Sugarfish (a popular sushi chain) in the middle of Beverly Hills, this secret omakase (chef's choice) sushi spot has only 10 seats, where master chef Osamu Fujita slices up the freshest cuts of raw fish from a 20-course tasting menu. If you ever wanted to get a one-on-one with a culinary wizard, this is your chance as you sit a foot away from the chef while he prepares your perfect portions. **Known for:** omakase sushi; bluefin tuna hand rolls; hard-to-get reservations needed. $ *Average main: $225* ⊠ *212 N. Canon Dr., Beverly Hills* ☎ *424/216–6158* ⊕ *www.nozawabar.com* ⊗ *Closed Sun.*

Polo Lounge

$$$$ | **AMERICAN** | Nothing says Beverly Hills quite like the Polo Lounge inside the Beverly Hills Hotel. This classic, monied spot is home to Hollywood royalty and entertainment luminaries noshing on lobster Nicoise or the famed Wagyu burger during power lunches. **Known for:** celebrity sightings; mouthwatering Wagyu burgers; dress code of no ripped jeans or baseball caps. $ *Average main: $45* ⊠ *The Beverly Hills Hotel, 9641 Sunset Blvd., Beverly Hills* ☎ *310/887– 2777* ⊕ *www.dorchestercollection.com/ en/los-angeles/the-beverly-hills-hotel/ restaurants-bars/the-polo-lounge.*

★ Spago Beverly Hills

$$$ | **MODERN AMERICAN** | Wolfgang Puck's flagship restaurant is a modern L.A. classic. Spago centers on a buzzing red-brick outdoor courtyard (with retractable roof) shaded by 100-year-old olive trees, and a daily-changing menu that offers dishes like smoked salmon pizza or off-menu schnitzel. **Known for:** great people-watching; off-menu schnitzel; sizzling smoked salmon pizza. $ *Average main:*

$35 ✉ *176 N. Canon Dr., Beverly Hills* ☎ *310/385–0880* 🌐 *www.wolfgangpuck.com* 🕒 *Closed Mon.*

Sprinkles Cupcakes

$ | **BAKERY** | The haute cupcake craze isn't going away, so expect lines that extend out the door and down the block here. If you need an after-hours fix, not to worry: Sprinkles also has the world's first cupcake (and cookie) ATM, open round the clock. **Known for:** red velvet cupcakes; banana peanut butter cupcakes; long lines. [$] *Average main: $5* ✉ *9635 S. Santa Monica Blvd., Beverly Hills* ☎ *310/274–8765* 🌐 *www.sprinkles.com.*

Hotels

Beverly Hills Hotel

$$$$ | **HOTEL** | **FAMILY** | Nicknamed the "Pink Palace," this luxury spot with giant marble bathrooms continues to attract Hollywood's elite after more than 100 years. **Pros:** iconic Polo Lounge; swanky spa and pool; ultraluxurious private bungalows. **Cons:** pricey fare at the Polo Lounge; expensive valet parking ($60); controversial ownership by the Sultan of Brunei. [$] *Rooms from: $1200* ✉ *9641 Sunset Blvd., Beverly Hills* ☎ *310/276–2251, 800/283–8885* 🌐 *www.beverlyhillshotel.com* 🛏 *210 rooms, 23 bungalows* 🍴 *No Meals.*

Beverly Wilshire, a Four Seasons Hotel

$$$$ | **HOTEL** | Built in 1928, this Rodeo Drive–adjacent hotel is part Italian Renaissance (with elegant details like crystal chandeliers) and part contemporary. **Pros:** complimentary car service; Wolfgang Puck restaurant on-site; first-rate spa. **Cons:** small lobby; valet parking is $65/night; might be too sceney for some. [$] *Rooms from: $735* ✉ *9500 Wilshire Blvd., Beverly Hills* ☎ *310/275–5200, 800/427–4354* 🌐 *www.fourseasons.com/beverlywilshire* 🛏 *395 rooms* 🍴 *No Meals.*

Four Seasons Hotel, Los Angeles at Beverly Hills

$$$$ | **HOTEL** | High hedges and patio gardens make this hotel a secluded retreat that even the hum of traffic can't permeate—one reason it's a favorite of Hollywood's elite, whom you might spot at the pool and espresso bar. **Pros:** tropical terrace with pool; high-end Italian eatery, Culina, on-site; great massages and nail salon. **Cons:** entertainment events can often limit access to parts of hotel; sometimes snooty atmosphere; breakfast not included. [$] *Rooms from: $735* ✉ *300 S. Doheny Dr., Beverly Hills* ☎ *310/273–2222, 800/819–5053* 🌐 *www.fourseasons.com/losangeles* 🛏 *285 rooms* 🍴 *No Meals.*

★ **L'Ermitage Beverly Hills**

$$$$ | **HOTEL** | This all-suites hotel is the picture of luxury: French doors open to a mini-balcony with views of the Hollywood sign; inside the very large rooms you'll find soaking tubs and oversize bath towels. **Pros:** stellar on-site restaurant; free shuttle service within 2-mile radius; all rooms are large suites with balconies. **Cons:** small spa and pool; valet $60/night; a bit of a trek to Beverly Hills shopping. [$] *Rooms from: $595* ✉ *9291 Burton Way, Beverly Hills* ☎ *310/278–3344* 🌐 *www.lermitagebeverlyhills.com* 🛏 *116 rooms* 🍴 *No Meals.*

★ **The Maybourne Beverly Hills**

$$$$ | **HOTEL** | The nine-story, Mediterranean-style palazzo is dedicated to welcoming those who relish luxury, providing classic style and exemplary service. **Pros:** Italian cocktail bar on the roof; obliging, highly trained staff; one-of-a-kind spa. **Cons:** breakfast not included with standard rooms; not all rooms have balconies; valet parking $60/night. [$] *Rooms from: $995* ✉ *225 N. Canon Dr., Beverly Hills* ☎ *310/860–7800* 🌐 *www.maybournebeverlyhills.com* 🛏 *201 rooms* 🍴 *No Meals.*

Mr. C Beverly Hills
$$ | **HOTEL** | An Italian getaway in the middle of Los Angeles, Mr. C Beverly Hills of the famed Cipriani family welcomes guests to their European home. **Pros:** free shuttle with a 3-mile radius including Beverly Hills and Century City; Italian restaurant serving classic Cipriani dishes; welcome Bellini at check-in. **Cons:** not directly in prime Beverly Hills; views of Beverly Hills are often 15% extra; breakfast not included. [$] *Rooms from: $345* ✉ *1224 Beverwil Dr., Beverly Hills* ☎ *310/277–2800* 🌐 *www.mrchotels.com/mrcbeverlyhills* 🛏 *138 rooms* 🍴 *No Meals.*

★ **Peninsula Beverly Hills**
$$$$ | **HOTEL** | This French Riviera–style palace overflowing with antiques and art is a favorite of boldface names, and visitors consistently describe a stay here as near perfect. **Pros:** 24-hour check-in/check-out policy; sunny pool area with cabanas; complimentary Rolls-Royce takes you to nearby Beverly Hills. **Cons:** valet parking $65/night; room decor might feel too ornate for some; room views are limited to a private garden or city streets. [$] *Rooms from: $980* ✉ *9882 S. Santa Monica Blvd., Beverly Hills* ☎ *310/551–2888, 800/462–7899* 🌐 *www.peninsula.com/en/beverly-hills/5-star-luxury-hotel-beverly-hills* 🛏 *195 rooms* 🍴 *No Meals.*

SLS Hotel Beverly Hills
$$$ | **HOTEL** | From the sleek, Philippe Starck–designed lobby and lounge with fireplaces, hidden nooks, and a communal table to luxurious poolside cabanas, this hotel offers a cushy, dreamlike stay. **Pros:** outstanding rooftop views; complimentary house car for use within 3-mile radius; dreamy Ciel spa. **Cons:** standard rooms are compact; valet parking $70/night; on a busy intersection outside Beverly Hills. [$] *Rooms from: $440* ✉ *465 S. La Cienega Blvd., Beverly Hills* ☎ *310/247–0400* 🌐 *slshotels.com/beverlyhills* 🛏 *297 rooms* 🍴 *No Meals.*

Sonder The Crescent Beverly Hills
$ | **HOTEL** | Built in 1927 as a dorm for silent-film actors, the Crescent is now a fanciful boutique hotel with a great location—within the Beverly Hills shopping triangle—and with an even better price (for the area). **Pros:** incredible prints throughout hotel; lively on-site restaurant, Crescent Bar and Terrace; cheapest room rates in Beverly Hills. **Cons:** no direct phone to the hotel; no elevator; rooms on the small side. [$] *Rooms from: $175* ✉ *403 N. Crescent Dr., Beverly Hills* ☎ *310/247–0505* 🌐 *www.sonder.com/destinations/los_angeles* 🛏 *35 rooms.*

★ **Waldorf Astoria Beverly Hills**
$$$$ | **HOTEL** | The belle of Beverly Hills, this Pierre-Yves Rochon–designed five-star property impresses with a top-notch spa, state-of-the-art amenities, and a rooftop pool with VIP cabanas and a restaurant program created by Jean-Georges Vongerichten. **Pros:** impeccable service; free shuttle within 5-mile radius; excellent La Prairie Spa. **Cons:** one of L.A.'s priciest rooms; on the busy corner of Wilshire and Santa Monica; valet parking $70/night. [$] *Rooms from: $815* ✉ *9850 Wilshire Blvd., Beverly Hills* ☎ *310/860–6666* 🌐 *www.waldorfastoriabeverlyhills.com* 🛏 *170 rooms* 🍴 *No Meals.*

Shopping

AllSaints Westfield Century City
MIXED CLOTHING | The British store invaded Beverly Drive, bringing with it a rock-and-roll edge mixed with a dash of Downton Abbey. Look for leather biker jackets, tough shoes, edgy prints, and long sweaters and cardigans, which, worn correctly, let them know you're with the band. ✉ *10250 Santa Monica Blvd., Beverly Hills* ☎ *310/499–0971* 🌐 *www.us.allsaints.com.*

Alo Yoga
SPORTING GOODS | In a city that takes its yoga seriously, it only makes sense that

this locally designed activewear brand would take its very first Los Angeles storefront to the next level. For Alo Yoga's flagship, that means an 8,000-square-foot space complete with an organic coffee bar, kombucha on tap, and a rooftop deck that hosts daily sweat-and-stretch sessions. As for the clothing, the model-favorite line offers stylish leggings, sports bras, tanks, and more pieces that look as cool outside the fitness studio as they do during downward dog. ⊠ *370 N. Canon Dr., Beverly Hills* ☎ *310/295–1860* ⊕ *www.aloyoga.com.*

Anto Distinctive Shirtmaker

MEN'S CLOTHING | A who's who of Hollywood's leading men, including Ryan Gosling and Tom Cruise, have been wearing Anto's bespoke shirts both on- and offscreen since 1955. An expertly tailored, customized shirt from this iconic showroom is decidedly an investment piece (you'll need to make an appointment for that service ahead of time), but you can also shop ready-made ties and button-downs here if you're just dropping by. ⊠ *258 N. Beverly Dr., Beverly Hills* ☎ *310/278–4500* ⊕ *www.antoshirt.com.*

Bijan

MEN'S CLOTHING | The House of Bijan is hard to miss with its trademark canary yellow Bugatti or Rolls-Royce always parked right out front. Inside, a Mediterranean palazzo welcomes high-end menswear shoppers into what is billed as the most expensive store in the world (by appointment only, of course). Some of the famous clientele includes George W. Bush, Bill Clinton, and Barack Obama. ⊠ *443 N. Rodeo Dr., Beverly Hills* ☎ *310/273–6544* ⊕ *bijan.com.*

Cartier

JEWELRY & WATCHES | Cartier has a bridal collection to sigh for in its chandeliered and respectfully hushed showroom, along with more playful pieces (chunky, diamond-encrusted panther cocktail rings, for example), watches, and accessories. The shop itself feels like the ultimate playground for A-list clientele, complete with a red-carpeted spiral staircase. ⊠ *411 N. Rodeo Dr., Beverly Hills* ☎ *310/275–4272* ⊕ *www.cartier.com.*

Céline

MIXED CLOTHING | Under designer Hedi Slimane's creative direction, the Parisian brand has entered a new chapter. At the Beverly Hills brick-and-mortar, fashion lovers looking for French Cool Girl clothing will love the selection of the label's leather handbags, heels, and chic ready-to-wear clothing. ⊠ *456 N. Rodeo Dr., Beverly Hills* ☎ *310/888–0120* ⊕ *www.celine.com.*

Chanel

MIXED CLOTHING | Fans of the French luxury retailer will be happy to find that the Beverly Hills flagship store stocks the brand's trademark pieces, like quilted leather bags, tweed jackets, and jewelry designed with the signature double C logo. Beyond those essentials are plenty of other pieces from Chanel's ready-to-wear collection. ⊠ *9560 Wilshire Blvd., Beverly Hills* ☎ *310/278–5500* ⊕ *www.chanel.com.*

Gearys of Beverly Hills

SOUVENIRS | Since 1930, this has been the ultimate destination for those seeking the most exquisite fine china, crystal, silver, and jewelry, mostly from classic sources like Christofle, Baccarat, and Waterford. No wonder it's a favorite for registries of the rich and famous. ⊠ *351 N. Beverly Dr., Beverly Hills* ☎ *310/273–4741* ⊕ *www.gearys.com.*

Harry Winston

JEWELRY & WATCHES | Perhaps the most locally famous jeweler is Harry Winston, *the* source for Oscar-night jewelry. The three-level space, with a bronze sculptural facade, velvet-panel walls, private salons, and a rooftop patio, is as glamorous as the gems. ⊠ *310 N. Rodeo Dr., Beverly Hills* ☎ *310/271–8554* ⊕ *www.harrywinston.com.*

Jimmy Choo

SHOES | This footwear designer is practically synonymous with flat-out sexy, sky-high stilettos. But there's also plenty more eye candy for fashionistas within the Rodeo Drive location's posh, monochromatic interior. ⊠ *250 N. Rodeo Dr., Beverly Hills* ☎ *310/860–9045* ⊕ *www. jimmychoo.com.*

Louis Vuitton

JEWELRY & WATCHES | Holding court on a prominent corner, Louis Vuitton carries its sought-after monogram (the ultimate symbol of luxury for many) on all manner of accessories and leather goods. ⊠ *295 N. Rodeo Dr., Beverly Hills* ☎ *310/859–0457* ⊕ *www.louisvuitton.com.*

Neiman Marcus

DEPARTMENT STORE | This couture salon frequently trots out designer trunk shows, and most locals go right to the shoe department, which features high-end footwear favorites like Giuseppe Zanotti and Christian Louboutin. A café on the third floor keeps your blood sugar high during multiple wardrobe changes, while a bar on the fourth is for celebrating those perfect finds with a glass of champagne. ⊠ *9700 Wilshire Blvd., Beverly Hills* ☎ *310/550–5900* ⊕ *www. neimanmarcus.com.*

Prada

MIXED CLOTHING | Prada's Rodeo Drive haven sits inside the incredibly cool Rem Koolhaas–designed Italian showcase space, which features 20-foot-wide staircases and fun-house curves. ⊠ *343 N. Rodeo Dr., Beverly Hills* ☎ *310/278–8661* ⊕ *www.prada.com.*

Saint Laurent

MIXED CLOTHING | Celebrities with the coolest, edgiest styles know they can head to the slick storefront to score the label's signature pieces, like moto jackets, skinny jeans, and platform pumps. A men's store with equally rock star–worthy clothing and accessories is just down

the street. ⊠ *326 N. Rodeo Dr., Beverly Hills* ☎ *310/271–5051* ⊕ *www.ysl.com.*

Taschen

BOOKS | Philippe Starck designed the Taschen space to evoke a cool 1920s Parisian salon—a perfect showcase for the publisher's design-forward coffee-table books about architecture, travel, culture, and photography. A suspended glass cube gallery in back hosts art exhibits and features limited-edition books. ⊠ *354 N. Beverly Dr., Beverly Hills* ☎ *310/274–4300* ⊕ *www.taschen.com.*

Tiffany & Co.

JEWELRY & WATCHES | Who can resist a gift that comes in those iconic blue boxes? Discover three floors of classic and contemporary jewelry (including plenty of sparklers perfect for popping the question) as well as watches, crystal, and china. ⊠ *210 N. Rodeo Dr., Beverly Hills* ☎ *310/273–8880* ⊕ *www.tiffany.com.*

Versace

MIXED CLOTHING | With its columned facade, temple dome ceiling, and recherché design, this is just the place for a dramatic red-carpet gown, bold bags, sunglasses, and accessories. It also stocks sleek menswear for fashion-forward fellows. ⊠ *240 N. Rodeo Dr., Beverly Hills* ☎ *310/205–3921* ⊕ *www. versace.com/us.*

Westfield Century City

MALL | FAMILY | This mall that sits between Beverly Hills and Brentwood is home to dozens of great stores, restaurants, and a massive movie theater. The best options here include L.A.'s iteration of Eataly, the ultimate Italian market; Din Tai Fung, an award-winning dumpling house; and Shake Shack, the famous East Coast burger joint. Some unique stores include a Tesla showroom, a Peloton shop, and the new Venus et Fleur flower boutique. ⊠ *10250 Santa Monica Blvd., Century City* ☎ *310/277–3898* ⊕ *www.westfield. com/centurycity.*

Chapter 7

WEST HOLLYWOOD, FAIRFAX, AND MID-WILSHIRE

7

Updated by
Paul Feinstein

Sights	Restaurants	Hotels	Shopping	Nightlife
★★☆☆☆	★★★★★	★★★★☆	★★★☆☆	★★★★★

NEIGHBORHOOD SNAPSHOT

TOP EXPERIENCES

■ **Wander the Grove and feast at the Farmers Market:** Visit for a shopping respite or to take in and appreciate the Farmers Market's over 75-year-old history and atmosphere.

■ **Drive down Sunset Boulevard to the Ocean:** The quintessential Los Angeles experience, it's best to start at La Cienega headed west on Sunset, which will take you through the Sunset Strip.

■ **Experience the '60s, '70s, and '80s all over again:** To truly experience the L.A. music scene of decades past, wander into the venues where everyone from the Doors to Guns N' Roses used to play: the Troubadour, the Whisky A Go Go, and the Rainbow Bar and Grill.

■ **Get cultured on Miracle Mile:** Check out Museum Row, which includes LACMA, the Petersen Automotive Museum, the Academy Museum of Motion Pictures, and La Brea Tar Pits.

■ **Laugh your butt off:** This area is home to the Hollywood Improv, the Laugh Factory, the Comedy Store, and Largo at the Coronet where A-list comedians test out new material and headline epically funny shows.

GETTING HERE

All main west–east roads will get you toward West Hollywood and the Fairfax District. Santa Monica Boulevard is the easiest. It starts in Santa Monica, heads straight into West Hollywood, and intersects with Fairfax. But traffic can be a nightmare, as it can be for another one of L.A.'s main arteries, Sunset Boulevard, which also hits West Hollywood. Secret streets that can be easier to zip around on include San Vicente, which cuts diagonally from Sunset down to West 3rd Street, or Fountain, which will take you from La Cienega to La Brea and beyond. For Mid-Wilshire, the main thoroughfares include Wilshire, Olympic, and Pico Boulevards, but to avoid traffic, try using 6th Street. Luckily, there is also direct Metro access that runs across both neighborhoods with stops at LACMA on the Westside all the way to Wilshire/Vermont on the Eastside.

VIEWFINDER

■ **Paul Smith Pink Wall:** A giant pink box, the Paul Smith store is notorious for gangs of photo hounds looking to glam up their social feeds. The earlier in the morning you come, the fewer people you'll have to navigate around for that perfect pink pic. ✉ *8221 Melrose Ave.*

■ **The Vanderpump Trifecta:** Bravo fans can get their entire fill of the Vanderpump empire and can take photos in front (or inside of) SUR, PUMP, and TomTom as they're all right around the corner from each other. ✛ *Start at 606 N. Robertson*

■ **Urban Light at LACMA:** 202 cast-iron antique street lamps are lined up outside L.A.'s most famous art museum. Come at night, set a longer exposure time on your camera, and look like a movie star as the lights rain down on you from all angles. ✉ *5905 Wilshire Blvd.*

■ **Levitated Mass:** On the grounds behind LACMA, there's a 340-ton boulder that "hovers" over a 456-foot viewing path. The concept art was created by Michael Heizer and offers keen picture takers an opportunity to snap shots of themselves holding up the giant rock. You'll need a tripod or a friend to help you get the angle just right. Come early in the morning to avoid crowds.

West Hollywood is not a place to see things (like museums or movie studios) as much as it is a place to do things—like go to a nightclub, eat at a world-famous restaurant, or attend an art gallery opening. Since the end of Prohibition, the Sunset Strip has been Hollywood's nighttime playground, where stars headed to such glamorous nightclubs as the Trocadero, the Mocambo, and Ciro's.

It's still going strong, with crowds still filing into well-established spots like Whisky A Go Go and paparazzi staking out the members-only Soho House. But hedonism isn't all that drives West Hollywood. Also thriving is an important interior design and art gallery trade exemplified by the Cesar Pelli–designed Pacific Design Center.

West Hollywood has also emerged as one of the most progressive cities in Southern California. It's one of the most gay-friendly cities anywhere, with a large LGBTQ+ community. Its annual Gay Pride Parade is one of the largest in the nation, drawing tens of thousands of participants each June.

The neighborhood maps are squiggly, but bordering and penetrating WeHo is the Fairfax District and Mid-Wilshire. Fairfax has become one of the trendiest streets in L.A. and features a bevy of streetwear shops and hot new restaurants. Running from the Sunset Strip all the way down to Wilshire (and beyond) Fairfax is also where you'll find the historic Farmers Market and The Grove shopping mall, which are both great places to people-watch over breakfast or to shop for ethnic eats and designer wares.

Heading further south on Fairfax, you'll enter the Mid-Wilshire neighborhood, which is home to Little Ethiopia, with its amazing Ethiopian restaurants, and Miracle Mile, where you'll get your culture on. Museums like LACMA, the Petersen Automotive Museum, La Brea Tar Pits, and the Academy Museum of Motion Pictures sit side by side.

West Hollywood and Fairfax

Sights

★ The Grove
STORE/MALL | FAMILY | Come to this popular outdoor mall for familiar names like Apple, Nike, and Nordstrom; stay for the central fountain with "dancing" water and light shows, people-watching from the trolley, and, during the holiday

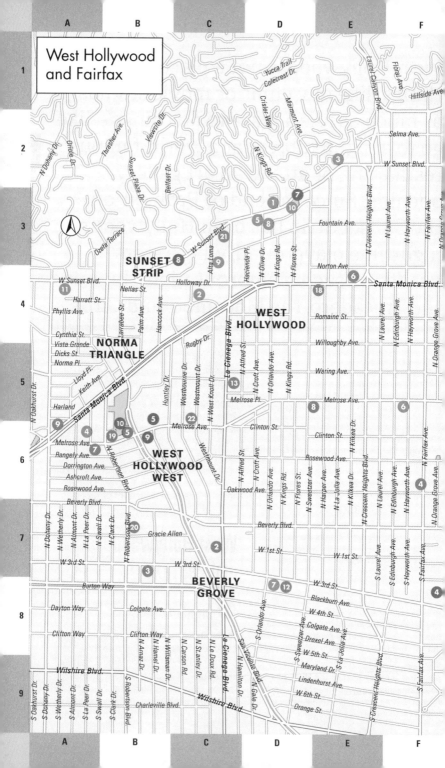

Sights ▼

Restaurants ▼

Hotels ▼

season, artificial snowfall and a winter wonderland. Feel-good pop blasting over the loudspeakers aims to boost your mood while you spend, and a giant cineplex gives shoppers a needed break with the latest box office blockbusters. ⊠ *189 The Grove Dr., Fairfax District* ☎ *323/900–8080* ⊕ *www.thegrovela.com.*

Holocaust Museum LA

HISTORY MUSEUM | A museum dedicated solely to the Holocaust, it uses its extensive collections of photos and artifacts as well as award-winning audio tours and interactive tools to evoke European Jewish life in the 20th century. The mission is to commemorate the lives of those who perished and those who survived the Holocaust. The building is itself a marvel, having won two awards from the American Institute of Architects. Throughout the week, the museum hosts talks given by Holocaust survivors, while other events include a lecture series, educational programs, and concerts. ⊠ *100 The Grove Dr., Los Angeles* ☎ *323/651–3704* ⊕ *www.holocaustmuseumla.org* 🎟 *Free.*

Melrose Avenue

STREET | Melrose Avenue is a tale of two streets: west of Fairfax Avenue is a haven of high-end boutique shopping, chichi restaurants, and avant-garde galleries while east of Fairfax is much grittier, where street style is more in vogue, with sneaker stores, head shops, fast-casual food, and vintage boutiques. Fans of *Melrose Place* will be excited to learn that the eponymous street actually exists and is home to upscale shops and restaurants. Instagram junkies will recognize a number of photo hot spots like the shockingly pink Paul Smith store or graffitied angel wings along numerous storefronts. ⊠ *Melrose Ave., West Hollywood* ⊕ *www.melrose-avenue.com.*

★ The Original Farmers Market

MARKET | FAMILY | Called the Original Farmers Market for a reason, this special piece of land brought out farmers to sell their wares starting in 1934. Today, the market has more permanent residences, but fresh produce still abounds among the dozens of vendors. Some purveyor standouts include gourmet market Monsieur Marcel, Bob's Coffee & Doughnuts, and Patsy D'Amore's Pizzeria, which has been serving slices since 1949. The market is adjacent to The Grove shopping center, and locals and tourists flock to both in droves. ⊠ *6333 W. 3rd St., Fairfax District* ☎ *323/933–9211* ⊕ *www.farmersmarketla.com.*

Pacific Design Center

NOTABLE BUILDING | World-renowned architect Cesar Pelli's original vision for the Pacific Design Center was three buildings that together housed designer showrooms, office buildings, parking, and more—a sleek shrine to design. These architecturally intriguing buildings were built years apart: the building sheathed in blue glass (known as the Blue Whale) opened in 1975; the green building opened in 1988. The final "Red" building opened in 2013, completing Pelli's grand vision many years later. Altogether the 1.6-million-square-foot complex covers more than 14 acres, housing more than 100 design showrooms as well as 2,200 interior product lines. ⊠ *8687 Melrose Ave., West Hollywood* ☎ *310/657–0800* ⊕ *www.pacificdesigncenter.com.*

Santa Monica Boulevard

STREET | From Fairfax Avenue in the east to Doheny Drive in the west, Santa Monica Boulevard is the commercial core of West Hollywood's gay community, with restaurants and cafés, bars and clubs, bookstores and galleries, and other establishments catering largely to the LGBTQ+ scene. Twice a year—during June's L.A. Pride and on Halloween—the boulevard becomes an open-air festival. ⊠ *Santa Monica Blvd. between Fairfax Ave. and Doheny Dr., West Hollywood* ☎ *323/848–6400* ⊕ *weho.org.*

Sunset Boulevard

STREET | One of the most fabled avenues in the world, Sunset Boulevard began humbly enough in the 18th century as a route from El Pueblo de Los Angeles to the Pacific Ocean. Today, as it passes through West Hollywood, it becomes the sexy and seductive Sunset Strip, where rock and roll had its heyday and cocktail bars charge a premium for the views. It slips quietly into the tony environs of Beverly Hills and Bel-Air, twisting and winding past gated estates and undulating vistas. ✉ *Sunset Blvd., West Hollywood* 🌐 *www.weho.org.*

Sunset Plaza

PLAZA/SQUARE | With a profusion of sidewalk cafés, Sunset Plaza is one of the best people-watching spots in town. Sunny weekends reach the highest pitch, when people flock to this stretch of Sunset Boulevard for brunch or lunch and to browse in the trendy shops that offer a range of price points. There's free parking in the lot behind the shops. ✉ *8623 W. Sunset Blvd., West Hollywood* 🌐 *www.sunsetplaza.com.*

West Hollywood Design District

STORE/MALL | More than 200 businesses—art galleries, antiques shops, fashion outlets (including Rag & Bone and James Perse), and interior design stores—are found in the design district. There are also about 30 restaurants, including the famous paparazzi magnet, the Ivy. All are clustered within walking distance of each other—rare for L.A. ✉ *Melrose Ave. and Robertson and Beverly Blvds., West Hollywood* ☎ *310/289–2534* 🌐 *westhollywooddesigndistrict.com.*

West Hollywood Library

LIBRARY | Across from the Pacific Design Center, this library, designed by architects Steve Johnson and James Favaro, is a charming part of the city. Replete with floor-to-ceiling glass, a modern and airy interior, a huge mural by Shepard Fairey, and other art by Kenny Scharf and Retna, the three-story building and the adjoining park are a great place to take a break from your tour of the city. They also have an impressive LGBTQ+ book collection. There's inexpensive parking and a café below. ✉ *625 N. San Vicente Blvd., West Hollywood* ☎ *310/652–5340* 🌐 *lacountylibrary.org/west-hollywood-library.*

🍴 Restaurants

★ Angelini Osteria

$$$ | **ITALIAN** | With a buzzy indoor dining room and ample outdoor seating, this is one of L.A.'s most celebrated Italian restaurants. The keys are chef-owner Gino Angelini's consistently impressive dishes, like whole branzino, *tagliolini al limone,* veal chop *alla* Milanese, as well as lasagna oozing with *besciamella* (Italian béchamel sauce). **Known for:** large Italian wine selection; bold flavors; savory pastas. [$] *Average main: $40* ✉ *7313 Beverly Blvd., Beverly–La Brea* ☎ *323/297–0070* 🌐 *www.angelinirestaurantgroup.com.*

Angler

$$ | **SEAFOOD** | Don't balk when you see that Angler is in the Beverly Center mall. If you do, you'll be missing out on one of the most interesting seafood restaurants in the entire city. **Known for:** excellent cocktails and wine list; Michelin-starred team behind Angler SF; surprising and imaginative seafood. [$] *Average main: $30* ✉ *8500 Beverly Blvd., Suite 117, West Hollywood* ☎ *424/332-4082* 🌐 *anglerla.com* 🕒 *Closed Sun. and Mon.*

A.O.C.

$$ | **MEDITERRANEAN** | Not to be confused with the congresswoman from New York, the acronym here stands for Appellation d'Origine Contrôlée, the regulatory system that ensures the quality of local wines and cheeses in France. Fittingly, A.O.C. upholds this standard of excellence in its shared plates and perfect wine pairings in the stunning exposed-brick and vine-laden courtyard. **Known for:** amazing cocktail hour; quaint outdoor courtyard; charming indoor fireplaces.

Continued on page 133

CRUISING THE SUNSET STRIP

For more than half a century, Hollywood's night owls have headed for the 1¾-mile stretch of Sunset Boulevard between Crescent Heights Boulevard on the east and Doheny Drive on the west, known as the Sunset Strip. The experience of driving it from end to end gives you a sampling of everything that makes L.A. what it is, with all its glamour and grit, and its history of those who rose fast and fell faster.

Left, Sunset Boulevard. Top right, The Chateau Marmont. Bottom right, Mel's Drive-in Diner.

In the 1930s and '40s, stars such as Errol Flynn and Rita Hayworth came for wild evenings of dancing and drinking at nightclubs like Trocadero, Ciro's, and Mocambo.

The Strip's image as Tinseltown's glamorous nighttime playground began to die in the '50s, and by the mid-'60s it was the center of L.A.'s raucous music-and-nightlife scene. Bands like the Doors and the Byrds played the Whisky a Go Go, and the city's counterculture clashed with police in the famous Sunset Strip curfew riots in the summer of 1966.

In the '70s, the Strip was all about glam rock, with David Bowie, T. Rex, and Queen hitting the venues. But this was when it began a decline that would last almost two decades, until it became a seedy section of the city where hookers hung out on every corner.

It's only been in the last decade that the Strip has seen a true revitalization, with new hotels, restaurants, and bars opening that have become haunts for celebs and A-listers. It retains its rough-and-tumble image in some sections but overall is a much classier spot to spend a night out.

A CLASSIC DRIVE THROUGH L.A.

Depending on the time of day, driving the Strip is a different experience. In the afternoon grab lunch at a hotel and hobnob with industry types. At night, drive with the top down and come to hear music, hit a club, or have cocktails at a rooftop bar. Either way, it's good to park the car and walk (yes, walk!).

WHERE TO EAT & DRINK

See and be seen at **Skybar at the Mondrian Hotel** (✉ 8440 Sunset Blvd. ☎ 323/848–6025), the luxe outdoor lounge and pool deck. The bar opens to the public at 8 pm daily. Come early to enjoy sweeping views of the city before turning your gaze inward to the beautiful people milling around. **Daughter's Deli** (✉ 8555 Sunset Blvd., ☎ 310/652-6552) is run by the grand-daughter of Langer's, LA's most beloved sandwich joint. The pastrami is just as good, but the Turkey Nana gives it a run for its money. Open 10am-9pm weekdays and Sat. 9-6, Sun. 9-5.

Stop in for a burger and shake at **Mel's Drive-In** (✉ 8585 Sunset Blvd. ☎ 310/854–7201), open 24 hours a day. The iconic 1950s-inspired diner in

TIPS FOR PARKING

Parking and traffic around the Strip can be tough on weekends. Although there's some parking on side streets, it may be worth it to park in a lot and pay $10-$25. Most of the hotels have garages as well.

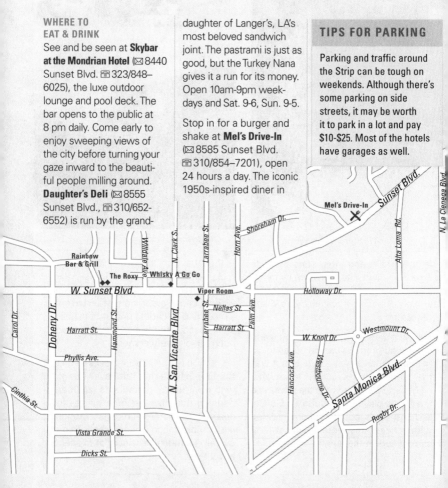

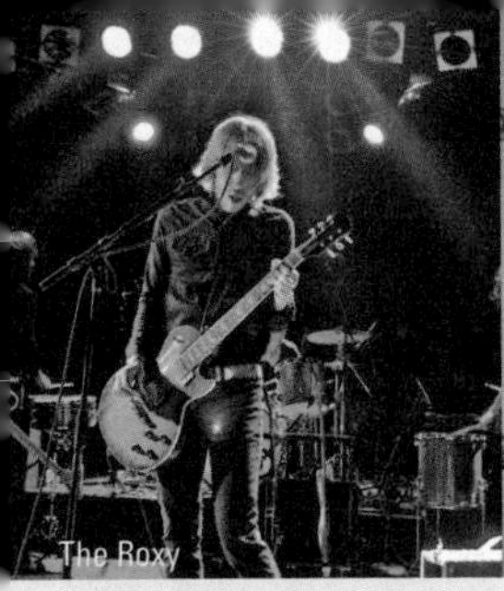
The Roxy

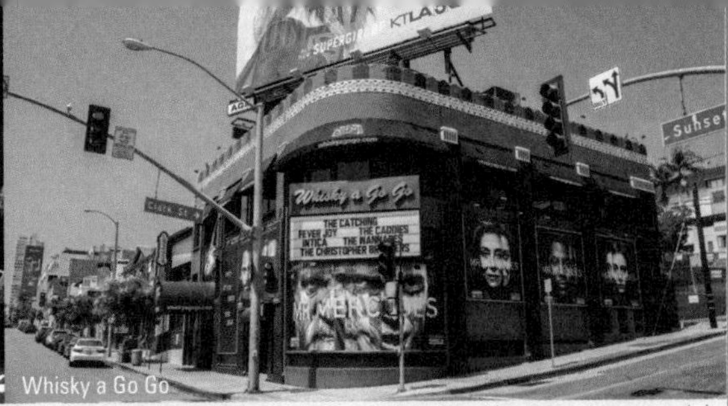
Whisky a Go Go

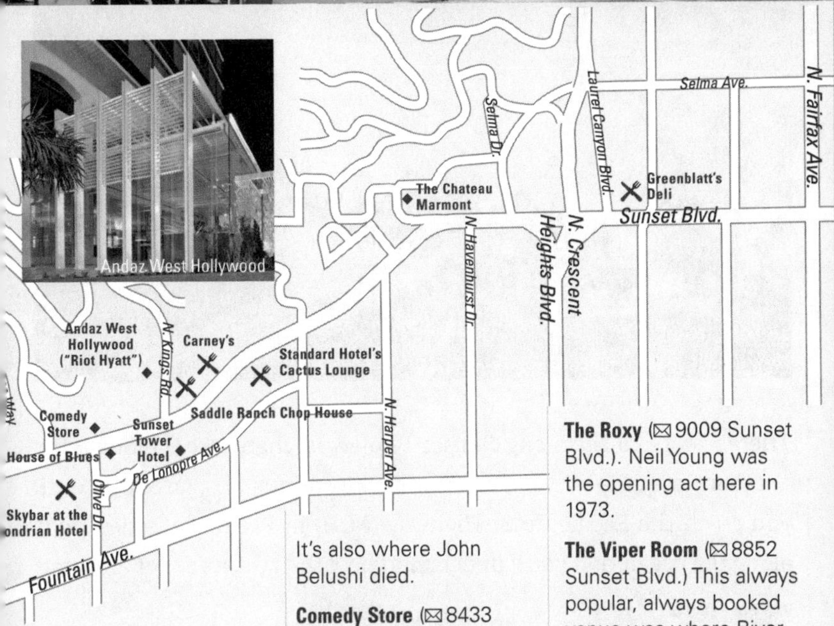
Selma Ave.
N. Fairfax Ave.
Laurel Canyon Blvd.
Selma Dr.
The Chateau Marmont
Greenblatt's Deli
Sunset Blvd.
N. Havenhurst Dr.
Heights Blvd.
N. Crescent
Andaz West Hollywood ("Riot Hyatt")
N. Kings Rd.
Carney's
Standard Hotel's Cactus Lounge
Comedy Store
Sunset Tower Hotel
Saddle Ranch Chop House
House of Blues
De Longpre Ave.
N. Harper Ave.
Skybar at the Mondrian Hotel
Olive Dr.
Fountain Ave.
Andaz West Hollywood

the heart of the Strip is a fun place to people-watch, day or night.

For the city's best hot dogs, chili fries, and frozen chocolate-dipped bananas, head to **Carney's** (✉ 8351 Sunset Blvd. ☎ 323/654-8300), a popular spot for a quick bite. You can't miss it—look for the yellow railcar.

SIGHTS TO SEE

The Chateau Marmont (✉ 8221 W. Sunset Blvd.). Greta Garbo once called this castle-like hotel home. It's also where John Belushi died.

Comedy Store (✉ 8433 Sunset Blvd.). David Letterman and Robin Williams rose to fame here.

Andaz West Hollywood ("Riot Hyatt") (✉ 8401 Sunset Blvd.). Led Zeppelin, the Rolling Stones, and the Who stayed and played here when they hit town.

Rainbow Bar & Grill (✉ 9015 Sunset Blvd.). Jimi Hendrix and Bob Marley began their climb to the top of the charts here.

The Roxy (✉ 9009 Sunset Blvd.). Neil Young was the opening act here in 1973.

The Viper Room (✉ 8852 Sunset Blvd.) This always popular, always booked venue was where River Phoenix OD'd in 1993.

Whisky a Go Go (✉ 8901 W. Sunset Blvd.). Granted Landmark status in 2019, this iconic club has been hosting hot bands since it opened in 1964.

Saddle Ranch Chop House (✉ 8371 Sunset Boulevard). Originally the Thunder Roadhouse, this raucous steakhouse has a mechanical bull featured on many a TV show, including *Sex and the City*.

A DRIVE BEYOND THE STRIP

California's Pacific Coast Highway

There's more to see along Sunset Boulevard than just the Strip. For another classic L.A. drive, just before dusk, continue west on Sunset until you reach the Pacific Coast Highway (PCH) in Pacific Palisades, right along the ocean, and you'll understand how the boulevard got its name.

WHEN TO GO

Time it right so you can catch that famous L.A. sunset, or drive down Sunset Boulevard late morning after rush hour and arrive just in time for lunch at a waterfront restaurant or a picnic on the beach.

The PCH is also known for its fresh seafood shacks along the roadside. For a cocktail with a great view, try **Gladstone's 4 Fish** (⊠ 17300 Pacific Coast Hwy.), where Sunset Boulevard hits the PCH.

TRIP TIPS

While it's hard to tear your eyes away from sites along the way, there are hairpin turns on the Boulevard, and driving can be a challenge. Stop-and-go traffic—especially along the Strip—means lots of fender benders, so be careful and keep a safe distance.

Sunset view from Gladstone's

$ Average main: $30 ⊠ 8700 W. 3rd St., West Hollywood ☎ 310/859–9859 ⊕ www.aocwinebar.com.

Canter's

$ | SANDWICHES | FAMILY | This granddaddy of L.A. delicatessens (it opened in 1931) cures its own corned beef and pastrami and features delectable desserts from the in-house bakery. It's not the best (or friendliest) deli in town, but it's a classic. **Known for:** location adjacent to Kibitz Room bar; plenty of seating and short wait times; open 24 hours. $ Average main: $18 ⊠ 419 N. Fairfax Ave., Fairfax District ☎ 323/651–2030 ⊕ www.canters-deli.com.

Catch LA

$$$$ | ASIAN FUSION | Boasting the best see-and-be-seen crowd in West Holly-wood, this rooftop restaurant also has some of the best views. As you enter through a pergola, you'll find an extreme-ly good-looking crowd of well-heeled din-ers and drinkers flirting at the large bar or getting cozy in the teal brushed-leather booths. **Known for:** some of the city's best celeb sightings; rooftop views; excellent crab tempura. $ Average main: $45 ⊠ 8715 Melrose Ave., West Hollywood ☎ 323/347–6060 ⊕ catchrestaurants. com/catchla ⊗ No brunch weekdays.

Connie and Ted's

$$ | SEAFOOD | Inspired by the classic clam, oyster, and fish houses of New England, this beautiful space (the roof is arched like a wave) is occupied by a dressed-up crowd dipping fried calamari or spooning up Jo's wicked-good chow-da. Lobster rolls are insanely good, and you can never go wrong with the catch of the day. **Known for:** buttery lobster rolls; catch of the day; classic New England seafood spot atmosphere. $ Average main: $30 ⊠ 8171 Santa Monica Blvd., West Hollywood ☎ 323/848–2722 ⊕ www.connieandteds.com ⊗ Closed Mon. and Tues. No lunch Wed. and Thurs.

Craig's

$$$ | AMERICAN | Behind the unremarkable facade is an übertrendy—yet decidedly old-school—den of American cuisine that doubles as a safe haven for the movie industry's most important names and well-known faces. Be aware that this joint is always busy so you might not even get a table and reservations are hard to come by. **Known for:** lots of celebrities; delicious chicken Parm; strong drinks. $ Average main: $35 ⊠ 8826 Melrose Ave., West Hollywood ☎ 310/276–1900 ⊕ craigs.la ⊗ No lunch Mon.–Sat. No dinner Sun.

★ Crossroads

$$ | VEGETARIAN | From its famous Impossible Burger (you can't believe it's not meat) to its Sicilian pepperoni pizza (again, not meat), Crossroads's level of plant-based inventiveness knows no bounds. The space itself is dimly lit, with red-leather booths and a full bar illuminat-ing its A-list clientele. **Known for:** high-end plant-based cuisine; great bar menu; popular celebrity hangout. $ Average main: $24 ⊠ 8284 Melrose Ave., West Hollywood ☎ 323/782–9245 ⊕ www. crossroadskitchen.com.

Dan Tana's

$$$ | ITALIAN | If you're looking for an Italian vibe straight out of Goodfellas, your search ends here. Checkered table-cloths cover the tightly packed tables as Hollywood players dine on the city's best chicken and veal Parm, and down Scotches by the finger. **Known for:** elbow-room-only bar; lively atmosphere; celeb spotting. $ Average main: $35 ⊠ 9071 Santa Monica Blvd., West Hollywood ☎ 310/275–9444 ⊕ www.dantanasrestau-rant.com ⊗ No lunch.

★ El Coyote Mexican Food

$ | MEXICAN | FAMILY | Open since 1931, this landmark spot is perfect for those on a budget or anyone after an authen-tic Mexican meal. The traditional fare is decadent and delicious while the margaritas are sweetened to perfection.

Known for: affordable, quality cuisine; festive atmosphere; being an L.A. staple. [$] *Average main: $18* ✉ *7312 Beverly Blvd., Beverly–La Brea* ☎ *323/939–2255* 🌐 *www.elcoyotecafe.com* ⏲ *Closed Mon. and Tues.*

Happy Ice
$ | **AMERICAN** | From a food truck to a brick-and-mortar space, Happy Ice is a rainbow-colored icee shop that keeps the crowds coming. Customers can combine up to three of the nine flavors, including the world-famous Rainbow Rocket, Mango Madness, Sour Apple Lush, and more. **Known for:** colorful, Instagram-worthy atmosphere; creative slushies and icees; vegan-friendly ingredients. [$] *Average main: $5* ✉ *7324 Melrose Ave., West Hollywood* ☎ *855/934–2779* 🌐 *www.happyicela.com.*

★ **Joan's on Third**
$ | **CAFÉ** | **FAMILY** | Part restaurant, part bakery, part market, Joan's on Third has a little bit of everything. This roadside French-style café caters to families, the occasional local celebrity, and lovers of all things wholesome. **Known for:** crispy baguettes and fresh pastries; deli sandwiches and imported cheeses; long lines (get there before 9 am). [$] *Average main: $16* ✉ *8350 W. 3rd St., West Hollywood* ☎ *323/655–2285* 🌐 *www.joansonthird.com.*

Koi
$$$ | **ASIAN FUSION** | Koi first opened its doors in 2002 and immediately became one of the buzziest restaurants in Los Angeles, attracting a who's who clientele salivating over their unique Asian-fusion cuisine. Today, it continues to deliver on every level: fun atmosphere, incredible food, and solid celebrity sightings. **Known for:** beautiful setting; cult following; Koi Crispy Rice and signature rolls. [$] *Average main: $40* ✉ *734 N. La Cienega Blvd., West Hollywood* ☎ *310/659–9449* 🌐 *koirestaurant.com/los-angeles* ⏲ *No lunch.*

Milk Bar LA
$ | **BAKERY** | A longtime darling for Angelenos, Milk Bar is a sweets shop that will cure any sugary cravings. The Milk Bar pie and cereal-milk soft serve are favorites, but you can also take classes with owner Christina Tosi to become you own baking master. **Known for:** famous Milk Bar pie; cereal-milk soft serve; long lines. [$] *Average main: $6* ✉ *7150 Melrose Ave., West Hollywood* ☎ *213/341–8423* 🌐 *milkbarstore.com.*

★ **MozzaPlex**
$$$ | **ITALIAN** | A trio of restaurants by star chef Nancy Silverton, MozzaPlex consists of Pizzeria Mozza, a casual pizza and wine spot; Osteria Mozza, an upscale Italian restaurant with incredible pastas; and chi SPACCA, an Italian steak house with succulent cuts of steak. The restaurant complex is one of the most beloved in the whole city and if you're craving any kind of Italian food, you'll want to get yourself inside. **Known for:** great pizzas; intimate atmosphere; the chi SPACCA burger. [$] *Average main: $3* ✉ *641 N. Highland Ave., Beverly–La Brea* ☎ *323/297–1130* 🌐 *www.mozzarestaurantgroup.com.*

Petty Cash Taqueria and Bar
$ | **MODERN MEXICAN** | A boisterous vibe permeates PCT as groups of twenty- and thirtysomethings feast on fresh guacamole under the graffitied walls. There are 10 or so tacos on the ever-changing menu, from grilled octopus and Baja fish to pork belly and shrimp. **Known for:** house-made tortillas; delicious mezcal cocktails; lively atmosphere. [$] *Average main: $15* ✉ *7360 Beverly Blvd., Beverly–La Brea* ☎ *323/933–5300* 🌐 *www.pettycashtaqueria.com* ⏲ *Closed Mon. No lunch weekdays.*

★ **Pink's Hot Dogs**
$ | **HOT DOG** | **FAMILY** | Since 1939, Angelenos and tourists alike have been lining up at this roadside hot dog stand. But Pink's is more than just an institution, it's a beloved family-run joint that serves

a damn good hot dog. **Known for:** the famous Brando Dog; late-night dining; chili fries. [$] *Average main: $7* ✉ *709 N. La Brea Ave., Hollywood* ☎ *323/931–4223* ⊕ *www.pinkshollywood.com.*

Pura Vita

$$ | **VEGETARIAN** | At the first 100% plant-based Italian restaurant and wine bar in the whole country, chef Tara Punzone makes you believe her caprese has real mozzarella, her meatballs come from cows, and her *cacio e pepe* is filled with dairy. The food is exceptional, the atmosphere screams New York, and the best part is that no animals were harmed for any of it. **Known for:** all-vegan cuisine; incredible pastas; stellar wine list. [$] *Average main: $20* ✉ *8247 Santa Monica Blvd., West Hollywood* ☎ *323/688–2303* ⊕ *www.puravitalosangeles.com* ⊗ *Closed Mon.*

SUR Restaurant & Lounge

$$$$ | **MODERN AMERICAN** | Fans of Lisa Vanderpump and the *Vanderpump Rules* reality show on Bravo will instantly recognize SUR as the backdrop for the series's endless drama, broken relationships, one-night stands, and countless drinks. The actual restaurant serves a melange of new American items that range from fried goat cheese balls to prime pork chops. **Known for:** celebrity sightings; crafty cocktails; bachelorette parties galore. [$] *Average main: $42* ✉ *606 N. Robertson Blvd., West Hollywood* ☎ *310/340–1725* ⊕ *www.surrestaurant. com* ⊗ *Closed Mon. No lunch weekdays.*

Sushi Tama

$$ | **JAPANESE** | A calming effect comes over you as you enter this simple sushi bar on one of L.A.'s most fashionable streets. Chef Yoshimoto actually sharpened his skills inside Tokyo's Tsukiji Fish Market where he learned what the best quality fish really means, resulting in sushi that transports you to Japan. **Known for:** fresh fish; donburi bowls; traditional sushi. [$] *Average main: $25* ✉ *116 N. Robertson Blvd., West Hollywood* ☎ *424/249–3009* ⊕ *www.sushitama-la. com.*

Tesse

$$$$ | **FRENCH FUSION** | Jaws drop upon entering this French hot spot in West Hollywood, thanks to the marvelous interior design with sloping wood ceilings, lush leather banquettes, angled mirrors, and open kitchen. But more important, French-food fanatics will salivate over the gooey cheese plates and duck leg confit. **Known for:** duck leg confit; stunning interior design; great cocktail program. [$] *Average main: $45* ✉ *8500 W. Sunset Blvd., Suite B, West Hollywood* ☎ *310/360–3866* ⊕ *www.tesserestaurant.com* ⊗ *Closed Mon. and Tues.*

Urth Caffé Melrose

$ | **AMERICAN** | The ultratrendy Urth Caffé is full of beautiful people refueling on organic coffee and tea with a range of health-conscious sandwiches, salads, and juices. The outdoor patio is a great place to take in the scene or spot celebrities. **Known for:** healthy eats; organic coffee and tea; celeb spotting. [$] *Average main: $14* ✉ *8565 Melrose Ave., West Hollywood* ☎ *310/659–0628* ⊕ *www. urthcaffe.com.*

Hotels

ANdAZ West Hollywood

$$ | **HOTEL** | On the north side of the Sunset Strip, the ANdAZ is Hyatt's fun younger sister, catering to hipsters, techies, and rock stars lounging in the lobby as "hosts" check them in via tablets (there's no front desk). **Pros:** fridge stocked with healthy drinks and snacks; ambitious hotel dining and bar concepts; gym overlooks Sunset Boulevard. **Cons:** traffic congestion impedes access; Sunset Strip can get loud and rowdy on nights and weekends; expensive parking. [$] *Rooms from: $330* ✉ *8401 Sunset Blvd., West Hollywood* ☎ *323/656–1234, 800/233–1234* ⊕ *www.hyatt.com/brands/andaz* ⤳ *239 rooms* ⦿ *No Meals.*

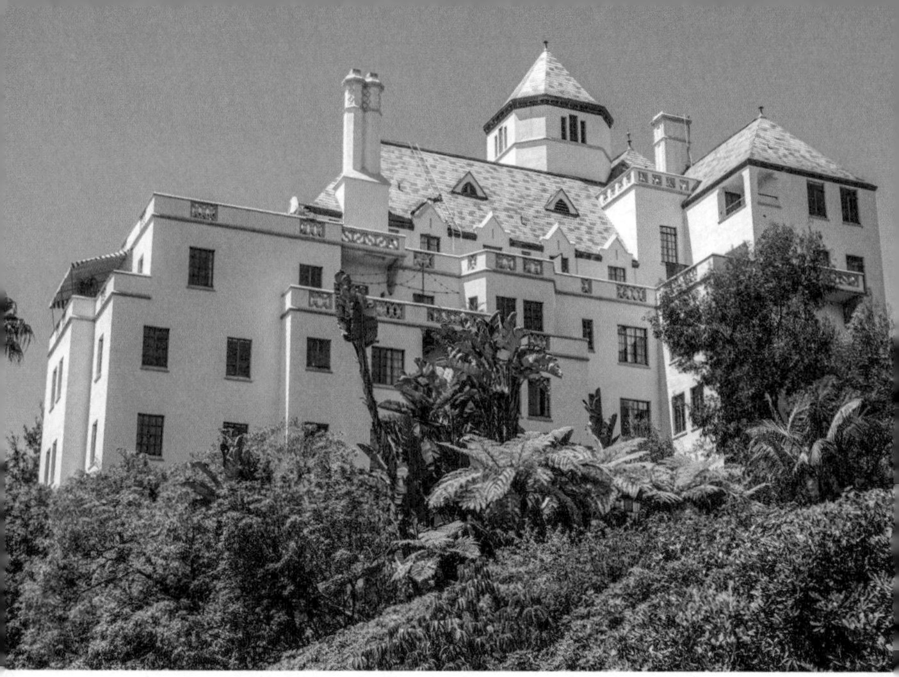

Celebrity hot spot Chateau Marmont is one of the most famous hotels in Los Angeles.

Chamberlain

$$ | **HOTEL** | On a leafy residential side street, the Chamberlain is steps from Santa Monica Boulevard and close to the Sunset Strip, bringing in fashionable young professionals and 24-hour party people looking to roam West Hollywood. **Pros:** excellent guests-only dining room and bar; suites come with fireplace and balcony; 24-hour fitness center. **Cons:** compact bathrooms; uphill climb to the Sunset Strip; party-friendly crowds might be too noisy for some. [$] *Rooms from: $249* ✉ *1000 Westmount Dr., West Hollywood* ☎ *310/657–7400, 888/377–7181* 🌐 *www.chamberlainwesthollywood.com* 🛏 *114 suites* 🍴 *Free Breakfast.*

Chateau Marmont

$$$$ | **HOTEL** | Built in 1929 as a luxury apartment complex, the Chateau is now one of the most unique see-and-be-seen hotel hot spots in all of the city. **Pros:** private and exclusive vibe; famous history; beautiful pool. **Cons:** some may find it pretentious; celeb guests will take priority over you; some of the rooms are underwhelming. [$] *Rooms from: $595* ✉ *8221 Sunset Blvd., West Hollywood* ☎ *323/656–1010* 🌐 *www.chateaumarmont.com* 🛏 *63 rooms* 🍴 *No Meals.*

Kimpton La Peer Hotel

$$$ | **HOTEL** | One of the newer boutique hotels in West Hollywood, the Kimpton La Peer sits in the West Hollywood Design District and attracts an in-crowd of creative types. **Pros:** fashionable location; chic bar scene; great outdoor pool. **Cons:** daily amenity fee is $56 plus tax for very few amenties; expensive parking; rooms by pool can be noisy. [$] *Rooms from: $395* ✉ *627 N. La Peer Dr., West Hollywood* ☎ *213/296–3038, 800/373–6365* 🌐 *www.lapeerhotel.com/hotels-in-west-hollywood* 🛏 *105 rooms* 🍴 *No Meals.*

Mondrian Los Angeles

$$$ | **HOTEL** | The Mondrian has a city club feel; socializing begins in the lobby bar and lounge and extends from the restaurant to the scenic patio and pool, where you can listen to music underwater, and the lively Skybar. **Pros:** acclaimed

Skybar on property; flirty social scene; best views in the city. **Cons:** pricy valet parking; late-night party scene not for everyone; Alice in Wonderland theme might be too much for some. $ *Rooms from: $352* ⊠ *8440 Sunset Blvd., West Hollywood* ☎ *323/650–8999, 800/606–6090* ⊕ *www.mondrianhotel.com* ↝ *236 rooms* ⦿❘ *No Meals.*

Palihotel Melrose Avenue

$$ | **HOTEL** | A mostly young and creative clientele flocks here, to one of the only boutique hotels on Melrose Avenue. **Pros:** great decor; walking distance to Melrose shops and restaurants; good on-site dining. **Cons:** no gym, spa, or pool; the area can be unsafe after dark; need to request alarm clocks and phones from front desk. $ *Rooms from: $269* ⊠ *7950 Melrose Ave., West Hollywood* ☎ *323/272–4588* ⊕ *www.pali-hotel.com* ↝ *33 rooms* ⦿❘ *No Meals.*

Palihouse West Hollywood

$$ | **HOTEL** | Part of the ever-growing Pal-isociety lifestyle-hotel brand, Palihouse West Hollywood is the latest addition and a much-needed hotel in the lodging-bare stretch of West 3rd Street. **Pros:** great sushi bar and happy hour; central location; all rooms have kitchenettes. **Cons:** tiny gym; parking $50/night; $35 resort fee for a nonresort hotel. $ *Rooms from: $300* ⊠ *8384 W. 3rd St., Los Angeles* ☎ *323/658–6600* ⊕ *www.palisociety. com/hotels/west-hollywood* ↝ *95 rooms* ⦿❘ *No Meals.*

★ Pendry West Hollywood

$$ | **HOTEL** | Part of a proliferation of new hotels in West Hollywood, the Pendry has a legitimate claim to being the best of them all. **Pros:** high level of service; Wolfgang Puck–led restaurants; free use of Cadillacs. **Cons:** valet parking $65/night; on-site social club access a little confusing; some rooms only have street views. $ *Rooms from: $300* ⊠ *8430 Sunset Blvd., West Hollywood* ☎ *310/928–9000* ⊕ *www.pendry.com/west-hollywood* ↝ *149 rooms* ⦿❘ *No Meals.*

★ Sunset Marquis Hotel and Villas

$$$ | **HOTEL** | If you're in town to cut your new hit single, you'll appreciate this near-the-Strip hidden retreat in the heart of WeHo, with two on-site recording studios. **Pros:** favorite among rock stars; 53 villas with lavish extras; exclusive Bar 1200. **Cons:** rooms can feel dark; small balconies; no direct car access to the Sunset Strip. $ *Rooms from: $450* ⊠ *1200 N. Alta Loma Rd., West Hollywood* ☎ *310/657–1333, 800/858–9758* ⊕ *www.sunsetmarquis.com* ↝ *152 rooms* ⦿❘ *No Meals.*

Sunset Tower Hotel

$$$$ | **HOTEL** | A 1929 art deco landmark, this boutique hotel on the Sunset Strip brings out as many locals as it does tourists. **Pros:** incredible city views; Tower Bar, a favorite of Hollywood's elite; exclusive spa favored by locals. **Cons:** wedged into the Strip, so the driveway is a challenge; small standard rooms; parts of the hotel feel dated. $ *Rooms from: $525* ⊠ *8358 Sunset Blvd., West Hollywood* ☎ *323/654–7100* ⊕ *www.sunsettowerhotel.com* ↝ *81 rooms* ⦿❘ *No Meals.*

West Hollywood EDITION

$$$$ | **HOTEL** | Fans of EDITION hotels from around the world will find a lot to love at this Sunset Strip iteration, thanks to its balance of a chic space and minimalist vibe alongside a pool table and hopping bar in the lobby. **Pros:** exceptional rooftop pool; fun social scene; great location on the Sunset Strip. **Cons:** parking $65/night; high room prices for the area; might be too party-friendly for some. $ *Rooms from: $550* ⊠ *9040 W. Sunset Blvd., West Hollywood* ☎ *310/953–9899* ⊕ *www.marriott.com/hotels/travel/lax-eb-the-west-hollywood-edition* ↝ *190 rooms* ⦿❘ *No Meals.*

 Nightlife

★ The Abbey

DANCE CLUBS | The Abbey in West Hollywood is one of the most famous

Legendary music venue The Troubadour is still a great place to see live music.

LGBTQ+ bars in the world. And rightfully so. Seven days a week, a mixed and very good-looking crowd comes to eat, drink, dance, and flirt. Creative cocktails are whipped up by buff bartenders with a bevy of theme nights and parties each day. ✉ *692 N. Robertson Blvd., West Hollywood* ☎ *310/289–8410* ⊕ *www.theabbeyweho.com.*

Barney's Beanery

BARS | Open since 1920, Barney's Beanery is an iconic spot along the original Route 66 that drew legendary regulars Janis Joplin and Jim Morrison (among others) to its doorstep. There's an extensive menu, but all anyone talks about is the famous chili and the list of more than 85 beers. There are plenty of distractions, including three pool tables, a foosball table, and arcade games. There's great trivia on Tuesdays. ✉ *8447 Santa Monica Blvd., West Hollywood* ☎ *323/654–2287* ⊕ *www.barneysbeanery.com.*

Comedy Store

COMEDY CLUBS | Three stages give seasoned and unseasoned comedians a place to perform and try out new material, with big-name performers dropping by just for fun. The front bar along Sunset Boulevard is a popular hangout after or between shows, oftentimes with that night's comedians mingling with fans. ✉ *8433 Sunset Blvd., West Hollywood* ☎ *323/650–6268* ⊕ *www.thecomedystore.com.*

Delilah

THEMED ENTERTAINMENT | Reservations are definitely required for this swanky, New York–style space in West Hollywood. Waiters in white coats serve a mix of upscale American cuisine, but the true reason to come happens a little later when live jazz and burlesque dancers turn the night into a sultry singles scene that's visited by a see-and-be-seen crowd. ✉ *7969 Santa Monica Blvd., West Hollywood* ☎ *323/745–0600* ⊕ *www.delilahla.com.*

Employees Only

COCKTAIL LOUNGES | If you're looking for the best cocktail program in L.A., you'll find it at Employees Only. This very chic spot is a sister of the New York original and is consistently awarded worldwide for its delicious drinks. At this iteration, there are various themed nights with burlesque on Sunday and sporadic live music. In the back is a speakeasy called Henry's Room, which is a more intimate space where you can get up close and personal with the master barkeeps to tailor the perfect drink for you. ⊠ *7953 Santa Monica Blvd., West Hollywood* ☎ *323/536–9045* ⊕ *www.employeesonly-la.com.*

Hollywood Improv

COMEDY CLUBS | Arguably the best comedy club in the city, set apart from its competitors on the Sunset Strip, the Hollywood Improv (which is not technically in Hollywood) is known to bring in heavy-hitting A-list comics that range from Craig Robinson and Adam Carolla to Maria Bamford and Whitney Cummings. Don't be surprised if major stars like Dave Chappelle pop in to try out a set. The club features theme nights throughout the week, so check the schedule online. ⊠ *8162 Melrose Ave., West Hollywood* ☎ *323/651–2583* ⊕ *www.improv.com/hollywood.*

Jones

BARS | Italian food and serious cocktails are the mainstays at Jones. Whiskey is a popular choice for the classic cocktails, but the bartenders also do up martinis properly (read: strong). The Beggar's Banquet is their version of happy hour (10:30 pm to 2 am, Sunday through Thursday), with specials on drinks and pizza. ⊠ *7205 Santa Monica Blvd., West Hollywood* ☎ *323/850–1726* ⊕ *www.jonesholly-wood.com.*

Laugh Factory

COMEDY CLUBS | Top stand-up comics regularly appear at this Sunset Boulevard mainstay, often working out the kinks in new material in advance of national tours. Stars such as Tiffany Haddish and Dan Ahdoot sometimes drop by unannounced, and theme nights like

Chocolate Sundaes and Tehran Thursdays are extremely popular, with comics performing more daring sets. ⊠ *8001 W. Sunset Blvd., West Hollywood* ☎ *323/656–1336* ⊕ *www.laughfactory.com.*

Rainbow Bar and Grill

BARS | Its location next door to a long-running music venue, the Roxy, helped cement this bar and restaurant's status as a legendary watering hole for musicians (as well as their entourages and groupies). The Who, Guns N' Roses, Poison, Kiss, and many others have all passed through the doors. ⊠ *9015 W. Sunset Blvd., West Hollywood* ☎ *310/278–4232* ⊕ *www.rainbowbarand-grill.com.*

Skybar

COCKTAIL LOUNGES | This beautiful poolside bar is well worth a visit, but it can be a hassle to get into if you're not staying at the hotel, on the guest list, or know someone who can pull strings. The drinks are on the pricier side, but in this part of town that's to be expected, and the views might just make it all worthwhile. ⊠ *Hotel Mondrian, 8440 Sunset Blvd., West Hollywood* ☎ *323/848–6025* ⊕ *www.sbe.com/nightlife/skybar/los-angeles.*

★ The Troubadour

LIVE MUSIC | The intimate vibe of the Troubadour helps make this club a favorite with music fans. Around since 1957, this venue has a storied past where legends like Elton John and James Taylor have graced the stage. These days, the eclectic lineup is still attracting crowds, with the focus mostly on rock, indie, and folk music. Those looking for drinks can imbibe to their heart's content at the adjacent bar. ⊠ *9081 Santa Monica Blvd., West Hollywood* ⊕ *www.troubadour.com.*

The Viper Room

LIVE MUSIC | This 21-plus rock club on the edge of the Sunset Strip has been around for more than 30 years and is famously known as the site of much controversial Hollywood history—River Phoenix overdosed and died here, and Johnny Depp used to be a part owner. Today the venue books rising alt-rock acts, and covers typically range from $10 to $15, but its history has also seen legends like Tom Petty and Lenny Kravitz on their stage. ✉ *8852 Sunset Blvd., West Hollywood* ☎ *310/358–1881* ⊕ *www.viperroom.com.*

Whisky A Go Go

LIVE MUSIC | The hard-core metal and rock scene is alive and well at the legendary Whisky A Go Go (the full name includes the prefix "World Famous"), where Janis Joplin, Led Zeppelin, Alice Cooper, Van Halen, the Doors (they were the house band for a short stint), and Frank Zappa have all played. On the Strip for more than five decades, the club books both underground acts and huge names in rock. ✉ *8901 W. Sunset Blvd., West Hollywood* ☎ *310/652–4202* ⊕ *www.whiskyagogo.com.*

👜 Shopping

West Hollywood is prime shopping real estate. And as they say with real estate, it's all about location, location, location.

Melrose Avenue is part bohemian-punk shopping district (from North Highland to Sweetzer) and part upscale art and design mecca (upper Melrose Avenue and Melrose Place). Discerning locals and celebs haunt the posh boutiques around Sunset Plaza (Sunset Boulevard at Sunset Plaza Drive), on Robertson Boulevard (between Beverly Boulevard and 3rd Street), and along upper Melrose Avenue.

The huge, blue Pacific Design Center, on Melrose at San Vicente Boulevard, is the focal point for this neighborhood's art- and interior design–related stores, including many on nearby Beverly Boulevard. The Beverly–La Brea neighborhood also claims a number of trendy

clothing stores. Perched between Beverly Hills and West Hollywood, 3rd Street (between La Cienega Boulevard and Fairfax Avenue) is a magnet for small, friendly designer boutiques.

Melrose Place, not to be confused with the cheaper and trendier Melrose Avenue, is an in-the-know haven to savvy Los Angeles fashionistas and a charming antidote to the city's addiction to strip malls and mega shopping centers. This three-block-long strip, east of La Cienega and a block north of Melrose Avenue, lacks the pretentiousness of Rodeo Drive.

Finally, the Fairfax District, along Fairfax Avenue below Melrose Avenue, is filled with streetwear shops, trendy restaurants, the historic Farmers Market at Fairfax Avenue and 3rd Street, and the adjacent shopping extravaganza, The Grove.

★ American Rag Cie

SECOND-HAND | Half the store features new clothing from established and emerging labels, while the other side is stocked with well-preserved vintage clothing organized by color and style. You'll also find plenty of shoes and accessories being picked over by the hippest of Angelenos. ✉ *150 S. La Brea Ave., West Hollywood* ☎ *323/935–3154* ⊕ *americanrag.com.*

Beverly Center

MALL | This eight-level shopping center is home to luxury retailers like Gucci, Louis Vuitton, and Salvatore Ferragamo but also offers plenty of outposts for more affordable brands including Aldo, H&M, and Uniqlo. Don't miss the bevy of great dining options like Eggslut, an extraordinarily popular breakfast joint; Angler, an upscale and modern seafood haven; and Yardbird, a fried-chicken lovers' favorite, plus many, many more. ✉ *8500 Beverly Blvd., West Hollywood* ☎ *310/854–0070* ⊕ *www.beverlycenter.com.*

Blackman Cruz

ANTIQUES & COLLECTIBLES | Not your grandmother's antiques shop, David Cruz and Adam Blackman's celebrity-loved shopping destination is known for selecting beautifully offbeat pieces (there's no shortage of ceremonial masks and animal figurines at any given time) as well as fine European and Asian furniture from the 18th to the mid-20th century. ⊠ *836 N. Highland Ave., West Hollywood* ☎ *323/466–8600* ⊕ *www.blackmancruz. com.*

Book Soup

BOOKS | One of the best independent bookstores in the country, Book Soup has been serving Angelenos since 1975. Given its Hollywood pedigree, it's especially deep in books about film, music, art, and photography. Fringe benefits include an international newsstand, a bargain-book section, and author readings several times a week. ⊠ *8818 Sunset Blvd., West Hollywood* ☎ *310/659–3110* ⊕ *www.booksoup.com.*

Boot Star

SHOES | This huge selection of Western-style boots is heaven for urban cowboys and cowgirls. You can find materials ranging from calfskin to alligator, and most boots are handmade in Mexico and Texas. Custom sizing is available for a guaranteed perfect fit. ⊠ *8633 Sunset Blvd., West Hollywood* ☎ *323/650–0475* ⊕ *www.bootstarusa.com.*

Decades

WOMEN'S CLOTHING | A-listers scour these racks for dresses to wear during awards season. Owner Cameron Silver's stellar selection includes dresses by Pucci and bags by Hermès. On the street level, Decades Two resells contemporary designer and couture clothing and accessories. ⊠ *8214 Melrose Ave., West Hollywood* ☎ *323/746–0480* ⊕ *www. decadesinc.com.*

★ Fred Segal

MIXED CLOTHING | One of the most well-known boutiques in all of Los Angeles, Fred Segal is a fashion design mecca that has been clothing the rich, famous, and their acolytes since the 1960s. Since moving from its original location on Melrose, the flagship store sits atop Sunset Boulevard with more than 21,000 square feet of space that showcases innovative brands and high-end threads. ⊠ *8500 Sunset Blvd., West Hollywood* ☎ *310/432–0560* ⊕ *www.fredsegal.com.*

Golf Wang

OTHER ACCESSORIES | Right in the middle of streetwear haven Fairfax Avenue, Golf Wang stands apart with its avant-garde clothes and accessories created from the mind of rapper Tyler, the Creator. Whether you're shopping for hats, beanies, socks, or even custom skateboard decks, Golf Wang will continuously keep you surprised and delighted with an ever-changing showroom. ⊠ *350 N. Fairfax Ave., Fairfax District* ☎ *No phone* ⊕ *www.golfwang.com.*

H. Lorenzo

MIXED CLOTHING | Funky, high-end designer clothes (Ann Demeulemeester, Walid, and Comme des Garçons, to name a few) attract a young Hollywood crowd that doesn't mind paying top dollar for such fresh finds. Next door, H. Men provides equally hot styles for guys. ⊠ *8660 Sunset Blvd., West Hollywood* ☎ *310/659–1432* ⊕ *www.hlorenzo.com.*

Heath Ceramics

CERAMICS | This loftlike outpost of the beloved Sausalito-based ceramics company stocks everything from the Coupe Line (created by founder Edith Heath herself in the 1940s) to glass tumblers handblown in West Virginia. Also look for table linens, bud vases, and specialty foods like Milla chocolates from Culver City. ⊠ *7525 Beverly Blvd., Beverly–La Brea* ☎ *323/965–0800* ⊕ *www.heathceramics.com.*

Unique artwork abounds at Melrose Trading Post.

Isabel Marant

WOMEN'S CLOTHING | Even before falling for the French designer's effortlessly cool clothing, footwear, and bags (think Paris meets Los Angeles), shoppers will already be enamored of the lush location on fashionable Melrose Place. Inside, the model-favorite destination has a modern rustic vibe, but the outside is a plant paradise, loaded with cacti and succulents. ⊠ *8454 Melrose Pl., West Hollywood* ☎ *323/651–1493* ⊕ *www.isabelmarant. com.*

★ Maxfield

WOMEN'S CLOTHING | This modern concrete structure is one of L.A.'s most desirable destinations for ultimate high fashion. The space is stocked with sleek offerings from Givenchy, Saint Laurent, Valentino, and Rick Owens, plus occasional pop-ups by fashion's labels-of-the-moment. For serious shoppers (or gawkers) only. ⊠ *8825 Melrose Ave., West Hollywood* ☎ *310/274–8800* ⊕ *www.maxfieldla.com.*

MedMen

OTHER SPECIALTY STORE | The legalization of marijuana in California has led to an explosion of cannabis shops around Los Angeles. One of the most reputable is MedMen, a more refined dispensary that traffics in high-quality buds in a very welcoming environment. Here you can find edibles, vaporizers, concentrates, topical ointments, and more cannabis-laced products. A cannabis shop with a cause, MedMen is also actively involved in criminal justice reform. ⊠ *8208 Santa Monica Blvd., West Hollywood* ☎ *323/579–1449* ⊕ *www.medmen.com/ stores/los-angeles-west-hollywood.*

★ Melrose Trading Post

MARKET | Hollywood denizens love this hip market, where you're likely to find recycled rock T-shirts or some vinyl to complete your collection in addition to antique furniture and quirky arts and crafts. Live music and fresh munchies entertain vintage hunters and collectors. The market is held 9 to 5 every Sunday—rain or shine—in Fairfax High School's parking lot and admission is $5. ✉ *Fairfax Ave. and Melrose Ave., Fairfax District* ☎ *323/655–7679* ⊕ *www.melrosetradingpost.org.*

OK

SOUVENIRS | An überclassy gift shop, OK stocks items such as Scandinavian stemware and vintage phones; it also specializes in architecture and design books. There's also a second Silver Lake location. ✉ *8303 W. 3rd St., West Hollywood* ☎ *323/653–3501* ⊕ *okthestore.com.*

Paul Smith

MIXED CLOTHING | You can't miss the massive, minimalist pink box that houses Paul Smith's fantastical collection of clothing, boots, hats, luggage, and objets d'art (seriously, there will be hordes of Instagrammers shooting selfies in front of the bright facade). Photos and art line the walls above shelves of books on pop culture, art, and Hollywood. As for the clothing here, expect the British brand's signature playfully preppy style, with vibrant colors and whimsical patterns mixed in with well-tailored closet staples. ✉ *8221 Melrose Ave., West Hollywood* ☎ *323/951–4800* ⊕ *www.paulsmith.com/uk.*

Reformation

WOMEN'S CLOTHING | Local trendsetters flock here for the sexy, easy-to-wear silhouettes of Reformation's dresses (including a totally affordable bridal line), jumpsuits, and separates—it's a welcome bonus that the pieces here are sustainably manufactured using recycled materials. ✉ *8000 Melrose Ave., West Hollywood* ☎ *213/408–4154* ⊕ *www.thereformation.com.*

The Row

MIXED CLOTHING | This Olsen twin–owned luxury outfitter quickly became an it-girl's staple after its opening in 2006. Offering women's, men's, and children's clothing, the brand focuses on top-of-the-line fabrics and chef's-kiss tailoring to set it apart from other high-end designers with the "less is more" mentality. This place is a neutrals-lover's dream closet, where classic pieces meet modern silhouettes and even the sweatpants are supremely chic. ✉ *8440 Melrose Pl., West Hollywood* ☎ *310/853–1900* ⊕ *www.therow.com/storelocator.*

Supreme

MIXED CLOTHING | The L.A. location for NYC's premier streetwear brand regularly sees crowds of sneakerheads and skaters, who know that this is the place to get the freshest urban gear around. When new merchandise drops, lines can easily wrap around the block—but getting your hands on the goods (namely shoes, shirts, outerwear, hats, and backpacks) before anyone else just might be worth the trouble. ✉ *439 N. Fairfax Ave., Fairfax District* ☎ *323/655–6205* ⊕ *www.supremenewyork.com.*

The Way We Wore

WOMEN'S CLOTHING | Beyond the over-the-top vintage store furnishings, you'll find one of the city's best selections of well-cared-for and one-of-a-kind items, with a focus on sequins and beads. Upstairs, couture from Halston, Dior, and Chanel can cost up to $20,000. ✉ *334 S. La Brea Ave., Beverly–La Brea* ☎ *323/937–0878* ⊕ *www.thewaywewore.com.*

Mid-Wilshire

The 1½-mile strip of Wilshire Boulevard between La Brea and Fairfax Avenues was bought up by developers in the 1920s, and they created a commercial district that catered to automobile traffic. Nobody thought the venture could be successful, so the burgeoning strip became known as Miracle Mile. It was the world's first linear downtown, with building designs incorporating wide store windows to attract attention from passing cars. As L.A.'s art deco buildings have come to be appreciated, preserved, and restored over the years, the area's exemplary architecture is a highlight. The surrounding Mid-Wilshire area encompassing Miracle Mile includes the notable Petersen Automotive Museum (clad in steel racing-stripe ribbons) and the years-in-the-making Academy Museum of Motion Pictures, with its massive spherical extension that beckons visitors to the many wonders of the film industry.

◉ Sights

★ Academy Museum of Motion Pictures

OTHER MUSEUM | FAMILY | The long-awaited Academy Museum of Motion Pictures sits on the corner of Wilshire and Fairfax, and is highlighted by a giant spherical dome that features a 1,000-seat theater and stunning terrace with views of the Hollywood Hills. Inside, the museum has seven floors of exhibition space that delves into the history of cinema with interactive exhibits, features on award-winning storytellers, multiple theaters, and immersive experiences. Dedicated to the art and science of movies, the Academy Museum is the premier center that is a must-stop for film buffs and casual moviegoers alike. ✉ 6067 Wilshire Blvd., Mid-Wilshire ☎ 323/930–3000 ⊕ www.academymuseum.org ✆ $25.

Craft Contemporary

ART MUSEUM | This small but important cultural landmark pioneered support for traditional folk arts. The two-story space has a global outlook, embracing social movements and long-established trends. It mounts rotating exhibitions where you might see anything from costumes of carnival celebrations around the world to handmade quilts. The ground-level gift shop stocks a unique collection of handcrafts, jewelry, ceramics, books, and textiles. ✉ 5814 Wilshire Blvd., Mid-Wilshire ☎ 323/937–4230 ⊕ www.craftcontemporary.org ✆ $9 ⊘ Closed Mon.

La Brea Tar Pits Museum

NATURE SIGHT | FAMILY | Show your kids where Ice Age fossils come from by taking them to the stickiest park in town. The area formed when deposits of oil rose to the earth's surface, collected in shallow pools, and coagulated into asphalt. In the early 20th century, geologists discovered that all that goo contained the largest collection of Pleistocene (Ice Age) fossils ever found at one location: more than 600 species of birds, mammals, plants, reptiles, and insects. Roughly 100 tons of fossil bones have been removed in excavations during the last 100 years, making this one of the world's most famous fossil sites. You can see most of the pits through chain-link fences, and the Excavator Tour gets you as close as possible to the action.

Pit 91 and Project 23 are ongoing excavation projects; tours are offered, and you can volunteer to help with the excavations in the summer. Several pits are scattered around Hancock Park and the surrounding neighborhood; construction in the area has often had to accommodate them, and in nearby streets and along sidewalks, little bits of tar occasionally ooze up. The museum displays fossils from the tar pits and has a glass-walled laboratory that allows visitors to view paleontologists and volunteers as they work on specimens.

■ TIP→ Museum admission is free for L.A. County residents weekdays 3–5 pm. ✉ 5801 Wilshire Blvd., Miracle Mile ☎ 323/934–7243 ⊕ www.tarpits.org ✆ $15 ⊘ Closed 1st Tues. of every month and every Tues. in Sept. ☞ Excavator Tour 1 pm weekdays and 10 am weekends.

★ Los Angeles County Museum of Art (LACMA)

ART MUSEUM | Los Angeles has a truly fabulous museum culture and everything that it stands for can be epitomized by the massive, eclectic, and ever-changing Los Angeles County Museum of Art. Opened at its current location in 1965,

Learn about the history of cars and check out rare vehicles at the Petersen Automotive Museum.

today the museum boasts the largest collection of art in the western United States with more than 135,000 pieces from 6,000 years of history across multiple buildings atop over 20 acres. Highlights include the *Urban Light* sculpture by Chris Burden (an Instagram favorite), *Levitated Mass* by Michael Heizer, and prominent works by Frida Kahlo, Wassily Kandinsky, Henri Matisse, and Claude Monet. With an illustrative permanent collection to go along with an ever-rotating array of temporary exhibits, film screenings, educational programs, and more, the museum is a beacon of culture that stands alone in the middle of the city.

■ TIP→ **Temporary exhibitions sometimes require tickets purchased in advance.** ✉ *5905 Wilshire Blvd., Miracle Mile* ☎ *323/857–6000* ⊕ *www.lacma.org* ✆ *$20* ⊘ *Closed Wed.*

Petersen Automotive Museum
OTHER MUSEUM | FAMILY | L.A. is a mecca for car lovers, which explains the popularity of this museum with a collection of more than 300 automobiles and other motorized vehicles. But you don't have to be a gearhead to appreciate the Petersen; there's plenty of fascinating history here for all to enjoy. Learn how Los Angeles grew up around its freeways, how cars evolve from the design phase to the production line, and how automobiles have influenced film and television. To see how the vehicles, many of them quite rare, are preserved and maintained, take the 90-minute self-guided tour of the basement-level Vault. ✉ *6060 Wilshire Blvd., Mid-Wilshire* ☎ *323/964–6331* ⊕ *www.petersen.org* ✆ *From $25.*

🍽 Restaurants

★ Meals by Genet
$$ | ETHIOPIAN | In a tucked-away stretch along Fairfax Avenue is Little Ethiopia, where Angelenos of all stripes flock for the African country's signatures like *tibs*, *wat*, and *kitfo*. And while there is a plethora of Ethiopian options, no one does the cuisine justice quite like Meals by Genet. **Known for:** authentic Ethiopian

cuisine; jovial atmosphere; unreal tibs. [$] *Average main: $20* ✉ *1053 S. Fairfax Ave., Mid-Wilshire* ☎ *323/938–9304* 🌐 *www.mealsbygenetla.com* 🕒 *Closed Mon.–Wed.*

Merkato Ethiopian Restaurant and Market

$ | **ETHIOPIAN** | For a wholly authentic Ethiopian experience, you can't really go wrong with Merkato. Not only does it serve the classics like spongy injera bread, spicy beef, and grilled fish, but there's also a market where you can buy Ethiopian ingredients to make your own mouthwatering cuisine at home. **Known for:** authentic Ethiopian cuisine; market products; friendly staff. [$] *Average main: $15* ✉ *1036½ S. Fairfax Ave., Mid-Wilshire* ☎ *213/816–3318.*

Ray's and Stark Bar

$$ | **AMERICAN** | Whether you want to fill up before perusing L.A.'s best art galleries or simply grab a drink to soak in the priceless sculptures at the LACMA, Ray's and Stark Bar is the perfect complement to any museumgoer's experience. Situated just outside the main entrance of the museum, the restaurant/bar offers a variety of Americana cuisine like pizza, burgers, and pastas. **Known for:** good happy hour; fun (dog-friendly) brunch; excellent signature cocktails. [$] *Average main: $25* ✉ *5905 Wilshire Blvd., Miracle Mile* ☎ *323/857–6180* 🌐 *www.patinagroup.com/rays-and-stark-bar* 🕒 *Closed Wed.*

★ République

$$$ | **FRENCH** | **FAMILY** | This stunning expansive space, originally built for Charlie Chaplin back in the 1920s, serves French delicacies for breakfast, lunch, and dinner every day of the week. The scent of homemade croissants wafts through the building in the morning; steak frites can be enjoyed at night. **Known for:** French classics; unbeatable pastries; nice bar menu. [$] *Average main: $35* ✉ *624 S. La Brea Ave., Beverly–La Brea* ☎ *310/362–6115* 🌐 *www.republiquela.com* 🕒 *No dinner Sun. or Mon.*

Sky's Gourmet Tacos

$ | **MEXICAN** | If you're searching for some of the spiciest and most succulent tacos in L.A., look no further than Sky's. This quaint taco joint offers up beef, chicken, turkey, seafood, and vegan options that will leave your mouth on fire and your belly full in all the best ways possible. **Known for:** amazing tacos with a variety of fillings (including breakfast tacos); lots of spices; jovial atmosphere. [$] *Average main: $10* ✉ *5303 W. Pico Blvd., Mid-Wilshire* ☎ *323/672–4062* 🌐 *www.skysgourmettacos.com.*

Uovo

$ | **ITALIAN** | It's hard to fathom that the pasta inside this small counter restaurant is flown in weekly from Bologna. But once you take a bite of the perfect cacio e pepe, *amatriciana,* or tortellini with *crema parmigiano,* you'll become an instant believer. **Known for:** perfect pasta flown in from Italy; decadent sauces; chill atmosphere. [$] *Average main: $18* ✉ *6245 Wilshire Blvd., Suite 103, Mid-Wilshire* ☎ *323/642–6386* 🌐 *www.uovo.la.*

🍸 Nightlife

★ El Rey Theater

LIVE MUSIC | This former art deco movie house from the 1930s has been given a second life as a live music venue. Legends and rising stars grace the stage of El Rey. Everyone from the Pixies and Ringo Starr to the Jonas Brothers and Lana Del Rey have performed here. ✉ *5515 Wilshire Blvd., Mid-Wilshire* ☎ *323/936–6400* 🌐 *www.theelrey.com.*

Chapter 8

HOLLYWOOD

8

Updated by
Michelle Rae Uy

 Sights
★★★★★

 Restaurants
★★★☆☆

 Hotels
★★★☆☆

 Shopping
★★★☆☆

 Nightlife
★★★☆☆

NEIGHBORHOOD SNAPSHOT

TOP EXPERIENCES

■ **Walk in famous footsteps:** Outside the TCL Chinese Theatre are footprints of more than 200 of the silver screen's biggest stars. The Hollywood Walk of Fame has stars honoring more than 2,500 of the entertainment industry's most famous on its sidewalks.

■ **Hike up to the Hollywood Sign.** Pack your hiking or running shoes, and partake in the locals' favorite pasttime. Hiking up to the Hollywood Sign is an easy one, and you'll be rewarded with Instagram-worthy snaps and sweeping views of the city.

■ **Picnic at the Hollywood Bowl:** Even if you don't get tickets for a show, stop at this L.A. landmark just north of Hollywood Boulevard for a great outdoor meal.

■ **Check out Hollywood memorabilia:** The Hollywood Museum has an incredible collection of Tinseltown's most glamorous costumes, photos, and more.

■ **Catch a movie at a historic movie theater.** El Capitan and the TCL Chinese Theatre aren't just photo ops. They're working movie theaters that have daily showings of the latest releases. Though watching a movie might be the last thing on your list during your vacation, doing so in one of these are a uniquely L.A. experience.

GETTING HERE

Coming from the north or south requires using the Golden State Freeway (I-5) then hopping on Hollywood Freeway (U.S. 101/Highway 170) to get into the heart of the neighborhood.

If you're heading in from Burbank, try skipping the freeways, and take Cahuenga Boulevard heading south instead. If you're driving from the beach, go on the Santa Monica Freeway (I-10) to La Brea Ave or take Santa Monica Boulevard all the way. Either way, plan around rush hour, which is typically 7–9 am and 4–6 pm. If you're near the subway, the Metro's Red Line makes two stops in the heart of Hollywood: the Hollywood/Vine Station and the Hollywood/Highland Station.

PLANNING YOUR TIME

■ Hollywood has several fabulous and central hotels that will keep you within walking distance of most of the area's top attractions. You'll need at least a day, even two if you want to sample the restaurants and bars, as well as the essential attractions. There are two ways to plan your time: 1. Play peak tourist and hit all the "star" attractions, stopping for brunch and ending with a special dinner and setting at a lively clubstaurant. 2. Hike up to the Hollywood Sign along the Bronson Canyon Trail in the morning, linger Hollywood-style on a pretty patio with a healthy lunch, and then see a concert at the Hollywood Bowl in the evening.

VIEWFINDER

■ **Brush Canyon Trail:** For epic views of the Hollywood Hills and that iconic Hollywood Sign, hike the six-mile roundtrip Brush Canyon Trail to Mulholland Trail early in the morning for sunrise photo ops. ⊹ *Start at 3000 Canyon Dr.*

The Tinseltown mythology of Los Angeles was born in Hollywood, so if it's your first time in L.A., it's kind of required that you make at least a brief stop here. Hollywood has a reputation for being touristy, and that's because this famous neighborhood has some top attractions worthy of a visit. A Hollywood hit list usually includes the Hollywood Walk of Fame, a movie in one of its opulent movie palaces, a tour at the Icons of Darkness if you love sci-fi or horror, and a morning hiking up to the Hollywood Sign.

Like Downtown L.A., Hollywood continues to undergo a transformation designed to lure a hip, younger crowd and big money back into the fold. New sleek clubs and restaurants seem to pop up every month drawing in celebrities, influencers, and starry-eyed newcomers to create a colorful nighttime landscape (and some parking headaches).

Many daytime attractions can be found on foot around the home of the Academy Awards at the **Dolby Theatre,** part of the Ovation Hollywood entertainment complex. The adjacent **TCL Chinese Theatre** delivers silver-screen magic with its iconic facade and ornate interiors from a bygone era. A shining example of a successful Hollywood revival can be seen and experienced just across Hollywood Boulevard at the 1926 **El Capitan Theatre,** which offers live stage shows and a Wurlitzer organ concert before select movie engagements.

Walk the renowned **Hollywood Walk of Fame** to find your favorite celebrities, and you can encounter derelict diversions literally screaming for your attention (and dollar), numerous panhandlers, and an occasional costumed superhero not sanctioned by Marvel Comics. At Sunset and Vine, a developer-interpreted revival with sushi, stars, and swank condos promises to continue the ongoing renovations of the area. In summer, visit the crown jewel of Hollywood, the **Hollywood Bowl,** which features shows by the Los Angeles Philharmonic and many guest stars.

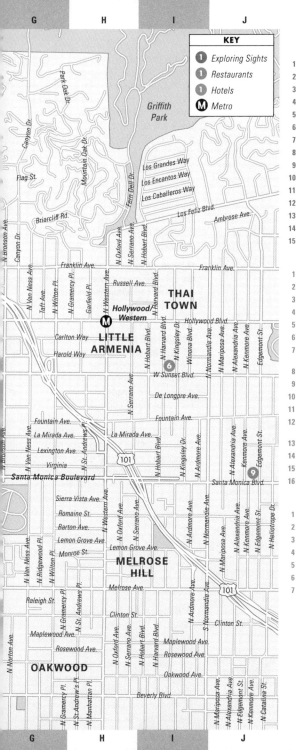

KEY

1 *Exploring Sights*

1 *Restaurants*

1 *Hotels*

M *Metro*

Sights ▼

1 Dolby Theatre C4
2 El Capitan Theatre C4
3 Hollywood Bowl C2
4 Hollywood Bowl Museum C2
5 Hollywood Forever Cemetery F7
6 Hollywood Heritage Museum.... D3
7 Hollywood Museum C4
8 Hollywood RockWalk A5
9 Hollywood Sign C1
10 Hollywood Walk of Fame E4
11 Icons of Darkness C4
12 Japan House C4
13 Pantages Theatre...................E4
14 Paramount Pictures F8
15 TCL Chinese Theatre C4

Restaurants ▼

1 The Barish..........................C4
2 Beauty & Essex E4
3 Cactus Taqueria #1 ....E7
4 For the Win F3
5 Gwen................................D5
6 Jitlada...............................I5
7 La Mesa Restaurant
   and Lounge.........................E5
8 L'antica Pizzeria da Michele.......C5
9 Marouch.............................J6
10 Petit Trois C7
11 Providence D8
12 Roscoe's House of
   Chicken and Waffles F5
13 Salt's Cure C6
14 Superba Food + Bread D5
15 TAO Hollywood......................D5
16 Tropicana Pool and Cafe.......... B4

Hotels ▼

1 Dream Hollywood.................. D5
2 Hollywood Roosevelt Hotel........C4
3 Loews Hollywood...................C4
4 Magic Castle Hotel C4
5 Mama Shelter Los Angeles....... D5
6 Moment Hotel...................... A5
7 W Hollywood........................E4

Sights

Dolby Theatre

PERFORMANCE VENUE | More than just a prominent fixture on Hollywood Boulevard, the Dolby Theatre has a few accolades under its belt as well, most notably as home to the Academy Awards. The theater is the blend of the traditional and the modern, where an exquisite classical design inspired by the grand opera houses of Europe meets a state-of-the-art sound and technical system for an immersive, theatrical experience. Watch a concert or a show here to experience it fully, but before you do, take a tour for an informative, behind-the-scenes look and to step into the VIP lounge where celebrities rub elbows on the big night. ✉ *6801 Hollywood Blvd., Hollywood* ☎ *323/308–6300* ⊕ *www.dolbytheatre. com* ☎ *Tour $25.*

El Capitan Theatre

OTHER ATTRACTION | Home to Los Angeles's first home of spoken drama, El Capitan Theatre carries on that tradition by way of film showings—specifically Disney films, having been acquired by the company in the 1980s. Watching movies in this classic movie palace, originally built in 1926, is an elevated experience, thanks to its special screenings and its elegant East Indian Revival interior. Having survived several transformations, it has been restored to almost exactly how it looked in 1926. It's also the grand venue for all Disney movie premieres during which movie fans can spot (and perhaps even meet) celebrities as they walk the red carpet on Hollywood Boulevard. ✉ *6838 Hollywood Blvd., Hollywood* ☎ *800/347–6396* ⊕ *elcapitantheatre.com.*

★ Hollywood Bowl

PERFORMANCE VENUE | For those seeking a quintessential Los Angeles experience, a concert on a summer night at the Bowl, the city's iconic outdoor venue, is unsurpassed. The Bowl has presented world-class performers since it opened in 1920. The L.A. Philharmonic plays here from June to September; its performances and other events draw large crowds. Parking is limited near the venue, but there are additional remote parking locations serviced by shuttles. You can bring food and drink to any event, which Angelenos often do, though you can only bring alcohol when the L.A. Phil is performing. (Bars sell alcohol at all events, and there are dining options.) It's wise to bring a jacket even if daytime temperatures have been warm—the Bowl can get quite chilly at night.

■**TIP**➔ **Visitors can sometimes watch the L.A. Phil practice for free, usually on a weekday; call ahead for times.** ✉ *2301 N. Highland Ave., Hollywood* ☎ *323/850–2000* ⊕ *www.hollywoodbowl.com.*

Hollywood Bowl Museum

HISTORY MUSEUM | Originally the tearoom for the Hollywood Bowl, this unassuming, two-story museum not only recounts the history of one of L.A.'s most renowned landmarks, but also commemorates some of the major and unforgettable performances that have taken place here. While the second floor mostly touts temporary exhibits, the first floor boasts permanent displays, a few of which are interactive. A quick visit to this museum is a definite must`whether you're a musicophile or you're coming to see a performance at the Hollywood Bowl. ✉ *2301 N. Highland Ave., Hollywood* ☎ *323/850–2058* ⊕ *www.hollywoodbowl. com/visit/hollywood-bowl-museum* ☎ *Free* ☉ *Closed Sat.–Mon. during offseason.*

★ Hollywood Forever Cemetery

CEMETERY | One of the many things that makes this cemetery in the middle of Hollywood so fascinating is that it's the final resting place of many of the Hollywood greats, from directors like Cecil B. DeMille and actors like Douglas Fairbanks and Judy Garland to musicians like Johnny Ramone. Beyond its famous residents, however, the Hollywood Forever Cemetery is also frequented for its serene grounds peppered with intricately designed tombstones, not to mention by cinephiles in the summer and fall months for the outdoor movie screenings that take place under the stars on the Fairbanks Lawn. If you're looking for both tourist and local experiences while in town, this sight lets you tick off both in one visit. ⊠ *6000 Santa Monica Blvd., Hollywood* ☎ *866/706–4826* ⊕ *www.hollywoodforever.com* ⊠ *Free; check online for film screenings.*

Hollywood Heritage Museum

HISTORY MUSEUM | This unassuming building across from the Hollywood Bowl is a treasure trove of memorabilia from the earliest days of Hollywood filmmaking, including a thorough look back at Cecil B. DeMille's starry career. Large sections of the original stone statues from *The Ten Commandments* lay like fallen giants among smaller items in glass cases around the perimeter of this modest museum. A documentary tracking Hollywood's golden era is worth taking in. The building itself is the restored Lasky-De-Mille Barn, designated a California State Historic Landmark in 1956. ⊠ *2100 N. Highland Ave., Hollywood* ☎ *323/874–2276* ⊕ *www.hollywoodheritage.org* ⊠ *$10* ⊙ *Closed Mon.–Thurs.*

★ Hollywood Museum

HISTORY MUSEUM | Don't let its kitschy facade turn you off: the Hollywood Museum, nestled at the busy intersection of Hollywood and Highland, is worth it, especially for film aficionados. A museum deserving of its name, it boasts an impressive collection of exhibits from the moviemaking world, spanning several film genres and eras. Start in its pink, art deco lobby where the Max Factor exhibit pays tribute to the cosmetics company's pivotal role in Hollywood, make your way to the dark basement, where the industry's penchant for the macabre is on full display, and wrap up your visit

by admiring Hollywood's most famous costumes and set props on the top floor. ⊠ *1660 N. Highland Ave., at Hollywood Blvd., Hollywood* ☎ *323/464–7776* ⊕ *www.thehollywoodmuseum.com* ⊠ *$15* ⊙ *Closed Mon. and Tues.*

Hollywood RockWalk

PUBLIC ART | Providing equipment for countless Los Angeles bands since the 1960s, Guitar Center pays tribute to its rock-star clientele with the Hollywood RockWalk in front of the building. The concrete slabs are imprinted with the talented hands of Van Halen, Bonnie Raitt, Chuck Berry, Dick Dale, Def Leppard, Carlos Santana, KISS, and others. Two standouts are Joey Ramone's upside-down hand and Lemmy of Motörhead's "middle finger salute." The store's minimuseum displays signed sheet music and memorabilia like Bob Dylan's hat and harmonica. ⊠ *Guitar Center, 7425 W. Sunset Blvd., Hollywood* ☎ *323/874–1060* ⊠ *Free.*

★ Hollywood Sign

HISTORIC SIGHT | With letters 50 feet tall, Hollywood's trademark sign can be spotted from miles away. The icon, which originally read "Hollywoodland," was erected in the Hollywood Hills in 1923 to advertise a segregated housing development and was outfitted with 4,000 light bulbs. In 1949 the "land" portion of the sign was taken down. By 1973 the sign had earned landmark status, but because the letters were made of wood, its longevity came into question. A makeover project was launched and the letters were auctioned off (rocker Alice Cooper bought an "O" and singing cowboy Gene Autry sponsored an "L") to make way for a new sign made of sheet metal. Inevitably, the sign has drawn pranksters who have altered it over the years, albeit temporarily, to spell out "Hollyweed" (in the 1970s, to push for more lenient marijuana laws), "Go Navy" (before a Rose Bowl game), and "Perotwood" (during businessman Ross Perot's 1992

There are more than 2,500 stars honored on the Hollywood Walk of Fame.

presidential bid). A fence and surveillance equipment have since been installed to deter intruders, but another vandal managed to pull the "Hollyweed" prank once again in 2017 after Californians voted to make recreational use of marijuana legal statewide. And while it's still very illegal to get anywhere near the sign, several area hikes will get you as close as possible for some photo ops; you can hike just over 6 miles up behind the sign via the Brush Canyon trail for epic views, especially at sunset.

⚠ **Use caution if driving up to the sign on residential streets; many cars speed around the blind corners.** ⊠ *Griffith Park, Mt. Lee Dr., Hollywood* ⊕ *www.hollywoodsign. org.*

Hollywood Walk of Fame

OTHER ATTRACTION | Along Hollywood Boulevard (and part of Vine Street) runs a trail of affirmations for entertainment-industry overachievers. On this mile-long stretch of sidewalk, inspired by the concrete handprints in front of TCL Chinese Theatre, names are embossed in brass, each at the center of a pink star embedded in dark gray terrazzo. They're not all screen deities; many stars commemorate people who worked in a technical field, such as sound or lighting. The first eight stars were unveiled in 1960 at the northwest corner of Highland Avenue and Hollywood Boulevard: Olive Borden, Ronald Colman, Louise Fazenda, Preston Foster, Burt Lancaster, Edward Sedgwick, Ernest Torrence, and Joanne Woodward (some of these names have stood the test of time better than others). Since then, more than 2,000 others have been immortalized, though that honor doesn't come cheap—upon selection by a special committee, the personality in question (or more likely his or her movie studio or record company) pays about $30,000 for the privilege. To aid you in spotting celebrities you're looking for, stars are identified by one of five icons: a motion-picture camera, a radio microphone, a television set, a record, or a theatrical mask. ⊠ *Hollywood Blvd. and Vine St., Hollywood* ⊕ *www.walkoffame. com.*

Icons of Darkness

OTHER MUSEUM | Movie buffs rejoice in director, producer, and actor Rich Correll's expansive sci-fi, fantasy, and horror movie memorabilia collection, the world's largest privately owned collection of screen-used props, costumes, and special effects. Icons are found in spades, from the original helmets and costumes from the *Star Wars* franchise to costumes and props from 1979 to present-day *Alien* films, and *Jurassic Park*'s T-Rex heads, stunt suits, puppet heads, and cage raptors. A guided tour ensures you can both geek out and not miss out on any details. Watch out for jump scares! ⊠ *6801 Hollywood Blvd., Suite 151, Hollywood* ☎ *323/380–7548* ⊕ *www.iconsofdarkness.com* ✉ *$25.*

Japan House

OTHER MUSEUM | FAMILY | Highlighting the best of Japanese art, food, and culture with a goal to nurture a deeper understanding of Japan in the world, Japan House is an oasis of serenity on frenetic Hollywood Boulevard. This two-floor, multiuse space, whose interior and exterior were designed by leading Japanese designers, is made up of a gallery, a store with beautiful Japanese wares for sale, a library, an event space, and a fine-dining restaurant. The gallery hosts touring and original exhibitions focused on photography, architecture, manga, paper culture, and more. The library and reading nooks welcome further exploration. ⊠ *6801 Hollywood Blvd., Levels 2 and 5, Hollywood* ☎ *800/516–0565* ⊕ *www.japanhousela. com* ✉ *Free.*

Pantages Theatre

PERFORMANCE VENUE | Besides being home to the Academy Awards for a decade in the '50s, this stunning art deco–style theater near Hollywood and Vine has been playing host to many of the musical theater world's biggest and greatest productions, from the classics like *Cats*, *West Side Story*, and *Phantom of the Opera* to modern hits like *Hamilton*

and *Wicked*. During your Los Angeles jaunt, see a show or two in order to really experience its splendor. While guided tours are not being offered to the public, an annual open house is available to season pass holders for an exclusive and informative tour of the theater and its history. ⊠ *6233 Hollywood Blvd., Hollywood* ☎ *323/468–1770* ⊕ *www.broadwayinhollywood.com.*

★ Paramount Pictures

FILM/TV STUDIO | With a history dating to the early 1920s, the Paramount lot was home to some of Hollywood's most luminous stars, including Mary Pickford, Rudolph Valentino, Mae West, Marlene Dietrich, and Bing Crosby. Director Cecil B. DeMille's base of operations for decades, Paramount offers probably the most authentic studio tour, giving you a real sense of the film industry's history. This is the only major studio from film's golden age left in Hollywood—all the others are now in Burbank, Universal City, or Culver City.

Memorable movies and TV shows with scenes shot here include *Sunset Boulevard, Forrest Gump,* and *Titanic.* Many of the *Star Trek* movies and TV series were shot entirely or in part here, and several seasons of *I Love Lucy* were shot on the portion of the lot Paramount acquired in 1967 from Lucille Ball. You can take a two-hour studio tour or a 4½-hour VIP tour, led by guides who walk and trolley you around the backlots. As well as gleaning some gossipy history, you'll spot the sets of TV and film shoots in progress. Reserve ahead for tours, which are for those ages 10 and up.

■ **TIP→ You can be part of the audience for live TV tapings (tickets are free), but you must book ahead.** ⊠ *5515 Melrose Ave., Hollywood* ☎ *323/956–1777* ⊕ *www. paramountstudiotour.com* ✉ *$63.*

TCL Chinese Theatre

HISTORIC HOME | The stylized Chinese pagodas and temples of the former

You can take tours of several classic Hollywood studios, including Paramount Pictures.

Grauman's Chinese Theatre have become a shrine both to stardom and the combination of glamour and flamboyance that inspire the phrase "only in Hollywood." Although you have to buy a movie ticket to appreciate the interior trappings, the courtyard is open to the public. The main theater itself is worth visiting, if only to see a film in the same setting as hundreds of celebrities who have attended big premieres here.

And then, of course, outside in front are the oh-so-famous cement hand- and footprints. This tradition is said to have begun at the theater's opening in 1927, with the premiere of Cecil B. DeMille's *King of Kings,* when actress Norma Talmadge just happened to step in wet cement. Now more than 160 celebrities have contributed imprints for posterity, including some oddball specimens, such as casts of Whoopi Goldberg's dreadlocks. ✉ *6925 Hollywood Blvd., Hollywood* ☎ *323/461–3331* ⊕ *www.tclchinesetheatres.com* 🎟 *Tour $16.*

🍴 Restaurants

Hollywood has two faces; while it's a hub for tourists who come here to take photos along the Hollywood Walk of Fame, it is still in touch with its irreverent rock-and-roll roots while also keeping things culturally relevant. The result is a complex dining scene made up of cheap fast food, upscale eateries, and provocative hot spots helmed by celebrity chefs.

The Barish

$$$ | ITALIAN | Located in the historic lobby of the Hollywood Roosevelt hotel, this old-world Italian steak house features a glamorous, Old Hollywood feel with mirrored columns, floor-to-ceiling windows, and Spanish Colonial Revival details alongside an open kitchen, comfortable banquettes, a wood-fire hearth, and a menu that showcases chef Nancy Silverton's flair for Californian-Italian flavors. The deconstructed steak tartare has obtained cult status as have the dry-aged steaks, pasta *al forno,* poultry cooked over a wood fire, and the Barish

Farmhouse rolls, served warm with Rodolphe Le Meunier butter on the side. **Known for:** Old Hollywood ambience; pasta al forno; steak tartare. $ *Average main: $40* ⊠ *7000 Hollywood Blvd., Hollywood* ☎ *323/769–8888* ⊕ *www.the-barishla.com* ⊘ *Closed Mon. and Tues.*

Beauty & Essex

$$$ | **MODERN AMERICAN** | With vintage decor, grand chandeliers, gilded walls, and luxe jewel tones, the Hollywood outpost of popular New York "club-staraunt" Beauty & Essex more than lives up to its Tinseltown address. Hidden speakeasy-style behind a collector's storefront (beware impulse pricey jewelry purchases on the way out), this gigantic celebrity-frequented restaurant with a double-height main dining room with skylight, a ground-floor courtyard, and a patio on the second level, isn't all just glam smoke and mirrors. **Known for:** glamorous setting perfect for special occasions; party vibe (it can be loud); creative cocktails. $ *Average main: $35* ⊠ *1615 Cahuenga Blvd., Hollywood* ☎ *323/676–8880* ⊕ *taogroup.com/venues/beauty-essex-los-angeles* ⊘ *Closed Mon.*

Cactus Taqueria #1

$ | **MEXICAN** | **FAMILY** | A humble taco shack on the side of the road, Cactus offers up $4 tacos with all types of meat you could imagine, even beef tongue. They also have carne asada and chicken for the less adventurous. **Known for:** California burritos; delicious fries; excellent street-style tacos. $ *Average main: $11* ⊠ *950 Vine St., Hollywood* ☎ *323/464–5865* ⊕ *www.cactustaqueriainc.com.*

★ For The Win

$ | **BURGER** | Are you even in L.A. if you haven't had a smashburger yet? Usurping all other burgers and burger joints, For the Win has become a power player on the burger scene in L.A., growing from this unassuming location in a strip mall in Hollywood to a collection of storefronts throughout the region. **Known for:** smashburger; house-made sauce; recognized

as one of the best burgers in L.A.. $ *Average main: $9* ⊠ *6221 Franklin Ave., Hollywood* ☎ *323/871–2026* ⊕ *www.forthewinla.com.*

★ Gwen

$$$$ | **STEAKHOUSE** | Heaven for carnivores, this upscale European-style butcher shop and fine-dining restaurant serves wood-fire-cooked meats in a copper-and-marble art deco setting. From Australian celeb-chef Curtis Stone and his brother, Luke, and named for their grandmother, Gwen's butcher shop serves up quality cuts of humanely raised meats to locals during the day, while the elegant dining space within view of the glass-enclosed dry-age rooms, charcuterie curing, and roaring firepit elevates the smoking, searing, and roasting of those quality meats to an art form by night. **Known for:** house-made charcuterie; wood-fire grilled steaks; strong cocktails and good wine list. $ *Average main: $50* ⊠ *6600 Sunset Blvd., Hollywood* ☎ *323/946–7513* ⊕ *www.gwenla.com.*

Jitlada

$$ | **THAI** | Los Angeles is known for wonderful hole-in-the-wall eateries tucked inside tiny strip malls, and family-owned Jitlada is Exhibit A, churning out delicious, spicy, southern Thai dishes since 2006. If the colorful yet low-key dining area doesn't astound you, then the menu with more than 300 options just might. **Known for:** coco mango salad; crying tiger beef; huge menu of over 300 options. $ *Average main: $20* ⊠ *5233½ W. Sunset Blvd., Hollywood* ☎ *323/667–9809* ⊕ *www.jitladala.com* ⊘ *Closed Mon.*

La Mesa Restaurant and Lounge

$$$ | **CONTEMPORARY** | If you like dining out to feel like an event, then tropical, Tulum-inspired La Mesa is for you, especially if you are visiting with a group or celebrating a special event. With lush greenery and palm trees, ambient mood lighting from candles and hanging lanterns and lamps, live music and outlandish live shows, and specialty cocktails,

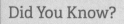

Did You Know?

At the top of the Capitol Records Tower, a blinking light spells out "Hollywood" in Morse code.

you might be forgiven for forgetting to eat. **Known for:** reservations recommended; 21-plus party vibes; DJ and live music and entertainment. $ *Average main: $35* ✉ *1430 N. Cahuenga Blvd., Hollywood* ☎ *323/463–0006* ⊕ *lamesalounge.com* ☽ *Closed Sun.–Wed.* ☞ *21-plus only.*

L'antica Pizzeria da Michele
$$ | **ITALIAN** | **FAMILY** | Tucked away from the frenzy of Hollywood, this Los Angeles outpost of the famous Naples-based pizza spot (featured in *Eat Pray Love*) attracts patrons of all L.A. varieties, from industry folks looking for hearty Italian classics to tourists needing respite from the touristing. L'antica serves comforting yet elevated Neapolitan pie and pasta dishes in an expansive and relaxed classic Italian-meets-modern-Californian indoor-outdoor space accented with lush greenery. **Known for:** century-old pizza recipe; delicious pastas; indoor-outdoor dining. $ *Average main: $30* ✉ *1534 N. McCadden Pl., Hollywood* ☎ *323/366–2408* ⊕ *damicheleusa.com.*

Marouch
$$ | **LEBANESE** | **FAMILY** | Family-run Marouch is somewhat of a rarity in Hollywood in that it deviates from all the usual fanfare and instead delivers a more casual and authentic home-cooking approach with a you're-part-of-our-family attitude. So, while it doesn't constantly reinvent itself a la buzzy Hollywood spots to get you to come back, you will return for the quality and flavor of the traditional Lebanese and Armenian meze plates that have been passed down in the family for generations. **Known for:** iconic Lebanese-Armenian restaurant; combination platters; walnut baclava. $ *Average main: $25* ✉ *4905 Santa Monica Blvd., Hollywood* ☎ *323/662–9325* ⊕ *www.hollywoodmarouch.com.*

Petit Trois
$$$ | **MODERN AMERICAN** | With a modest, you'll-hardly-notice-it's-there exterior and a small, packed-like-sardines interior, you're likely to have to wait in line

to get into Petit Trois. But the wait is worth it for the incredible classic French dishes inside. **Known for:** Big Mec double cheeseburger; trout almondine; cozy atmosphere. $ *Average main: $34* ✉ *718 N. Highland Ave., Hollywood* ☎ *323/468–8916* ⊕ *petittrois.com.*

★ **Providence**
$$$$ | **SEAFOOD** | This is widely considered one of the best seafood restaurants in the country, and chef-owner Michael Cimarusti elevates sustainably driven fine dining to an art form. The elegant space is the perfect spot to sample exquisite seafood with the chef's signature application of French technique, traditional American themes, and Asian accents. **Known for:** fresh seafood; honey and zero-waste chocolate programs; exquisite dessert options. $ *Average main: $150* ✉ *5955 Melrose Ave., Hollywood* ☎ *323/460–4170* ⊕ *www.providencela. com* ☽ *Closed Sun. and Mon.*

Roscoe's House of Chicken and Waffles
$ | **SOUTHERN** | **FAMILY** | Roscoe's is *the* place for down-home Southern cooking in Southern California. Just ask the patrons who drive from all over L.A. for bargain-priced fried chicken and waffles. The name of this casual eatery honors a late-night combo popularized in Harlem jazz clubs. **Known for:** simple yet famous chicken and waffles; classic soul food dishes; eggs with cheese and onions. $ *Average main: $15* ✉ *1514 N. Gower St., Hollywood* ☎ *323/466–7453* ⊕ *www. roscoeschickenandwaffles.com.*

Salt's Cure
$$ | **AMERICAN** | **FAMILY** | Featuring all locally sourced meat, seafood, and produce, an all-day lunch menu, and a popular patio, this former West Hollywood spot proves that despite appearances, Californians love traditional meat-based staples and cocktails just as much as they love their kale salads and smoothies. If you're in doubt, just take a good look at this joint's hearty sandwiches. **Known for:** oatmeal griddle cakes; hearty sandwiches; all

California-grown ingredients. $ *Average main: $20* ⊠ *1155 N. Highland Ave., Hollywood* ☎ *323/465–7258* ⊕ *www.saltscure.com* ☉ *Closed Mon. and Tues.*

Superba Food + Bread

$$ | **CONTEMPORARY** | Bread is in this restaurant's name and should be front and center on your dining plan here as it is freshly baked and delicious served with sides like fresh cheese and smoked trout. The light, bright, and open space and umbrella- and tree-filled patio is popular for coffee and baked bread and pastries early in the day; grain bowls, salads, and avocado toast for lunch and brunch (on weekends); and the oyster bar, Hippie burgers, sandwiches, pastas, and creative cocktails as lunch rolls in to dinner. **Known for:** popular patio; Superba grain bowl; fresh baked breads and pastries. $ *Average main: $28* ⊠ *6530 Sunset Blvd., Hollywood* ☎ *323/364–9844* ⊕ *www.lifesuperba.com.*

TAO Hollywood

$$$ | **ASIAN FUSION** | Feast on Pan-Asian fare and dark and atmospheric faux-Asian decor as A- and B-listers do the same at neighboring tables in this dramatic 300-seat two-level restaurant and lounge next to the Dream Hotel. It's all about vibes here, and it definitely attracts celebratory groups for the sharing plates, DJ, moody candle- and red-lamp light, Asian-themed decor including the giant Quan Yin statue looking out over the ornate main dining room, and the lively patio, lounge, and bar. **Known for:** always busy and always loud; fresh sushi and dim sum; clubby setting and scene. $ *Average main: $40* ⊠ *6421 Selma Ave., Hollywood* ☎ *323/593–7888* ⊕ *taogroup.com/venues/tao-asian-bistro-los-angeles.*

★ Tropicana Pool and Cafe

$$ | **AMERICAN** | Despite being set in the middle of Hollywood's mad dash, the surprisingly serene oasis that is the Tropicana Pool and Cafe is where California fare meets refreshing tropical cocktails in a vintage Hollywood setting. While the poolside loungers are technically restricted to hotel guests, visitors are welcome (at the hotel's discretion) to take advantage of the bar and kitchen service in view of that glorious heated pool with its David Hockney mural. **Known for:** small bites; creative cocktails; poolside dining. $ *Average main: $20* ⊠ *Hollywood Roosevelt Hotel, 7000 Hollywood Blvd., Hollywood* ☎ *323/466–7000* ⊕ *www.thehollywoodroosevelt.com/about/food-drink/tropicana-pool-cafe.*

Hotels

Dream Hollywood

$$ | **HOTEL** | Live out your Hollywood dreams in—where else?—Dream Hollywood, whose modern suites and floor-to-ceiling windows that afford great views of the town are not even its best parts. **Pros:** rooftop pool with cabanas; bedside tablets for hotel and other services; mobile keys and electronic luggage tags. **Cons:** on the pricey side; surrounding area can be sketchy at night; noise in some rooms. $ *Rooms from: $300* ⊠ *6417 Selma Ave., Hollywood* ☎ *323/844–6417* ⊕ *www.dreamhotels.com/hollywood/default-en.html* ⟿ *178 rooms* ⊙| *No Meals.*

★ Hollywood Roosevelt Hotel

$$$ | **HOTEL** | The historic, party-centric Hollywood Roosevelt Hotel, known for hosting the first Academy Awards ceremony, has played host and been home to some of the movie industry's most important people and events. **Pros:** refreshed rooms with great amenities; pool is a popular weekend hangout; great burgers at the on-site 25 Degrees restaurant. **Cons:** reports of noise and staff attitude; stiff parking fees ($45); busy location. $ *Rooms from: $365* ⊠ *7000 Hollywood Blvd., Hollywood* ☎ *323/856–1970* ⊕ *www.hollywoodroosevelt.com* ⟿ *300 rooms* ⊙| *No Meals.*

Local Chains to Try

It's said that the drive-in burger joint was invented in L.A., probably to meet the demands of an ever-mobile car culture. Burger aficionados line up at all hours outside **In-N-Out Burger** (⊕ www.in-n-out.com, multiple locations), still a family-owned operation whose terrific made-to-order burgers are revered by Angelenos. Visitors may recognize the chain as the infamous spot where Paris Hilton got nabbed for drunk driving, but locals are more concerned with getting their burger fix off the "secret" menu, with variations like "Animal Style" (mustard-grilled patty with grilled onions and extra spread), a "4 x 4" (four burger patties and four cheese slices, for big eaters), or the bun-less "Protein Style" that comes wrapped in a bib of lettuce. Go online for a list of every "secret" menu item.

Tommy's is best known for its delightfully sloppy chili burger. Visit its no-frills original location (⊠ 2575 Beverly Blvd., Downtown ☎ 213/389–9060)—a culinary landmark. One-of-a-kind-sausage lovers will appreciate **Wurstküche** (⊠ 800 E. 3rd St., Downtown ☎ 213/457–7462 ⊕ www. wurstkuche.com), where the menu includes items like rattlesnake and rabbit or pheasant with herbes de Provence. Meanwhile, health nuts will go crazy over the plant-based yet still incredibly satisfying burgers, fries, and shakes at **Monty's Good Burger** (⊠ 1533 W. Sunset Blvd, Echo Park) which gives a whole new meaning to fast food with its locally sourced ingredients, house-made sauce, and plant-based Impossible patty.

Loews Hollywood

$$$ | **HOTEL** | **FAMILY** | Part of the massive Ovation Hollywood shopping, dining, and entertainment complex, the 20-story Loews is at the center of Hollywood's action but manages to deliver a quiet night's sleep. **Pros:** large rooms with contemporary furniture; nice pool with great views; Red Line Metro station adjacent. **Cons:** corporate feeling; very touristy; pricey parking ($20 per night). ⓢ Rooms from: $385 ⊠ 1755 N. Highland Ave., Hollywood ☎ 323/856—1200, 877/875–1604 ⊕ www.loewshotels.com/en/hollywood-hotel ⇄ 628 rooms ¶○¶ No Meals.

★ **Magic Castle Hotel**

$$ | **HOTEL** | **FAMILY** | Guests at the hotel can secure advance dinner reservations and attend magic shows at the Magic Castle, a private club in a 1908 mansion next door for magicians and their admirers. **Pros:** heated pool and lush patio; central location near Hollywood & Highland; access to fun Magic Castle shows. **Cons:** strict dress code; no elevator; highly trafficked street. ⓢ Rooms from: $250 ⊠ 7025 Franklin Ave., Hollywood ☎ 323/851–0800, 800/741–4915 ⊕ magiccastlehotel.com ⇄ 43 rooms ¶○¶ Free Breakfast.

★ **Mama Shelter Los Angeles**

$$ | **HOTEL** | Mama Shelter Los Angeles is not just a cool hotel, it's an attitude, with its tropical rooftop bar populated with beautiful people having fun, a lively lobby restaurant and café, and eclectic, playful design, throughout like masks in rooms and a foosball table in the lobby. **Pros:** delicious food and cocktails on the property; affordable rooms that don't skimp on style; a block from Hollywood Boulevard. **Cons:** some rooms are noisy; creaky elevators; bar and restaurant often get crowded. ⓢ Rooms from: $265 ⊠ 6500 Selma Ave., Hollywood ☎ 323/785–6600

🌐 *www.mamashelter.com/en/los-angeles* 🛏 *70 rooms* 🍴 *No Meals.*

Moment Hotel

$$ | **HOTEL** | Hollywood's best-value property housed in a former motor inn caters to young partygoers, who breeze in and out of the lobby (which doubles as a bar and breakfast lounge). **Pros:** very affordable; fun rooftop bar; free Wi-Fi. **Cons:** not the safest neighborhood for walking at night; tends to draw a partying crowd and thus noise; smallish rooms. [$] *Rooms from: $275* ✉ *7370 Sunset Blvd., Hollywood* ☎ *323/822–5030* 🌐 *th-emomenthotel.com* 🛏 *39 rooms* 🍴 *No Meals.*

W Hollywood

$$$ | **HOTEL** | This centrally located, ultra-modernly lit location is outfitted for the wired traveler and features a rooftop pool deck and popular on-site bars, like the Station Hollywood and the mod Living Room lobby bar. **Pros:** Metro stop outside the front door; comes with in-room party necessities, from ice to cocktail glasses; comfy beds with petal-soft duvets. **Cons:** small pool; pricey dining and valet parking; location in noisy part of Hollywood. [$] *Rooms from: $479* ✉ *6250 Hollywood Blvd., Hollywood* ☎ *323/798–1300, 888/625–4988* 🌐 *www.marriott.com/en-us/hotels/laxwh-w-hollywood* 🛏 *305 rooms* 🍴 *No Meals.*

🍸 Nightlife

Hollywood is no longer just a tourist magnet. With the renewed interest in discovering Hollywood history, this area is once again a nightlife destination for locals, visitors, and celebrities alike. Its blend of glitz and grime is reflected here in the after-hours scene.

Avalon

LIVE MUSIC | This multitasking art deco venue offers both live music and club nights. The killer sound system, cavernous space, and multiple bars make it a perfect venue for both. The club is best known for its DJs, who often spin well past the 2 am cutoff for drinks. The crowd can be a mixed bag, depending on the night, but if you're looking to dance, you likely won't be disappointed. Upstairs is **Bardot,** which hosts special events including a free Monday night showcase of up-and-coming artists. ✉ *1735 Vine St., Hollywood* ☎ *323/462–8900* 🌐 *www.avalonhollywood.com.*

Birds

PUBS | They call it your neighborhood bar, because even if you don't live in the neighborhood you'll feel at home at this Alfred Hitchcock–themed eatery. Located in Franklin Village, a block-long stretch of bars, cafés, and bookstores, come here for pub food or a cheap poultry-centric dinner. Weekend nights mean cheap beer and well drinks, crowds spilling onto the streets, and a few rounds of oversize Jenga. ✉ *5925 Franklin Ave., Hollywood* ☎ *323/465–0175* 🌐 *www.birdshollywood.com.*

Boardner's

PUBS | Priding itself as one of the last remaining neighborhood bars in Los Angeles's ever-evolving bar scene, Boardner's has maintained its no-nonsense vibe for more than 70 years. Leave your self-importance at the door, order ice-cold beer and hearty mac and cheese, and keep an eye out for any weird apparitions—this place is known to be one of the most haunted spots in the city. ✉ *1652 N. Cherokee Ave., Hollywood* ☎ *323/462–9621* 🌐 *www.boardners.com.*

Burgundy Room

BARS | Around since 1919, Burgundy Room attracts a fiercely loyal crowd of locals, as well as the occasional wandering tourist. The bar is supposedly haunted (check out the Ouija boards toward the back), but that just adds to its charm. Its rock-and-roll vibe, strong drinks, and people-watching opportunities make this a worthy detour on any night out on the town. ✉ *1621½ N. Cahuenga Blvd., Hollywood* ☎ *323/465–7530.*

The Cat and Fiddle

PUBS | A British pub might look out of place in Hollywood, but the Cat and Fiddle's punk-rock influence and 40-year stint give it more than enough street cred. Besides, classic pub grub like fish-and-chips, bangers and mash, and shepherd's pie are a nice counterpoint to L.A.'s vegetarian and gluten-free offerings. There have been a few changes over the years, with Ashley Gardner now running it with her mother, Paula, and a new chef, Alan Rodriguez, at the helm, but it remains the perfect spot to just grab a pint and a savory pie or to satisfy one's inner Anglophile. There's even afternoon tea during the weekends. ⊠ *742 N. Highland Ave., Hollywood* ☎ *323/468–3800* ⊕ *www.thecatandfiddle.com.*

★ **Dirty Laundry**

COCKTAIL LOUNGES | Tucked away in a basement on quiet Hudson Avenue, Dirty Laundry is a former speakeasy turned proper cocktail bar with live music and DJs spinning both fresh and throwback music. There's beer on hand, but here, cocktails are king. ⊠ *1725 Hudson Ave., Hollywood* ☎ *323/462–6531.*

The Fonda Theatre

LIVE MUSIC | Right on the edge of the Walk of Fame, this historic venue was one of the area's first theaters when it opened in the 1920s. The Spanish Colonial–style theater now hosts some of the biggest names in indie music, but don't expect any major acts on the calendar. Drinks are pricey—so grab a cocktail on Hollywood Boulevard before the show—as is parking, which will cost you at least $20 in the adjacent lot. ⊠ *6126 Hollywood Blvd., Hollywood* ☎ *323/464–6269* ⊕ *www.fondatheatre.com.*

Frolic Room

BARS | Once frequented by one of L.A.'s most famous sons, Charles Bukowski, the Frolic Room was also owned at one point by Howard Hughes and has served as a filming location for period flicks like *L.A. Confidential*. Despite its impressive history, its down-to-earth atmosphere and proximity to the Pantages Theatre makes it the perfect place to start off your night. ⊠ *6245 Hollywood Blvd., Hollywood* ☎ *323/462–5890.*

★ **Good Times at Davey Wayne's**

BARS | It's a fridge; it's a door; it's the entrance to Davey Wayne's, a bar and lounge that pulls out all the stops to transport you back in time to the '70s. The interior is your living room; the outside is an ongoing backyard barbecue with all your friends. Come early to beat the crowds or be prepared to get up close and personal with your neighbors. ⊠ *1611 N. El Centro Ave., Hollywood* ☎ *323/498–0859* ⊕ *www.goodtimesatdaveywaynes.com.*

Harvard and Stone

LIVE MUSIC | An interior that's one part industrial, one part mid-century modern, and one part ski lodge plays witness to the coolest live music this side of the city and serves some of the most exquisite cocktails you'll ever try in your life. Of course, if live music isn't exactly your thing, there are also dark, quiet corners where you can enjoy your drinks in peace. ⊠ *5221 Hollywood Blvd., Hollywood* ☎ *818/848–4016* ⊕ *harvardandstone.com.*

Hotel Cafe

LIVE MUSIC | This intimate venue caters to fans of folk, indie rock, and music on the softer side. With red velvet backdrops, hardwood furnishings, and the occasional celebrity surprise performance—notably John Mayer—music lovers will not only be very happy but will receive a respite from the ordinary Hollywood experience. ⊠ *1623½ N. Cahuenga Blvd., Hollywood* ⊕ *www.hotelcafe.com.*

★ **Musso and Frank Grill**

GATHERING PLACES | FAMILY | The prim and proper vibe of this old-school steak house won't appeal to those looking for a raucous night out; instead, its appeal lies in its history and sturdy drinks. Established over a century ago, its dark wood decor, red tuxedo–clad waiters, and highly skilled bartenders can easily shuttle you back to its Hollywood heyday when Marilyn Monroe, F. Scott Fitzgerald, and Greta Garbo once hung around and sipped martinis. ⊠ *6667 Hollywood Blvd., Hollywood* ☏ *323/467–7788* ⊕ *www. mussoandfrank.com.*

No Vacancy

BARS | At first glance, No Vacancy might convey an air of exclusivity and pretentiousness, but its relaxed interiors and welcoming staff will almost instantly make you feel like you're at a house party. You know, the kind with burlesque shows, tightrope performances, a speakeasy secret entrance, and mixologists who can pretty much whip up any drink your heart desires. ⊠ *1727 N. Hudson Ave., Hollywood* ☏ *323/465–1902* ⊕ *www.novacancyla.com.*

Sassafras Saloon

DANCE CLUBS | Put on your dancing shoes (or your cowboy boots) and step back in time. The Sassafras boasts not only an oddly cozy, Western atmosphere, but also plenty of opportunities to strut your moves on the dance floor. Indulge in exquisite craft mezcal, whiskey, and tequila cocktails for some liquid courage before you two-step the night away. ⊠ *1233 N. Vine St., Hollywood* ☏ *323/467–2800* ⊕ *www.sassafrassaloon.com.*

The Spare Room

PIANO BARS | While your typical Hollywood crowd might be a permanent fixture at this Hollywood Roosevelt cocktail bar, it's still worth a visit for its luscious cocktails, hearty fare, and collection of classic board games. It can get a little too crowded, especially on the weekends, but if you come early, you should be able to admire its art deco appeal and perhaps enjoy a game at one of its two vintage bowling lanes. ⊠ *7000 Hollywood Blvd., Hollywood* ☏ *323/769–7296* ⊕ *www. spareroomhollywood.com.*

Three Clubs

BARS | Cocktail bars are a dime a dozen in Hollywood, but there's something about this Vine Street joint that makes patrons keep coming back for more. Maybe it's the down-to-earth attitude, delicious no-frills cocktails, and the fact that a taco stand serving greasy grub is right next door. Come to see one of the burlesque or comedy shows for a full experience. ⊠ *1123 Vine St., Hollywood* ⊕ *www. threeclubs.com.*

The Woods

PIANO BARS | Don't let the forest fairy-tale vibe—one that'll make you think that a woodsman fell in love with a tree nymph and then went on to open a bar—or the baffling strip mall location fool you. When the occasion calls for it, this little dive bar knows how to throw a party and show you a good time with the simple concoction of jukebox music, DJ spins, and signature drinks. ⊠ *1533 N. La Brea Ave., Hollywood* ☏ *323/876–6612* ⊕ *www. thewoodshollywood.com.*

🎞 Performing Arts

Fountain Theatre

THEATER | The multiple award–winning (Los Angeles Drama Critics Circle, NAACP Theater Awards, Ovation Award, to name a few) Fountain Theatre is committed to diverse theater and dance performances. Although the 80-seat venue may be intimate, it's a powerhouse at producing original plays in addition to revivals. ⊠ *5060 Fountain Ave., Hollywood* ☏ *323/663–1525* ⊕ *www.fountaintheatre.com.*

Ricardo Montalban Theatre

THEATER | The Ricardo Montalban Theatre is more than just a live performance and outdoor movie screening space. While it is famous for its comedy shows, small film festivals, and rooftop movie screenings, collaborating with well-known chefs for its food service as well as artists to create art and commerce together, its

Laurel Canyon and Mulholland Drive

The hills that separate Hollywood from the Valley are more than a symbolic dividing line between the city slickers and the suburbanites; they have a community in their own right and a reputation as a hideaway for celebrities and wealthy creatives.

The 2002 movie *Laurel Canyon* showed the lifestyle of one kind of Canyon dweller—freethinking entertainment industry movers and shakers seeking peaceful refuge in their tree-shaded homes. By day they're churning out business deals and working on projects; by night they're living it up with private parties high above the bustle of the city streets. Landslides can cause road closures in Laurel Canyon, so do some research beforehand.

Drive through Laurel Canyon and you'll pass estates and party pads dating back to the silent film era. If you have time to cruise Mulholland Drive, expect breathtaking views that show the city's serene side.

8

Hollywood

biggest goals are to support performing arts and create employment in Hollywood. So, beyond having that quintessentially L.A. experience of watching movies outdoors, you're also supporting a local business that in turn supports the local community. For a true local experience in Hollywood, this is the spot to go and check out a show. ⊠ *1615 Vine St., Hollywood* ☎ *323/461–6999* ⊕ *www.themontalban.com.*

🛍 Shopping

Browsing Hollywood Boulevard, you'll find a mixed bag of offerings including lingerie, movie memorabilia, souvenir, and wig shops, while the crowd-heavy Ovation Hollywood complex is home to more familiar retailers and eateries.

Outside the main drag, Hollywood has a few other pockets for picking up high-end goods, including La Brea Avenue, where you'll find a handful of design-happy shops. Take a leisurely stroll as you browse upscale clothing, antiques, and furniture stores.

★ Amoeba Records

MUSIC | Touted as the "World's Largest Independent Record Store," Amoeba is a playground for music lovers, with a knowledgeable staff and a focus on local artists. Catch free in-store appearances and signings by artists and bands that play sold-out shows at venues down the road. There's a massive and eclectic collection of vinyl records, CDs, and cassette tapes, not to mention VHS tapes, DVDs, and Blu-Ray discs. It's a paradise for both music and movie lovers. ⊠ *6200 Hollywood Blvd., Hollywood* ☎ *323/245–6400* ⊕ *www.amoeba.com.*

Hollywood Farmers' Market

MARKET | Among L.A.'s many farmers' markets, the Hollywood Farmers' Market is one of the most well-known. This family-friendly, open-air market, which has been around for over 30 years, is also the city's largest with more than 160 local producers and farmers touting their seasonal yields every Sunday. Start your day right and stop by to shop organic, locally grown produce, see live music, and sample some delicious California fare. ⊠ *Hollywood* ⊹ *Ivar Ave. and Selma*

Ave., between Hollywood Blvd. and Sunset Blvd. ☎ *323/463–3171.*

Larry Edmunds Bookshop

BOOKS | Cinephiles have long descended upon this iconic 70-plus-year-old shop that in addition to stocking tons of texts about motion picture history offers film fans the opportunity to pick up scripts, posters, and photographs from Hollywood's golden era to the present. ✉ *6644 Hollywood Blvd., Hollywood* ☎ *323/463–3273* ⊕ *www.larryedmunds. com.*

Ovation Hollywood

SHOPPING CENTER | If you're on the hunt for unique boutiques, look elsewhere. However, if you prefer the biggest retail chains America has to offer, Ovation Hollywood is a great spot for a shopping spree. Sadly, the original courtyard that pays tribute to the city's film legacy is no longer there, replaced by a more modern space, but if you head to the north-facing balconies, you will find a picture-perfect view of the Hollywood sign. Heads up that this place is a huge tourist magnet. ✉ *6801 Hollywood Blvd., at Highland Ave., Hollywood* ⊕ *www.ovationholly-wood.com.*

The Record Parlour

MUSIC | Vinyl records and music memorabilia abound in this hip yet modest record store–slash–music lover magnet that also touts vintage audio gear and retro jukeboxes. A visit here is usually a multi-hour affair, one that involves more than just browsing through display cases, digging through wooden carts of used vinyls, and playing your picks at the listening station. ✉ *6408 Selma Ave., Hollywood* ☎ *323/464–7757* ⊕ *www.facebook.com/ therecordparlour.*

Activities

★ Runyon Canyon Trail and Park

HIKING & WALKING | Is Runyon Canyon the city's most famous trail? To the world, it just might be, what with so many A-listers frequenting it. Many folks visiting L.A. take the trail specifically for celebrity spotting. But, if that's not something you're into, this accessible trail right in the middle of Hollywood is also a good place to hike, run, see the Hollywood sign, photograph the city skyline, or simply get a bit of fresh air. If you just happen to run into a famous face, well that's just the cherry on the cake. ✉ *2000 N. Fuller Ave., Hollywood* ☎ *323/644–6661 Park Ranger* ⊕ *www.laparks.org/runyon.*

THE VALLEY

BURBANK, STUDIO CITY, NORTH HOLLYWOOD, AND UNIVERSAL CITY

Updated by
Michelle Rae Uy

⊙ **Sights**
★★★☆☆

🍴 **Restaurants**
★★★☆☆

🛏 **Hotels**
★☆☆☆☆

🛍 **Shopping**
★★☆☆☆

🍸 **Nightlife**
★☆☆☆☆

NEIGHBORHOOD SNAPSHOT

TOP EXPERIENCES

Get your Super Mario overalls on: Pony up for a Power-Up-Band so you can smash bricks, hit question boxes, and unlock hidden levels of awesomeness to feel like you are truly transported inside a Nintendo game at the already fun Super Nintendo World at Universal Studio Hollywood.

Tour a working film studio: Whether it's the highly popular Studio Tour at Universal or the one at Warner Bros. Studios, a guided tour of at least one of the working film studios in the Valley is a must experience when visiting L.A. You might even get to visit a "hot set" or witness a production filming a scene.

Indulge in pastries at Porto's: Porto's Bakery is a beloved institution in Los Angeles and for good reason. Whether you've got a hankering for a sweet pastry or you're just looking to try a Cuban delicacy, waiting in line here is an essential local experience.

Shop for vintage items along Magnolia Boulevard: L.A. has more than its share of vintage and antique shopping strips, but the one on Magnolia Boulevard has long been a favorite among locals. You'll find everything from old film cameras and curiosities to antique furniture worth shipping home.

GETTING HERE

Traffic jams on the Hollywood Freeway (U.S. 101/ Highway 170), San Diego Freeway (I–405), and Ventura Freeway (U.S. 101/Highway 134) can make for lengthy trips to or from the Valley. The best way to the valley from Hollywood is to skip the freeways and take Hollywood Boulevard to Cahuenga Boulevard heading north. If you're heading to Burbank, take a right on Barham Boulevard. The Metro's Red Line subway cuts through Hollywood and terminates in North Hollywood. While you can easily take a rideshare from there to Universal Studios or the rest of the valley, don't expect to get around the valley without a car, whether it's a rental or a rideshare.

PLANNING YOUR TIME

■ The San Fernando Valley might not have a lot of tourist attractions, but the ones it does have require quite a bit of time. The Warner Bros. Tour needs at least three hours while Universal Studios Hollywood demands at least a full day and maybe more if you are really into movies. Find a nearby hotel like The Garland, to minimize time traveling to and from the parks.

VIEWFINDER

■ **Circus Liquor:** There's a 32-foot neon clown sign. Enough said? Bonus: it served as a crime scene in Snoop Dogg's music video for "Murder was the Case" and as a backdrop in *Clueless*. Visit by night to see him in all his neon glory. ⊠ *5600 Vineland Ave.*

■ **Toothsome Chocolate Emporium & Savory Feast Kitchen:** For the sweetest photo op, head to one of the newest additions to Universal CityWalk for cool, steampunk gadgetry and backdrops and characters who pay table visits. The delicious and over-the-top milkshakes are especially Gram-worthy. ⊠ *100 Universal City Plaza*

The polarizing San Fernando Valley has its share of haters and ardent devotees, but its contributions to L.A. as well as the movie and music scenes are undeniable. Though the Laurel Canyon '70s counterculture era is long gone, it remains an integral part of the movie industry, being home to several of the biggest movie studios in the world.

Warner Bros. Studios and nearby Universal Studios both host stellar studio tours, with the former involving a three-hour tram tour through the 100-acre backlot to all types of filming locations and photo ops and props, and the latter also providing a full day of entertainment with its surrounding theme park and shopping district, the Universal CityWalk Hollywood. And, there's some surprisingly robust shopping as well, particularly along Burbank's Magnolia Avenue, where you'll find an assortment of vintage and thrift shops to get into the L.A. spirit.

These sleepy communities north of the Hollywood Hills are more than just where the movie magic happens and home to the Valley Girl accent (though there's a *Clueless* landmark or two here). North Hollywood, or NoHo, is unique for L.A. in that it is walkable, unhurried, and easygoing. Linger in outdoor cafés, take in some "off-Broadway"–type theater, and just generally take a break from the greater L.A. area.

Burbank

Johnny Carson, host of *The Tonight Show,* used to ironically refer to downtown Burbank as "beautiful," but it's since become one of the area's most desirable suburbs. It's also home to Warner Bros. Studios, Disney Studios, and the Burbank Studios (formerly NBC Studios), and to Bob Hope Airport (BUR), one of the two major airports serving L.A.

Sights

★ Warner Bros. Studios

FILM/TV STUDIO | FAMILY | Tour an actual working studio, visit hot sets, and marvel at the costumes and props from the biggest blockbusters at Warner Bros. Studios. The exterior sets and soundstages here have been used to film some of the most famous TV shows and films in Hollywood, making a visit here a vital part of the Los Angeles experience.

After a short film on the studio's movies and TV shows, hop aboard a tram for a ride through the sets and soundstages used for classics such as *Casablanca* and

Visit one of the busiest working studios in Hollywood with a tour of Warner Bros. Studios.

Rebel Without a Cause. You'll see the bungalows where Marlon Brando, Bette Davis, and other icons relaxed between takes, and the current production offices for famous directors. You might even spot a celeb or see a shoot in action—tours change from day to day depending on the productions taking place on the lot. Finally, you can spend a couple of hours pretending like you're part of your favorite shows and movies, whether it's at a working replica of Central Perk from *Friends* or taking part in a Sorting Hat ceremony from the *Harry Potter* movies. ✉ *3400 W. Riverside Dr., Burbank* ☎ *818/977–8687* 🌐 *www.wbstudiotour.com* 🎟 *From $69.*

🍴 Restaurants

Home to movie and television studios, there's a quiet sophistication to this part of town. Great restaurants are tucked away in strip malls and side streets.

Bea Bea's

$ | DINER | FAMILY | Just because Bea Bea's is a no-nonsense kind of place, it doesn't mean the food isn't special. This diner serves breakfast food that is about as close to extraordinary as the most important meal of the day can be. **Known for:** pancakes and French toast; friendly staff; classic diner grub. [$] *Average main: $15* ✉ *353 N. Pass Ave., Burbank* ☎ *818/846–2327* 🌐 *www.beabeas.com.*

Centanni Trattoria

$$ | ITALIAN | In a city full of adventurous restaurants touting innovation and all things new and gimmicky, Centanni Trattoria focuses on executing traditional, comforting fare to perfection. From lasagna and ravioli to tiramisu, this authentic dinner spot offers reasonably priced, delicious food. **Known for:** pumpkin ravioli; risotto di funghi; great appetizers. [$] *Average main: $23* ✉ *117 N. Victory Blvd., Burbank* ☎ *818/561–4643* 🌐 *www.centannila.com.*

Chili John's

$ | **DINER** | **FAMILY** | Hearty home cooking may not be a big part of L.A.'s dining scene, but that doesn't mean you can't have it when you're visiting the city. Tucked in the heart of Burbank, this diner-style spot serves chili everything, from traditional chili bowls to open-faced chili burgers. **Known for:** beef chili; lemon pie; organic and locally sourced comfort food. [$] *Average main: $9* ✉ *2018 W. Burbank Blvd., Burbank* ☎ *818/846–3611* 🌐 *www.chilijohnsofca.com* 🕒 *Closed Sun.*

Los Amigos

$ | **MEXICAN** | **FAMILY** | If you're in the mood for good old-fashioned fun coupled with hearty Mexican fare and delicious margaritas, then you'll want to consider Los Amigos, whose legendary fruity margaritas alone are worth the drive. Pair those with something from the Platillos Mexicanos menu on karaoke night, and you're guaranteed a good time until the wee hours of the night. **Known for:** classic Mexican food; massive portions; casual dining. [$] *Average main: $18* ✉ *2825 W. Olive Ave., Burbank* ☎ *818/842–3700* 🌐 *www.losamigosbarandgrill.com.*

Porto's Bakery

$ | **CUBAN** | **FAMILY** | Waiting in line at Porto's is as much a part of the experience as is indulging in one of its roasted pork sandwiches or chocolate-dipped croissants. This Cuban bakery and café has been an L.A. staple for more than 50 years, often drawing crowds during lunch. **Known for:** famous potato balls; must-try desserts; fast-moving counter service. [$] *Average main: $8* ✉ *3614 W. Magnolia Blvd., Burbank* ☎ *818/846–9100* 🌐 *www.portosbakery.com.*

Summer Buffalo

$ | **THAI** | While there are plenty of great Thai restaurants in Los Angeles, if you're looking for something a little different, Summer Buffalo isn't just about classic Thai fare. Yes, you'll still find favorites like *larb*, curry, and pad Thai, but you'll also be able to sample chicken wings that come in four different sauces, including traditional *grapow*. **Known for:** city's best Thai chicken wings; drunken noodles; cozy ambience. [$] *Average main: $12* ✉ *449 S. Glenoaks Blvd., Burbank* ☎ *818/561–4777* 🌐 *www.summerbuffalo.com.*

Hotels

Hotel Amarano Burbank

$$ | **HOTEL** | Close to Burbank's TV and movie studios, the smartly designed Amarano feels like a Beverly Hills boutique hotel, complete with 24-hour room service, a homey on-site restaurant and lounge, and lovely rooms. **Pros:** amenities include saltwater pool and complimentary bike rentals; convenient to studios and restaurants; lively bar. **Cons:** some street noise; away from most of the city's action; $25 amenity fee. [$] *Rooms from: $280* ✉ *322 N. Pass Ave., Burbank* ☎ *818/842–8887* 🌐 *www.hotelamarano.com* 🛏 *132 rooms* 🍴 *No Meals.*

Nightlife

Flappers Comedy Club

COMEDY CLUBS | Even though this live comedy club doesn't exactly have as long a history as others in town (it opened in 2010), it's attracted an impressive list of big names like Jerry Seinfeld, Maria Bamford, and Adam Sandler thanks to its Celebrity Drop-In Tuesdays. The food and drinks are good though not great, but you're here for the laughs not the grub. ✉ *102 E. Magnolia Blvd., Burbank* ☎ *818/845–9721* 🌐 *www.flapperscomedy.com.*

Tony's Darts Away

PUBS | Pubs serving vegan food aren't exactly a dime a dozen, but it's no surprise you can find one in Los Angeles. Tony's Darts Away is one such place, touting a predominantly vegan menu with dishes tasty enough to satisfy even the most steadfast meat lover. And craft beer lovers will be sure to appreciate the all-Californian craft beer selection. ✉ *1710*

W. Magnolia Blvd., Burbank ☎ *818/253–1710* 🌐 *www.tonysda.com.*

🛍 Shopping

It's not a major shopping destination, but Burbank has some offbeat shops that are well worth exploring. Given its close proximity to some major studios, the area has a few hidden gems for finding postproduction castaways, like mint-condition designer and vintage clothing.

It's a Wrap

OTHER SPECIALTY STORE | For nearly four decades, the wardrobe departments of movie and TV studios and production companies have been shipping clothes and props here daily. Besides scoring occasional gems from designers like Georgio Armani, Versace, Chanel, and more for between 35% and 95% off retail price, insiders flock here to get their hands on a piece of history. Good news for the serious collectors: your purchase includes the title and code from the production it was used on, so you can properly place each piece of memorabilia. ✉ *3315 W. Magnolia Blvd., Burbank* ☎ *818/567–7366* 🌐 *www.itsawraphollywood.com.*

Magnolia Park Vintage

NEIGHBORHOODS | Melrose Avenue might be Los Angeles's most well-known vintage shopping destination, but to many locals, especially those on the Eastside, Burbank's Magnolia Park is, in many ways, better. Spanning several blocks around Magnolia Avenue, this revitalized area blends vintage, thrift, and antiques shopping opportunities with the laid-back small-town vibe that Melrose lacks. Great dining spots and modern coffee shops abound, as well as foot and nail spas for a bit of pampering. ✉ *W. Magnolia Blvd., between N. Niagara and N. Avon St., Burbank* 🌐 *www.visitmagnoliapark.com.*

Playclothes Vintage Fashions

MIXED CLOTHING | Productions including *Mad Men, Austin Powers*, and *Catch Me If You Can* (among many, many others) have turned to this vintage shop for mint-condition pieces from the 1930s through the 1980s. Ladies who love the pinup look will adore the selection of curve-hugging pencil skirts, cardigans, and lingerie, while men will have their pick of Hawaiian shirts, suits, and skinny ties. The time-warped interior also features decorative home accents and furniture from decades past. ✉ *3100 W. Magnolia Blvd., Burbank* ☎ *818/557–8447* 🌐 *www.vintageplayclothes.com.*

Studio City

Ventura Boulevard, the famed commercial strip, cuts through the lively neighborhood of Studio City. This area, located west of Universal City, is home to several smaller film and TV studios.

🍴 Restaurants

The dining scene here continues to grow as restaurateurs realize how many locals are looking for stylish and swanky places to eat. Japanese, Mexican, and Italian eateries can all be found in this dynamic city.

Asanebo

$$ | **JAPANESE** | One of L.A.'s finest sushi restaurants, Asanebo is an inviting, no-frills establishment serving top-quality sushi and a wealth of innovative dishes to an A-list clientele. The affable chefs will regale you with memorable specialties such as succulent seared *toro* (tuna belly), halibut truffle sashimi, or just simple morsels of pristine fish dusted with sea salt. **Known for:** omakase (chef's choice) dinners; halibut truffle; excellent sushi. [$] *Average main: $30* ✉ *11941 Ventura Blvd., Studio City* ☎ *818/760–3348* 🌐 *www.asanebo-restaurant.com/.*

Firefly

$$$ | **AMERICAN** | One minute you're in an old library quickly converted into a lounge, the next you're in the cabana of a modest country club. Yet Firefly's eclectic design is part of its appeal, and its excellent, if a bit pricey, French-American fare will make you forget all about it. **Known for:** prix-fixe and à la carte dining; reputation as a date spot; seasonal fare. [$] *Average main: $34* ✉ *11720 Ventura Blvd., Studio City* ☎ *818/762–1833* 🌐 *www.fireflystudiocity.com.*

Good Neighbor Restaurant

$ | **DINER** | Its walls may be heavy with framed photographs of film and TV stars, and folks from the biz might regularly grace its tables, but this Studio City diner is every bit as down-to-earth as your next-door neighbor, even after 40-some years. It gets pretty busy, but a plateful of that home cooking is worth the wait; or if you're in a mad dash, grab a caffeine or fruit smoothie fix from the Neighbarista. **Known for:** craft-your-own omelet; cottage fries; excellent breakfast food. [$] *Average main: $15* ✉ *3701 Cahuenga Blvd. W, Studio City* ☎ *818/761–4627* 🌐 *goodneighborrestaurant.com* 🕒 *Closed Mon.*

Miceli's

$$ | **PIZZA** | **FAMILY** | If the charming, Italian square–inspired interior doesn't turn you into a sappy mush, then Miceli's musical servers serenading you with Italian opera will. Studio City might not be the most romantic place in L.A., but one dinner at this restaurant might make you feel like you're in a Hollywood version of Rome. **Known for:** specialty pastas; singing servers; touristy crowd. [$] *Average main: $25* ✉ *3655 Cahuenga Blvd. W, Studio City* ☎ *323/851–3344* 🌐 *www.micelisrestaurant.com.*

🍸 Nightlife

Baked Potato

LIVE MUSIC | Baked Potato might be a strange name to give a world-famous jazz club that's been holding performances of well-known acts (Allan Holdsworth and Michael Landau) under its roof since the '70s, but it only takes a quick peek at the menu to understand. Twenty-four different types of baked potatoes dominate its otherwise short menu, each of which come with sour cream, butter, and salad to offset all that carb intake. ✉ *3787 Cahuenga Blvd., Studio City* ☎ *818/980–1615* 🌐 *www.thebakedpotato.com.*

The Fox and Hounds

PUBS | With bangers and mash, fish-and-chips, and shepherd's pie rolling out of the kitchen and 16 imported draft beers being poured into glasses, this pub is as British as it can get—even if football matches share screen time with the NFL and NBA. ✉ *11100 Ventura Blvd., Studio City* ☎ *818/763–7837.*

The Rendition Room

PIANO BARS | A speakeasy cocktail lounge seems a little out of place in Studio City, especially on a middle-of-the-road commercial strip paved with quaint boutique stores, but the Rendition Room makes it work. It's a member's club with pretty laid-back rules about letting nonmembers in—so long as there's room, of course. Even as a tourist, you, too, can sample the Rendition's exciting cocktails, crafted by talented mixologists. ✉ *4349 Tujunga Ave., Studio City* ☎ *818/769–0905* 🌐 *therenditionroom.wildapricot.org.*

North Hollywood

Originally called Lankershim after the family of ranchers and farmers who first settled here, this area took the name North Hollywood in the 1920s to capitalize on the popularity of the city just over the hill to the south. Today, the large and bustling neighborhood serves as the terminus of the Metro Red Line subway, around which the NoHo Arts District thrives.

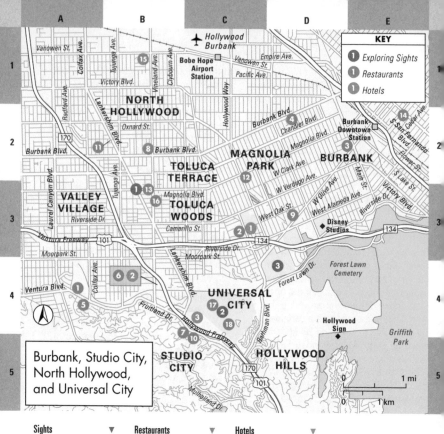

KEY

- 1 Exploring Sights
- 1 Restaurants
- 1 Hotels

Burbank, Studio City, North Hollywood, and Universal City

0 — 1 mi
0 — 1 km

Sights

NoHo Arts District

NEIGHBORHOOD | In only a few years, North Hollywood's performance arts hub has grown from the residential home of aspiring actors who frequent a few small theaters and several chain restaurants to a completely revitalized district that boasts its own, albeit small, collection of new coffee shops and restaurants, bars serving up craft beer, and colorful street art. ✉ *Lankershim and Magnolia Blvds., North Hollywood* 🌐 *www.nohoartsdistrict.com.*

Restaurants

The Front Yard

$$ | **AMERICAN** | **FAMILY** | Big hotel restaurants are rarely ever good, let alone adventurous with their dishes, but the Front Yard is one of the very few exceptions. It has one of the best patios in the Valley, which like the hotel is furnished in that retro '70s style that makes you feel like you should linger all day. **Known for:** lovely sycamore-filled patio; Valley fried chicken; fun weekend brunch. [$] *Average main: $25* ✉ *4222 Vineland Ave., North Hollywood* ☎ *818/255–7290* 🌐 *www.thefrontyardla.com.*

Hayat's Kitchen

$ | **LEBANESE** | Sit down here to a table piled high with assorted hot and cold mezes, baba ghanoush, garlic fries, falafel, and kebabs piled on a bed of rice. Fresh, satisfying, and with excellent service, this reasonably priced hidden gem in the Valley is worth the trek over the hill. **Known for:** Lebanese home cooking; delicious appetizers; Kabob-shish Tawook. [$] *Average main: $18* ✉ *11009 Burbank Blvd., Suite 117, North Hollywood* ☎ *818/761–4656* 🌐 *www.hayats.kitchen.*

★ **Mofongo's**

$ | **PUERTO RICAN** | Mofongo's small storefront represents one of the best and only venues to get authentic Puerto Rican food in L.A. Stop by and try the namesake dish (a delectable mash of fried plantains), but stay for the *pasteles* (cakes) and *rellenos de papa* (stuffed potatoes). **Known for:** mofongo de Pollo Guisado (fried mashed plantains with chicken stew); hard-to-find Puerto Rican food; flan de queso (cream cheese flan). [$] *Average main: $14* ✉ *5757 Lankershim Blvd., North Hollywood* ☎ *818/754–1051* 🌐 *www.mofongosrestaurant.com.*

Rodini Park

$ | **MEDITERRANEAN** | Nestled in the heart of the NoHo Arts District amid newly minted high-rises, Rodini Park's "build your own" concept and highly rated homemade pastries make it the place to go for a quick, fresh, and delicious take on Greek cuisine. Between the multiple protein, topping, and sauce offerings, it offers something for all palates. **Known for:** chicken shawarma; baklava cheesecake; Mount Olympus sauce. [$] *Average main: $13* ✉ *11049 Magnolia Blvd., North Hollywood* ☎ *818/358–4802* 🌐 *www.rodinipark.com.*

The Swingin Door BBQ

$$ | **BARBECUE** | **FAMILY** | Los Angeles is not known for barbecue so when a place like the Swingin Door does it right, it's worth taking note. Take a gander around and you'll see smokers slowly cooking all that meaty goodness, ready to be enjoyed on plastic-covered tables and doused with a variety of different hot sauces (which you can buy to take home). **Known for:** baby back ribs; assorted hot sauces; rare Texas-style barbecue in the city. [$] *Average main: $20* ✉ *11018 Vanowen St., North Hollywood* ☎ *818/763–8996* 🌐 *bbqnorthhollywood.wixsite.com/swingindoor* ⏲ *Closed Mon.*

TeaPop

$ | **CAFÉ** | At first glance, TeaPop may seem to be doing too many things at once, but this tea-centric café, with its art gallery–slash–industrial modern interior and picturesque patio, is a perfect spot to not only study or take a breather, but also to catch pop-up events like comedy nights and workshops. Don't let the hipster vibes turn you off—the service is fantastic and the drinks delicious. **Known for:** vintage milk tea; hipster vibes; community events. $ *Average main: $4* ✉ *5050 Vineland Ave., North Hollywood* ☎ *323/927–0429* ⊕ *teapopla.com.*

Hotels

The Garland

$$ | **HOTEL** | **FAMILY** | The cool kid of the Valley with a Hollywood pedigree, the 7-acre hideaway that is the Garland isn't technically a resort, but it might as well be considering the long list of activities and amenities it has on offer for guests. **Pros:** large pool and play area; private balcony or patio in each room; plenty of in-house activities and amenities. **Cons:** close to the freeway; weekly nonrefundable $75 pet fee; far from other major Los Angeles sights. $ *Rooms from: $319* ✉ *4222 Vineland Ave., North Hollywood* ☎ *818/980–8000, 800/238–3759* ⊕ *www.beverlygarland.com* ⤳ *256 rooms* ⦿| *No Meals.*

Shopping

Circus Liquor

WINE/SPIRITS | It might seem strange to include a liquor store on your Valley itinerary, but this particular liquor store is a quintessential L.A. photo op. There's a 32-foot neon clown sign outside, which was already L.A. famous but was made even more so by being featured in *Clueless*. And, while here, you might as well pick up some booze. ✉ *5600 Vineland Ave., North Hollywood* ☎ *818/769–1500.*

The Iliad Book Shop

BOOKS | For over 30 years, Iliad not only has been selling used books but has been a set piece on a number of TV shows and movies, including *Lethal Weapon 3*. But with a collection of 150,000 books of all genres, including a solid selection of graphic novels, it's worth a visit just to peruse the aisles and find your next favorite novel. ✉ *5400 Cahuenga Blvd., North Hollywood* ☎ *818/509–2665* ⊕ *www.iliadbooks.com.*

Midcenturyla

FURNITURE | The idea of going to Los Angeles to buy furniture may sound nuts, but go ahead, indulge your inner designer at Midcenturyla, a curated furniture store brimming with custom and vintage mid-century modern desks, sofas, and more. ✉ *5333 Cahuenga Blvd., North Hollywood* ☎ *818/509–3050* ⊕ *midcenturyla.com.*

Universal City

Although it has its own zip code and subway station, Universal City, over the hill from Hollywood, is simply the name for the unincorporated area of Los Angeles where Universal Studios Hollywood and CityWalk are located.

Sights

★ Universal Studios Hollywood

THEME PARK | **FAMILY** | A theme park with classic attractions like roller coasters and thrill rides, Universal Studios Hollywood also provides that unique brand of thrill you get from the magic of the movies, with tours of sets and movie-themed rides. Unlike other amusement parks, this one is centered around the biggest blockbusters, with rides like Jurassic World – The Ride and Harry Potter and the Forbidden Journey as well as worlds like the brand-new Super Nintendo World, which boasts the fun and highly interactive Mario Kart: Bowser's Challenge and is, in and of itself, a game—exactly the kind of experience that Super Mario fans truly enjoy. If you're in town in October, the park's Halloween Horror Nights is a must-visit, featuring mazes full of monsters, murderers, and jump scares.

The world-famous Studio Tour takes you around the Universal backlot, home to working soundstages and exterior sets where many popular movies and shows have been filmed. During the tram tour, you'll witness King Kong save you from massive predators, see the airplane wreckage from *War of the Worlds,* ride along with the cast of the *Fast and the Furious,* and have a close call with Norman Bates from *Psycho.*

■ TIP→ **The tram ride is usually the best place to begin your visit, because the lines become longer as the day goes on.**

Geared more toward adults, CityWalk is a separate venue run by Universal Studios, where you'll find shops, restaurants, nightclubs, and movie theaters. ✉ *100 Universal City Plaza, Universal City* ☎ *800/864–8377* 🌐 *www.universalstudioshollywood.com* 🎟 *$139.*

🍴 Restaurants

Three Broomsticks/Hog's Head
$ | BRITISH | FAMILY | While theme-park food is notoriously bad, the Three Broomsticks and Hog's Head, both at the Wizarding World of Harry Potter, are exceptions. Yes, you have to go into the park itself to grab a bite, but if you happen to be here (which, let's be honest, is probably the only reason you're in Universal City), you should wander in and feast on large helpings of traditional British fare and gulp down frozen butterbeer. **Known for:** pretty good fish-and-chips; iconic butterbeer; ultimate dining mecca for Harry Potter fans. [$] *Average main: $17* ✉ *Universal Studios Hollywood, 100 Universal City Plaza, Universal City* ☎ *800/864–8377* 🌐 *www.universalstudioshollywood.com.*

The Toothsome Chocolate Emporium & Savory Feast Kitchen
$$ | AMERICAN | FAMILY | It's a lot, from the mouthful of a restaurant name, and the caters-to-everyone extensive menu, to the oversized steampunk-style decor (think: airship mural and nearly 100-foot-high smokestacks), and the characters who interact with diners. But set in Universal CityWalk, it is the perfect amount of "a lot" to meet your fanciful, over-the-top mood after visiting theme parks. **Known for:** broad menu so something for everyone; steampunk gadgets and decor; sweets and more sweets. [$] *Average main: $23* ✉ *100 Universal City Plaza, Hollywood* ☎ *818/622–2222* 🌐 *www.universalstudioshollywood.com/web/en/us/things-to-do/dining/citywalk/toothsome-chocolate-emporium-and-savory-feast-kitchen.*

🛏 Hotels

Sheraton Universal
$$ | HOTEL | FAMILY | With large meeting spaces and a knowledgeable staff, this Sheraton buzzes year-round with business travelers and families, providing easy access to the free shuttle that takes guests to adjacent Universal Studios and CityWalk. **Pros:** pool area with cabanas and bar; convenient for visitors to Universal Studios; family friendly. **Cons:** parking is pricey; touristy crowd; chain hotel feel. [$] *Rooms from: $250* ✉ *333 Universal Hollywood Dr., Universal City* ☎ *818/980–1212, 888/627–7184* 🌐 *www.sheratonuniversal.com* 🛏 *461 rooms* 🍽 *No Meals.*

Chapter 10

DOWNTOWN AND KOREATOWN

Updated by
Paul Feinstein

 Sights
★★★★☆

 Restaurants
★★★★★

 Hotels
★★★★☆

 Shopping
★★★☆☆

 Nightlife
★★★★★

NEIGHBORHOOD SNAPSHOT

TOP EXPERIENCES

■ **Visit Frank Gehry's Disney Concert Hall:** Be wowed by the genius architecture, and grab tickets for an L.A. Phil performance led by Gustavo Dudamel.

■ **See a Lakers or Kings game:** Catch the action at the Crypto.com Arena and see famous faces on and off the court.

■ **Take a historic walking tour:** The L.A. Conservancy offers several tours, such as the Art Deco tour, where you can see old architectural glamour all over the streets of downtown. ⊕ *www.laconservancy.org/tours*

■ **Peruse the Last Bookstore:** This is not only one of the best bookstores in Los Angeles, it's also one of the most fantastical. Find rare and used books and LPs downstairs, then go upstairs into a labyrinth of oddities.

■ **Get pampered and go sing in K-town:** Koreatown is known for its bevy of open-late Korean spas like Wi and Aroma, but after getting a full body scrub, head out to for late-night karaoke sessions at spots like Pharaoh, Break Room 86, and Brass Monkey.

VIEWFINDER

Hotel Cecil: If you watched the Netflix show, *The Vanishing at the Cecil Hotel,* stand on Main St. closer to 7th St., to snap yourself pointing up at the Cecil Hotel sign. ⊠ *640 S. Main St.*

Chinatown Gateway Monument: Hovering over Broadway are two giant, golden dragons who look like they're about to do battle. For an uncrowded shot underneath, you'll want to go right before daybreak on a weekend morning. ⊠ *603 N. Broadway*

Tom's One Hour Photo: This one-hour photo shop in Koreatown specializes in classic 80s and 90s portrait photography, made famous after country superstar Kacey Musgraves did an Instagram-fueled shoot here. ⊠ *4158 Beverly Blvd.*

GETTING HERE

The good news is that freeways 5, 101, 110, and 10 all get you to Downtown; the bad news is that the traffic can delay your travels. If you're coming from the Hollywood area, skip the freeways altogether and take Sunset Boulevard, which turns into César Chávez Boulevard. If you're coming from LAX, take the 105 East to the 110 North. Be warned: parking can be very expensive. It's better to rideshare or take the Metro.

For Koreatown, it's all side streets. The official borders of Koreatown are Western Ave. on the west side running north–south between Third St. and Olympic Blvd. to Vermont Ave. on the east side. But if you're heading Downtown on the 10 or the 101, Western and Vermont both have freeway exits that will lead you straight there.

PLANNING YOUR TIME

■ Visit weekdays during the day, when the area is bustling and restaurants are open for lunch. The streets are packed weekend nights, and wait times can be long at restaurants and bars. Weekday evenings tend to be much quieter and it's easy to get yourself a table or a barstool. Seeing everything in one day is possible, but it's best to spread it out over two.

If there's one thing Angelenos love, it's a makeover, and city planners have put the wheels in motion for a dramatic revitalization of this area in recent years. Downtown is both glamorous and gritty and is an example of Los Angeles's complexity as a whole. There's a dizzying variety of experiences not to be missed here if you're curious about the artistic, historic, ethnic, or sports-loving sides of L.A.

Downtown Los Angeles isn't just one neighborhood: it's a cluster of pedestrian-friendly enclaves where you can sample an eclectic mix of flavors, wander through world-class museums, and enjoy great live performances or sports events.

As you venture into the different neighborhoods of Downtown—**Chinatown, Little Tokyo,** and **El Pueblo de Los Angeles**—take advantage of the tastes, sounds, and sights. Eat roast duck in Chinatown, red bean cakes in Little Tokyo, or pickled cactus on Olvera Street. Spend time browsing the **Grand Central Market,** where stalls are filled with colorful locally grown produce and homemade treats from tamales and olive bread to Texan barbecue and Thai-style chicken over rice. For art lovers, the **Broad Museum** has one of the most important modern and contemporary art collections, while those who are fans of architecture should make a point to see the Gehry creation, the **Walt Disney Concert Hall,** or the massive, geometrically designed **Cathedral of Our Lady for the Angels.**

To see the glory of Broadway's golden years, look up above the storefront signs, and you'll find the marvelous architecture and theater marquees of the majestic buildings they reside in. From the late 19th century to the 1950s—before malls and freeways—**Broadway** glittered with the finest shops and the highest number of luxurious theaters in the world, making it a rich, cultural haven. Though it remains the main road through Downtown's Historic Core, the area has changed dramatically over the years. Though it once exclusively housed businesses catering to mostly Mexican and Central American immigrants, there are now trendy pockets for shopping and dining. However, you can still find the classic experience of mariachi and *banda* music blaring from electronics-store speakers between 1st and 9th Streets, street-food vendors hawking sliced papaya sprinkled with chili powder, and fancy dresses for a girl's *quinceañera* (15th birthday). Bordering Downtown L.A. to the west, Koreatown is one of the most diverse

Tulips by Jeff Koons is just one of the many modern art exhibits at the Broad Museum.

neighborhoods in the entire city. Though its history is steeped in Korean culture (it houses the largest Korean population outside of Korea), there is much more that makes this eclectic neighborhood unique. Spanning 3 square miles, Koreatown is home to some of the most vibrant nightlife in L.A. from late-night karaoke bars and nightclubs to classic bars and lounges. The dining scene is also varied with a bevy of Korean BBQ gems but also burger joints, seafood spots, Oaxacan cuisine, and French fine dining. If late-night drinking isn't your thing, you can also indulge in late-night spa'ing as Koreatown is home to several classic and unique Korean spas that will make your body melt.

One important note for visitors. L.A.'s unhoused population has unofficial numbers reaching 100,000 people. Nowhere is this more prevalent than in Downtown L.A. You'll be confronted with the dichotomy of the city's rich and poor as sparkling new high-rises are flanked by tent encampments. Walking around downtown at night can be dangerous, not because people are unhoused in general, but because of the problem of drugs, crime, etc., that are an unfortunate byproduct of the overwhelming number of people on the streets.

Downtown

Sights

★ Angels Flight Railway

HISTORIC SIGHT | The turn-of-the-20th-century funicular, dubbed "the shortest railway in the world," operated between 1901 and 1969, when it was dismantled to make room for an urban renewal project. Almost 30 years later, Angels Flight returned with its original orange-and-black wooden cable cars hauling travelers up a 298-foot incline from Hill Street to the fountain-filled Watercourt at California Plaza. Your reward is a stellar view of the neighborhood. Tickets are $1 each way, but you can buy a souvenir round-trip ticket for $2 if you want something to take home with you. ⊠ *351 S. Hill St., between 3rd and 4th Sts., Downtown* ☎ *213/626–1901* ⊕ *www.angelsflight.org.*

Avila Adobe

HISTORIC HOME | Built as a private home for cattle rancher and pueblo of L.A. mayor Francisco Ávila in 1818, this museum preserves seven of what were originally 18 rooms in the city's oldest standing residence. The graceful structure features 3-foot-thick walls made of adobe brick over cottonwood timbers, a traditional interior courtyard, and 1840s-era furnishings that bring to life an era when the city was still part of Mexico. The museum is open daily from 9 am to 4 pm and the complex is a California Historical Landmark. ⊠ *10 Olvera St., Downtown* ☎ *213/485–6855* ⊕ *elpueblo.lacity.org* Ⓜ *Union Station.*

Bradbury Building

NOTABLE BUILDING | Stunning wrought-iron railings, ornate plaster moldings, pink marble staircases, a birdcage elevator, and a skylighted atrium that rises almost 50 feet—it's easy to see why the Bradbury Building leaves visitors awestruck. Designed in 1893 by a novice architect who drew his inspiration from a science-fiction story and a conversation with his dead brother via an Ouija board, the office building was originally the site of turn-of-the-20th-century sweatshops, but now it houses a variety of businesses. Scenes from *Blade Runner, Chinatown,* and *500 Days of Summer* were filmed here, which means there's often a barrage of tourists snapping photos. Visits are limited to the lobby and the first-floor landing.

■ TIP→ **Historic Downtown walking tours hosted by the L.A. Conservancy cost $15 and include the Bradbury Building.** ⊠ *304 S. Broadway, Downtown* ☎ *213/626–1893*

⊕ *www.laconservancy.org/locations/bradbury-building* Ⓜ *Pershing Square.*

★ The Broad Museum

ART MUSEUM | The talk of Los Angeles's art world when it opened in 2015, this museum in an intriguing, honeycomb-looking building was created by philanthropists Eli and Edythe Broad (rhymes with "road") to showcase their stunning private collection of contemporary art, amassed over five decades and still growing. With upward of 2,000 pieces by more than 200 artists, the collection has in-depth representations of the work of such prominent names as Jean Michel Basquiat, Jeff Koons, Ed Ruscha, Cindy Sherman, Cy Twombly, Kara Walker, and Christopher Wool. The "veil and vault" design of the main building integrates gallery space and storage space (visitors can glimpse the latter through a window in the stairwell): the veil refers to the fiberglass, concrete, and steel exterior; the vault is the concrete base. Temporary exhibits and works from the permanent collection are arranged in the small first-floor rooms and in the more expansive third floor of the museum, so you can explore everything in a few hours. Next door to the Broad is a small plaza with olive trees and seating, as well as the museum restaurant, Otium. Admission to the museum is free, but book timed tickets in advance to guarantee entry. ⊠ *221 S. Grand Ave., Downtown* ☎ *213/232–6200* ⊕ *www.thebroad.org* 🎟 *Free* ☉ *Closed Mon.* ⚏ *Tickets required in advance* Ⓜ *Civic Center/Grand Park.*

California African American Museum

ART MUSEUM | With more than 4,500 historical artifacts, this museum showcases contemporary art of the African diaspora. Artists represented here include Betye Saar, Charles Haywood, and June Edmonds. The museum has a research library with more than 6,000 books available for public use.

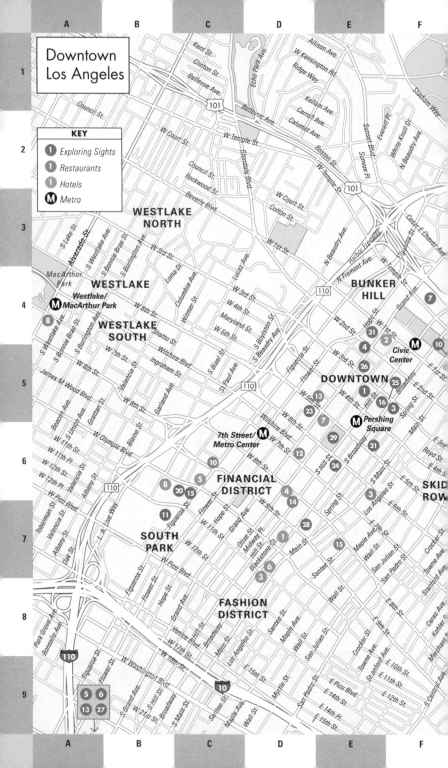

Sights ▼

1 Angels Flight Railway ... **E5**
2 Avila Adobe **G4**
3 Bradbury Building **F5**
4 The Broad Museum **E5**
5 California African
   American Museum..... **A9**
6 California
   Science Center **A9**
7 Cathedral of Our Lady
   of the Angels **F4**
8 Chinatown **G3**
9 Chinese American
   Museum **G4**
10 City Hall of
   Los Angeles **F5**
11 Crypto.com Arena **B7**
12 El Pueblo de
   Los Angeles **G4**
13 Exposition Park **A9**
14 Geffen Contemporary
   at MOCA **G5**
15 GRAMMY Museum...... **C6**
16 Grand Central Market... **E5**
17 Italian American Museum
   of Los Angeles **G4**
18 Japanese American
   Cultural and
   Community Center...... **G6**
19 Japanese American
   National Museum....... **G5**
20 L.A. Live **C6**
21 The Last Bookstore...... **E6**
22 Little Tokyo.............. **G5**
23 Los Angeles
   Central Library **D5**
24 Los Angeles Theatre **E6**
25 Million Dollar Theater... **F5**
26 MOCA Grand Avenue ... **E5**
27 Natural History
   Museum of
   Los Angeles County **A9**
28 Orpheum Theatre **D7**
29 Pershing Square......... **E6**
30 Union Station............ **H4**
31 Walt Disney
   Concert Hall **E4**

Restaurants ▼

1 Bavel **H7**
2 Bestia **I9**
3 Cole's French Dip **E7**
4 Damian..................... **I9**
5 De La Nonna **G6**
6 The Factory Kitchen.... **H7**
7 Howlin' Ray's............ **G3**
8 Langer's Delicatessen-
   Restaurant............... **A4**
9 Majordomo **I2**
10 Original Pantry Cafe..... **C6**
11 Philippe The Original ... **G4**
12 Q Sushi.................... **D6**
13 71Above.................... **E5**
14 Shibumi **D6**
15 Sonoratown **E7**
16 Sushi Gen................ **G6**

Hotels ▼

1 Ace Hotel Downtown
   Los Angeles **D7**
2 Conrad Los Angeles..... **F4**
3 Downtown L.A.
   Proper Hotel............. **D7**
4 Freehand
   Los Angeles **D6**
5 Hotel Figueroa **C6**
6 The Hoxton **D7**
7 Millennium
   Biltmore Hotel............ **E5**
8 The Ritz-Carlton,
   Los Angeles **B6**

■TIP➔ **If possible, visit on a Sunday or Thursday, when there's almost always a diverse lineup of speakers and performances.** ⊠ *600 State Dr., Exposition Park* ☎ *213/744–7432* ⊕ *www.caamuseum.org* ⊠ *Free; parking $15* ⊗ *Closed Mon. and Tues.* Ⓜ *Expo/Vermont Station.*

California Science Center

SCIENCE MUSEUM | FAMILY | You're bound to see excited kids running up to the dozens of interactive exhibits here that illustrate the prevalence of science in everyday life. Clustered in different "worlds," the center keeps young guests busy for hours. They can design their own buildings and learn how to make them earthquake-proof; watch GLOBAL ZONE, where you can see Earth's global cycles of air, water, land, and life exhibited on a giant interactive globe. One of the exhibits in the Air and Space section shows how astronauts Pete Conrad and Dick Gordon made it to outer space in the Gemini 11 capsule in 1966. The IMAX theater screens science-related large-format films that change throughout the year. ⊠ *700 Exposition Park Dr., Exposition Park* ☎ *323/724–3623* ⊕ *www. californiasciencecenter.org* ⊠ *Permanent exhibits free; fees for some attractions, special exhibits, and IMAX screenings vary; parking $15* Ⓜ *Expo/Vermont.*

Cathedral of Our Lady of the Angels

CHURCH | A half block from Frank Gehry's curvaceous Walt Disney Concert Hall sits the austere Cathedral of Our Lady of the Angels—a spiritual draw as well as an architectural attraction. Controversy surrounded Spanish architect José Rafael Moneo's unconventional design for the seat of the Archdiocese of Los Angeles. But judging from the swarms of visitors and the standing-room-only holiday masses, the church has carved out a niche for itself in Downtown L.A.

The plaza in front is glaringly bright on sunny days, though a children's play garden with bronze animals mitigates the starkness somewhat. Head underground to wander the mausoleum's mazelike white-marble corridors. Free self-guided tours start at the entrance fountain at 1 pm on weekdays.

■TIP➔ **There's plenty of underground visitors' parking; the vehicle entrance is on Hill Street.** ⊠ *555 W. Temple St., Downtown* ☎ *213/680–5200* ⊕ *www.olacathedral.org* ⊠ *Free* Ⓜ *Civic Center/Grand Park.*

Chinatown

HISTORIC DISTRICT | Smaller than San Francisco's Chinatown, this neighborhood near Union Station still represents a slice of East Asian life. Sidewalks are usually jammed with tourists, locals, and residents hustling from shop to shop picking up goods, spices, and trinkets from small shops and mini-plazas that line the street. Although some longtime establishments have closed in recent years, the area still pulses with its founding culture. During Chinese New Year, giant dragons snake down the street. And, of course, there are the many restaurants and quick-bite cafés specializing in Chinese feasts. In recent years, a slew of hip eateries like Howlin' Ray's and Majordomo have injected the area with vibrancy.

An influx of local artists has added a spark to the neighborhood by taking up empty spaces and opening galleries along Chung King Road, a faded pedestrian passage behind the West Plaza shopping center between Hill and Yale. Also look for galleries along a little side street called Gin Ling Way on the east side of Broadway. Chinatown has its main action on North Broadway. There are several garages available for parking here that range from $15 to $25 per day. ⊠ *Bordered by the 110, 101, and 5 freeways, Downtown* ⊕ *chinatownla.com* Ⓜ *Union Station.*

Chinese American Museum

HISTORY MUSEUM | Because it's in El Pueblo Plaza, you might assume that this

L.A.'s Chinatown has its share of Chinese restaurants, shops, and cultural institutions, but you'll also find a growing community of artists and galleries.

museum features Mexican American art, but it's actually the last surviving structure of L.A.'s original Chinatown. Three floors of exhibits reveal the different cultures that have called this area home, as well as how the original residents paved the way for what is now a vibrant and varied Chinatown. Rotating exhibits feature the work of Chinese American artists. ⊠ *425 N. Los Angeles St., Downtown* ☎ *213/485–8567* ⊕ *www. camla.org* ⊡ *$3* ⊘ *Closed Mon.–Thurs.* Ⓜ *Union Station.*

City Hall of Los Angeles
GOVERNMENT BUILDING | This gorgeous 1928 landmark building is a TV star—it was in the opening scenes of *Dragnet* and served as the Daily Planet building in the original *Adventures of Superman*. During extensive renovations, the original Lindburg Beacon was put back in action atop the hall's 13-story tower. The revolving spotlight, inaugurated by President Calvin Coolidge from the White House via a telegraph key, was used from 1928 to 1941 to guide pilots into the Los Angeles airport. The observation deck, located on the 27th floor, is free to the public and has a stellar view of the greater Los Angeles area. ⊠ *200 N. Spring St., Downtown* ☎ *213/473–3231* ⊕ *www.lacity. org* ⊘ *Closed weekends* Ⓜ *Civic Center/ Grand Park.*

Crypto.com Arena
SPORTS VENUE | Home to the Lakers, the Sparks, and the ice hockey team Los Angeles Kings, the Crypto.com Arena is Downtown's top sports destination. It's also the preferred venue for superstars like Bruce Springsteen, Ariana Grande, and Justin Bieber. Though not open for visits except during events, the saucer-shape building is eye-catching. ⊠ *1111 S. Figueroa St., Downtown* ☎ *213/742– 7100* ⊕ *www.staplescenter.com* Ⓜ *Pico.*

★ El Pueblo de Los Angeles
HISTORIC SIGHT | The oldest section of the city, known as El Pueblo de Los Angeles, represents the rich Mexican heritage of L.A. It had a close shave with

disintegration in the early 20th century, but key buildings were preserved, and eventually **Olvera Street,** the district's heart, was transformed into a Mexican American marketplace. Today vendors still sell puppets, leather goods, sandals, and woolen shawls from stalls lining the narrow street. You can find everything from salt and pepper shakers shaped like donkeys to gorgeous glassware and pottery.

At the beginning of Olvera Street is the Plaza, a Mexican-style park with plenty of benches and walkways shaded by a huge Moreton Bay fig tree. On weekends, mariachi bands and folkloric dance groups perform. Nearby places worth investigating include the historic Avila Adobe, the Chinese American Museum, the Plaza Firehouse Museum, and the America Tropical Interpretive Center. Exhibits at the Italian American Museum of Los Angeles chronicle the area's formerly heavy Italian presence. ⊠ *Avila Adobe/Olvera Street Visitors Center, 125 Paseo De La Plaza, Downtown* ☎ *213/485–6855* ⊕ *elpueblo.lacity.org* ⌕ *Free for Olvera St. and self-guided tours; fees at some museums.*

Exposition Park

CITY PARK | Originally developed in 1872 as an agricultural park, this 160-acre park has a lovely sunken rose garden and three museums—the California African American Museum, the California Science Center, and the Natural History Museum of Los Angeles County—as well as an IMAX theater. There's also Los Angeles Memorial Coliseum where Olympic festivities were held in 1932 and 1984 and where USC games are now played. The newest addition to the park is the Banc of California Stadium, a 22,000-seat arena that's home to the LAFC soccer club. Good news for commuters: the Metro Expo Line, which connects the Westside to Downtown Los Angeles, has a stop at Exposition Park.

⚠ **Note that the park and neighborhood are sketchy at night.** ⊠ *700 Exposition Park Dr., Exposition Park* ☎ *213/744–2294* ⊕ *expositionpark.ca.gov* ⌕ *Parking $15* Ⓜ *Expo/Vermont.*

Geffen Contemporary at MOCA

ART MUSEUM | The Geffen Contemporary is one of architect Frank Gehry's boldest creations. One of three MOCA branches, the 40,000 square feet of exhibition space was once used as a police car warehouse. The museum's permanent collection includes works from artists like Willem de Kooning, Franz Kline, Jackson Pollock, Mark Rothko, and Cindy Sherman.

■ TIP→ **Present your TAP metro card to get two-for-one admission.** ⊠ *152 N. Central Ave., Downtown* ☎ *213/626–6222* ⊕ *www.moca.org/visit/geffen-contemporary* ⌕ *Free; special exhibitions $18 or free every Thurs. 5–8; parking $9* ⊙ *Closed Mon.*

GRAMMY Museum

OTHER MUSEUM | The GRAMMY Museum brings the music industry to life. Throughout four floors and 30,000 square feet of space, the museum showcases rare footage of GRAMMY performances, plus rotating and interactive exhibits on award-winning musicians and the history of music. A 200-seat theater is great for live events that include screenings, lectures, interviews, and intimate music performances. ⊠ *800 W. Olympic Blvd., Downtown* ☎ *213/765–6800* ⊕ *www.grammymuseum.org* ⌕ *$18* ⊙ *Closed Tues.* Ⓜ *Pico.*

★ Grand Central Market

MARKET | With options that include handmade white-corn tamales, warm olive bread, dried figs, Mexican fruit drinks, and much more, this mouthwatering gathering place is the city's largest and most active food market. The spot bustles nonstop with locals and visitors surveying the butcher shop's display of everything from lambs' heads to pigs' tails. Produce stalls are piled high with locally grown avocados and heirloom tomatoes. Stop by Chiles Secos at stall No. 30 for a remarkable selection of rare chilies and spices; Ramen Hood at No. 23, for sumptuous vegan noodles and broth; or Sticky Rice at stall No. 24, for fantastic Thai-style chicken. Even if you don't plan on buying anything, it's a great place to browse and people-watch. ⊠ *317 S. Broadway, Downtown* ☎ *213/624–2378* ⊕ *www.grandcentralmarket.com* ⊠ *Free* Ⓜ *Pershing Square.*

Italian American Museum of Los Angeles

HISTORY MUSEUM | This landmark, constructed in 1908, is noteworthy because its south wall bears an infamous mural. Famed Mexican muralist David Alfaro Siqueiros shocked his patrons in the 1930s by depicting an oppressed worker of Latin America being crucified on a cross topped by a menacing American eagle. The anti-imperialist mural was promptly whitewashed but was later restored by the Getty Museum. It can be seen on the Italian Hall building today. Today the site functions as a museum and has seven color-coded exhibits on the history of Italian Americans. The site is also home to Taste of Italy, an annual event that celebrates the Italian culinary history of Los Angeles. ⊠ *644 N. Main St., Downtown* ☎ *213/485–8432* ⊕ *iamla. org* ⊙ *Museum closed Mon.* Ⓜ *Union Station.*

Japanese American Cultural and Community Center

ARTS CENTER | Plenty of traditional and contemporary cultural events make this center well worth the trip. Founded in 1980, JACCC is home to a number of civic and arts organizations. Through the center's basement you reach the James Irvine Garden, a serene sunken space where local plants mix with bamboo, Japanese wisteria, and Japanese maples. The main floor of the museum houses the George J. Doizaki Gallery, which has 2,000 square feet of exhibition space and has housed everything from national treasures of Japan to the Bugaku costumes from the Kasuga Grand Shrine in Nara. An 880-seat theater is known for any number of performing arts shows including Bunraku Puppet Theater and the Grand Kabuki of Japan. ⊠ *244 S. San Pedro St., Downtown* ☎ *213/628–2725* ⊕ *www.jaccc.org* ⊙ *Doizaki Gallery closed Mon. and Tues.; Japanese garden closed Mon.* Ⓜ *Pershing Square.*

Japanese American National Museum

HISTORY MUSEUM | What was it like to grow up on a sugar plantation in Hawaii? How difficult was life for Japanese Americans interned in concentration camps during World War II? These questions are addressed by changing exhibitions at this museum in Little Tokyo that also include fun tributes to anime and Hello Kitty. Volunteer docents are on hand to share their own stories and experiences. The museum occupies its original site in a renovated 1925 Buddhist temple and an 85,000-square-foot adjacent pavilion.

■TIP➔ **Take the Metro and get $2 off general admission and a 10% discount at adjoining Chado Tea Room.** ⊠ *100 N. Central Ave., off E. 1st St., Downtown* ☎ *213/625–0414* ⊕ *www.janm.org* ⊠ *$16; free Thurs. 5–8 and all day every 3rd Thurs. of month* ⊙ *Closed Mon.* Ⓜ *Civic Center/Grand Park.*

L.A. Live

PLAZA/SQUARE | The mammoth L.A. Live entertainment complex was opened in 2007 when there was little to do or see in this section of Downtown. Since its inception, this once creepy ghost town has become a major hub for sports, concerts, award shows, and more. The first things you'll notice as you emerge from the parking lot are the giant LED screens and sparkling lights, and the buzz of crowds as they head out to dinner before or after a Lakers game, movie, or live

The Los Angeles Metro

Long ago, Los Angeles had an enviable public transportation system known as the Pacific Electric Red Cars, trolleys that made it possible to get around this sprawling city without an automobile. In the mid-1900s, the last of the Red Cars disappeared, and L.A. lost itself in the car culture.

That culture is here to stay, but in recent years, a new rail system has emerged. You can now take the subway through parts of Downtown, Hollywood, Pasadena, and North Hollywood. The Red Line starts at Downtown's Union Station, then curves northwest to Hollywood and on to Universal City and North Hollywood. The Blue and Green light-rail lines are designed for commuters. The Gold Line goes from Union Station up to Azusa, stopping in Pasadena. Take the Expo Line from Downtown to Santa Monica, or the Purple Line from Union Station through Koreatown and into Mid-City and its Restaurant Row. Future plans include a line that runs all the way to the Los Angeles International Airport (LAX).

The Metro Rail stations are worth exploring themselves as you can see the colorful murals, sculptures, and architectural elements that illustrate themes of Los Angeles history.

The Universal City station is next to the site of the Campo de Caheunga, where Mexico relinquished control of California to the United States in 1847. The station features a time line of the area's past done in the traditional style of colorful Mexican folk art.

The North Hollywood station also celebrates local history, including native Gabrielino culture, many immigrant communities, Amelia Earhart (a local), Western wear designer Nudie, and the history of transportation in L.A. County.

There are film reels on the ceiling of the Hollywood and Vine station as well as original Paramount Pictures film projectors from the 1930s, and floor paving modeled after the yellow brick road from *The Wizard of Oz.* Imposing, glass-clad columns juxtaposed with rock formations can be seen at the Vermont and Beverly station. The old Red Car trolley makes an appearance in the Hollywood and Western station.

show at the Microsoft Theater. There are dozens of restaurants and eateries here, including Los Angeles favorite Katsuya, the spot for sizzling Kobe beef platters and excellent sushi (the crab rolls are not to be missed).

■ **TIP→ Park for free on weekdays from 11 am to 2 pm if you eat at one of the dozen or so restaurants here.** ✉ *800 W. Olympic Blvd., Downtown* ☎ *213/763–5483* ⊕ *www.lalive.com* Ⓜ *Pico.*

★ **The Last Bookstore**

STORE/MALL | California's largest used and new book and record shop is a favorite for both book lovers and fans of a good photo op, thanks to elements like an archway created from curving towers of books, a peephole carved into the stacks, and an in-store vault devoted to horror texts. Aside from the awesome aesthetics, shoppers will love to get lost in the store's collection of affordable books, art, and music. ✉ *453 S. Spring St., ground fl., Downtown* ☎ *213/488–0599* ⊕ *www.lastbookstorela.com* Ⓜ *Pershing Square.*

★ Little Tokyo

HISTORIC DISTRICT | One of three official Japantowns in the country—all of which are in California—Little Tokyo is blossoming again thanks to the next generation of Japanese Americans setting up small businesses. Besides dozens of sushi bars, tempura restaurants, and karaoke bars, there's a lovely garden at the Japanese American Cultural and Community Center and a renovated 1925 Buddhist temple with an ornate entrance at the Japanese American National Museum.

On 1st Street you'll find a strip of buildings from the early 1900s. Look down when you get near San Pedro Street to see the art installation called *Omoide no Shotokyo* ("Remembering Old Little Tokyo"). Embedded in the sidewalk are brass inscriptions naming the original businesses, quoted reminiscences from residents, and steel time lines of Japanese American history up to World War II. Nisei Week (a *nisei* is a second-generation Japanese American) is celebrated every August with traditional drums, dancing, a carnival, and a huge parade.

TIP→ Docent-led walking tours are available by appointment on occasional Saturdays starting at 10:15 am. The cost is $15 and should be reserved in advance at littletokyohs.org. ✉ *Bounded by 1st and 3rd Sts., the 101 and 110 freeways, and L.A. River, Downtown* ☎ *213/880–6875* ⊕ *www.visitlittletokyo.com* Ⓜ *Civic Center/Grand Park Station.*

Los Angeles Central Library

LIBRARY | The nation's third-largest public library, the handsome Los Angeles Central Library was designed in 1926 by Bertram Goodhue. Restored to their pristine condition, a pyramid tower and a torch symbolizing the "light of learning" crown the building. The Cook rotunda on the second floor features murals by Dean Cornwell depicting the history of California, and the Tom Bradley Wing, named for a famed L.A. mayor, has a soaring eight-story atrium.

The library offers frequent special exhibits, and don't ignore the gift shop, which is loaded with unique items for readers and writers. Free art and architecture tours are offered Friday at 12:30, Saturday at 11, and Sunday at 2. An Art-in-the-Garden tour happens once a month on Saturday at 12:30 pm. A self-guided tour map is also available on the library's website. ✉ *630 W. 5th St., Downtown* ☎ *213/228–7000* ⊕ *www.lapl.org* ✉ *Free* Ⓜ *Pershing Square.*

Los Angeles Theatre

HISTORIC SIGHT | Built in 1931, the 2,200-seat Los Angeles Theatre opened with the premiere of Charlie Chaplin's classic *City Lights*. Full of glorious French baroque–inspired details, the six-story lobby is awe-inspiring with its dramatic staircase, enormous fountain, grandiose chandeliers, and ornate gold detailing. You can occasionally witness the old Hollywood glamour by catching a special movie screening. ✉ *615 S. Broadway, Downtown* ☎ *213/629–2939* ⊕ *www. losangelestheatre.com* Ⓜ *Pershing Square.*

Million Dollar Theater

HISTORIC SIGHT | The Million Dollar Theater opened in 1918 as part of Sid Grauman's famed chain of movie theaters. This Spanish baroque–style venue had the special feature of having its own organ. Film stars such as Gloria Swanson, Rudolph Valentino, and a young Judy Garland frequently made appearances. In the '40s, the venue swung with jazz and big band performers including Billie Holiday. The theater is open for special events and is worth a stop if you're walking past to inspect the lavish exterior with entertainment figures carved into the molding. ✉ *307 S. Broadway, Downtown* ☎ *213/359–6007.*

MOCA Grand Avenue

ART MUSEUM | The main branch of the Museum of Contemporary Art, designed by Arata Isozaki, contains underground galleries and presents

Watts Towers

Take a 20-minute drive south of Downtown and gaze upon one of the city's most stunning sights: the Watts Towers.

It took 33 years for Italian immigrant Simon Rodia to construct the Watts Towers—a massive steel structure comprising 17 interlaced mosaic-tiled spirals. Rodia settled in Los Angeles in the early 20th century and in 1921 bought a parcel of land in the Watts neighborhood of South Los Angeles. Over the next three and half decades, he single-handedly constructed the towers—without the use of construction equipment or scaffolding.

He was asked over and over a simple question: Why? And he gave a lot of different answers—it kept him away from the bottle, he didn't have a job, he just wanted to do something grand.

Rodia died in 1965, the same year the Watts riots erupted. Though much of the area was completely destroyed, the towers stood tall. They became a symbol, not only for the strength of that community, but for the enduring creativity of the entire city.

elegant exhibitions. A huge Nancy Rubins sculpture fashioned from used airplane parts graces the museum's front plaza. The museum gift shop offers apothecary items, modernist ceramics, and even toys and games for children to appease any art lover.

■TIP➜ **Take advantage of the free audio tour.** ☒ *250 S. Grand Ave., Downtown* ☎ *213/626–6222* ⊕ *www.moca.org* ☚ *General admission free; special exhibitions $18 or free Thurs. 5–8* ☽ *Closed Mon.* Ⓜ *Civic Center/Grand Park.*

Natural History Museum of Los Angeles County

HISTORY MUSEUM | FAMILY | The hot ticket at this beaux arts–style museum completed in 1913 is the Dinosaur Hall, whose more than 300 fossils include adult, juvenile, and baby skeletons of the fearsome *Tyrannosaurus rex.* The Discovery Center lets kids and curious grown-ups touch real animal pelts, and the Insect Zoo gets everyone up close and personal with the white-eyed assassin bug and other creepy crawlers. A massive hall displays dioramas of animals in their natural habitats. Also look for

pre-Columbian artifacts and crafts from the South Pacific, or priceless stones in the Gem and Mineral Hall. Outdoors, the 3½-acre Nature Gardens shelter native plant and insect species and contain an expansive edible garden.

■TIP➜ **Don't miss out on the Dino lab, where you can watch paleontologists unearth and clean real fossils.** ☒ *900 W. Exposition Blvd., Exposition Park* ☎ *213/763–3466* ⊕ *www.nhm.org* ☚ *$15* ☽ *Closed first Tues. of the month* Ⓜ *Expo/Vermont.*

Orpheum Theatre

HISTORIC SIGHT | Opened in 1926, the opulent Orpheum Theatre played host to live attractions including classic comedians, burlesque dancers, jazz greats like Lena Horne, Ella Fitzgerald, and Duke Ellington, and later on rock-and-roll performers such as Little Richard. After extensive restorations, the Orpheum once again revealed a stunning white-marble lobby, majestic auditorium with fleur-de-lis panels, and two dazzling chandeliers. A thick red velvet and gold-trimmed curtain opens at showtime, and a white Wurlitzer pipe organ (one of the last remaining

organs of its kind from the silent movie era) is at the ready. The original 1926 rooftop neon sign again shines brightly, signaling a new era for this theater. Today the theater plays host to live concerts, comedy shows, and movie screenings. ✉ *842 S. Broadway, Downtown* ☏ *877/677–4386* ⊕ *www.laorpheum. com/events.*

Pershing Square

PLAZA/SQUARE | FAMILY | The city's cultures come together in one of its oldest parks, named in honor of World War I general John J. Pershing. Opened in 1866, the park was renovated in the 1990s by architect Ricardo Legorreta and landscape architect Laurie Olin with faded pastel-color walls, fountains, and towers. However, most Downtown residents and architecture lovers are not fans of the design and have long lobbied for a makeover, which is perennially rumored to be unveiled. From mid-November to mid-January, an outdoor ice-skating rink attracts ice-skaters and families. Every Wednesday 10–2 is the Pershing Square Farmers' Market. ⚠ **The park will undergo a significant overhaul for much of 2023 and into 2024.** ✉ *532 S. Olive St., Downtown* ☏ *213/847–4970* ⊕ *www.laparks.org/ pershingsquare* ▦ *Free* Ⓜ *Pershing Square.*

Union Station

TRAIN/TRAIN STATION | Even if you don't plan on traveling by train anywhere, head here to soak up the ambience of a great rail station. Envisioned by John and Donald Parkinson, the architects who also designed the grand City Hall, the 1939 masterpiece combines Spanish Colonial Revival and art deco elements that have retained their classic warmth and quality. The waiting hall's commanding scale and enormous chandeliers have provided the backdrop for countless scenes in films, TV shows, and music videos. Recently added to the majesty are the Homebound Brew Haus and the Traxx Bar, two bars that pay homage to

the station's original architecture while serving homemade brews and inventive classic cocktails. ■TIP→ **Walking tours of Union Station are on Saturday at 11 and cost $15.** ✉ *800 N. Alameda St., Downtown* ⊕ *www.unionstationla.com* Ⓜ *Union Station.*

★ Walt Disney Concert Hall

CONCERTS | One of the architectural wonders of Los Angeles, the 2,265-seat hall is a sculptural monument of gleaming, curved steel designed by Frank Gehry. It's part of a complex that includes a public park, gardens, shops, and two outdoor amphitheaters, one of them atop the concert hall. The acoustically superlative venue is the home of the city's premier orchestra, the Los Angeles Philharmonic, whose music director, Gustavo Dudamel, is an international celebrity in his own right. The orchestra's season runs from late September to early June, before it heads to the Hollywood Bowl for the summer. ✉ *111 S. Grand Ave., Downtown* ☏ *323/850–2000* ⊕ *www.laphil.org* ▦ *Free self-guided tours* Ⓜ *Civic Center/ Grand Park.*

🍴 Restaurants

Downtown Los Angeles is also home to L.A.'s Arts District, Financial District, Chinatown, Little Tokyo, the Theater District, and everything in between. The neighborhood has experienced a culinary renaissance that has rippled through the area, making it a popular dining destination where people come in search of edgy and creative menus that celebrate its eclectic nature. Here you'll find plenty of cozy wine bars, quaint bistros, historical landmarks, ethnic eats, and upscale restaurants that lack pretension.

★ Bavel

$$$$ | MIDDLE EASTERN | Fans of Bestia have been lining up for stellar Mediterranean cuisine at this Arts District hot spot, which is owned by the same restaurateurs. Rose-gold stools give way

Frank Gehry's Walt Disney Concert Hall was an instant L.A. icon.

to marble tabletops as the open kitchen bangs out hummus and baba ghanoush spreads, along with flatbreads and lamb-neck shawarma. **Known for:** delicious Mediterranean cuisine; reservations recommended; great vibes. $ *Average main: $50* ✉ *500 Mateo St., Downtown* ☎ *213/232–4966* ⊕ *baveldtla.com.*

Bestia

$$$ | **ITALIAN** | One of the most exciting and popular Italian restaurants in L.A. is housed inside a converted warehouse in the Arts District Downtown. Exposed air ducts and brick dominate the enormous space as in-the-know eaters chow down on spicy lamb sausage pizza and spaghetti Rustichella with Dungeness crab. **Known for:** eclectic pizzas; excellent date spot; upscale modern decor. $ *Average main: $40* ✉ *2121 E. 7th Pl., Downtown* ☎ *213/514–5724* ⊕ *www.bestiala.com* ⊙ *No lunch.*

★ Cole's French Dip

$ | **AMERICAN** | There's a fight in Los Angeles over who created the French dip sandwich. The first contender is Cole's, whose sign on the door says it's the originator of the salty, juicy, melt-in-your-mouth meats. **Known for:** historic L.A. dining; one of the top contenders for best French dip sandwich in the country; secret speakeasy in back. $ *Average main: $18* ✉ *118 E. 6th St., Downtown* ☎ *213/622–4090* ⊕ *www.pouringwith-heart.com/coles.*

Damian

$$$ | **MODERN MEXICAN** | The Arts District in DTLA continues to trot out some of the most exciting restaurants in all of Los Angeles, and Damian is simply the latest and greatest example to enter the space. Across from Bestia, the Enrique Olvera–helmed joint serves contemporary Mexican fare combined with California's bounty of excellent produce. **Known for:** buzzy spot; great cocktails; modern Mexican cuisine. $ *Average main: $40* ✉ *2132 E. 7th Pl., Downtown* ☎ *213/270–0178* ⊕ *www.damiandtla.com* ⊙ *Closed Mon. and Tues.* ⊂ *Open for brunch Sat. and Sun.*

Diners can sit and enjoy lunch at the Wexler's Deli counter inside Grand Central Market.

De La Nonna
$$ | **PIZZA** | Meaning, 'from the grandma' in Italian, De La Nonna is the newest, hippest, most fun pizza restaurant in DTLA. Owned by three friends, chef Patrick Costa, restaurateur Jose Cordon, and bar manager Lee Zaremba, the outlet features a bevy of focaccia-styled pizzas with engaging toppings like Japanese sweet potato or roasted mushrooms with garlic cream sauce. **Known for:** late-night pizza slice window; Italian cocktails; great pizzas. [$] *Average main: $20* ✉ *710 E. 4th Pl., Downtown* ☎ *213/221–1268* 🌐 *www.delanonna.com* 🕒 *Closed Sun. and Mon.*

The Factory Kitchen
$$$ | **ITALIAN** | The homemade pasta here, kneaded from imported Italian flour, guarantees this place a spot on the "must eat" list. The large Arts District eatery is carved from a converted warehouse and is held up inside by towering pillars. **Known for:** Ligurian Focaccina; incredible cannoli; best pesto in the city. [$] *Average main: $32* ✉ *1300 Factory Pl., Downtown* ☎ *213/996–6000* 🌐 *www.thefactory-kitchen.com* 🕒 *Closed Mon. No lunch weekends* ☞ *No cash accepted.*

★ **Howlin' Ray's**
$ | **SOUTHERN** | **FAMILY** | Don't let the hour-long waits deter you—if you want the best Nashville fried chicken in L.A., Howlin' Ray's is worth the effort. Right in the middle of Chinatown, this tiny chicken joint consists of a few bar seats, a few side tables, and a kitchen that sizzles as staff yell out "yes, chef" with each incoming order. **Known for:** spicy fried chicken; classic Southern sides; long waits. [$] *Average main: $15* ✉ *727 N. Broadway, Suite 128, Downtown* ☎ *213/935–8399* 🌐 *www.howlinrays.com* 🕒 *Closed Mon. and Tues.* [M] *Union Station.*

★ **Langer's Delicatessen-Restaurant**
$$ | **SANDWICHES** | **FAMILY** | This James Beard Award winner not only has the look and feel of a no-frills Jewish deli from New York, it also has the food to match. The draw here is the hand-cut pastrami: lean, peppery, robust—and

with a reputation for being the best in town. **Known for:** #19 sandwich; Jewish deli classics like matzo ball soup and rugelach; no-frills atmosphere. [$] *Average main: $23* ✉ *704 S. Alvarado St., Downtown* ☎ *213/483–8050* 🌐 *www.langersdeli.com* 🕒 *Closed Sun. No dinner* [M] *Westlake/MacArthur Park.*

★ Majordomo

$$$$ | **ECLECTIC** | You would never just stumble upon this out-of-the-way spot in Chinatown, but world-famous celeb chef David Chang likes it that way. The beautifully designed minimal spot with spacious patio, an exposed-duct ceiling, and elongated wood bar has a cuisine style that defies any singular category. **Known for:** chuck short rib; rice-based drinks; hard-to-get reservations (try to eat at the bar). [$] *Average main: $55* ✉ *1725 Naud St., Downtown* ☎ *323/545–4880* 🌐 *www.majordomo.la* 🕒 *Closed Mon. and Tues.*

Original Pantry Cafe

$ | **AMERICAN** | Opened in 1924 by Dewey Logan, this classic diner's former claim to fame is that it never closed in the entirety of its run. Currently owned by former L.A. mayor Richard Riordan, the diner has more limited hours and serves American food for breakfast, lunch, and dinner, and is known for cakes, pies, steaks, and chops. **Known for:** long lines; amazing breakfast; historic restaurant. [$] *Average main: $15* ✉ *877 S. Figueroa St., Downtown* ☎ *213/972–9279* 🌐 *www.pantrycafe.com* 🕒 *Closed Mon. and Tues. No dinner Wed.–Fri.* [M] *7th Street/Metro Center.*

★ Philippe the Original

$ | **AMERICAN** | **FAMILY** | First opened in 1908, Philippe's is one of L.A.'s oldest restaurants and claims to be the originator of the French dip sandwich. While the debate continues around the city, one thing is certain: the dips made with beef, pork, ham, lamb, or turkey on a freshly baked roll stand the test of time. Join locals as they chow down at communal tables while debating Dodgers games and politics. **Known for:** 50¢ coffee; communal tables; post–Dodgers game eats. [$] *Average main: $11* ✉ *1001 N. Alameda St., Downtown* ☎ *213/628–3781* 🌐 *www.philippes.com* [M] *Union Station.*

Q Sushi

$$$$ | **JAPANESE** | Every night is different at this elegant, one-Michelin-starred omakase (chef-selected) sushi joint. It all depends on what's the freshest and what's the absolute best. **Known for:** pricey multicourse omakase menu; elegant ambience; fresh bluefin tuna and Hokkaido scallops. [$] *Average main: $300* ✉ *521 W. 7th St., Downtown* ☎ *213/225–6285* 🌐 *www.qsushila.com* 🕒 *Closed Sun. and Mon. No lunch Sat.* [M] *7th Street/Metro Center.*

71Above

$$$$ | **ECLECTIC** | As its name suggests, this sky-high dining den sits on the 71st floor, 950 feet above ground level. With that elevation comes the most stunning views of any restaurant in L.A., and the food is close to matching it. **Known for:** sky-high views; fine dining with a seafood focus; classy atmosphere and loosely enforced dress code (no shorts or flip-flops). [$] *Average main: $45* ✉ *633 W. 5th St., 71st fl., Downtown* ☎ *213/712–2683* 🌐 *www.71above.com* 🕒 *No lunch* [M] *Pershing Square.*

Shibumi

$$$$ | **JAPANESE** | This *kappo* (cooking and cutting) restaurant in the middle of Downtown is offering up some of the most inventive raw, steamed, grilled, and fried Japanese dishes you'll ever try. Chef David Schlosser serves you personally from the 400-year-old cypress bar. **Known for:** kappo and omakase dining with a Michelin star; actual Kobe beef; creative off-menu options (be sure to ask!). [$] *Average main: $125* ✉ *815 S. Hill St., Downtown* ☎ *323/484–8915* 🌐 *www.shibumidtla.com* 🕒 *Closed Mon. and Tues.* [M] *7th Street/Metro Center.*

Sonoratown

$ | **MEXICAN** | Paying homage to the Mexican border town where owner Teo Diaz-Rodriguez Jr. grew up, Sonoratown is a Downtown L.A. joint that serves some of the best tacos in the entire city. Handmade tortillas, mesquite wood-fired carne asada, and supercheap prices have made this spot a neighborhood favorite and a must-have on any trip Downtown. **Known for:** excellent Sonoran-style tacos; great prices; friendly neighborhood spot. [$] *Average main: $8* ✉ *208 E. 8th St., Downtown* ☎ *213/628–3710* 🌐 *www.sonoratown.com.*

Sushi Gen

$$ | **JAPANESE** | Consistently rated one of the top sushi spots in L.A., Sushi Gen continues to dole out the freshest and tastiest fish in town. Sit at the elongated bar and get to know the sushi masters while they prepare your lunch. **Known for:** chef-recommended sushi selections; limited seating; great lunch specials. [$] *Average main: $25* ✉ *422 E. 2nd St., Downtown* ☎ *213/617–0552* 🌐 *www.sushigen-dtla.com* 🕒 *Closed Sun. and Mon. No lunch Sat.*

Hotels

An ongoing revitalization in Downtown, anchored around the L.A. Live complex, makes this a great place to see Los Angeles in transition: think affordable accommodations rubbing elbows with business hotels, streets lined with coffeehouses, and edgy boutiques that can be explored on foot. If you're traveling alone, some parts of Downtown are better to drive rather than walk through after dark.

★ Ace Hotel Downtown Los Angeles

$ | **HOTEL** | The L.A. edition of this bohemian-chic hipster haven is at once a hotel, theater, and poolside bar (called Upstairs), housed in the gorgeous Spanish Gothic–style United Artists building in the heart of Downtown. **Pros:** lively rooftop lounge/pool area; gorgeous building and views; location in the heart of Downtown. **Cons:** expensive parking rates compared to nightly rates ($55); some kinks in the service; compact rooms. [$] *Rooms from: $165* ✉ *929 S. Broadway, Downtown* ☎ *213/623–3233* 🌐 *www.acehotel.com/losangeles* 🛏 *183 rooms* 🍴 *No Meals.*

Conrad Los Angeles

$$$ | **HOTEL** | The Conrad is Hilton's top-of-the-line hotel brand, and the DTLA iteration, designed by Frank Gehry and packed with priceless art and meticulous design, exudes top-of-the-line and luxury in every way. **Pros:** endless views; José Andrés restaurants; great downtown location. **Cons:** Downtown can be dangerous at night; parking $55/night; confusing entryway. [$] *Rooms from: $350* ✉ *100 S. Grand Ave., Downtown* ☎ *213/349–8585* 🌐 *www.hilton.com/en/hotels/laxavci-conrad-los-angeles* 🛏 *305 rooms* 🍴 *No Meals.*

★ Downtown L.A. Proper Hotel

$$ | **HOTEL** | The new Downtown L.A. Proper Hotel is a design-lover's dream as renowned interior decorator Kelly Wearstler infuses the property with touches of Mexican modernism to Moroccan and Spanish flourishes. **Pros:** stunning interior design; speakeasy off lobby; restaurants and bars by renowned L.A. chefs. **Cons:** smallish rooms; parking $55/night; the area can be dangerous at night. [$] *Rooms from: $269* ✉ *1100 S. Broadway, Downtown* ☎ *213/806–1010* 🌐 *www.properhotel.com/downtown-la* 🛏 *147 rooms* 🍴 *No Meals.*

★ Freehand Los Angeles

$ | **HOTEL** | Part hotel, part shared accommodation space, the Freehand is one of the newer hotels in Downtown Los Angeles and also one of the coolest. **Pros:** range of affordable rooms from lofts to bunk beds; active social scene; great rooftop pool and bar. **Cons:** area can be dangerous at night; free lobby Wi-Fi attracts nonhotel guests; most affordable rooms are shared accommodations. $ *Rooms from: $77* ✉ *416 W. 8th St., Downtown* ☎ *213/612–0021* 🌐 *freehandhotels.com/los-angeles* 🛏 *59 shared rooms* 🍴 *No Meals* [M] *Pershing Square.*

Hotel Figueroa

$$ | HOTEL | The 12-story Hotel Figueroa was originally built in 1926, and touches of that originality are still seen throughout with original skylights, wood beams, and tiles. **Pros:** a short walk to L.A. Live and the convention center; great poolside bar; buzzy nightlife scene. **Cons:** the area can be dangerous at night; expensive parking ($52/night); smallish pool. $ *Rooms from: $219* ✉ *939 S. Figueroa St., Downtown* ☎ *866/734–6018* 🌐 *www.hotelfigueroa.com* 🛏 *268 rooms* 🍴 *No Meals* [M] *Olympic/Figueroa.*

The Hoxton

$$ | HOTEL | One of the chicest Downtown hotels, the Hoxton is an open-house hotel where the lobby is the hub of activity and welcoming to all, and has thoughtful design touches that permeate throughout. **Pros:** stellar restaurant; welcoming lobby; great rooftop pool. **Cons:** area can be dangerous at night; no gym; some rooms on the small side. $ *Rooms from: $249* ✉ *1060 S. Broadway, Downtown* ☎ *213/725–5900* 🌐 *www.thehoxton.com/downtown-la* 🛏 *174 rooms* 🍴 *No Meals.*

Millennium Biltmore Hotel

$ | HOTEL | As the local headquarters of John F. Kennedy's 1960 presidential campaign and the location of some of the earliest Academy Awards ceremonies, this Downtown treasure, with its gilded 1923 beaux arts design, exudes ambience and history. **Pros:** 24-hour fitness center; tiled indoor pool; impressive history. **Cons:** business groups can overwhelm common areas; standard rooms are compact; some decor feels outdated. $ *Rooms from: $150* ✉ *506 S. Grand Ave., Downtown* ☎ *213/624–1011, 866/866–8086* 🌐 *www.millenniumhotels.com* 🛏 *683 rooms* 🍴 *No Meals* [M] *Pershing Square.*

The Ritz-Carlton, Los Angeles

$$$$ | HOTEL | This citified Ritz-Carlton on the 23rd–26th floors of a 54-story tower within Downtown's L.A. Live entertainment complex features skyline views through expansive windows, blond woods, and smartened-up amenities including a flat-screen TV hidden in the bathroom mirror. **Pros:** designer spa; rooftop pool; daily buffet for Club Level. **Cons:** expensive valet parking ($54); corporate feel; mandatory daily fee of $30. $ *Rooms from: $600* ✉ *900 W. Olympic Blvd., Downtown* ☎ *213/743–8800* 🌐 *www.ritzcarlton.com* 🛏 *123 rooms* 🍴 *No Meals* ☞ *A daily $30 destination fee can be partially applied to food and beverages ($20). Fee also gets access to the GRAMMY Museum and daily yoga classes.* [M] *Pico.*

🍸 Nightlife

With choice music venues, upscale bars, and divier clubs, Downtown Los Angeles is high on the list of after-dark options.

Broadway Bar

BARS | This watering-hole-meets-dive sits in a flourishing section of Broadway (neighbors include the swank Ace Hotel). Bartenders mix creative cocktails while DJs spin tunes nightly. The two-story space includes a smoking balcony overlooking the street. The crowd is often dressed to impress. ✉ *830 S. Broadway, Downtown* ☎ *213/614–9909* 🌐 *www.broadwaybarla.com.*

Clifton's Republic

THEMED ENTERTAINMENT | Part marketplace, part bazaar of bars, part curio museum, Clifton's Republic is a wild, weird, and glorious establishment. Enter the ground floor and you'll find an indoor forest and a whole lot of grub. Upstairs is a maze of bars, dance floors, and intimate corners. ✉ *648 S. Broadway, Downtown* ☎ *213/613–0000* ⊕ *www. theneverlands.com/cliftons-republic* Ⓜ *Pershing Square.*

★ Golden Gopher

BARS | Craft cocktails, beers on tap, an outdoor smoking patio, and retro video games—this bar in the heart of Downtown is not to be missed. With one of the oldest liquor licenses in Los Angeles (issued in 1905), the Golden Gopher is the only bar in Los Angeles with an on-site liquor store for to-go orders—just in case you want to buy another bottle before you head home. ✉ *417 W. 8th St., Downtown* ☎ *213/614–8001* ⊕ *www. pouringwithheart.com/golden-gopher* Ⓜ *7th Street/Metro Center.*

La Cita

BARS | This dive bar may not look like much, but it more than makes up for it with an interesting mix of barflies, urban hipsters, and reasonable drink prices. Friday and Saturday night, DJs mix Top 40 hits and a tiny dance floor packs in the crowd. For those more interested in drinking and socializing, head to the back patio where a TV plays local sports. Every day has a differently themed happy hour—Tropico Tuesday or Cumbia Fever on Thursday. Specials vary from inexpensive beers to free pizza. ✉ *336 S. Hill St., Downtown* ☎ *213/687–7111* ⊕ *www. lacitabar.com* Ⓜ *Pershing Square.*

The Let's Go! Disco & Cocktail Club

COCKTAIL LOUNGES | Home to one of the best Italian liqueur collections in the city, The Let's Go is DTLA's newest, and most fun, cocktail bar and dance spot. The space is attached to (and co-owned by) the standout pizza joint De La Nonna, and is the perfect after-dinner spot to drink well-crafted Italian cocktails and dance like the pandemic never happened. Behind the bar is Lee Zaremba, whose cocktail bona fides include opening the legendary Italian drinks spot Billy Sunday in Chicago. Here, you'll find rare amari, superbitter fernets, challenging Italian vermouths, and so many more that are whipped into the tastiest cocktails in the city. ✉ *710 E. 4th Pl., Downtown* ☎ *213/221–1268* ⊕ *www.theletsgodisco. com.*

The Love Song Bar

BARS | Lovers of T. S. Eliot and vinyl will find themselves instantly at home inside this cozy establishment named after Eliot's "The Love Song of J. Alfred Prufrock." When not pouring drinks, bartenders often act as DJs, playing records (the best of the '60s through the '80s) in their entirety. As it's housed inside the Regent Theater, the cozy nature of the place can be disrupted when there's a concert scheduled. For those with an appetite, fantastic food can be ordered from the pizza parlor next door—naturally, it's called Prufrock's. ✉ *450 S. Main St., Downtown* ☎ *323/284–5728* ⊕ *www.spacelandpresents.com/events/ the-love-song.*

Redwood Bar & Grill

LIVE MUSIC | If you're looking for a place with potent drinks and a good burger, this kitschy bar fits the bill perfectly. Known today as the "pirate bar" because of its nautical decor, the place dates back to the 1940s, when it was rumored to attract mobsters, politicians, and journalists due to its proximity to city hall, the Hall of Justice, and the original location of the *Los Angeles Times*. There's nightly live music, though it comes with a cover charge. ✉ *316 W. 2nd St., Downtown* ☎ *213/680–2600* ⊕ *www.theredwoodbar. com* Ⓜ *Civic Center/Grand Park.*

★ Resident

LIVE MUSIC | Catch a lineup of indie tastemakers inside this converted industrial space, or hang outdoors in the beer garden while trying bites from on-site food truck KTCHN (on cooler evenings you can congregate around the firepits). A wide variety of draft beers and a specially curated cocktail program are available inside at the bar or at the trailer bar outside. ⊠ *428 S. Hewitt St., Downtown* ☎ *213/628–7503* ⊕ *www.residentdtla. com.*

★ Seven Grand

BARS | The hunting lodge vibe makes you feel like you need a whiskey in hand—luckily, this Downtown establishment stocks more than 700 of them. Attracting whiskey novices and connoisseurs, the bartenders here are more than willing to help you make a selection. Live jazz, blues, folk, and other bands play almost every night, so even if you're not a big drinker, there's still some appeal (although you're definitely missing out). For a more intimate setting, try the on-site Bar Jackalope, a bar within a bar, which has a "whiskey tasting library" specializing in Japanese varieties and seats only 18. ⊠ *515 W. 7th St., 2nd fl., Downtown* ☎ *213/614–0736* ⊕ *www. sevengrandbars.com* Ⓜ *7th Street/Metro Center.*

The Varnish

COCKTAIL LOUNGES | Beeline through the dining room of Cole's to find an unassuming door that leads to this small, dimly lit bar within a bar. Wooden booths line the walls, candles flicker, and live jazz is performed Sunday through Tuesday. The bartenders take their calling to heart and shake and stir some of the finest cocktails in the city. Those who don't have a drink of choice can list their wants ("gin-based and sweet," "strong whiskey and herbaceous") and be served a custom cocktail. Be warned: patrons requiring quick drinks will want to go elsewhere—perfection takes time. ⊠ *118 E. 6th St., Downtown* ☎ *213/265–7089* ⊕ *www. pouringwithheart.com/the-varnish.*

🎭 Performing Arts

Ahmanson Theatre

THEATER | The largest of L.A.'s Center Theatre Group's three theaters, the 2,100-seat Ahmanson Theatre presents larger-scale classic revivals, dramas, musicals, and comedies like *Into the Woods,* which are either going to or coming from Broadway and the West End. The ambience is a theater lover's delight. ⊠ *135 N. Grand Ave., Downtown* ☎ *213/972–7211* ⊕ *www.musiccenter. org/visit/Our-Venues/ahmanson-theatre* Ⓜ *Civic Center/Grand Park.*

★ Dorothy Chandler Pavilion

CONCERTS | Though half a century old, this theater maintains the glamour of its early years, richly decorated with crystal chandeliers, classical theatrical drapes, and a 24-karat gold dome. Part of the Los Angeles Music Center, this pavilion is home to the L.A. Opera though a large portion of programming is made up of dance and ballet performances as well. Ticket holders can attend free talks that take place an hour before opera performances.

◾**TIP**→ **Reservations for the talks aren't required, but it's wise to arrive early, as space is limited.** ⊠ *135 N. Grand Ave., Downtown* ☎ *213/972–0711* ⊕ *www. musiccenter.org/visit/Our-Venues/dorothy-chandler-pavilion* Ⓜ *Civic Center/ Grand Park.*

East West Players

THEATER | Plays at this Little Tokyo theater focus on the Asian American experience and feature an Asian American cast. Its Theatre for Youth Program is a traveling production that promotes racial tolerance and understanding among students. It is also home to the David Henry Hwang Writers Institute. ⊠ *120 Judge John Aiso St., Little Tokyo* ☎ *213/625–7000* ⊕ *www. eastwestplayers.org* Ⓜ *Union Station.*

Mark Taper Forum

THEATER | Both dramas and comedies dominate the stage at the Mark Taper Forum, next door to the Ahmanson Theatre in Downtown. A showcase for new and experimental plays, quite a few shows that premiered here have gone on to Broadway and off-Broadway theaters (a number of Pulitzer Prize–winning plays have also been developed here). ⊠ 135 N. Grand Ave., Downtown ☎ 213/628–2772 ⊕ www.musiccenter.org/visit/Our-Venues/mark-taper-forum Ⓜ Civic Center/Grand Park.

Microsoft Theater

CONCERTS | The Microsoft Theater is host to a variety of concerts and big-name awards shows—the Emmys, American Music Awards, BET Awards, and the ESPYs. This theater and the surrounding L.A. Live complex are a draw for those looking for a fun night out. The building's emphasis on acoustics and versatile seating arrangements means that all 7,100 seats are good, whether you're at an intimate acoustic concert or an awards show. Outside, the L.A. Live complex is home to restaurants and attractions, including the GRAMMY Museum, to keep patrons entertained before and after shows (though it's open whether or not there's a performance). ⊠ 777 Chick Hearn Ct., Downtown ☎ 213/763–6030 ⊕ www.microsofttheater.com Ⓜ Pico.

The REDCAT (Roy and Edna Disney/Cal Arts Theater)

FILM | Located inside the Walt Disney Concert Hall, this 288-seat theater serves as a space for innovative performance and visual art in addition to film screenings and literary events. The gallery features changing art installations. Tickets are reasonably priced and many are free. ⊠ 631 W. 2nd St., Downtown ☎ 213/237–2800 ⊕ www.redcat.org Ⓜ Civic Center/Grand Park.

Shrine Auditorium

CONCERTS | Since opening in 1926, the auditorium has hosted nearly every major awards show at one point or another, including the Emmys and the GRAMMYs. Today, the venue and adjacent Expo Hall hosts concerts, film premieres, award shows, pageants, and special events. The Shrine's Moorish Revival–style architecture is a spectacle all its own. ⊠ 665 W. Jefferson Blvd., Downtown ☎ 213/748–5116 ⊕ www.shrineauditorium.com.

🛍 Shopping

Downtown L.A. is dotted with international neighborhoods (Olvera Street, Chinatown, Koreatown, Little Tokyo) and several large, open-air shopping venues (the Fashion District, the Flower Market, Grand Central Market, the Toy District, and the Jewelry District).

It offers an urban bargain hunter's dream shopping experience if you know precisely what you're looking for (like diamonds and gems from the Jewelry District) or if you're willing to be tempted by unexpected finds (piñatas from Olvera Street, slippers from Chinatown, or lacquered chopsticks from Little Tokyo).

Fashion District

NEIGHBORHOODS | With the influx of emerging designers in this pocket of Downtown, it's become much more than just a wholesale market. Besides containing the plant paradise that is the Los Angeles Flower Market as well as the Fabric District and Santee Alley, the neighborhood now boasts a bevy of boutiques and cool coffee shops, thanks in part to the Row DTLA, a towering complex with curated stores, restaurants, and design spaces. ⊠ Roughly between I–10 and 7th St., and S. Los Angeles St. and S. Central Ave., Downtown ☎ 213/741–2661 ⊕ www.fashiondistrict.org.

Continued on page 207

Hard Rock Cafe, Hollywood

L.A. STORY
THE CITY'S HISTORY THROUGH ITS BARS

Los Angeles is known as a place where dreams are realized, but it is also a place where pasts are forgotten. Despite what people say about L.A.'s lack of memory, however, there are quite a few noteworthy old-school bars that pay tribute to the city's vibrant past and its famous patrons.

Collectively, these eclectic watering holes have hosted everyone from ex-presidents to rock legends to famed authors and, of course, a continual stream of countless movie stars.

The bars are located in virtually every corner of the city—from Downtown to West Hollywood to Santa Monica.

In terms of character, they run the gamut from dive to dressy and serve everything from top-shelf whisky to bargain-basement beer.

While it's their differences that have kept people coming back through the decades, they all have something in common: Each has a story to tell.

EIGHT OF L.A.'S BEST

Chez Jay

Mixing at Cole's

Cole's

Frolic Room

CHEZ JAY RESTAURANT (1959)

Noteworthy for: Located down the block from the Santa Monica Pier, this steak-and-seafood joint walks the line between celebrity hangout and dive bar.

Signature drink: Martini

Celeb clientele: Members of the Rat Pack, Leonard Nimoy, Sean Penn, Julia Roberts, Renée Zellweger, Owen Wilson, Drew Barrymore

Don't miss: The little booth in the back of the restaurant, known to insiders as Table 10, is a favorite celebrity hideout.

Filmed here: *A Single Man, Goliath*

Join the crowd: *1657 Ocean Ave., Santa Monica, 310/395–1741*

COLE'S (1908)

Noteworthy for: Found inside the Pacific Electric building, touted as Los Angeles's oldest public house, and once the epicenter of the Red Car railway network, this watering hole has its original glass lighting, penny-tile floors, and 40-foot mahogany bar.

Signature drink: Old-fashioned

Celeb clientele: The men's room boasts that Charles Bukowski and Mickey Cohen once relieved themselves here.

Don't miss: The Varnish at Cole's is an in-house speakeasy with 11 booths that can be accessed through a hidden door marked by a tiny framed picture of a cocktail glass.

Filmed here: *Forrest Gump, L.A. Confidential, Mad Men*

Join the crowd: *118 E. 6th St., Los Angeles, 213/622–4049*

CLIFTON'S REPUBLIC (1931)

Noteworthy for: This historical cafeteria/playground featuring a giant redwood tree in the center and intimidating wildlife taxidermy throughout, serves tasty comfort food and houses three lively bars: the Monarch, the Gothic, and the Pacific Seas.

Signature drink: The Mind Eraser at the Tiki bar; El Presidio at the Monarch; the Hyperion at The Gothic Bar (careful—this one's strong).

Claim to fame: Clifton's whimsical forest-themed dining area inspired Walt Disney to create Disneyland.

Frolic Room

Harvelle's

Kibitz Room

Dresden Restaurant

Don't miss: The 40's-era Tiki Bar. Located at the top of a secret stairway, it features deliciously strong drinks, dancing cigarette girls and the occasional appearance of a sequined mermaid.

FROLIC ROOM (1935)

Noteworthy for: This Hollywood favorite next door to the famed Pantages Theater has served actors and writers from Elizabeth Short to Charles Bukowski.

Signature drink: Cheap Budweiser during happy hour.

Celeb clientele: Kiefer Sutherland

Don't miss: A bowl of popcorn from the old-fashioned machine; the Hirschfeld mural depicting Marilyn Monroe, Charlie Chaplin, Louis Armstrong, Frank Sinatra, and others.

Filmed here: *L.A. Confidential, Southland*

Join the crowd: *6245 Hollywood Blvd., Los Angeles, 323/462–5890*

HARVELLE'S (1931)

Noteworthy for: Located one block off the Third Street Promenade, this dark and sexy jazz bar is said to be the oldest live music venue on the Westside.

Signature drink: The Deadly Sins martini menu offers house made mixes named after the seven sins, from Pride to Lust.

Don't miss: The Toledo Show is a pulse-quickening weekly burlesque-and-jazz performance on Sunday nights.

Join the crowd: *1432 4th St., Santa Monica, 310/395–1676.*

THE KIBITZ ROOM AT CANTER'S DELI (1961)

Noteworthy for: Adjacent to the famous Canter's Deli, which opened in 1948, this Fairfax District nightspot is definitely a dive bar, but that doesn't keep the A-listers away. Joni Mitchell, Jakob Dylan, and Fiona Apple have all played here.

Signature drink: Cheap beer

Celeb clientele: Jim Morrison, Frank Zappa, Juliette Lewis, Julia Roberts, Javier Bardem, Penélope Cruz

Don't miss: The decor is pure retro 1960s, including vinyl booths and a fall-leaf motif on the ceiling.

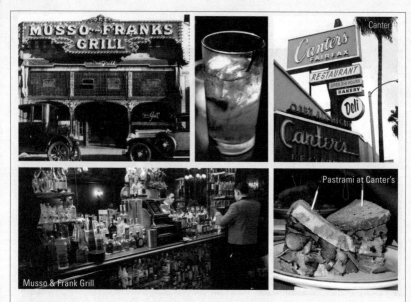

Musso & Frank Grill

Canter's

Pastrami at Canter's

Filmed here: *I Ought to Be in Pictures, Entourage, Curb Your Enthusiasm, Sunset Strip, Enemy of the State, What's Eating Gilbert Grape*
Join the crowd: *419 N. Fairfax Ave., Los Angeles, 323/651–2030.*

DOLCE VITA (1966)

Noteworthy for: Located in tony Beverly Hills, this staple for northern Italian has a classy clubhouse atmosphere, round leather booths, white tablecloths, and exposed-brick walls.

Signature drink: Martini

Celeb clientele: Members of the Rat Pack; several ex-presidents, including Ronald Reagan. The place prides itself on being a safe haven from pesky paparazzi.

Don't miss: The burgundy-hued round leather booths.

Join the crowd: *9785 Santa Monica Blvd., Los Angeles, 310/278–1845*

MUSSO & FRANK GRILL (1919)

Noteworthy for: This swanky old-timer is called the oldest bar in Hollywood. While that title may spark jealousy among some of its Tinseltown counterparts, there is no doubt that this famed grill conjures Hollywood's halcyon days with its authentic '30s-era decor—and serves a mean martini.

Signature drink: The Mean Martini

Celeb clientele: Charlie Chaplin, Greta Garbo, Ernest Hemingway, F. Scott Fitzgerald, Marilyn Monroe

Don't miss: The red tuxedo-clad waiters are famous in their own right; some have been at the restaurant for more than 40 years.

Filmed here: *Ocean's Eleven, Charlie's Angels 2, Mad Men*

Join the crowd: *6667 Hollywood Blvd., Los Angeles, 323/467–7788*

The Musso & Frank Grill — THE OLDEST RESTAURANT IN HOLLYWOOD — Since 1919

Olvera Street, at the heart of the city's oldest neighborhood, is the place to experience many aspects of L.A.'s Mexican American culture.

Jewelry District

NEIGHBORHOODS | Filled with bargain hunters, these crowded sidewalks resemble a slice of Manhattan with nearly 5,000 individual vendors and businesses. While you can save big on everything from wedding bands to sparkling belt buckles, the neighborhood also offers several more upscale vendors for those in search of super-special pieces. ⊠ *Between Olive St. and Broadway from 5th to 8th St., Downtown* ☎ *213/928–7889* ⊕ *www.the-jewelry-district.com* Ⓜ *Pershing Square.*

★ Olvera Street

MARKET | FAMILY | Known as the birthplace of Los Angeles, this redbrick walkway is lined with historic buildings and overhung with grapevines. At dozens of clapboard stalls you can browse south-of-the-border goods—leather sandals, woven blankets, and devotional candles—as well as cheap toys and souvenirs—and sample outstanding tacos. With the musicians and cafés providing the soundtrack, the area is constantly lively. Annual events include a tree-lighting ceremony and Día de los Muertos celebrations. ⊠ *Between Cesar Chavez Ave. and Arcadia St., Downtown* ⊕ *www.olvera-street.com* Ⓜ *Union Station.*

Row DTLA

SHOPPING CENTER | The city's newest shopping, food, and cultural destination in the venerable L.A. Arts District, Row DTLA is spread across an entire campus, with around 100 curated boutique stores like Poketo, Bodega, A+R, Flask & Field, and Tokyo Bike. Additionally, new restaurants like Rappahannock Oyster Bar and Michelin-starred Hayato seem to be popping up weekly. A weekend highlight is Smorgasburg, where every Sunday dozens of food stalls pop up in the next-door parking lot serving tasty favorites across every cuisine imaginable. ⊠ *777 Alameda St., Downtown* ☎ *213/988–8890* ⊕ *rowdtla.com.*

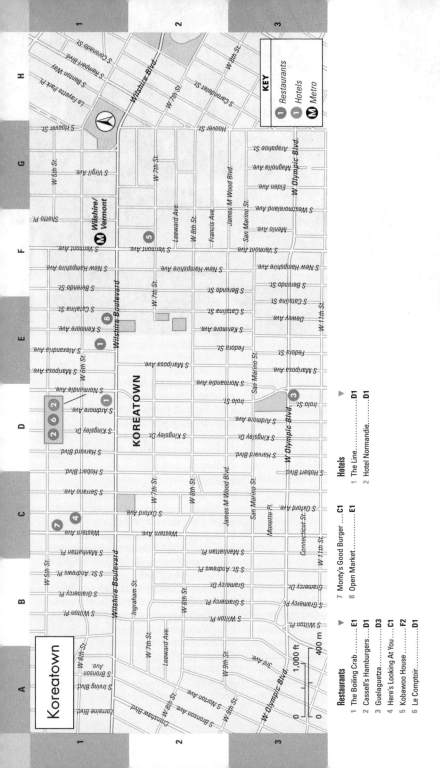

Koreatown

KEY

- **1** Restaurants
- **1** Hotels
- **M** Metro

KOREATOWN

M Wilshire/Vermont

Restaurants ▶

1 The Boiling Crab............	**E1**
2 Cassell's Hamburgers....	**D1**
3 Guelaguetza.................	**D3**
4 Here's Looking At You....	**C1**
5 Kobawoo House.............	**F2**
6 Le Comptoir..................	**D1**
7 Monty's Good Burger	**C1**
8 Open Market.................	**E1**

Hotels ▶

1 The Line.....................	**D1**
2 Hotel Normandie.........	**D1**

The Santee Alley

NEIGHBORHOODS | Situated in the Fashion District, the Santee Alley is known for back-alley deals on knockoffs of designer sunglasses, jewelry, handbags, shoes, and clothing. Be prepared to haggle, and don't lose sight of your wallet. Weekend crowds can be overwhelming, but there's plenty of street food to keep your energy up. ✉ *Santee St. and Maple Ave. from Olympic Blvd. to 12th St., Downtown* ☎ *213/488–1153* 🌐 *www.fashiondistrict.org/santee-alley*.

Koreatown

Despite its name, Koreatown is one of the most eclectic neighborhoods in all of Los Angeles, particularly when it comes to dining. Obviously, you can find drool-worthy Korean restaurants, but there are also gems like the Oaxacan eatery Guelaguetza; the genre-defying Here's Looking at You; and the vegan burger joint Monty's Good Burger. Combine the food with the wonderful Korean spas and incredible nightlife, and you'll find a mix of everything that makes L.A. great.

🍴 Restaurants

Home to the largest and densest Korean population outside of Korea, Koreatown is also an ethnically diverse neighborhood. While Korean cuisine is ubiquitous here, like in most of L.A., you can find incredible Asian fusion and even classic burger joints.

The Boiling Crab

$$ | **SEAFOOD** | **FAMILY** | Put on your bib and prepare to get messy, because this crab shack is not for stodgy eaters. Choices of blue, Dungeness, snow, and king are brought out in plastic bags where you can rip, tear, twist, and yank the meaty goodness out of their shells. **Known for:** giant crab legs; unfussy environment; long lines. [$] *Average main: $21* ✉ *3377 Wilshire Blvd., Suite 115, Koreatown* ☎ *213/389–2722* 🌐 *www.theboilingcrab.com* [M] *Wilshire/Normandie*.

Cassell's Hamburgers

$ | **DINER** | **FAMILY** | Since 1948, Cassell's has been grilling up some of the city's best burgers and remains on just about every top burger list in town. In-the-know burger lovers come here for the reliability of a perfectly cooked patty, a toasted bun, and fries with the right amount of crunch. **Known for:** perfectly cooked burgers and fries; no-frills diner setting; late-night eats. [$] *Average main: $15* ✉ *3600 W. 6th St., Koreatown* ☎ *213/387–5502* 🌐 *www.cassellshamburgers.com* [M] *Wilshire/Normandie*.

Guelaguetza

$$ | **MEXICAN** | **FAMILY** | A classic L.A. Mexican eatery, Guelaguetza serves the complex but not overpoweringly spicy cooking of Oaxaca, one of Mexico's most renowned culinary capitals. Inside, you'll find a largely Spanish-speaking clientele bobbing their heads to nightly jazz, marimba, and rock while wolfing down the restaurant's specialty: the moles. **Known for:** mole; chili-marinated pork; family-owned restaurant. [$] *Average main: $21* ✉ *3014 W. Olympic Blvd., Koreatown* ☎ *213/427–0608* 🌐 *www.ilovemole.com* 🕒 *Closed Mon.*

★ **Here's Looking At You**

$$ | **ECLECTIC** | Hawaiian and Asian-inspired dishes can be found on this menu featuring veggie, meat, poultry, and seafood. The environment is eclectic, as is the food, with signature dishes like frogs' legs with salsa negra and blue crab tostadas with *yuzu kosho*. **Known for:** friendly atmosphere; exceptional cocktails; inventive dishes. [$] *Average main: $25* ✉ *3901 W. 6th St., Koreatown* ☎ *213/568–3573* 🌐 *www.hereslookingatyoula.com* 🕒 *Closed Tues. and Wed.*

★ Kobawoo House

$$$ | **KOREAN** | **FAMILY** | Nestled into a dingy strip mall, this Korean powerhouse is given away by the lines of locals waiting outside. Once inside, scents of grilled meats and kimchi immediately fill your nostrils, and soon enough, your table will be littered with sides, *kalbi* beef, *dolsot* bibimbap, *wang bosam* (cabbage wraps with boiled pork), and tall bottles of Hite beer. **Known for:** perfect kalbi beef; long lines; cheap eats. [$] *Average main: $35* ✉ *698 S. Vermont Ave., Suite 109, Koreatown* ☎ *213/389–7300* 🌐 *www.kobawoo-house.com* 🕒 *Closed Mon.* [M] *Wilshire/Vermont.*

Le Comptoir

$$$$ | **FRENCH** | Situated inside the Hotel Normandie in a minuscule space, Le Comptoir is a 10-seat French restaurant helmed by chef Gary Menes that features veggie-forward food in an unstuffy setting. The counter spot earned a Michelin star for its organic kitchen and intimate atmosphere that gives guests one-on-one attention from the chef who is making and plating your food right in front of you. **Known for:** eight-course tasting menu of innovative French cuisine; intimate setting; vegetarian-friendly dishes. [$] *Average main: $175* ✉ *Hotel Normandie, 3606 W. 6th. St., Koreatown* ☎ *213/290–0750* 🌐 *www.lecomptoirla.com* 🕒 *Closed Sun.–Wed.* [M] *Wilshire/Normandie.*

Monty's Good Burger

$ | **BURGER** | A 100% plant-based establishment in Koreatown shouldn't be a thing that works, but Monty's Good Burger has the neighborhood fooled, as its Impossible Burger makes believers out of the most devout carnivores. Perfectly pressed plant-based patties come with oozing vegan cheese and fries or tots that melt in your mouth. **Known for:** plant-based burgers; epic shakes; late-night eats and long lines. [$] *Average main: $15* ✉ *516 S. Western Ave., Koreatown* ☎ *213/915–0257* 🌐 *montysgoodburger.com* [M] *Wilshire/Western.*

★ Open Market

$ | **SANDWICHES** | One of the newer (and better) additions to the Koreatown dining scene, Open Market is part restaurant, part corner store, specializing in sandwiches, coffee, and a meticulously curated selection of wines, chocolates, tinned fish, and more. Run by husband-and-wife team Brian and Yoona Lee, the minimalist market attracts everyone from midday construction workers to oenophiles looking for the next best thing. **Known for:** L.A. goods and gifts; locally made chips, hot sauces, and snacks; excellent sandwiches. [$] *Average main: $15* ✉ *3339 Wilshire Blvd., Koreatown* ☎ *213/232–3851* 🌐 *www.openmarket.la* 🕒 *Closed Sun.*

Hotels

Hotel Normandie

$$ | **HOTEL** | Originally built in 1926, this Renaissance Revival gem has been renovated to today's standards and is now a hip and not-terribly-pricey spot to post up in the ever-booming center of Koreatown. **Pros:** Michelin-starred French restaurant; daily wine reception; historic burger joint. **Cons:** feels dated; tiny bathrooms; neighborhood can be dangerous at night. [$] *Rooms from: $250* ✉ *605 Normandie Ave., Koreatown* ☎ *213/388–8138* 🌐 *www.hotelnormandiela.com* 🔑 *92 rooms* 🍴 *No Meals* [M] *Wilshire/Normandie.*

The Line

$$ | **HOTEL** | This boutique hotel pays homage to its Koreatown address with dynamic dining concepts and a hidden karaoke speakeasy. **Pros:** Room service by Michelin chef Josiah Citrin; unique decor; fun bars on-site (ask about the speakeasy). **Cons:** valet parking $54/night; lobby bar crowds public spaces; hotel is a bit isolated from common tourist attractions. [$] *Rooms from: $210* ✉ *3515*

Wilshire Blvd., Koreatown ☎ *213/381– 7411* ⊕ *www.thelinehotel.com* ↯ *384 rooms* ⦿ *No Meals* Ⓜ *Wilshire/ Normandie.*

▼ Nightlife

Known primarily for its boundless Korean barbecue spots and karaoke, this off-the-beaten-path segment of Central L.A. is also home to unique must-visit bars.

Cafe Brass Monkey

BARS | Karaoke every night, yes you heard that right, *every night.* Cafe Brass Monkey is K-town dive bar royalty, a perfect place to belt out your ballads without fear of the judgment you might find in snootier spots. The ambience is relaxed and the food is bar style. If you're looking to sing, be prepared to wait your turn as the line to perform can get lengthy. Sprinkled in with tried-and-true regulars, celebrities looking to have a good ol' fashioned sing-along filter through Cafe Brass Monkey from time to time. The wall features photos of famous friends of the Monkey like Adam Levine, Seth Macfarlane, and Chelsea Handler. Parking is free after 5 pm with a validation, but the glory of knowing you hit the high note is priceless. ✉ *3440 Wilshire Blvd., Koreatown* ☎ *213/381–7047* ⊕ *www.cafebrassmonkey.com* Ⓜ *Wilshire/Normandie.*

Dan Sung Sa

BARS | Step through the curtained entrance and back in time to 1970s Korea at Dan Sung Sa, which gained wider popularity after Anthony Bourdain paid a visit. At this quirky time-capsule bar, woodblock menus feature roughly 100 small eats. You'll see much that looks familiar, but fortune favors the bold. Take a chance on corn cheese, or try the *makgeolli:* a boozy Korean rice drink you sip from a bowl. It pairs perfectly with good conversation and snacking all night long. ✉ *3317 W. 6th St., Koreatown* ☎ *213/487–9100* ⊕ *dansungsala.com* Ⓜ *Wilshire/Vermont.*

★ HMS Bounty

BARS | This super-kitschy nautical-theme bar in the heart of Koreatown offers drink specials and food at prices that will make you swoon. Come for the wings, all-day breakfast specials, cheap drinks, and very eclectic crowds. ✉ *3357 Wilshire Blvd., Koreatown* ☎ *213/385–7275* ⊕ *www.the-hmsbounty.com* Ⓜ *Wilshire/Normandie.*

The Normandie Club

COCKTAIL LOUNGES | With a reputation for great takes on classic cocktails and even better conversation among patrons, this dimly lit haunt is a fantastic place to mingle. Tucked inside the Normandie Hotel, the lounge is a party without the affection for chaos afforded by other late-night spots. The menu features a slew of old standards, but mixologists are eager to play: they'll ask you what the mood is and mix a drink to match. The cocktails are seriously good, and the ambience is comforting yet classy. Plus, if you're looking to dance off a well-made whiskey sour, you don't have to go far, as The Normandie Club houses "damn fine" in back, a live-DJ dance party Thursday, Friday, and Saturday nights from 9 pm–2 am. ✉ *Hotel Normandie, 3612 W. 6th St., Koreatown* ☎ *213/263–2709* ⊕ *www.the-normandieclub.com* Ⓜ *Wilshire/Vermont.*

The Prince

BARS | *Mad Men* and *New Girl* both had multiple scenes filmed in this Old Hollywood relic, which dates back to the early 1900s. The Prince is trimmed with vintage fabric wallpaper and bedecked with a stately mahogany bar; the grand piano waits in the wings. Squire lamps punctuate red-leather booths where you can enjoy Korean fare and standard cocktails, wine, and beer. Whatever you do, get the deep-fried chicken. ✉ *3198 W. 7th St., Koreatown* ☎ *213/389–1586* ⊗ *Closed Sun.* Ⓜ *Wilshire/Vermont.*

 Performing Arts

Wiltern Theater

CONCERTS | Built in 1931, this historical art deco landmark, named for its location at the intersection of Wilshire Boulevard and Western Avenue, serves mainly as a space for music (it's a top destination for touring musicians), but other live entertainment can be seen here as well, including comedy and dance. The main floor is standing room only for most shows, but there are some seating areas available if desired. ✉ *3790 Wilshire Blvd., Koreatown* ☎ *213/388–1400* ⊕ *www.wiltern.com* Ⓜ *Wilshire/Western.*

Activities

Aroma Spa & Sports

SPAS | It's not difficult to find amazing spa experiences throughout Koreatown. Most places will offer up standard scrubs, hot and cold baths, dry and wet saunas, and more. Aroma takes things to another level as the spa is just the centerpiece of an entire entertainment complex. Spa services include all the traditional treatments, but when you're done getting pampered, the rest of the facility includes a gym, a swimming pool, restaurants, and a state-of-the-art golf driving range. ✉ *3680 Wilshire Blvd., Koreatown* ☎ *213/387–2111* ⊕ *www. aromaresort.com* Ⓜ *Wilshire/Western.*

★ **Wi Spa**

SPAS | Koreatown is filled with endless spa experiences, but there are a few that rise above the rest. Wi Spa is a 24/7 wonderland of treatments that includes hot and cold baths, unique sauna rooms, and floors for men, women, or co-ed family spa fun. Signature sauna rooms vary from intense 231-degree thermotherapy to salt-enriched stations and specialty clay imported from Korea. Just remember, Korean spas are not for the shy at heart—you will be nude, you will get scrubbed, and you will feel like a million bucks after. ✉ *2700 Wilshire Blvd., Koreatown* ☎ *213/487–2700* ⊕ *www.wispausa. com* ✉ *For services under $150, there is an admission fee of $30* Ⓜ *Wilshire/ Vermont.*

Chapter 11

LOS FELIZ, SILVER LAKE, AND THE EASTSIDE

Updated by
Michelle Rae Uy

◉ Sights	🍴 Restaurants	🛏 Hotels	🛍 Shopping	🍸 Nightlife
★★★☆☆	★★★★★	★★☆☆☆	★★★★☆	★★★★★

A DAY AT GRIFFITH PARK

On the trail in Griffith Park

The 4,100-acre Griffith Park (the largest municipal park and urban wilderness area in the United States) stands out as an oasis in a city covered in cement and asphalt.

On warm weekends, there are parties, barbecues, mariachi bands, and strolling vendors selling fresh fruit. Joggers, cyclists, and walkers course its roadways. There are also top attractions within the park, including the Griffith Observatory and the Los Angeles Zoo.

The park was named after Col. Griffith J. Griffith, a mining tycoon who donated 3,000 acres of land to the city for the park in 1896. It has been used as a film and television location since the early days of motion pictures. One early Hollywood producer advised, "A tree is a tree, a rock is a rock, shoot it in Griffith Park."

GETTING HERE

The park has several entrances: off Los Feliz Boulevard at Western Canyon Avenue, Vermont Avenue, Crystal Springs Drive, and Riverside Drive; from the Ventura/134 Freeway at Victory Boulevard, Zoo Drive, or Forest Lawn Drive; from the Golden State Freeway (I–5) at Los Feliz Boulevard and Zoo Drive. The park is open from 6 am to 10 pm.

Top Experiences

Visit the Griffith Observatory. The Griffith Observatory offers breathtaking panoramic views, and the structure itself is a pristinely maintained art deco spectacle. Visit during a scheduled talk or show at the Leonard Nimoy Event Horizon Theater, look through the Zeiss Telescope on a clear night, or check out the Samuel Oschin Planetarium and its incredible dome.

The Griffith Observatory

The expansive grounds are open to the public and include a monument dedicated to James Dean; several scenes from *Rebel Without a Cause* were filmed here (if you've never seen the film, it's a definite must-watch before visiting). To see the lights of the city twinkle at night from above, stay late and head up to the Observatory Deck, open until 10 pm every evening except Monday.

Climb Mount Hollywood. There are plenty of scenic routes throughout the park, but one of the best trails is to the top of Mount Hollywood. Park at the Griffith Observatory lot and pick up the trail from there. It's an easy half-hour hike to the top. On clear days you'll be able to see all the way to the Pacific Ocean and Catalina Island. About two-thirds of the way up is Dante's View, an area

A resident of the park's zoo

with benches where you can stop for a break or snack. You'll likely cross paths with horseback riders on the way.

An up-close view of the Hollywood sign from below means hiking a little more than 6 miles round-trip from the parking lot.

Check Out the Los Angeles Zoo and Botanical Gardens. In the northeast corner of the park, the zoo's highlights include a gorilla reserve, a Sumatran tiger, a snow leopard, and an acre dedicated to one of the largest troops of chimpanzees in the United States. In addition, the zoo claims to have more flamingoes than any other zoo worldwide.

Enjoy a Bike Tour. There's a flat, family-friendly 4.7-mile path that runs along Crystal Springs Drive and Zoo Drive. Rentals are available inside the park at Spokes n' Stuff Bike Shop (✉ *4730 Crystal Springs Dr., at ranger station parking lot* ☎ *323/662–6573*).

See a Concert at the Greek Theatre. The 6,100-seat Greek Theatre (☎ *323/665–1927*) is an outdoor venue where top artists such as Elton John and Paul Simon have performed.

NEIGHBORHOOD SNAPSHOT

TOP REASONS TO GO

■ **Hike at Griffith Park:** This is without a doubt the best place to partake in L.A.'s favorite pastime—exercising. With over 4,210 acres, it's one of the largest urban parks in the country and happens to have one of the most glorious views of the city.

■ **Stargaze at the Griffith Observatory:** Most visitors may flock to this observatory for its mesmerizing panoramas, but the more discerning travelers come for its night sky viewings and star parties.

■ **Get some culture at Barnsdall Art Park:** Architecture, art, drama, and wine all come together in one of L.A.'s best-kept secrets, where a day can be spent taking an art class, touring the appealing Frank Lloyd Wright–designed Hollyhock House, and sipping wine.

■ **See a new movie at the old-school Vintage Theatre:** An L.A. trip isn't complete without seeing a movie at one of the city's oldest cinemas. If you aren't a fan of the classics, this quaint 1920s movie theater in the heart of Los Feliz plays newly released titles as well.

■ **Eat your way around the neighborhood:** Los Feliz is home to a host of fantastic restaurants. Indulge in Middle Eastern at Kismet, Italian at Little Dom's, and drink good wine and beer at Bar Covell. For a morning or midday boost, Maru is a caffeine hot spot.

VIEWFINDER

Griffith Park: Griffith Park is one of the most Instagrammable spots in L.A. For the quintessential Hollywood shot, head to the Griffith Park Observatory parking lot to pose your face next to a bust of James Dean (*Rebel Without a Cause* was shot here) with the iconic Hollywood sign in the background. There are several trails from here to get you a little closer to the sign and for panoramic views of the city skyline. Note that the Hollywood sign is not lighted at night. ⊠ *2800 E. Observatory Ave.*

GETTING HERE

■ When driving from the east, take either I–10 to I–5 heading north or State Route 134 to I–5 heading south; from the west, take I–10 to I–5 heading north or brave the U.S. 101 traffic, getting off in Hollywood then heading east. The closest Metro station is Vermont and Sunset, which puts you within walking distance of Los Feliz's most bustling streets, Vermont and Hillhurst. Metered street parking is available along Vermont and Hillhurst, while some free parking can be found on residential side streets—though pay attention to posted signs.

PLANNING YOUR TIME

■ Los Feliz is a delightfully intimate neighborhood, and it won't take long to tick off its most important highlights. However, a decent, get-your-heart-pumping hike at Griffith Park may take a couple of hours or more, and it's definitely worth spending a few more strolling around to experience all of its offerings, including Griffith Observatory. Silver Lake and Echo Park can easily take up a whole lazy day of eating, drinking, and shopping but can also be done in an afternoon.

The neighborhoods in L.A.'s Eastside are talked about with the same oh-my-god-it's-so-cool reverence by Angelenos as Brooklyn is by New Yorkers. These streets are dripping with the coolest boutiques, cafés, boho-chic bars, and trendy hot spots and their corresponding trendsetters and trend-seekers.

While there has been heated debate, and even local Council votes, as to the exact location and makeup of L.A.'s Eastside, the rebranding of neighborhoods like Los Feliz, Silver Lake, and Echo Park as the Eastside when they began gentrifying in the late 1990s, has been hard to undo—despite the fact that the name "Eastside" was already being used to refer to neighborhoods located east of the L.A. River, like Boyle Heights, El Sereno, and Lincoln Heights.

In 2009, *The Los Angeles Times* triggered a lot of conversation around neighborhood boundaries when it conducted its Mapping LA project, which documented neighborhood boundaries using census information, reader feedback, and historical and anecdotal definitions. According to this map, the Eastside was defined as comprising Boyle Heights, El Sereno, Lincoln Heights, and East Los Angeles.

While the debate flares up occasionally, the battle for the cool Eastside title has never definitively been settled, and for many Angelenos, it depends on where they grew up or how long they have lived in L.A. In 2014, the Silver Lake Neighborhood Council even went so far as to officially declare that it was not part of the Eastside umbrella, but the City of Los Angeles still includes it and Echo Park, Atwater, and Highland, along with the "original" Eastside neighborhoods in its list of communities in the official East Area Planning Commission.

For many, there's the original Eastside and the newer Eastside, but you may want to avoid the topic altogether and just stick with the actual neighborhood names. Whether they are Eastside, or newer Eastside, or just Los Feliz, Silver Lake, and Echo Park, these neighborhoods have each taken turns as the hottest and trendiest neighborhoods in Los Angeles. As each one became more expensive, the cool kids relocated, leaving behind their style and influence. Now Highland Park is the center of the oh-so-hip universe. But the epicenter is constantly shifting.

Los Feliz

In the rolling hills below the stunning Griffith Observatory, Los Feliz is one of L.A.'s most affluent neighborhoods. With Hollywood just a few miles west, its winding streets are lined with mansions belonging to some of the biggest celebrities. In recent years, both Vermont and

Hillhurst Avenues have come alive with hip restaurants, boutiques, and theaters.

Sights

Barnsdall Art Park

CITY PARK | FAMILY | The panoramic view of Hollywood alone is worth a trip to this hilltop cultural center. On the grounds you'll find the 1921 **Hollyhock House,** a masterpiece of modern design by architect Frank Lloyd Wright. It was commissioned by philanthropist Aline Barnsdall to be the centerpiece of an arts community. While Barnsdall's project didn't turn out the way she planned, the park now hosts the L.A. Municipal Art Gallery and Theatre, which provides exhibition space for visual and performance artists.

Wright dubbed this style "California Romanza" (*romanza* is a musical term meaning "to make one's own form"). Stylized depictions of Barnsdall's favorite flower, the hollyhock, appear throughout the house in its cement columns, roof line, and furnishings. The leaded-glass windows are expertly placed to make the most of both the surrounding gardens and the city views. On summer weekends, there are wildly popular wine tastings and outdoor movie screenings. Self-guided tours are available Thursday through Sunday from 11 to 4. ⊠ *4800 Hollywood Blvd., Los Feliz* ☎ *323/913–4030* ⊕ *www.barnsdall.org* 🖼 *Free; house tours $7* ⊗ *House closed Sun.–Wed.* ⚭ *Advance tickets required for house.*

★ Griffith Observatory

OBSERVATORY | Most visitors barely skim the surface of this gorgeous spot in the Santa Monica Mountains, but those in the know will tell you there's more to the Griffith Observatory than its sweeping views and stunning Greek Revival architecture. The magnificence of the cosmos and humankind's ingenuity to explore the deepest depths of the universe are in the spotlight here, with its space-focused exhibits, the free public telescopes, and shows at the Leonard Nimoy Event Horizon Theater and the Samuel Oschin Planetarium. For visitors who are looking to get up close and personal with the cosmos, monthly star-viewing parties with local amateur astronomers are also on hand. In the early mornings, the extensive trails of Griffith Park are the perfect venue to partake in L.A.'s favorite pastime: hiking.

■TIP➔ **For a fantastic view, come at sunset to watch the sky turn fiery shades of red with the city's skyline silhouetted.** ⊠ *2800 E. Observatory Ave., Los Feliz* ☎ *213/473–0800* ⊕ *www.griffithobservatory.org* ⊗ *Closed Mon.* ⚭ *Observatory grounds and parking are open daily.*

★ Griffith Park

CITY PARK | FAMILY | One of the country's largest municipal parks, the 4,210-acre Griffith Park is a must for nature lovers, the perfect spot for respite from the hustle and bustle of the surrounding urban areas. Plants and animals native to Southern California can be found within the park's borders, including deer, coyotes, and even a reclusive mountain lion. Bronson Canyon (where the Batcave from the 1960s *Batman* TV series is located) and Crystal Springs are favorite picnic spots.

The park is named after Colonel Griffith J. Griffith, a mining tycoon who donated 3,000 acres to the city in 1896. As you might expect, the park has been used as a film and television location for at least a century. Here you'll find the Griffith Observatory, the Los Angeles Zoo, the Greek Theater, two golf courses, hiking and bridle trails, a swimming pool, a merry-go-round, and an outdoor train museum. ⊠ *4730 Crystal Springs Dr., Los Feliz* ☎ *323/644–2050* ⊕ *www.laparks.org/dos/parks/griffithpk* 🖼 *Free; attractions inside park have separate admission fees.*

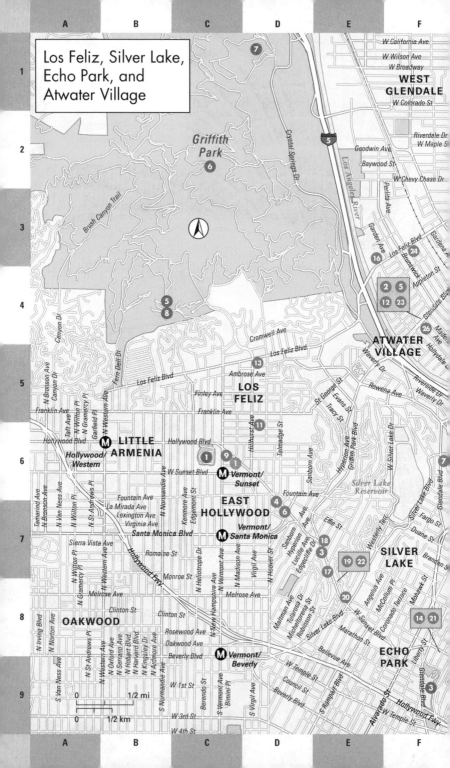

Los Feliz, Silver Lake,
Echo Park, and
Atwater Village

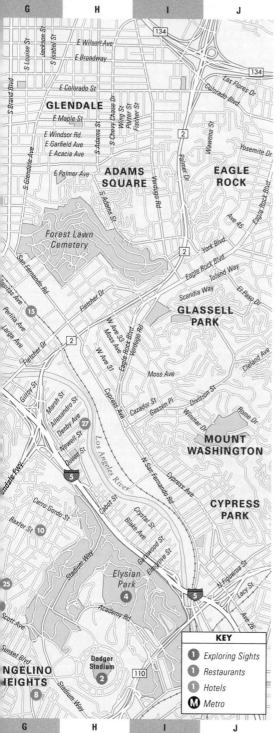

Los Angeles Zoo

ZOO | FAMILY | The sweeping grounds of the Los Angeles Zoo are a terrific place to introduce young minds (and all minds) to threatened species of animals from all over the world and to encourage empathy for them at an early age. This accredited zoo's main focus is cultivating a connection to nature in the community, while educating, advocating, and creating action around animal welfare and conservation. The zoo is home to more than 2,100 mammals, birds, amphibians, and reptiles representing more than 270 different species, of which more than 58 are endangered. While coordinating with different organizations around the world, the L.A. Zoo also has its own in-house conservation programs, including innovative breeding strategies for reptiles, a successful Masai giraffe breeding program, and participating in efforts to restore the pronghorn species population. The care of the adorable residents of this 133-acre zoo is priority number one, and every effort is made to allow animals plenty of space and the agency to roam in their enclosures, to create environments that mimic their wild habitats, and to make enrichment toys available for play. The sprawling, 6.56-acre Elephants of Asia habitat boasts more than 3 acres of outdoor space, deep bathing pools, a waterfall, sandy hills, enrichment opportunities, and care facilities for elephants of all sizes and ages. The enjoyment of visiting humans is considered, too. In summer, the Zoo Friday Nights program allows visitors an opportunity to witness the more nocturnal residents. The sustainable wine and dinner series (21-plus) features gourmet farm-to-table menus, expert wine pairings, and conversations with a curator or keeper.

You'll need at least three hours to explore this zoo, but a full day is even better. Amenities include several restaurants, free solar-powered charging stations, water-refilling stations, and electric shuttles that can take you around the zoo for a small fee. Passionate and knowledgeable docents are also available to tell you more about the animals. ⊠ *5333 Zoo Dr., Los Feliz* ☎ *323/644–4200* ⊕ *www.lazoo.org* 🖾 *$22.*

Samuel Oschin Planetarium

OTHER ATTRACTION | FAMILY | Located in the heart of the famed Griffith Observatory, the 290-seat Samuel Oschin Planetarium may be on the modest side as far as planetariums are concerned, but the shows held here are no less epic and electrifying. This state-of-the-art theater has an aluminum dome and a Zeiss star projector that plays awe-inspiring multimedia exhibitions that address the mystery of the cosmos. There are typically three 30-minute ticketed shows in rotation, so be sure to allow time to catch one while spending a day at the park. ■**TIP→ Be sure to sit in the back for the best experience.** ⊠ *2800 E. Observatory Rd., Griffith Park* ☎ *213/473–0800* ⊕ *griffithobservatory.org/exhibits/samuel-oschin-planetarium* 🖾 *$10.*

 # Restaurants

This affluent hillside community has a laid-back dining scene. Wine bars and an Italian deli or restaurants are among the options for a family night out.

Kismet

$$ | MEDITERRANEAN | You may feel like you're about to walk into a sauna rather than a restaurant because of its minimalist light-color wood on white-paint interior, but you'll find nothing but colorful, gorgeous, Middle Eastern dishes here at Kismet. This James Beard nominee perfectly blends comforting Middle Eastern and Israeli cuisine with California flavors and plant-based flair, all served in a modern space. **Known for:** Persian crispy rice; tasty lamb meatballs; Middle Eastern classics with a Cali twist. 🖹 *Average main: $20* ⊠ *4648 Hollywood Blvd., Los Feliz* ☎ *323/409–0404* ⊕ *www.kismetla.com.*

a Pergoletta

$ | **ITALIAN** | Just look for the swaying
talian flag at a strip mall on Hillhurst and
Melbourne, and you'll stumble into La
Pergoletta, a cozy little space. Though
the decor is decidedly frenzied, it still
maintains a chic yet rustic quality that
looks like it was cobbled together by an
talian *nonna*. **Known for:** fresh pasta you
can customize; Panna & Funghi; food
just like Nonna used to make. $ *Average
main: $25* ⊠ *1802 Hillhurst Ave., Los Feliz*
☎ *323/664–8259* ⊕ *www.lapergoletta.
com.*

ittle Dom's

$ | **ITALIAN** | With a vintage bar and
dapper barkeep who mixes up seasonally inspired retro cocktails, an attached
talian deli where you can pick up a pizza
it to take back to your Airbnb or kitch-
nette, and a $25 Monday-night supper,
it's not surprising that Little Dom's is a
neighborhood gem. Cozy and inviting,
with big leather booths you can sink into
for the night, the restaurant puts a modern spin on classic Italian dishes such
as rice balls, fish piccata, and spaghetti
and meatballs. **Known for:** ricotta cheese
and fresh blueberry pancakes; excellent
pizza margherita; fun weekend brunch.
$ *Average main: $25* ⊠ *2128 Hillhurst
Ave., Los Feliz* ☎ *323/661–0055* ⊕ *www.
littledoms.com.*

🛌 Hotels

★ Hotel Covell

$ | **HOTEL** | **FAMILY** | Each apartment-style
room at this nine-room boutique hotel is
unique, thanks to its designer handpick-
ing custom-made pieces and vintage
furnishings, from the bedside tables to
the lamps, to create a cute little pad you
wished you owned. **Pros:** rooms have
kitchenettes; complimentary parking;
stylish vintage and modern mix. **Cons:**
no room service; just nine suites so can
be hard to get a room; no 24-hour lobby.
$ *Rooms from: $345* ⊠ *4626 Hollywood

Blvd., Los Feliz ☎ *323/660–4300* ⊕ *www.
hotelcovell.com* 🛏 *9 suites* ⦿ *No Meals.*

🍸 Nightlife

While neighboring Hollywood champions
nightclubs, laid-back Los Feliz favors its
pubs, quirky neighborhood bars, and
casual lounges. The scene is buzzing,
especially on weekends, with locals
dominating it. But visitors hoping to get
away from the rowdiness of Hollywood
are always a welcome addition.

Bar Covell

WINE BARS | This laid-back spot is the
embodiment of an unpretentious wine
drinker's wine bar, complete with non-
judgey staff. What else would you expect
from a spot with repurposed furnishings
and a vintage motorcycle mounted to
the wall? There's a new menu of wine
and locally sourced beer every week
as well as delicious appetizers like the
popular deviled eggs and charcuterie
plate. ⊠ *4628 Hollywood Blvd., Los Feliz*
☎ *323/660–4400* ⊕ *www.barcovell.com.*

Dresden Room

PIANO BARS | This bar's 1940s lounge
decor makes it a favorite with folks in Los
Angeles. The long-running house band,
Marty and Elayne, entertained patrons
for more than four decades. (They found
a new generation of fans, thanks to the
film *Swingers*.) Other than the entertainment, perhaps the best reason to wander
in is to sip on a Blood and Sand cocktail,
self-proclaimed to be "the world's most
tantalizing drink." ⊠ *1760 N. Vermont
Ave., Los Feliz* ☎ *323/665–4294* ⊕ *www.
thedresden.com.*

Tabula Rasa Bar

WINE BARS | This unassuming spot feels
less like a wine bar and more of a neighborhood watering hole where the servers
take the time to chat with customers
rather than somberly educate them on
the complexities of wine. But make no
mistake: the wine selection is perfec-
tion and the snacks are delightful—they

simply want to ensure your enjoyment of your wine rather than have you bow down at the appreciation of their knowledge. ✉ *5125 Hollywood Blvd., Los Feliz* ☎ *213/290–6309* ⊕ *www.tabularasabar. com.*

 Performing Arts

Though Los Feliz has a bit of a theater scene—mostly a spillover from Hollywood—it's home to a couple of fantastic cinemas and one of L.A.'s best live music venues: the Greek.

★ Greek Theatre

CONCERTS | With a robust lineup from May through November, acts such as Bruce Springsteen, John Legend, and Aretha Franklin (RIP) have all graced the stage at this scenic outdoor venue. Located at the base of Griffith Park, there's usually slow pre-show traffic on concert nights, but that'll give you a chance to take in the beautiful park foliage and homes in the Hollywood Hills. Paid lots are available for parking, but wear comfortable shoes and expect to walk as some lots are fairly far from the theater. Or you can park and enjoy cocktails in trendy and chic Los Feliz before a show, then walk up to the venue. ✉ *2700 N. Vermont Ave., Los Feliz* ☎ *844/524–7335* ⊕ *www.lagreektheatre. com.*

Vintage Los Feliz Theatre

FILM | This theater is nothing fancy, but it is one of the most cherished in the city, and watching a movie here is a true L.A. experience. Recently acquired and updated by the American Cinemateque, this intimate three-auditorium theater has long been a part of Los Angeles's rich movie-watching history. Two of the rooms cater to the latest first-run releases and often host Netflix screenings, while the third and biggest of the rooms is host to exclusive American Cinemateque events and showings. Book in advance online for special screenings and events. ✉ *1822 N.*

Vermont Ave., Los Feliz ☎ *323/664–2169* ⊕ *vintagecinemas.com/losfeliz* 🎟 *$12.50.*

Shopping

Stroll past the mansions on Los Feliz Boulevard before hitting the vintage shops and sophisticated boutiques with old-school tendencies—think refurbished brick and classic decor.

Skylight Books

BOOKS | A neighborhood bookstore through and through, Skylight has excellent sections devoted to kids, fiction, travel, and food; it even has a live-in cat. The space also hosts book discussion groups, panels, and author readings with hip literati. Art lovers can peruse texts on design and photography, graphic novels, and indie magazines at Skylight's annex a few doors down. ✉ *1818 N. Vermont Ave., Los Feliz* ☎ *323/660–1175* ⊕ *www. skylightbooks.com.*

Soap Plant/Wacko

SOUVENIRS | This pop-culture supermarket offers a wide range of items, including rows of books on art and design. But it's the novelty stock that makes the biggest impression, with ant farms, X-ray specs, and anime figurines for sale. An adjacent gallery space, La Luz de Jesus, focuses on underground art. ✉ *4633 Hollywood Blvd., Los Feliz* ☎ *323/663–0122* ⊕ *www. soapplant.com.*

Spitfire Girl

SOUVENIRS | When the person you're shopping for is the nontraditional type, you can count on this quirky boutique to provide unique goods including taxidermy, printed wood flasks, white magic spell kits, and cheeky socks, much of which is created by Spitfire Girl's own house label. ✉ *1939½ Hillhurst Ave., Los Feliz* ☎ *323/912–1977* ⊕ *www.spitfiregirl. com.*

✦ Activities

Bronson Canyon

HIKING & WALKING | Bronson Canyon—or more popularly, Bronson Caves—is one of L.A.'s most famous filming locations, especially for Western and sci-fi flicks. This section of Griffith Park, easily accessible through a trail that's less than half a mile, is a great place to visit whether you're a film buff or an exercise junkie. ⊠ *3200 Canyon Dr., Hollywood.*

Silver Lake

This hilly, mostly residential neighborhood sits southeast of Los Feliz and northwest of Echo Park. Regarded as a bohemian enclave since the 1930s, it was the site of the first large film studio built by Walt Disney. Today Silver Lake is known for cute boutiques, bougie coffeehouses, and specialty restaurants along its stretch of Sunset Boulevard.

✦ Restaurants

With plenty of trendy appeal, the eateries of Silver Lake draw an eclectic crowd to its neighborhood hangouts.

Creamo by Donut Friend

$ | ICE CREAM | Started by former music producer and Donut Friend creator Mark Trombino, Creamo is to ice cream as Donut Friend is to doughnuts (and if you don't get those L.A. references, it's what In-N-Out is to burgers). Everything is vegan in the shop; nonetheless, non-vegans will love its 16 soy-based flavors, many of which are named after pop-punk and emo bands. **Known for:** Donut Friend doughnuts; vegan shakes and ice cream sandwiches; vegan ice cream. $ *Average main: $5* ⊠ *3534 Sunset Blvd., Silver Lake* ☎ *213/863–0979* ⊕ *creamoicecream.com* ☽ *Closed Mon.*

Dinosaur Coffee

$ | CAFÉ | By blending geometrical shapes and horizontal lines together in an airy place with big windows, Dinosaur Coffee has utilized its space well, bringing a touch of the new into a section of Silver Lake that feels a little old. Yet it's more than just the interiors that draw people in—the coffee is excellent, as are the pastries. **Known for:** perfect oat milk latte; great cold brew; no Wi-Fi. $ *Average main: $6* ⊠ *4334 W. Sunset Blvd., Silver Lake* ⊕ *dinosaurcoffee.com.*

El Cid

$$ | TAPAS | A popular local venue for live bands, DJ sets, and burlesque shows, El Cid has been presenting flamenco performances since the early '60s. The weekend flamenco dinner and show includes a four-course meal and a lively, engrossing Spanish dance performance. **Known for:** flamenco shows; live performances; paella. $ *Average main: $22* ⊠ *4212 W. Sunset Blvd., Silver Lake* ☎ *323/668–0318* ⊕ *www.elcidsunset. com* ☽ *Flamenco on weekends only.*

Gingergrass

$ | VIETNAMESE | FAMILY | With minimalist decor marked by tropical wood banquettes, Silver Lake's bohemian past and übertrendy present converge at Gingergrass. Traditional Vietnamese favorites emerge from the café's open kitchen, sometimes with a California twist. **Known for:** roasted pork chop with rice; bánh mì sandwiches; great desserts. $ *Average main: $15* ⊠ *2396 Glendale Blvd., Silver Lake* ☎ *323/644–1600* ⊕ *www.gingergrass.com.*

★ Night + Market Song

$ | THAI | There are a lot of Thai restaurants in Los Angeles, but none have quite reached the level of cult status of Night + Market Song. Tucked between a free clinic, a small clothing store, and a tax office, this second rendition of chef Kris Yenbamroong's popular WeHo restaurant might be easy to miss, but keep an eye out, as its authentic (and properly spicy)

Thai dishes are practically mandatory when you're in the neighborhood. **Known for:** Moo Sadoong ("startled pig"); khao soi; long weekend lines. [$] *Average main: $17* ✉ *3322 W. Sunset Blvd., Silver Lake* ☎ *323/665–5899* 🌐 *www.nightmarketsong.com* 🕑 *Closed Wed.*

Pine and Crane

$ | **TAIWANESE** | **FAMILY** | This is not the typical Chinese restaurant you might expect; it's a fast-casual, often locally sourced Taiwanese restaurant housed in a modern setting. The menu changes based on season, the wine and beer list updates constantly, and the tea menu is carefully curated. **Known for:** dan dan noodles; traditional panfried omelet; friendly staff. [$] *Average main: $15* ✉ *1521 Griffith Park Blvd., Silver Lake* ☎ *323/668–1128* 🌐 *www.pineandcrane.com* 🕑 *Closed Tues.*

Playita Mariscos

$ | **MEXICAN** | Essentially just a concrete shack with a roofed outdoor dining space populated by picnic tables, no-frills Playita Mariscos is a beloved local joint lauded for its Baja-style tacos. You'll also find beer-battered fish and shrimp tacos that evoke feelings of the sun-dappled Baja Mexico coast. Be sure to add the *aguachile* and ceviche to your order. **Known for:** beer-battered fish and shrimp tacos; aguachile; local haunt. [$] *Average main: $12* ✉ *3143 Sunset Blvd., Silver Lake* ☎ *323/928–2028* 🌐 *www.playitamariscos.com.*

Silverlake Ramen

$ | **RAMEN** | Now a franchise with several locations around Los Angeles (and a random one in Concord, NC), this spot in the heart of the city's hipsterville is the original and the best. The go-to ramen joint for Silverlake and Echo Park denizens is just the ticket if you're in dire need of some comfort food while also partaking in L.A.'s multicultural food scene. **Known for:** The Blaze, a spicy Tonkotsu ramen; crispy rice with spicy tuna; hearty Japanese fare. [$] *Average main: $16* ✉ *2927 Sunset Blvd., Silver Lake* ☎ *323/660–8100* 🌐 *www.silverlakeramen.com.*

Nightlife

Most of Silver Lake's best bars can be found in one condensed area, Sunset Junction, the intersection of Sunset and Santa Monica Boulevards. If you've spent your day shopping or dining here, return at night when coffee culture takes a breather and makes way for dark, eclectic bars patronized by locals and L.A.'s transplant community.

Akbar

BARS | Recently updated Akbar is not your fancy L.A. cocktail bar filled with sipping model types and beautiful celebrity-adjacent people. This local haunt is every inch a neighborhood bar, one that serves fast, cheap, and strong drinks; is inclusive of all people; and engages the local community through fun, unapologetically outrageous events like Craftaoke, Gaymer Night, and queer disco nights. ✉ *4356 W. Sunset Blvd., Silver Lake* ☎ *323/665–6810* 🌐 *www.akbarsilverlake.com.*

Cha Cha Lounge

BARS | If chaos and the assortment of ill-matched furnishings and decor is something you can forgive—or revel in—then this import from Seattle is a Silver Lake staple you should check out. Grab your (cheap) poison then meander through the Mexican fiesta–theme bar. Foosball tables, a photo booth, and a vending machine will give you plenty to occupy your time. ✉ *2375 Glendale Blvd., Silver Lake* ☎ *323/660–7595* 🌐 *www.chachalounge.com.*

★ **4100**

BARS | With swaths of fabric draped from the ceiling, this low-lit bar with a bohemian vibe is the perfect backdrop (and mood) for a date. Groups of locals also come through for the night, making for a good mix of people and energy. The bartenders pour drinks that are both tasty and potent. There's plenty of seating at the tables and stools along the central bar, which gets crowded on the weekends. ✉ *1087 Manzanita St., Silver Lake* ☎ *213/784–6595* ⊕ *www.4100bar.com.*

The Red Lion Tavern

BEER GARDENS | You wouldn't expect old European charm in the hipster enclave of Silver Lake, but Bavarian style is served right alongside irony at the Red Lion Tavern, just as it has for more than 60 years. So, grab a schnitzel and a bratwurst and wander the many rooms chockablock with German memorabilia or head toward the beer garden for a large selection of German-only beers on draft. ✉ *2366 Glendale Blvd., Silver Lake* ☎ *323/662–5337* ⊕ *www.redliontavern. net.*

Silverlake Lounge

LIVE MUSIC | Rock bands, burlesque performances, comedy sets, and LTGBQ+ nights all have a home at the cross section of Sunset and Silver Lake at a little dive bar called the Silverlake Lounge. This small-yet-famous venue, which received a recent refresh, is a neighborhood spot in the best way possible, with cheap drinks and local talent deserving of their time in the limelight. There are 10 signature cocktails, many of which are riffs on classics, and quite a few tequilas and mezcals on offer. If you come hungry, you can bring food in from the pizza place across the street or look for a restaurant pop-up in the newly updated back patio. ✉ *2906 W. Sunset Blvd., Silver Lake* ☎ *323/741–0032* ⊕ *www.thesilverlake-lounge.com.*

👜 Shopping

The action here is concentrated along Sunset Boulevard, where the young and hip come to sip artisanal coffee and peruse the one-of-a-kind wares.

Mohawk General Store

MIXED CLOTHING | Filled with a brilliant combination of indie and established designers, this upscale boutique is a mainstay for the modern minimalist. Pick up the wares of local favorites as well as internationally loved labels like Acne Studios, Issey Miyake, and Levi's. The Sunset Boulevard store stocks goods for men and women as well as children, plus accessories and some home goods. ✉ *4011 W. Sunset Blvd., Silver Lake* ☎ *323/669–1601* ⊕ *www.mohawkgeneralstore.com.*

Silver Lake Wine

WINE/SPIRITS | Boutique wineries from around the world provide this shop with the vintage bottles that fill the floor-to-ceiling racks. Looking relaxed and unassuming in jeans and T-shirts, the knowledgeable staff can steer you to the right wine or spirits for any occasion. Those who prefer to enjoy their wine in the privacy of their vacation rental or hotel will be pleased to know they also do deliveries around Silver Lake and the neighboring areas. ✉ *2395 Glendale Blvd., Silver Lake* ☎ *323/662—9024* ⊕ *www.silverlakewine.com.*

★ Yolk

SOUVENIRS | Woman-owned Yolk is the perfect spot to shop for home and lifestyle goods that are trendy in Los Angeles, stocked with all the nice things that you will want to buy as gifts for others, but will struggle to give away. Most of the offerings here are locally made and, therefore, hard to find elsewhere, and there's also a carefully curated selection of lovely designer goods. Look for unique kids' toys and furnishings, exquisite home accessories, stationery, and handcrafted items from California artisans. ✉ *3910 W. Sunset Blvd., Silver Lake* ☎ *323/426–9391* ⊕ *www.shopyolk. com.*

Echo Park

Silver Lake's edgier older cousin and neighbor, Echo Park is centered on a beautifully restored movie-famous lakefront park. The first residential neighborhood northwest of Downtown Los Angeles, Echo Park has long been under (deserved) scrutiny for gentrification, along with Highland Park and Silver Lake. This predominantly Latino and Mexican neighborhood has experienced an influx of young artists and industry hopefuls in recent years, as well as rent hikes, but it's not devoid of diversity or character. Film buffs take note: it was one of the principal locations of Roman Polanski's film *Chinatown.*

Sights

★ Dodger Stadium

SPORTS VENUE | FAMILY | Home of the Dodgers since 1962, Dodger Stadium is the third-oldest baseball stadium still in use and has had quite the history in baseball, including Sandy Koufax's perfect game in 1965 and Kirk Gibson's 1988 World Series home run. Not only has it played host to the Dodgers' ups and downs and World Series runs, it's also been the venue for some of the biggest performers in the world, including the Beatles, Madonna, and Beyoncé. The stadium can be tough to get into on game day, so consider getting dropped off in the park and walking up. Alternately, you can arrive early, as locals tend not to roll up until the third inning. If you have the opportunity to take in a Friday night game, make sure to stick around for the fireworks show that follows—if you're patient, you can even wait in line and watch it from the field. ⊠ *1000 Vin Scully Ave., Echo Park* ☎ *866/363–4377* ⊕ *mlb. com/dodgers/ballpark.*

Echo Park Lake

CITY PARK | FAMILY | If this charming little park and its lake of swan boats looks a little familiar to you, it's most likely because you've seen it in one L.A.-shot movie or another (*Chinatown,* for instance). After a major overhaul, the park has blossomed into a beautiful urban landscape, set against the backdrop of the Downtown skyline. Weekends are always bustling, as are mornings when joggers and early risers take laps around the lake. ⊠ *751 Echo Park Ave., Echo Park* ☎ *213/250–3578* ⊕ *www.laparks.org/aquatic/lake/ echo-park-lake.*

Elysian Park

HIKING & WALKING | FAMILY | Though not Los Angeles's biggest park—that honor belongs to Griffith Park—Elysian comes in second, and also has the honor of being the city's oldest. It's also home to one of L.A.'s busiest and most beloved attractions, Dodger Stadium, the home field to the Los Angeles Dodgers. For this reason, baseball fans flock to this 600-acre park for tailgate parties. The rest of the time, however, Elysian Park serves as the Echo Park residents' backyard, thanks to its network of hiking trails, picnic spaces, and public playgrounds. ⊠ *929 Academy Rd., Echo Park* ☎ *213/485–5054* ⊕ *www.laparks.org/ park/elysian.*

Restaurants

Echo Park's diversity manifests in its gastronomic scene. While vegan and Mexican restaurants are plentiful, there are other offerings to round out the selection and satisfy every taste bud, from French and Italian to Filipino and Thai.

★ Bacetti

$$ | ITALIAN | Though it's a relative newcomer to the dining scene, Bacetti instantly established itself as one of L.A.'s best Italian restaurants, serving Roman-inspired dishes with a California twist in a stylish, sprawling, wood-framed dining room and patio. This farm-driven, Roman trattoria–inspired

You'll find ducks, swan-shaped pedal boats for rent, and a fountain that continuously shoots a stream of water 200 feet into the air at Echo Park Lake.

spot, tucked in Echo Park's intimate commercial strip in the midst of a quiet residential neighborhood, is worth a trip, if only for the Focaccia Ebraica, which has gained a little cult following. **Known for:** stylish setting; Focaccia Ebraica; Italian wines. [$] *Average main: $24* ✉ *1509 Echo Park Ave., Echo Park* ☎ *213/995–6090* 🌐 *bacetti-la.com.*

★ Guisados

$ | MEXICAN | Family-owned Guisados has achieved cult status in L.A. with locations throughout the city (DTLA, Boyle Heights, WeHo) to accommodate its popularity. This Echo Park spot is worshipped and well supported locally for Nana's slow-cooked stew recipes, cooked to perfection for five to six hours and slapped on house-grilled tortillas. **Known for:** tacos with slow-cooked meats; breakfast tacos; cult favorite. [$] *Average main: $12* ✉ *1261 W. Sunset Blvd., Echo Park* ☎ *213/250–7600* 🌐 *www.guisados.la.*

Lady Byrd Cafe

$ | AMERICAN | Walking into woman-owned Lady Byrd Cafe is like walking through a portal to a fairy-tale land filled with whimsical decor, inventive greenhouse-sheltered tables, and grandma tableware, which explains its Insta-famous status. But, it's much more than just a pretty place to eat; dishes are pretty delectable. **Known for:** lemon poppy seed pancakes; variety of eggs Benedicts; juices and smoothies. [$] *Average main: $18* ✉ *2100 Echo Park Ave., Echo Park* ☎ *323/922–1006* 🌐 *ladybyrdcafe.com.*

Masa of Echo Park

$$ | PIZZA | FAMILY | While Masa of Echo Park does do excellent "bistro pizzas," as the restaurant calls them, it's mostly known for the delectable deep-dish pies that may just be the best you'll find this side of Chicago. Be prepared though—it can take a while to get seated and up to 45 minutes to get that deep dish you ordered, so it might be best to call ahead. **Known for:** vegan menu options; family-style dining; deep-dish pizza. $ *Average main: $24* ✉ *1800 W. Sunset Blvd., Echo Park* ☎ *213/989–1558* ⊕ *www. masaofechopark.com* ⊙ *Closed Mon. and Tues.*

Sage Vegan Bistro

$$ | **VEGETARIAN** | Vegan food can be satisfying, filling, and incredibly delicious; and Sage Vegan Bistro, situated in an industrial-modern space on busy Sunset Boulevard, is proof, with its vegan beer and anything made with jackfruit. And like any quality vegan place in L.A., the food is made from locally sourced and organic produce. **Known for:** vegan ice cream; cauliflower wings; vegan beer. $ *Average main: $22* ✉ *1700 Sunset Blvd., Echo Park* ☎ *213/989–1718* ⊕ *www.sageveganbistro.com.*

Spoon and Pork

$ | **FILIPINO** | In a city where food trucks can be successful enough to have their own brick-and-mortar spaces, and where Filipino food has quickly become a craze, it's no surprise that Spoon and Pork has found its rightful place in the neighborhood. With a name that cleverly plays on the traditional Filipino way of eating (using both spoon and fork), this modern Filipino food spot is the perfect introduction to the cuisine. **Known for:** adobo pork belly; lechon kawali; Filipino comfort food. $ *Average main: $16* ✉ *3131 W. Sunset Blvd., Echo Park* ☎ *323/922–6061* ⊕ *www.spoonandpork.com* ⊙ *Closed Mon.*

Valerie Confections

$ | **CAFÉ** | Most cafés treat tea as an afterthought, but at Valerie Confections, it's the main event. Different varieties of tea take over half the menu and many of the morsels advertised only serve to complement the tea. **Known for:** homemade chocolates; petit fours; excellent tea. $ *Average main: $15* ✉ *1665 Echo Park Ave., Echo Park* ☎ *213/250–9365* ⊕ *valerieconfections.com.*

Wax Paper

$ | **SANDWICHES** | While Wax Paper has a few outdoor tables set up for dining, this tiny sandwich place in Frogtown is tailor-made for to-go orders. The modest selection of brilliantly prepared sandwiches are made with fresh ingredients and named after NPR hosts; they're best enjoyed along the river or at a park nearby. **Known for:** creative to-go sandwiches; Kai Ryssdal tuna sandwich; friendly, low-key atmosphere. $ *Average main: $14* ✉ *2902 Knox Ave., Echo Park* ☎ *No phone* ⊕ *www.waxpaperco.com.*

Nightlife

See an up-and-coming local band, bring your own records to the bar, or impress a date in this eclectic neighborhood that manages to maintain its cultural authenticity more so than its neighbor, Silver Lake.

Bar Flores

BARS | Latina-owned Bar Flores may look like any indoor–outdoor bar you'll find in sun-kissed Puerto Vallarta in Mexico, but the elevated cocktails served here are very Los Angeles. Formerly, the pop-up speakeasy Sip, Bar Flores found its home in Echo Park back in 2012 and has established itself as a popular local hangout. Margarita Wednesdays are a must; the back patio has a taco stand in case you get hungry. ✉ *1542 Sunset Blvd., Echo Park* ☎ *213/266–8006* ⊕ *www.barflores.com.*

The Douglas

PUBS | If you're looking for that everybody-knows-your-name bar vibe in L.A., look no further than the Douglas where owners Dave and Johnny warmly wave to patrons, new and old alike, entering the front patio. Bonus that the draft beers and hard kombuchas are affordable enough to keep you coming back. The food is casual and no-nonsense, with chicken wings that are done right and served with house-made blue cheese, crowd-favorite breakfast burritos, and homemade falafels. Be prepared to rub elbows with Dodgers fans on game night. ⊠ *1400 Sunset Blvd., Echo Park* ☎ *213/947–3180* ⊕ *www.thedouglasla. com.*

★ The Echo

LIVE MUSIC | Echo Park is peppered with music venues, but if you want to be in the heart of the neighborhood's live music scene, you should head to the Echo. With a full bar and recurring theme nights, the spot hosts cutting-edge music from both up-and-coming local and touring acts as well as well-known bands. ⊠ *1822 Sunset Blvd., Echoplex entrance at 1154 Glendale Blvd., Echo Park* ☎ *213/413–8200* ⊕ *theecho.com.*

El Prado

BARS | A small selection of constantly rotating wine and beer ensures you'll get to try something new and interesting each time you visit. A record player serves as the main source of music—while the idea may seem twee, it's the heart of a popular Tuesday night record club, where patrons bring in their own vinyl. ⊠ *1805 W. Sunset Blvd., Echo Park* ⊕ *www.elpradobar.com.*

★ Mohawk Bend

PUBS | There are plenty of reasons to stop by Mohawk Bend: 72 craft beers on tap, a wide range of California-only liquor, a vegetarian and vegan-friendly menu that includes tailored-to-your-wants pizza, and a buffalo cauliflower that—rumor has it—started the whole trend. There might be a long line to get into this 100-year-old former theater in the evenings, but it's worth it. ⊠ *2141 Sunset Blvd., Echo Park* ☎ *213/483–2337* ⊕ *mohawk.la.*

The Semi-Tropic

BARS | This bar is part fancy Brooklyn café where you might study or linger and lounge over cold drinks with friends and part Instagram-worthy L.A. cocktail bar populated with cool locals. Chicken enchiladas and fajita bowls share the menu with roasted beef hummus and charcuterie. This being an L.A. watering hole, movie and TV show inspirations are everywhere, and being one of the filming locations for popular show *The L Word* is a frequently dropped accolade. Dana's Night is held here once a month to provide a venue for the local queer community. The outdoor patio is a newer addition and perfect for those nice Southern California summer nights, and board games are on hand to encourage those linger and lounge vibes. ⊠ *1412 Glendale Blvd., Echo Park* ☎ *213/568–3827* ⊕ *www.thesemitropic.com.*

★ 1642

LIVE MUSIC | This romantically lit hole-in-the-wall is easy to miss, but you should aim to check it out if you're a discerning wine connoisseur or looking to experience the best of California's microbreweries. Perfect for first dates, come here to experiment with craft beers or to warm up with wine while listening to some live old-time fiddle tunes. ⊠ *1642 W. Temple St., Echo Park* ☎ *213/989–6836* ⊕ *www.1642bar.com.*

Tilda

WINE BARS | Tucked into Echo Park's more residential area where its only other commercial companions are a cactus shop, a tiny neighborhood market, a juice store, and sister property Bacetti, Tilda may not be at the center of the city's buzzing nightlife scene. But wine connoisseurs would agree that it's the perfect place to sample California natural wines as well as offerings from Italy, Austria, and France. Pair your favorites with the wine bar's modest selection of simple fare. ⊠ *1507 Echo Park Ave., Echo Park* ☎ *213/995–6090* ⊕ *www.tildawine.com.*

🛍 Shopping

With a bit more edge than neighboring Silver Lake, this increasingly cool area has an artsy, do-it-yourself appeal. Secondhand stores squeeze in alongside vegan restaurants, hip dive bars, and friendly boutiques stocked with clothes by local designers.

Stories Books and Café
BOOKS | With an off-the-beaten-path collection of new and used literature, a café catering to freelancers and freethinkers, and a back patio that showcases singer-songwriters, Stories Books and Café is an authentic reflection of Echo Park. Readings, signings, and other events are a regular occurrence. ✉ *1716 Sunset Blvd., Echo Park* ☎ *213/413–3733* 🌐 *www.storiesla.com.*

Time Travel Mart
OTHER SPECIALTY STORE | **FAMILY** | You probably won't find anything useful in the Time Travel Mart and that's exactly the point. From dinosaur eggs to robot milk, this is a store that touts the absurdly hilarious—all of which should bring back memories of your childhood and maybe a little bit of joy. That's because the store holds a secret: it's really a fundraiser for the nonprofit 826LA, which tutors neighborhood kids in the back section. So even when you're buying something unnecessary but absolutely wonderful, remember it's for a noble and worthy cause. ✉ *1714 W. Sunset Blvd., Echo Park* ☎ *213/556–4861* 🌐 *timetravelmart.com.*

Atwater Village

Alongside nearby Glassell Park and Cypress Park, Atwater Village is one of the seven neighborhoods that make up the Northeast Los Angeles region, christened NELA by some locals. While it mostly mirrors the former two neighborhoods' predominantly residential status, it also swaggers with Los Feliz's upmarket, hip vibe. The main thoroughfares of Glendale and Los Feliz Boulevards are paved with neighborhood bars, elevated restaurants, and independent coffee shops, not to mention smart boutique shops touting artisanal goods.

🍴 Restaurants

Quality trumps quantity in Atwater Village. Expect modest yet eclectic menus stuffed with epicurean delights. Dropping by on a Sunday gives you the option to shop for fresh produce at the farmers' market.

Bon Vivant Market and Café
$$ | **AMERICAN** | With the extensive and eclectic breakfast, lunch, and dinner menus here, coupled with the fantastic cocktail menu and charming little marketplace, breakfast can easily turn into lunch and then late lunch. Patrons tend to adopt a slow pace, staggering orders of coffee, luscious crepes, small plates, and delicious entrées, all while adopting the laissez-faire attitude that is encouraged here. **Known for:** seasonal fromage and charcuterie boards; classic American fare; partially open-air setting. [$] *Average main: $26* ✉ *3155 Glendale Blvd., Atwater Village* ☎ *323/284–8013* 🌐 *www.bonvivantmarketcafe.com.*

Dune
$ | **MEDITERRANEAN** | **FAMILY** | Simple, small, and understated, it's easy to miss the best falafel spot in town. Hearty Middle Eastern falafel and chicken shawarma are piled on homemade flatbread. **Known for:** organic green-herb falafel sandwich; fried chicken shawarma; outdoor dining. [$] *Average main: $15* ✉ *3143 Glendale Blvd., Atwater Village* ☎ *323/486–7073* 🌐 *www.dunekitchen.com.*

Link N Hops
$ | **HOT DOG** | Almost just your typical sports bar, there are a couple of things that elevate Link N Hops above its competitors, like excellent hot dog sandwiches and 24 craft beers on tap. And about those signature links: there are around 20, some of which are made with more exotic ingredients like rattlesnake, duck, and bacon, not to mention a choice of toppings. **Known for:** Atwater knackwurst; smoked Portuguese Hawaiian sausage; happy hour specials. [$] *Average main:*

$13 ✉ 3111 Glendale Blvd., Atwater Village ☎ 323/426–9049 🌐 linknhops.com.

Momed

$$ | MIDDLE EASTERN | The perfect pairing of simplicity and complexity, Momed serves Mediterranean fare that is comforting yet upscale. The welcoming atmosphere is just as perfect for a romantic date night as it is for a more boisterous brunch with friends. **Known for:** excellent Atlantic salmon; short rib tagine; fun weekend brunch. [$] *Average main: $27 ✉ 3245 Casitas Ave., Atwater Village ☎ 323/522–3488 🌐 www.atmomed.com.*

The Morrison

$ | BURGER | FAMILY | A friendly neighborhood Scottish pub, the Morrison comes with a bit of an upmarket flair, a kids' menu, and believe it or not, dishes for your canine friends. And, since this is L.A., it serves a damn fine brunch. **Known for:** bacon bourbonator burger; cheese fries with bacon jam; eclectic whiskey menu. [$] *Average main: $20 ✉ 3179 Los Feliz Blvd., Atwater Village ☎ 323/667–1839 🌐 www.morrisonrestaurant.com.*

Tacos Villa Corona

$ | MEXICAN | You likely won't notice this cramped little spot on Glendale Boulevard unless there's a line or you're a fan of the late, great Anthony Bourdain, who was a big fan. About that line—it's almost always there, especially weekend mornings, when Tacos Villa Corona caters to the hungover crowd. **Known for:** chorizo and potato burrito; breakfast burritos; long lines. [$] *Average main: $5 ✉ 3185 Glendale Blvd., Atwater Village ☎ 323/661–3458 ⏲ Closed Mon.*

Tam O'Shanter

$$$ | IRISH | It's a bit of a specific recognition, but Tam O'Shanter is the oldest restaurant run by the same family in the same location in Los Angeles, operating for more than 90 years in its Tudor-style spot—that alone makes this place a worthy addition to any Atwater Village visit. Then there's their delicious food whose $30 prices are completely worth it, not to mention the fact that, once upon a time, it was Walt Disney's favorite restaurant. **Known for:** Tam O'Shanter cut of steak; interesting history; Scotch and whiskey flights. [$] *Average main: $32 ✉ 2980 Los Feliz Blvd., Atwater Village ☎ 323/664–0228 🌐 www.lawrysonline.com/tam-o-shanter.*

Wanderlust Creamery

$ | AMERICAN | FAMILY | This ice-cream shop showcases the flavors of the globe in artisanal frozen delights. Every single ice cream is light, creamy, and made with 100% organic milk. **Known for:** mango sticky rice vegan ice cream; ube malted crunch; seasonal flavors. [$] *Average main: $5 ✉ 3134 Glendale Blvd., Atwater Village ☎ 818/774–9888 🌐 www.wanderlustcreamery.com.*

🍸 Nightlife

★ Bigfoot Lodge

BARS | Don't be turned off by the glaring log cabin theme (which is intensified by signature cocktails called Scout's Honor and Roasted Marshmallow). Bigfoot Lodge is beloved by Eastside denizens, and despite appearances, it's every bit a low-key, unpretentious neighborhood bar that specializes in shots and beer and welcomes the occasional tourist that happens to stumble inside. *✉ 3172 Los Feliz Blvd., Atwater Village ☎ 323/662–9227 🌐 www.bigfootlodge.com.*

Golden Road Brewing

BREWPUBS | Sustainability and support of local community has always been a big part of this L.A. brewery's ethos, but more important, so is making great food and, of course, excellent beer. With several core brands, as well as a few specialty and seasonal brands, this is a must-stop for any craft beer lover vacationing in the City of Angels. *✉ 5410 W. San Fernando Rd., Atwater*

Village ☎ *818/243–2337* ⊕ *goldenroad.la/atwater-village.*

The Roost

BARS | Forget all your misconceptions about dive bars and walk into the Roost, whose comforting elements—a jukebox that comes fully loaded with Tom Petty, Springsteen, and the Allman Brothers Band, cozy leather booths, dimmed lights, and decent hearty food—will make you feel like you've flown back to your hometown for the holidays. The cocktails aren't too shabby either, but do bring cash. ⊠ *3100 Los Feliz Blvd., Atwater Village* ☎ *323/664–7272.*

Verdugo Bar

BEER GARDENS | It's hard to decide whether the best thing about this place is its selection of 20 craft beers on tap and menu of enticing cocktails or the large beer garden furnished with picnic tables. Be warned, this place can get crowded, but it's worth it, especially on a hot, sunny day (so pretty much every day). ⊠ *3408 Verdugo Rd., Atwater Village* ☎ *323/257–3408* ⊕ *www.verdugobar.com.*

Shopping

Atwater Village partakes in the tradition of independent boutique shops boasting a bright, modern look and touting artisanal and locally made goods from small businesses. It's a small neighborhood, so you wont exactly shop 'til you drop, but you can definitely knock off a good couple of hours popping in for a bit of retail therapy.

Potted

FLORIST | There's something comforting about Potted, like you've just walked into your parents' sunroom or a woodland fairy's home. This is a garden full of colors, nooks and crannies to tuck yourself into, and treasures of the botanic kind waiting to be discovered. It's every plant lover's paradise, but even those who wouldn't consider themselves to

be plant fiends will be tempted to spend a fortune here. ⊠ *3158 Los Feliz Blvd., Atwater Village* ☎ *323/665–3801* ⊕ *pottedstore.com.*

Treehaus

MIXED CLOTHING | The beauty of Treehaus isn't that it's an independent boutique—Los Angeles has plenty of those—but that it carries a great assortment of retail pieces, from women's and children's clothing to accessories and home goods, all in a cozy rectangular space. ⊠ *3153 Glendale Blvd., Atwater Village* ☎ *323/230–6776* ⊕ *www.treehausla.com.*

Highland Park

In the early 20th century, Highland Park was a bastion for artists who erected numerous Arts and Crafts movement houses. It evolved into a largely immigrant community in the middle of the century and in the last few years has become a hybrid of its history. Local business owners have revived beautiful historic buildings and turned them into exciting new restaurants, shops, and watering holes that pay homage to the area's past. These stand side by side with longtime establishments that serve up some of the best, and most authentic, tacos in town.

Sights

Heritage Square Museum

HISTORY MUSEUM | Looking like a prop street set up by a film studio, Heritage Square resembles a row of bright dollhouses in the modest Highland Park neighborhood. Five 19th-century residences, a train station, a church, a carriage barn, and a 1909 boxcar that was originally part of the Southern Pacific Railroad, all built between the Civil War and World War I, were moved to this small park from various locations in Southern California to save them from the wrecking ball. The latest addition, a re-creation

Sights

1 Heritage Square Museum **D5**

Restaurants

1 CaCao Mexicatessen **C2**
2 Cafe Birdie **D5**
3 Cindy's **C2**
4 Donut Friend **C3**
5 El Huarache Azteca **C4**
6 Goldburger . **D4**
7 Joy **C4**
8 Kitchen Mouse **D5**
9 Know-realitypie **C1**
10 Polka Polish Cuisine **A3**
11 Town Pizza **C3**

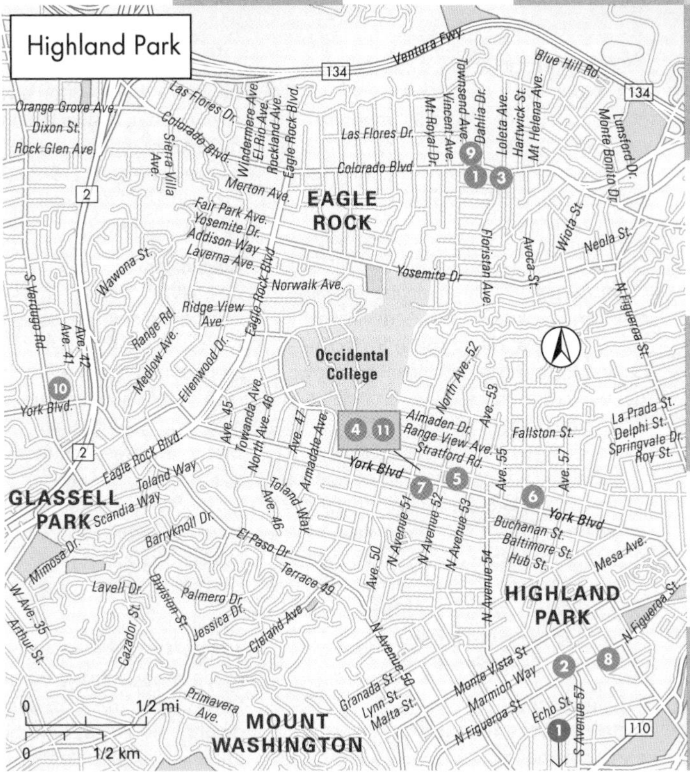

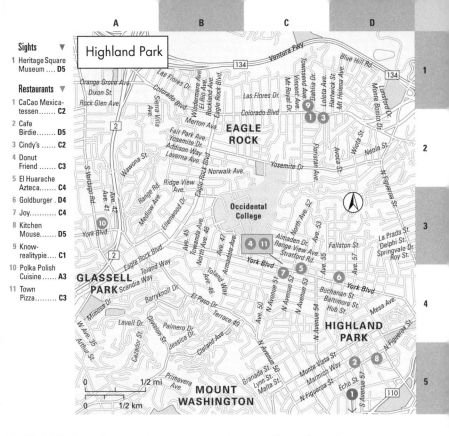

of a World War I–era drugstore, has a vintage soda fountain and traditional products. Docents dressed in period costume lead visitors through the lavish homes, giving an informative picture of Los Angeles in the early 1900s. Don't miss the unique 1893 Octagon House, one of just a handful of its kind built in California. ✉ *3800 Homer St., Highland Park* ☎ *323/225–2700* 🌐 *www.heritagesquare.org* 🎫 *$10* 🕒 *Closed Tues.–Fri. and federal holiday Mon.*

🍴 Restaurants

CaCao Mexicatessen

$ | **MEXICAN** | Opened by local Christie Lujan in 2009, CaCao Mexicatessen was one of the first places in town to showcase the creative potential of the street-style taco, offering options such as sea urchin and pork crackling as fillings. With handmade tortillas and a serious commitment to the flavors of Mexico, CaCao has embedded itself as one of the go-to places for Mexican food in Northeast L.A. **Known for:** duck carnitas taco; Korean short rib tacos; modern Mexican cuisine. [$] *Average main: $14* ✉ *1576 Colorado Blvd., Highland Park* ☎ *323/478–2791* 🌐 *www.cacaodeli.com* 🕒 *Closed Mon.*

Cafe Birdie

$$ | **MEDITERRANEAN** | This spacious 1920s-style spot along a quickly revitalizing stretch of Figueroa has established itself as a neighborhood bistro frequented by Highland Park residents, as well as folks from all over Los Angeles. The eclectic menu skillfully blends elements of European, North African, Southern, and Asian cuisines, tying them together with a fresh California flair and a gorgeously lush interior inspired by a fictional meeting-of-two-souls narrative. **Known for:** Moroccan-spiced fried chicken; seasonal cocktails; modern and luxurious yet lush and airy. [$] *Average main: $22* ✉ *5631 N. Figueroa St., Highland Park* ☎ *323/739–6928* 🌐 *www.cafebirdiela.com.*

Cindy's

$ | **DINER** | **FAMILY** | The husband-and-wife team that took over Cindy's never set out to create a trendy space for hipsters looking for their next artisanal fix; they just wanted to make great, accessible food. That's exactly what they've done, and by doing so they've established a neighborhood restaurant with reasonable prices and back-to-basics food that just so happens to look retro cool. **Known for:** brisket hash; barbecue cheeseburger with "cowboy candy"; retro diner–style space. [$] *Average main: $16* ✉ *1500 Colorado Blvd., Highland Park* ☎ *323/257–7375* 🌐 *cindyseaglerock.com.*

★ **Donut Friend**

$ | **BAKERY** | When this music-influenced doughnut shop first opened on York Boulevard in the early days of Highland Park's renaissance, there wasn't much there, and its arrival helped shape the now-bustling strip and its vegan inclinations. Donut Friend has evolved into a destination in its own right, touting both a signature and limited menu of purely vegan doughnuts—which also happen to be inspired by the pop punk and emo music scene. **Known for:** fun flavors like Green Teagan and Sara (with matcha tea glaze); all-vegan ingredients; ice cream and shakes. [$] *Average main: $4* ✉ *5107 York Blvd., Highland Park* ☎ *213/908–2745* 🌐 *www.donutfriend.com.*

El Huarache Azteca

$ | **MEXICAN** | **FAMILY** | While you definitely should try the flat shoe-shaped dish El Huarache Azteca is named after—think somewhere between a flatbread and a tostada—you cannot go wrong with any of the other options at this family restaurant that's been a fixture in the area for the last couple of decades. Just be aware there's often a wait for the food to come out. **Known for:** no-frills Mexican dishes; agua fresca; super huarache. [$] *Average main: $15* ✉ *5225 York Blvd., Highland Park* ☎ *323/478–9572* 🌐 *orderelhuaracheazteca.com.*

Goldburger

$ | **BURGER** | Smashburger spots in L.A. are a dime a dozen, but only a handful—like Goldburger—stand out. Tucked in a tiny spot on buzzing York Boulevard, this joint makes some of the juiciest, tastiest smashburgers in town, thanks in large part to the grass-fed beef and house-made sauces. **Known for:** smashburger; craft sodas; counter seating. [$] *Average main: $12* ✉ *5623 York Blvd., Highland Park* ☎ *323/274–4303* 🌐 *www.goldburgerla.com.*

Joy

$ | **TAIWANESE** | Bringing Taiwanese food made with California ingredients to a formerly Central American–dominated neighborhood may have been a reach, but Joy makes it work by keeping close ties with the community, preserving its building's history, and naturally, making delicious affordable food. Pine & Crane's sister restaurant is more accessible, spice-wise, but the simple-to-make dishes on its small menu are still comforting, wholesome, and familiar to those who grew up eating some versions of them. **Known for:** dan dan noodles; mince pork and rice; fast service. [$] *Average main: $10* ✉ *5100 York Blvd., Highland Park* ☎ *323/999–07642* 🌐 *www.joyonyork.com.*

Kitchen Mouse

$ | **DINER** | Born out of the owner's need for more kitchen space for her growing production catering business, Kitchen Mouse has blossomed into a wildly popular neighborhood restaurant with a cozy rustic-meets-modern look and an inspired, mostly organic vegan–vegetarian menu. The food is bright with vibrant flavors. **Known for:** Morning Glory

Bowl; oat corn and buckwheat pancakes; excellent breakfast and brunch. $ *Average main: $14* ✉ *5902 N. Figueroa St., Highland Park* ☎ *323/259–9555* ⊕ *www. kitchenmousela.com.*

★ Knowrealitypie

$ | **BAKERY** | The award-winning Knowrealitypie, hidden in a shop the size of a large walk-in closet, is truly a passion project, with co-owner Tracy Ann DeVore furiously paddling beneath the water's surface to make those homemade pies on her own. That's why it's only open from Thursday through Saturday until it sells out, which it often does. **Known for:** triple berry Cabernet pie; salted caramel mango rum pie; vegan and gluten-free options on request. $ *Average main: $6* ✉ *5106 Townsend Ave., Highland Park* ☎ *916/799–5772* ⊕ *www.knowrealitypie. com* ⊗ *Closed Mon.–Thurs.*

Polka Polish Cuisine

$ | **POLISH** | Polka Polish Cuisine, like most restaurants in L.A., went through a makeover during the lockdown, and now boasts a more modern interior and an airy patio that offers outdoor seating. But the food here—traditional Polish fare like pierogi, schnitzel, and stuffed cabbage rolls—is just as delicious and comforting as ever. **Known for:** hearty Polish comfort food; traditional pierogi and kielbasa; mom-and-pop ambience. $ *Average main: $20* ✉ *4112 Verdugo Rd., Highland Park* ☎ *323/255–7887* ⊕ *www.polkares-taurant.com* ⊗ *Closed Mon. and Tues.*

Town Pizza

$$ | **PIZZA** | The red building situated on the corner of York and North Avenue 51 houses a pizzeria that's as quirky and hip as the neighborhood it inhabits. Pizza purists, however, may cringe at some of the toppings, which include dried figs, corn, and mole. **Known for:** vegan topping options; creative pizzas like The Pig & The Fig (prosciutto and fig); trendy atmosphere. $ *Average main: $24* ✉ *5101 York Blvd., Highland Park* ☎ *323/344–8696* ⊕ *www.townla.com.*

Nightlife

Barcade LA

THEMED ENTERTAINMENT | This Highland Park outpost of an NYC institution started an arcade bar revolution in Los Angeles, serving elevated yet accessible (and more importantly, affordable) cocktails and American fare amidst rows of beloved retro arcade games and pinball machines. Barcade LA has built a community here, holding events like a pinball league to encourage loyal patrons to form bonds with like-minded individuals. The food and cocktail menus are fantastic as they are, with offerings like crispy fish tacos, the super smashburger, and Parmesan cauliflower wings being highly addictive. But, this spot loves to keep things interesting, which means dishes and cocktails are subject to change. You may want to block off the entire day as you visit or revisit classics like *Pac-Man, Marvel VS Capcom 2,* and *Mortal Kombat 2.* ✉ *5684 York Blvd., Highland Park* ☎ *323/274–4798* ⊕ *barcadelosangeles. com.*

Block Party

BEER GARDENS | This spot fills the beer-garden need in Highland Park, and it does it very well, with a large shuffleboard and a massive screen projecting LAFC matches, along with plenty of picnic tables where you can chug (or nurse) beer and wine. The selection, from small-batch and craft vendors, is on point; the more adventurous may want to grab a *michelada* and *paleta* combo. ✉ *5050 York Blvd., Highland Park* ☎ *323/741–2747* ⊕ *www. blockpartyhlp.com.*

The Hermosillo

PUBS | This is the kind of laid-back pub every neighborhood should have, with an excellent selection of locally focused draft beer on tap, a rotating wine list, and mouthwatering food. To add to its allure, award-winning Highland Park Brewery got its start in the pub's back storage room and is still featured prominently on the menu. ✉ *5125 York Blvd., Highland Park* ☎ *323/739–6459.*

★ Highland Park Bowl

THEMED ENTERTAINMENT | **FAMILY** | Once an ambitious restoration project, Highland Park Bowl now serves as a massive throwback to its Prohibition-era roots as an alcohol-prescribing doctor's office and drugstore with its own bowling alley. That bowling alley remains, complete with the original pin machine. The hooch-pushing doctor and druggist, however, are long gone. But now there's an Italian restaurant that serves excellent pizza made from scratch using a mother dough brought all the way from Italy. ✉ *5621 N. Figueroa St., Highland Park* ☎ *323/257–2695* ⊕ *www.highlandparkbowl.com.*

La Cuevita

BARS | Everyone could use a little more mezcal and tequila in their lives, and La Cuevita has a lot of it, often in its collection of tasty cocktails. This Mexico-themed bar—complete with free Taco Tuesdays, a dark red interior, and a picture of a bandito overlooking the patrons—has one of the best happy hours in L.A., making it the perfect place to start your evening. ✉ *5922 N. Figueroa St., Highland Park* ☎ *323/255–6871.*

The York

PUBS | Since 2007, before Highland Park became trendy, the York has been holding its own as the ultimate neighborhood bar. It's not just that the aesthetic gives off that neighborhood vibe (think exposed brick and chalkboard menus), but the craft beers on tap are great, and the pub food is delicious—the cheddar burger and the fish-and-chips are favorites. ✉ *5018 York Blvd., Highland Park* ☎ *323/255–9675* ⊕ *www.theyorkonyork.com.*

Shopping

Figueroa Boulevard isn't buzzing only with bars and restaurants but also with ample opportunities for retail therapy. Small style outposts pave this street, as well as the connecting York Boulevard, with adorable gift shops, record stores, and spots to satisfy your vintage shopping itch.

Galco's Soda Pop Stop

OTHER FOOD & DRINK | **FAMILY** | A local fixture in Highland Park for decades, Galco's is in some ways a trip down memory lane, carrying more than 600 sodas—most of which harken back to the days when soda was a regional affair—and options from all over the world. They also have a collection of retro candies, a soda creation station with more than 100 syrups to choose from, and a selection of alcohol that would put most liquor stores to shame. ✉ *5702 York Blvd., Highland Park* ☎ *323/255–7115* ⊕ *sodapopstop.com.*

Permanent Records

MUSIC | Part of the vinyl resurgence since 2013, Permanent Records stocks new and used vinyl for every musical taste and does it without any snobbery. The record store, which often has in-store performances, also runs its own label that focuses on local bands, limited-edition runs, and reissues. ✉ *1906 Cypress Ave., Highland Park* ☎ *323/332–2312* ⊕ *www.permanentrecordsla.com.*

TOPO by Kitchen Mouse

MARKET | Adjacent to its sister establishment, Kitchen Mouse, is this charming little market stop for all your pastry, grab 'n' go nourishment, and catering needs, complete with a small shop that touts adorable home and gift items. It's a must-stop after you've had your vegan fix at the restaurant. ✉ *5906 N. Figueroa St., Highland Park* ☎ *323/259–9555.*

Chapter 12

PASADENA

12

Updated by
Candice Yacono

⊙ Sights	🍴 Restaurants	🛏 Hotels	💼 Shopping	🍸 Nightlife
★★★☆☆	★★☆☆☆	★★☆☆☆	★★☆☆☆	★☆☆☆☆

NEIGHBORHOOD SNAPSHOT

TOP EXPERIENCES

■ **Visit the Huntington Library:** In addition to a collection of 18th-century British art, this library has 4 million manuscripts and 700,000 books, including the Gutenberg Bible.

■ **Walk through the Huntington's Botanical Gardens:** Set aside a couple of hours to enjoy the expansive lawns and stately trees surrounding the Huntington Library.

■ **See American craftsmanship at the Gamble House:** The teak staircase and cabinetry are just a few of the highlights at this home, built in 1908.

■ **Check out the Norton Simon Museum:** This small museum's fine collection features works by Renoir, Degas, Gauguin, and others

■ **Hang out in Old Town Pasadena:** Spend the afternoon walking around this 12-block historic town filled with cafés, restaurants, and shops.

VIEWFINDER

City Hall: Pasadena's iconic, century-old City Hall boasts a fairy-tale tower with Italian Renaissance and Spanish influences, and a rose garden that makes a heavenly backdrop when it's in bloom. ⊠ *100 Garfield Ave.*

Plaza Las Fuentes: An elaborate 2,500-square foot flower-filled tiled mural wall in the courtyard of this plaza across from City Hall makes a picture-perfect backdrop. ⊠ *135 N. Los Robles Ave.*

Colorado Street Bridge: Love *La La Land?* Head to the soaring arches of this bridge. The best spot to bag your selfie is under the east end of the bridge on North Arroyo Boulevard. Look for the parking area on the north side of the street and duck under the bridge there. ⊠ *504 W. Colorado Blvd.*

GETTING HERE

■ To reach Pasadena from Downtown Los Angeles, drive north on the Pasadena Freeway (I–110). From Hollywood and the San Fernando Valley, use the Ventura Freeway (Highway 134, east), which cuts through Glendale, skirting the foothills, before arriving in Pasadena. There are several city parking lots located in Old Town Pasadena with low rates, all close to Colorado Boulevard, the main drag. On-street parking here is also widely available.

PLANNING YOUR TIME

■ The Huntington Library should command most of your time. Just be sure to keep the summer heat in mind when you visit—the gardens are more pleasant during the cooler morning hours. A stop at the beautiful Gamble House shouldn't take more than an hour, leaving plenty of time for an afternoon visit to the Norton Simon Museum, one of the area's best spots to enjoy world-class art. Unless you're planning on seeing a game or hitting the world-class flea market, you will probably want to skip the Rose Bowl. Head to Old Pasadena in the evening, when the wide boulevards and leafy side streets come to life. Then catch a performance at A Noise Within.

Although seemingly absorbed into the general Los Angeles sprawl, Pasadena is a separate and distinct city. It's best known for the Tournament of Roses, or more commonly, the Rose Bowl, seen around the world every New Year's Day. But the city has sites worth seeing year-round—from gorgeous Craftsman homes to exceptional museums, particularly the Norton Simon and the Huntington Library, Art Museum, and Botanical Gardens. Note that the Huntington and the Old Mill reside in San Marino, a well-heeled, 4-square-mile residential area just over the Pasadena line.

First-time visitors to L.A. only here for a short time might find it hard to get out to Pasadena. However, if you've had your fill of city life and are looking for a nearby escape that feels much farther away than it is, with open space and fresher air, it's the perfect trip.

Start at the **Botanical Gardens,** then spend the afternoon strolling around **Old Town Pasadena,** with shops and restaurants filling its 19th-century brick buildings. Art and architecture lovers shouldn't miss the city's top sight, the **Norton Simon Museum,** most noted for its excellent collection of Degas, as well as works by Rembrandt, Goya, and Picasso. The **Gamble House** is an immense three-story house and one of the country's shining examples of American Arts and Crafts bungalow architecture. The thing that might surprise you most about visiting Pasadena is that even the drive here—on the freeway, though not during rush hour—is a scenic one. The Pasadena Freeway follows the curves of an arroyo (dry creek), lined with old sycamore trees. It was the main road north during the early days of Los Angeles, when horses and buggies made their way through the countryside to the small town of Pasadena. In 1939 the road became the Arroyo Seco Parkway, the first freeway in Los Angeles.

Pasadena

NORTH ARROYO

NORMANDIE HEIGHTS

PASADENA

SOUTH ARROYO

SOUTH PASADENA

OAK KNOLL

HIGHLAND PARK

0 1 mi
0 1 km

Sights

Descanso Gardens

GARDEN | Getting its name from the Spanish word for "rest," this 160-acre oasis is a respite from city life, shaded by massive oak trees. Known for being a smaller, mellower version of the nearby Huntington, Descanso Gardens features denser foliage, quaint dirt paths, and some hilly climbs that can make for good exercise. It's the perfect place to come in search of wonderful scents—between the lilacs, the acres of roses, and the forest of California redwoods, pines, and junipers, you can enjoy all sorts of fragrances. A forest of California live oak trees makes a dramatic backdrop for thousands of camellias and azaleas and the breathtaking 5-acre International Rosarium holding 1,700 varieties of antique and modern roses. There are also a gift shop, a historic home, and a café. ⊠ 1418 Descanso Dr., La Cañada/Flintridge ☎ 818/949–4200 ⊕ www. descansogardens.org ⊠ $15; often free 3rd Tues. of month.

The Gamble House

HISTORIC HOME | Built by Charles and Henry Greene in 1908, this American Arts and Crafts bungalow illustrates the incredible craftsmanship that went into early L.A. architecture. The term "bungalow" can be misleading, since the Gamble House is a huge three-story home. To wealthy Easterners such as the Gambles (as in Procter & Gamble), this type of vacation home seemed informal compared with their mansions back home. Admirers swoon over the teak staircase and cabinetry, the Greene and Greene–designed furniture, and an Emil Lange glass door. The dark exterior has broad eaves, with sleeping porches on the second floor. An hour-long, docent-led tour of the Gamble's interior will draw your eye to the exquisite details. For those who want to see more of the Greene and Greene homes, there are guided walks around the historic Arroyo Terrace neighborhood. Advance tickets are highly recommended.

■ **TIP→ Film buffs might recognize this as Doc Brown's house from** *Back to the Future.* ⊠ 4 Westmoreland Pl., Pasadena ☎ 626/793–3334 ⊕ gamblehouse.org ⊠ $15 ☉ Closed Mon. and Wed.

★ Huntington Library, Art Museum, and Botanical Gardens

GARDEN | If you have time for just one stop in the Pasadena area, be sure to see this sprawling estate built for railroad tycoon Henry E. Huntington in the early 1900s. Henry and his wife, Arabella (who was also his aunt by marriage), voraciously collected rare books and manuscripts, botanical specimens, and 18th-century British art. The institution they established became one of the most extraordinary cultural complexes in the world.

The library contains more than 700,000 books and 4 million manuscripts, including one of the world's biggest history of science collections and a Gutenberg Bible.

Don't resist being lured outside into the 130-acre Botanical Gardens, which extend out from the main building. The 10-acre Desert Garden has one of the world's largest groups of mature cacti and other succulents (visit on a cool morning or late afternoon). The Shakespeare Garden, meanwhile, blooms with plants mentioned in Shakespeare's works. The Japanese Garden features an authentic ceremonial teahouse built in Kyoto in the 1960s, and will soon see the addition of another historic building. A waterfall flows from the teahouse to the ponds below. The Chinese Garden, which is among the largest outside China, sinews around waveless pools. The Bing Children's Garden lets tiny tots explore the ancient elements of water, fire, air, and earth. Several on-site dining options are available, including the Rose Garden Tea Room, where afternoon tea is served (reserve in advance).

The Japanese Garden at the Huntington Botanical Gardens features an authentic ceremonial teahouse built in Kyoto in the 1960s.

A 1¼-hour guided tour of the Botanical Gardens is led by docents at posted times, and a free brochure with a map and property highlights is available in the entrance pavilion. Tickets for a monthly free-admission day are snapped up within minutes online, so plan carefully. ⊠ *1151 Oxford Rd., San Marino* ☎ *626/405–2100* ⊕ *www.huntington.org* ✉ *From $25; free admission 1st Thurs. of every month with advance ticket* ⊘ *Closed Tues.*

Los Angeles County Arboretum and Botanic Garden

GARDEN | FAMILY | Wander through a re-created tropical forest, a South African landscape, or the Australian outback at this family-friendly arboretum. One highlight is the tropical greenhouse, with carnivorous-looking orchids and a pond full of brilliantly colored goldfish. The house and stables of the eccentric real-estate pioneer Lucky Baldwin are well-preserved and worth a visit. Kids will love the many peacocks and waterfowl that roam the property. The most recent additions include a new forest pathway and the Garden of Quiet Reflection, filled with contemplative quotes, a sundial, and East Asian flora. ⊠ *301 N. Baldwin Ave., Arcadia* ☎ *626/821–3222* ⊕ *www. arboretum.org* ✉ *$15; free 3rd Tues. of month with advance ticket.*

★ Norton Simon Museum

ART MUSEUM | As seen in the New Year's Day Tournament of Roses Parade, this low-profile brown building is one of the finest midsize museums anywhere, with a collection that spans more than 2,000 years of Western and Asian art. It all began in the 1950s when Norton Simon (Hunt-Wesson Foods, McCalls Corporation, and Canada Dry) started collecting works by Degas, Renoir, Gauguin, and Cézanne. His collection grew to include works by old masters and impressionists, modern works from Europe, and Indian and Southeast Asian art. Today the museum is richest in works by Rembrandt, Picasso, and, most of all, Degas.

Head down to the bottom floor to see temporary exhibits and phenomenal

Southeast Asian and Indian sculptures and artifacts, where pieces like a Ban Chiang blackware vessel date back to well before 1000 BC. Don't miss a living artwork outdoors: the garden, conceived by noted Southern California landscape designer Nancy Goslee Power. The tranquil pond was inspired by Monet's gardens at Giverny. ⊠ *411 W. Colorado Blvd., Pasadena* ☎ *626/449–6840* ⊕ *www. nortonsimon.org* 🖾 *$15* ⊗ *Closed Tues. and Wed.*

The Old Mill (El Molino Viejo)

NOTABLE BUILDING | Built in 1816 as a gristmill for the San Gabriel Mission, the mill is the state's oldest commercial building and one of the last remaining examples in Southern California of Spanish Mission architecture. The thick adobe walls and textured ceiling rafters give the interior a sense of quiet strength. Be sure to step into the back room, now a gallery with rotating quarterly exhibits. Outside, a chipped section of the mill's exterior reveals the layers of brick, ground seashell paste, and ox blood used to hold the structure together. The surrounding gardens are reason enough to visit, with a flower-decked arbor and old sycamores and oaks. In summer, the Capitol Ensemble performs in the garden. ⊠ *1120 Old Mill Rd., San Marino* ☎ *626/449–5458* ⊕ *www.old-mill.org* 🖾 *Free* ⊗ *Closed Mon.*

Old Town Pasadena

NEIGHBORHOOD | This 22-block historic district contains a vibrant mix of restored 19th-century brick buildings interspersed with contemporary architecture. Chain stores have muscled in, but there are still some homegrown shops, plenty of tempting cafés and restaurants, and a bustling beer scene. In recent years, a vibrant Asian food scene has popped up in the vicinity as well. In the evening and on weekends, the streets are packed with people. Old Town's main action takes place on Colorado Boulevard between Pasadena Avenue and Arroyo

Parkway. ⊠ *Pasadena* ☎ *626/356–9725* ⊕ *www.oldpasadena.org.*

★ Rose Bowl and Flea Market

MARKET | With an enormous rose on its exterior, this 90,000-plus-seat stadium is home to the UCLA Bruins and the annual Rose Bowl Game on New Year's Day, and also regularly sees performances from the biggest recording artists in the world. Set at the bottom of a wide arroyo in Brookside Park, the facility is closed except during games, concerts, and special events like its famed Flea Market, a Southern California institution. The massively popular and eclectic event, which happens the second Sunday of each month (rain or shine), deservedly draws crowds that come to find deals from more than 2,500 vendors on goods including mid-century and antique furniture, vintage clothing, pop culture collectibles, books, and music. Food and drink options are on hand to keep shoppers satiated, parking is free, and general admission is just $9, but VIP/early-bird options are available for a little extra. Crowds tend to peak mid-day. Bring cash to avoid an inevitable line at the ATM, and feel free to try your hand at haggling. ⊠ *1001 Rose Bowl Dr., Pasadena* ☎ *626/577–3100* ⊕ *www.rosebowlstadium.com.*

Tournament House (Wrigley Mansion)

HISTORIC HOME | Chewing gum magnate William Wrigley purchased this white Italian Renaissance–style house in 1914. When his wife died in 1958, Wrigley donated the house to the city of Pasadena under the stipulation that it be used as the headquarters for the Tournament of Roses. The mansion features a green tile roof and manicured rose garden with 1,500 varieties. The interior provides a glimpse of the area's over-the-top style in the early 20th century. Tours of the house are every Thursday from 2 to 3 from April to August; fans of the Rose Parade can see the various crowns and tiaras worn by former Rose Queens, plus trophies and memorabilia. ⊠ *391 S. Orange Grove Blvd., Pasadena* ☎ *626/449–4100* ⊕ *www.visitpasadena.com/businesses/ tournament-house* 🎫 *Free.*

Restaurants

With the revitalization of Old Town Pasadena, more people are discovering the beauty of Rose City. They mingle at bistros, upscale eateries, and taco trucks, but are also discovering the newer innovative dining spots that are giving Pasadena a hipper feel.

The Arbour Pasadena

$$ | MODERN AMERICAN | This farm-to-table eatery uses all local ingredients to whip up creative cuisine in a chic environment. Savory musts include the oysters with grapefruit mignonette, as well as the outstanding Mediterranean sea bass. **Known for:** farm-to-table cuisine; chic atmosphere; mezcal paloma. Ⓢ *Average main: $30* ⊠ *527 S. Lake Ave., Suite 120, Pasadena* ☎ *626/396–4925* ⊕ *www. thearbourpasadena.com.*

Carmela Ice Cream

$ | ICE CREAM | Those who normally skip vanilla ice cream because it's so—well— *vanilla* should shelve their preconceptions and order a scoop of Carmela's beloved brown sugar vanilla bean. But this local fave also encourages a dive into more complex flavor profiles like carrot orange ginger sorbet. **Known for:** joy-inducing ice cream sandwiches; wild seasonal flavors; brown sugar vanilla bean decadence. Ⓢ *Average main: $7* ⊠ *2495 E. Washington Blvd., Pasadena* ☎ *626/797–1405* ⊕ *www.carmelaice-cream.com.*

Pie 'n Burger

$$ | DINER | Since 1963, this small and charming diner has done two things really well—pies and burgers. Most seats are counter-style, with a griddle searing up patties. **Known for:** simple burgers; enormous pie slices; retro-style decor. Ⓢ *Average main: $14* ⊠ *913 E. California Blvd., Pasadena* ☎ *626/795–1123* ⊕ *pien-burger.com.*

The Raymond 1886

$$$ | MODERN AMERICAN | The coolest kid on the Pasadena block, the Raymond 1886 is carved out of an old Craftsman cottage and has an expansive patio with long wooden tables and hanging lights. Chefs dish out everything from roasted acorn squash with "forbidden" rice to braised beef cheeks with mole sauce. **Known for:** solid happy hour; great bar food; expansive patio. Ⓢ *Average main: $36* ⊠ *1250 S. Fair Oaks Ave., Pasadena* ☎ *626/441–3136* ⊕ *theraymond.com* ☽ *Closed Mon.*

Saladang and Saladang Garden

$ | THAI | With pierced steel-paneled walls covered with fanciful designs, this tucked-away, twin-concept Thai palace has an extensive menu that varies a bit between the two neighboring locations; compare the menus before settling on a location. Next door to the indoor Saladang proper, Saladang Garden offers an outdoor dining space that's also used for special events. **Known for:** dual indoor and outdoor venues; mango and sweet sticky rice; secluded location. Ⓢ *Average main: $16* ⊠ *383 S. Fair Oaks Ave., Pasadena* ☎ *626/793–5200* ⊕ *www.saladang-thai. com.*

★ Union

$$$ | ITALIAN | There's a Michelin-quality Italian restaurant hiding in plain sight in Pasadena. The small and homey space where Northern Italy meets California is typically filled to the brim as diners await heaven-sent local wild mushrooms with polenta or the squid-ink *lumache* (shell pasta) with Maine lobster. **Known for:** superb wine list; excellent Italian food with a California twist; buzzy yet intimate atmosphere. Ⓢ *Average main: $31* ⊠ *37 E. Union St., Pasadena* ☎ *626/795–5841* ⊕ *www.unionpasadena.com* ☽ *No lunch.*

One of the most famous venues in sporting history, the Rose Bowl is best known as the host of the annual Rose Bowl college football game for which it is named.

⭐ Performing Arts

Fremont Centre Theatre

THEATER | This theater centers on original material and world premieres with professional actors year-round. The small venue is known for its dedication to diversity and its inclusive atmosphere, with "talkbacks" (Q&As between actors and audience members) after certain shows. Ray Bradbury regularly produced shows here for five years before his death in 2012, including a stage adaptation of *Fahrenheit 451.* ✉ *1000 Fremont Ave., South Pasadena* ☎ *626/441–5977* ⊕ *www.fremontcentretheatre.com.*

A Noise Within

THEATER | Named for one of Shakespeare's stage directions in *Hamlet*, A Noise Within is the Los Angeles area's preeminent place to see classic theater. The Bard's own works are told alongside those of Oscar Wilde and the Greek tragedies, often with a twist. The company boasts fierce talent among its revolving repertory of resident actors, many of whom also work in Hollywood. Audience members are never more than eight rows away from its platform stage, creating a sense of intimacy for all in attendance. ✉ *3352 E. Foothill Blvd., Pasadena* ☎ *626/356–3100* ⊕ *www.anoisewithin.org* 🎫 *$65.*

The Pasadena Playhouse

THEATER | Exceptional plays and musicals, occasionally featuring known TV and movie actors, are what this theater is mostly known for—that and it's a historical landmark that's been operating as a theater since 1925. The 650-seat playhouse also holds the title of official state theater of California. Tours of the venue are available by appointment. ✉ *39 S. El Molino Ave., Pasadena* ☎ *626/356–7529* ⊕ *www.pasadenaplayhouse.org.*

🛍 Shopping

The stretch of Colorado Boulevard between Pasadena Avenue and Arroyo Parkway, known as Old Town, is a popular pedestrian shopping destination, where retailers such as Crate & Barrel, H&M, and Tiffany and Co. rub elbows with clothing resale shops, dog treat bakeries, and gelaterias. A few blocks east on Colorado, the open-air "urban village" known as Paseo Colorado mixes residential, retail, dining, and entertainment spaces along Colorado Boulevard between Los Robles and Marengo Avenues. Enter on Colorado or Marengo for free parking.

Gold Bug

ANTIQUES & COLLECTIBLES | You'll see the works of more than 100 artists, including sculptures, animal specimens, crystals, antiques, paintings, and other unique oddities for the eccentric giftees on your list, inside this offbeat boutique located just behind bustling Colorado Boulevard. But the main draw here is the jewelry. Funky, whimsical finds like a black beaded bracelet with a diamond-flecked snake-head clasp or a fur-and-chain-mail cuff are stocked alongside more minimalist (yet still nature-inspired) pieces, all of which are created by independent designers and made of fine materials like gold or silver and semiprecious stones.

⚠ **No photos allowed inside.** ☒ *38 E. Holly, Pasadena* ☏ *626/744–9963* ⊕ *www. goldbugpasadena.com.*

Ten Thousand Villages

OTHER SPECIALTY STORE | At Pasadena's favorite fair-trade retailer, many of the shop workers are volunteers, which helps to maximize profits for the stable of artisans from more than 30 countries who produce eye-catching and unique home decor, accessories, gifts, art, and more here. Enticing options include a wool Nepalese shawl in the color palette of wild mushrooms, intricately cut metal wall hangings of birds and trees made in Haiti from oil drum lids, or a Bangladeshi Moses basket that wouldn't look out of place in a multimillion-dollar Malibu estate. ☒ *567 S. Lake Ave., Pasadena* ☏ *626/229–9892* ⊕ *www.tenthousandvillages.com/pasadena.*

Vroman's Bookstore

BOOKS | Southern California's oldest and largest independent bookseller is justly famous for its great service. A newsstand, café, literary-themed wine bar, and stationery store add to the appeal, and it's a favorite with locals for its on-trend, eclectic gift selection. A regular rotation of events including trivia night, kids' story time, author meet and greets, crafting sessions, discussions, and more get the community actively involved. ☒ *695 E. Colorado Blvd., Pasadena* ☏ *626/449–5320* ⊕ *www.vromansbookstore.com.*

Chapter 13

THE BEACHES

Updated by
Candice Yacono

👁 Sights	🍴 Restaurants	🛏 Hotels	🛍 Shopping	🍸 Nightlife
★★★★☆	★★★☆☆	★★★☆☆	★★☆☆☆	★★★☆☆

NEIGHBORHOOD SNAPSHOT

TOP EXPERIENCES

■ **Step back in time on the *Queen Mary*:** Experience the golden age of sea travel without the seasickness by stepping aboard this art deco masterpiece reminiscent of a pre-iceberg Titanic.

■ **Discover the wonders of the deep at the Aquarium of the Pacific:** Touch sea creatures, take in augmented reality exhibits and even get up close and personal with sharks at this world-class aquarium.

■ **Relive military history on the Battleship USS *Iowa*:** This battleship is the counterpoint to the prim *Queen Mary*, and many of her former sailors still roam the decks as volunteer docents.

■ **Have a bonfire at Dockweiler Beach:** Bonfires are pretty much illegal in L.A., except at Dockweiler. Pick up a grill and have a barbecue, or just toast marshmallows.

■ **Wander the old-fashioned Redondo Beach Pier:** This historic pier offers everything from fishing and whale-watching to shopping and dining, including some outstanding freshly made churros. Visit the arcade, grab a drink at a rooftop bar, or simply soak in the coastal views.

PLANNING YOUR TIME

Start in Long Beach, a vibrant waterfront city with plenty to see and do. Spend a day exploring the city's attractions, such as the Aquarium of the Pacific, the *Queen Mary*, and the Long Beach Museum of Art. Take a stroll along the scenic Shoreline Village or visit the historic Belmont Shore neighborhood for shopping and dining.

The South Bay is a great place to experience the quintessential California beach lifestyle. Manhattan Beach beckons with its family-friendly shores, or you can go whale-watching in Redondo Beach and explore its pier. In the evening, head to Hermosa Beach for fresh seafood and fresher nightlife. You might even catch a great like Jay Leno trying out new material at the comedy club.

GETTING HERE

Long Beach and the South Bay are accessible from downtown L.A. via freeway or public transportation. The most convenient way to get there is by car, taking the I-110 Freeway south. Via train, take the Metro A (or Blue) line south. The Metro Bus also offers several bus routes. Ride-hailing services are widely available and often preferred, given the many stops the buses make. For the South Bay, a car or Uber is your best bet; no Metro line goes straight to its coast, though the C (Green) line will get you to the general area.

Public parking is usually available at the beaches, though fees can range anywhere from $8 to $20. Also expect to pay to park in downtown Long Beach and many other neighborhoods.

VIEWFINDER

■ **Shoreline Aquatic Park in Long Beach:** Walk along the boardwalk and pose in front of the Long Beach Lighthouse with the ocean and palm trees in the background, or head carefully out onto the rocks to capture yourself and the lighthouse from a different perspective. For bonus points, try to get the *Queen Mary* in your shot; it's impossible to take a bad picture of her. ⊠ *200 Aquarium Way*

The beaches and coastal areas of Los Angeles collectively known as the South Bay and Long Beach are directly south of Venice and Santa Monica. They are an iconic symbol of the region's casual friendliness and endless optimism, and local love for them is as much a trope as it is a reality. From the beaches themselves to world-class attractions like the *Queen Mary* and the Aquarium of the Pacific, this region is worthy of its own vacation.

Angelenos are known for working hard and playing hard, and this less-touristed stretch of coast is one of their favorite places to unwind. Getting some sand on the floor of your car is a rite of passage here. Like its most ardent fans, this stretch of the Pacific is best known for its beauty: cosmetically enhanced in some areas and ruggedly pristine in others. The coastline is dotted with everything from exclusive resorts to quaint, family-owned hostelries. From compact Manhattan Beach to the rugged bluffs of Rancho Palos Verdes to the cultural dynamism of Long Beach, the gently arching coastline tells an L.A. story all its own as it transitions, north to south, from ultrarich to bohemian to working-class. Through it all, the sand remains the center of the action.

El Segundo

Just south of LAX, you'll find this quaint, sleepy beach community. Originally an oil town—Standard Oil set up its second refinery in El Segundo (hence the name, which means "the second" in Spanish)— now it's full of families, out wandering the cute residential streets.

Sights

Dockweiler Beach
BEACH | Is there a dreamier way to top off your day at the beach than a bonfire at twilight? Beach bonfires are largely illegal in L.A., but you can still live the dream along Dockweiler's 3.7-mile stretch. Here, lighting up isn't just permitted; it's practically encouraged, thanks to firepits peppered throughout. That's probably why this beach is almost always a scene where young twenty- and

thirtysomethings roast jumbo marshmallows on long, makeshift skewers, as they guzzle beer in red cups. **Amenities:** food and drink; parking; lifeguards; showers; toilets; water sports. **Best for:** partiers; sunset; surfing; swimming; walking. ⊠ *12001 Vista Del Mar, Playa del Rey* ☎ *310/322–4951* ⊕ *beaches.lacounty.gov/dockweiler-beach.*

 ## Hotels

Cambria Hotel LAX

$ | HOTEL | If you need a springboard for an LAX trip or a game at SoFi Stadium, consider the Cambria for a low-key, casual getaway. **Pros:** convenient to airport and events at SoFi Stadium; vibey outdoor patio area with firepit; gym is open 24/7 to accommodate jetlag or awkward flight times. **Cons:** bathroom doesn't offer complete privacy; paid parking (though this is ubiquitous near LAX); no shuttle service, but close to airport via Uber or Lyft. $ *Rooms from: $189* ⊠ *199 Continental Blvd, El Segundo* ☎ *310/965–0555* ⊕ *www.cambrialax.com* 🛏 *152 rooms* ¶◎¶ *No Meals.*

Sheraton Gateway Los Angeles

$$ | HOTEL | LAX's swanky hotel had some serious work done to its already sleek look, yet the appeal is in more than just the style; in-transit visitors love the 24-hour room service, pool (with private cabana rentals) and hot tub, fitness center, and airport shuttle, making this the perfect option for an early-morning flight. **Pros:** significantly lower weekend rates; free 24-hour LAX shuttle; good on-site Costero restaurant with vegetarian and vegan options and a craft beer menu. **Cons:** convenient to airport but not much else; chain hotel feel; on the expensive side for an airport hotel. $ *Rooms from: $279* ⊠ *6101 W. Century Blvd., Los Angeles International Airport* ☎ *310/642–1111, 800/325–3535* ⊕ *www.sheratonlosangeles.com* 🛏 *803 rooms* ¶◎¶ *No Meals.*

Manhattan Beach

Chic boutiques, multimillion-dollar homes, and some of the best restaurants in Los Angeles dot the hilly downtown streets of this tiny community. While the glamour and exclusivity are palpable, with attractive residents making deals over cocktails, this is still a beach town. Annual volleyball and surfing tournaments, crisp ocean breezes, and a very clean walking and biking path invite all visitors.

 ## Sights

Manhattan Beach

BEACH | A wide, sandy strip with good swimming and rows of volleyball courts, Manhattan Beach is the preferred destination of fit, tanned young professionals. There are also such amenities as a bike path, a playground, a bait shop, fishing equipment for rent, and a sizable fishing pier with a free aquarium at the end. It's the perfect place to unwind during a long layover at LAX. **Amenities:** parking (fee); lifeguards; toilets; food and drink; showers. **Best for:** swimming; walking. ⊠ *Manhattan Beach Blvd. at N. Ocean Dr., Manhattan Beach* ☎ *310/372–2166* ⊕ *beaches.lacounty.gov/manhattan-beach* 🚗 *Metered parking; long- and short-term lots.*

 ## Hotels

Ayres Hotel

$$ | HOTEL | The rates may be relatively modest, but the style here is grand, with the hotel resembling a stone-clad château. **Pros:** free Wi-Fi; very pet friendly with facilities; solid on-site restaurant. **Cons:** requires a drive to the ocean; not in the most centrally located neighborhood to other L.A. sights; rooms could use an update. $ *Rooms from: $209* ⊠ *14400 Hindry Ave., Manhattan Beach* ☎ *310/536–0400, 800/675–3550* ⊕ *www.ayreshotels.com/*

yres-hotel-manhattan-beach-hawthorne 🛏 *173 rooms* 🍴 *No Meals.*

hade
$$ | **HOTEL** | Super-contemporary design ıakes this hotel, rooftop pool, and kydeck feel like an adults-only play-round, and it's just a short walk to the horeline, the local pier, and Manhattan each's lively downtown. **Pros:** fun eebies like breakfast, cake pops, and ike use with $20 amenity fee; passes Equinox gym; cool amenities like chromatherapy" lighting. **Cons:** hotel is ndergoing renovations right now; rec-mmended for adults or older kids only; mall dipping pool. [$] *Rooms from: $449* ✉ *1221 N. Valley Dr., Manhattan Beach* ☎ *310/546–4995, 866/742–3377* 🌐 *www.hadehotel.com* 🛏 *38 rooms* 🍴 *Free reakfast.*

Hermosa Beach

his energetic beach city, whose name ppropriately means "gorgeous," boasts ome of the priciest real estate in the ountry. But down by the sand, the vibe decidedly casual, with plenty of pubs nd ambling young couples. Volleyball ourts line the wide beach, drawing ıany amateur and pro tournaments. he walkable 330-yard pier features ramatic views of the coastline winding outhward.

Sights

ermosa Beach
EACH | South of Manhattan Beach, ermosa Beach has all the amenities of s neighbor but attracts a rowdier crowd. wimming takes a back seat to the vol-yball games and parties on the pier and ustling boardwalk, but the water here is onsistently clean and inviting. **Amenities:** arking (fee); lifeguards; toilets; food and rink; showers. **Best for:** partiers; surfing; wimming. ✉ *1201 The Strand, Hermosa Ave. at 33rd St., Hermosa Beach* ☎ *310/372–2166* 🌐 *beaches.lacounty.gov/hermosa-beach/* 🅿 *Parking (metered) at 11th St. and Hermosa Ave., and 13th St. and Hermosa Ave.*

Restaurants

Baran's 2239
$$ | **CONTEMPORARY** | This gem of a restaurant, tucked into an unassuming strip mall, has taken Hermosa Beach and L.A. at large by storm; even the focaccia bread has a cult following. Diners love the revolving seasonal menu, with its eclectic mix of European, Mexican, and Asian influences reminiscent of the city's own diverse makeup. **Known for:** clever, rotating seasonal menu; hip California modern-farmhouse vibe; "secret" to-go breakfast burrito that locals swear by. [$] *Average main: $22* ✉ *502 Pacific Coast Hwy., Hermosa Beach* ☎ *424/247–8468* 🌐 *www.barans2239.com* 🕒 *Closed Mon.*

Fox and Farrow
$$ | **CONTEMPORARY** | If your vacation dreams run more British hunting lodge than SoCal beach scene, Fox and Farrow might be your place. Run by longtime South Bay chef Darren Weiss, this gastro-pub features classic fare like hunter's pie with wild boar alongside more creative concepts inspired by the Pacific Rim, all in a clubby ambience: think British-racing-green velvet Chesterfields and paneled wood walls. **Known for:** craft cocktail menu; savory duck pasta; speakeasy-meets-hunt-club vibes. [$] *Average main: $26* ✉ *1332 Hermosa Ave., Hermosa Beach* 🌐 *www.foxandfarrow.com* 🕒 *Closed Mon.*

Hotels

★ **Beach House Hotel at Hermosa**
$$$ | **HOTEL** | **FAMILY** | Bordering the Strand (SoCal's famous bike path on the beach), Beach House looks like a New England sea cottage from a century ago but has contemporary amenities in its bright studio suites. **Pros:** soaking tubs

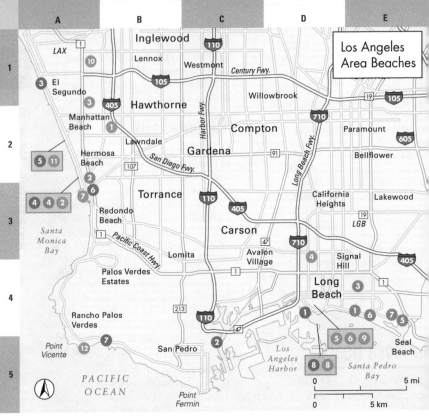

Los Angeles Area Beaches

with separate showers; enjoy delicious muffins and coffee (and more) in the breakfast room; oceanfront rooms and sunset views. **Cons:** noise from the busy Strand, especially on weekends; no pool; continental breakfast only. $ *Rooms from: $399 ⊠ 1300 The Strand, Hermosa Beach ☎ 310/374–3001, 888/895–4559 ⊕ www.beach-house.com ⇥ 96 suites ⦿ Free Breakfast.*

Nightlife

The Comedy and Magic Club

COMEDY CLUBS | With Los Angeles being Los Angeles, a disproportionate amount of comedians call the city home, from the would-be to the been-there-done-that. The decades-old Comedy and Magic Club attracts them all. One popular engagement is when 10 up-and-coming comedians perform, one right after the other, in a sort of comic brinksmanship. Other nights might see the occasional magician or an icon of the field like Jay Leno or Bob Saget, there to keep their timing fresh and try out new material for adoring crowds. Stiff drinks and decent entrées and appetizers reward those who arrive early for the best seats, but try grabbing a meal nearby before arriving 30 to 60 minutes prior to the show (budget a little more time for someone like Leno, who's a regular on Sunday nights but still draws crowds). ⊠ *1018 Hermosa Ave., Hermosa Beach ☎ 310/372–1193 ⊕ www.comedyandmagicclub.com.*

Lighthouse Cafe

LIVE MUSIC | Featured in *La La Land*, the 2016 musical set in Los Angeles, this onetime jazz bistro now offers a wide range of live entertainment, adding salsa, country, reggae, and pop to the repertoire. A jazz brunch and live music all day on weekends draw locals and tourists alike. Check out the weekday happy hour specials. ⊠ *30 Pier Ave., Hermosa Beach ☎ 310/376–9833 ⊕ www.thelighthouse-cafe.net.*

Underground Pub and Grill

BARS | Throw darts, shoot pool, or play shuffleboard at this British pub (its name refers to London's subway system), or watch a game on one of the many monitors. The adjacent Fox and Farrow gastropub is run by one of the co-owners. ⊠ *1334 Hermosa Ave., Hermosa Beach ☎ 310/318–3818 ⊕ www.undergroundpubandgrill.com.*

Redondo Beach

With its worn-in pier and cozy beach, Redondo is a refreshingly unglamorous counterpoint to neighboring beach cities. This was the first port in Los Angeles County in the early 1890s, before business shifted south to San Pedro Harbor, and the community still retains a working-class persona. The best way to soak up the scene these days is with a stroll along the sprawling pier, which features dozens of shops, casual restaurants, a live-fish market, and fantastic sunset views.

Sights

Redondo Beach

BEACH | The pier here marks the starting point of this wide, busy beach along a heavily developed shoreline community. Restaurants and shops flourish along the pier; excursion boats and privately owned crafts depart from launching ramps; and a reef formed by a sunken ship creates prime fishing and snorkeling conditions. If you're adventurous, you might try to kayak out to the buoys and hobnob with pelicans and sea lions. A series of free rock and jazz concerts takes place at the pier every summer. **Amenities:** parking; lifeguards; food and drink; toilets; showers; water sports. **Best for:** snorkeling; sunset; swimming; walking. ⊠ *Torrance Blvd. at Catalina Ave., Redondo Beach ☎ 310/372–2166 ⊕ www.redondopier.com.*

Did You Know?

Manhattan Beach (along with Hermosa Beach and Redondo Beach) make up the Beach Cities, which feature over two miles of stunning coastline.

Hotels

The Portofino Hotel & Yacht Club

$$$ | **HOTEL** | Open your balcony door and listen to the calls of seabirds and sea lions from ocean- and channel-side rooms here (earplugs are provided for humbugs); marina-side rooms overlook sailboats and docks. **Pros:** bike or walk to beach from the hotel's private peninsula; excellent Baleen restaurant overlooking the harbor; complimentary beach cruiser rentals. **Cons:** higher rates in summer and for ocean-view rooms; restaurant may be noisy due to the adjacent bar; sea lions may be too enthusiastic for some ocean-view room guests. [$] *Rooms from: $399* ✉ *260 Portofino Way, Redondo Beach* ☎ *310/379–8481, 800/468–4292* 🌐 *www.hotelportofino.com* 🛏 *166 rooms* 🍴 *No Meals.*

Rancho Palos Verdes

Rancho Palos Verdes is a picturesque, quiet coastal community perched on a peninsula. It's best known for its breathtaking views of the Pacific Ocean, rugged coastline, and impressive luxury homes. The city is home to several world-class golf courses, the five-star Terranea Resort, and good hiking trails, along with architectural landmarks like the Wayfarers Chapel. It's ideal for those looking to escape the hustle and bustle of the city and unwind in a peaceful coastal setting.

Sights

Wayfarers Chapel

CHURCH | Indoors and outdoors are inextricably linked in this mid-century stone-and-glass chapel designed by Lloyd Wright, Frank Lloyd Wright's son. An anomaly in this tony hillside bedroom community, the lighter-than-air cliff-top sanctuary also known as the Glass Church is nestled in a grove of redwoods above the Pacific. A popular wedding and filming location, it was designed for the Swedenborgian Church of North America and is still used for Wednesday and Sunday services, though the chapel and grounds are free to tour at other times. ✉ *5755 Palos Verdes Dr. S, Rancho Palos Verdes* ☎ *310/377–1650* 🌐 *www.wayfarerschapel.org* 🎟 *Free.*

Hotels

★ **Terranea**

$$$$ | **RESORT** | **FAMILY** | The Pacific Ocean and Catalina Island are within view at Terranea, L.A.'s only full-service ocean-front resort straddling 102 terraced acres at land's end on the scenic Palos Verdes Peninsula. Its location gives it the feel of a retreat. **Pros:** kid-friendly amenities and pool slide; blissful oceanfront spa; four saline pools and hot tubs. **Cons:** pricey on-site dining; with resort fee and parking, this luxury becomes very expensive; nearby beach is more rocky than sandy. [$] *Rooms from: $599* ✉ *100 Terranea Way, Rancho Palos Verdes* ☎ *310/265–2800* 🌐 *www.terranea.com* 🛏 *582 rooms* 🍴 *No Meals.*

Long Beach and San Pedro

About 25 miles southeast of Los Angeles, via I–110 south.

A beguiling blend of big city and eclectic small town, Long Beach has metamorphosed in recent years into a full-fledged tourist destination with a wide range of attractions rivaling many major cities. The biggest draw is the *Queen Mary,* a 1930s luxury ocean liner frozen in time in its permanent home, where tours, special events, and even floating hotel rooms draw visitors from around the world. The Aquarium of the Pacific is a hit with families; kids can't get enough of its sharks, penguins, sea lions, and more. Add in a variety of museums, restaurants, and outdoor recreation experiences ("Long Beach" isn't a misnomer), and you have all you need for an epic trip.

Nearby San Pedro is still very much a working port, but it houses another kind of floating attraction: the Battleship USS *Iowa*, which served in three wars and now lets visitors stand in the mess hall and wonder what life was like for its crew.

Sights

★ Aquarium of the Pacific

AQUARIUM | **FAMILY** | Sea lions, zebra sharks, and penguins—oh my! This aquarium focuses on creatures of the Pacific Ocean and is home to more than 12,000 animals. The main exhibits include large tanks of sharks, stingrays, and ethereal sea dragons, which the aquarium has successfully bred in captivity. The museum's first major expansion in years, Pacific Visions, features a 29,000-square-foot multisensory experience in which attendees can immerse themselves in humankind's relationship with the natural world through video projections, soundscapes, tactile exhibits, a touchscreen wall, interactive game tables, rumbling theater seats, and more. The aquarium focuses on its local environment in its refreshed Southern California Gallery, where you'll explore kelp forests, learn about local species, and learn about the aquarium's conservation efforts. Special events for kids, teens, and families abound; if you're interested in offsetting your travels with some local eco efforts, the whole family can join in local wetlands habitat restoration efforts held by the aquarium. Whale-watching trips on Harbor Breeze Cruises depart from the dock adjacent to the aquarium; summer sightings of blue whales are an unforgettable thrill. ⊠ *100 Aquarium Way, Long Beach* ☎ *562/590–3100* ⊕ *www. aquariumofpacific.org* ⊒ *$45.*

Battleship USS *Iowa* Museum

MILITARY SIGHT | **FAMILY** | For those seeking a more rough-hewn alternative or counterpoint to the genteel *Queen Mary*, the battleship USS *Iowa* in nearby San Pedro lets visitors of all ages clamber through hatches, peer through portholes, and climb into the seat of an antiaircraft gun, envisioning the past. The *Iowa*, the only such tourable battleship on the West Coast, was commissioned in 1943 as the lead of its class and served in World War II, Korea, and the Cold War. Volunteer "crew members," many of whom once served on the ship, happily offer their personal stories to kids and adults alike.

■ **TIP**→ **You're bound to be hungry after such an intrepid expedition. While many people might return to Long Beach or L.A., the nearby pedestrian-friendly, old-timey Downtown San Pedro strip, which centers on 6th and 7th Streets, boasts some outstanding dining options, from a British pub to killer Mediterranean and Italian options. There's also the tiny Little Fish Theatre.** ⊠ *250 S. Harbor Blvd., San Pedro* ☎ *877/446–9261* ⊕ *www.pacificbattleship.com* ⊒ *$24.*

★ Queen Mary

NAUTICAL SIGHT | **FAMILY** | The beautifully preserved art deco–style ocean liner, the *Queen Mary*, was launched in 1936 and made 1,001 transatlantic crossings before finally berthing in Long Beach in 1967. Today, it is a unique and historic hotel, one of Long Beach's top tour attractions, and an impressive example of 20th-century cruise ship opulence.

Take one of several daily themed tours such as the informative Glory Days historical walk, a traipse into the boiler rooms on the Steam and Steel Tour, or the downright spooky Haunted Encounters tour. (Spirits have reportedly been spotted in the pool and engine room.) You can add on a Winston Churchill exhibit and other holiday and special events, from a haunted Halloween experience to an annual Scottish festival. Stay for

On the historic *Queen Mary* (now permanently moored and turned into a floating hotel), you can pretend it's the 1930s. Wander the lido deck, take peek into the engine rooms, and even go on a ghost tour.

dinner at one of the ship's restaurants (call ahead to reserve), then listen to live jazz or order a cocktail in the Observation Bar (the sumptuous original first-class lounge). Even better, plan to spend the night in one of the 347 wood-paneled cabins. The ship's neighbor, a geodesic dome originally built to house Howard Hughes's *Spruce Goose* aircraft, now serves as a terminal for Carnival Cruise Lines, making the *Queen Mary* the perfect pit stop before or after a cruise. ✉ *1126 Queens Hwy., Long Beach* ☎ *877/342–0738* 🌐 *www.queenmary.com* 🕒 *Tours from $10.*

🍴 Restaurants

The Attic

$$ | MODERN AMERICAN | Long Beach's famous Craftsman bungalows were built en masse during an oil boom a century ago, and while many have been torn down to make way for McMansions and apartment blocks, one now plays home to the Attic, which serves up some of the best Southern-style cuisine in the region. The comfort food on the all-day menu delights, from the Flaming Hot Cheetos mac and cheese (don't overthink it; just try it) to the Three Little Pigs sandwich. **Known for:** modern Southern cooking; century-old cottage setting; Supper Club experience on weekends. [$] *Average main: $29* ✉ *3441 E. Broadway, Long Beach* ☎ *562/433–0153* 🌐 *www.theatticonbroadway.com.*

Cañadas Grill

$ | MEXICAN | Serving up authentic Mexican cuisine, the family-owned Cañadas Grill is where the locals go. Don't expect fancy decor or tableside service; this humble mom-and-pop shop is tucked into a tiny urban strip mall in an untouristed area, and shows *fútbol* matches on the corner TV. **Known for:** house-made salsa; carne en su jugo; super-authentic Mexican cuisine. [$] *Average main: $16* ✉ *3721 E. Anaheim St., Long Beach* ☎ *562/494–4903* 🌐 *www.canadasgrill.com.*

Nomad Asian Bistro

$ | **CHINESE** | Nomad Asian Bistro draws an army of dedicated locals to feast on Chinese halal dishes featuring hand-pulled noodles (at a nominal extra fee, but worth it in every way). Nomad offers a wide range of conventional and inventive options, with abundant vegetarian and gluten-free choices in addition to classics like short ribs and shrimp. **Known for:** sizzling rice soup that really sizzles; bargain lunch specials; delectable house-made noodles. $ Average main: $16 ✉ 6563 E. Pacific Coast Hwy., Long Beach ☎ 562/430–6888 ⊕ www.nomadasianbistrolongbeach.com.

Saint & Second

$$$ | **AMERICAN** | If Long Beach's 2nd Street is a treasure chest of casual communal experiences, Saint & Second is one of its gems. This on-trend modern American restaurant is the latest in a long line of successful concepts run on the same site by the same family for well over half a century. **Known for:** casual dishes in an industrial space; excellent happy hour offerings; huge whiskey list. $ Average main: $32 ✉ 4828 2nd St., Long Beach ☎ 562/433–4828 ⊕ www.saintandsecond.com ☞ Brunch served on weekends only.

Tantalum

$$ | **ASIAN FUSION** | Craving a modern fusion of Californian and Asian cuisines? Tantalizing Tantalum has been one of Long Beach's favorite bay-side gathering places for a generation. **Known for:** clever takes on Asian fusion; frequent live music; marina views. $ Average main: $29 ✉ 6272 E. Pacific Coast Hwy., Long Beach ☎ 562/431–1414 ⊕ www.tantalumrestaurant.com ☾ No lunch weekdays.

 Hotels

The Cove Hotel

$ | **HOTEL** | While you won't be beachside, complimentary champagne at check-in will set the resort mood, as will a bunch of boutique touches that normally cost extra. **Pros:** daily happy hour specials at the bar; suites have patios; extras that usually cost extra. **Cons:** no free breakfast or parking; not walking distance from the beach; walls are on the thinner side. $ Rooms from: $199 ✉ 200 E. Willow St., Long Beach ☎ 562/426–7611 ⊕ www.covelongbeach.com ⤴ 76 rooms ⦿ No Meals.

Hotel Royal

$ | **HOTEL** | **FAMILY** | A great value for Long Beach, the family-owned, European-style Hotel Royal makes up for in kindness what it lacks in fancy extras. **Pros:** stocked community kitchen good for families; lively happy hour; free breakfast and bike rentals. **Cons:** paid parking (but inexpensive for Long Beach); no elevator; some rooms share bathrooms. $ Rooms from: $159 ✉ 431 E. Broadway, Long Beach ☎ 562/283–8755 ⊕ www.hotelroyallb.com ⤴ 29 rooms ⦿ Free Breakfast.

★ Hyatt Centric the Pike Long Beach

$ | **HOTEL** | **FAMILY** | A boutique hotel with a playful modern nautical theme throughout, the highlight here is the rooftop pool and bar that offers panoramic views of the harbor complemented with craft cocktails. **Pros:** great pet-friendly location; rooftop offers views, a swimming pool, and the Top Sail Bar with craft cocktails; modern rooms. **Cons:** parking is at mall next door; some bathrooms can use a refresh; some rooms view a parking structure. $ Rooms from: $150 ✉ 285 Bay St., Long Beach ☎ 562/432–1234 ⊕ www.hyatt.com ⤴ 150 rooms ⦿ No Meals.

★ Queen Mary Hotel

$ | HOTEL | FAMILY | Experience the golden age of transatlantic travel without the seasickness: 1936 art deco style reigns on the *Queen Mary*, from the ship's mahogany paneling to its nickel-plated doors to the majestic Grand Salon. **Pros:** walkable, historic teakwood Promenade deck; views from Long Beach out to the Pacific; meticulous art deco detailing. **Cons:** spotty service; vintage soundproofing makes for a sometimes challenging night's sleep; mandatory facility fee. $ *Rooms from: $189* ⊠ *1126 Queens Hwy., Long Beach* ☎ *562/435–3511, 877/342–0742* ⊕ *www.queenmary.com* ⇘ *347 staterooms* ⦿❘ *No Meals.*

Renaissance Long Beach Hotel

$$ | HOTEL | Set in the heart of Long Beach's business district, directly across from the Long Beach Convention Center's side entrance, the Renaissance caters primarily to convention goers and business types. **Pros:** easy walk to Convention Center; near Shoreline Village dining and Aquarium of the Pacific; lively lobby bar. **Cons:** rooms facing south have best views; rooms facing street are noisy; corporate vibes. $ *Rooms from: $229* ⊠ *111 E. Ocean Blvd., Long Beach* ☎ *562/437–5900, 800/228–9898* ⊕ *www.marriott.com* ⇘ *374 rooms.*

Shopping

2nd Street

NEIGHBORHOODS | The stretch of 2nd Street that runs through Long Beach's tony residential neighborhood of Belmont Shore is a paradise for lovers of unique boutiques, coffee shops, bakeries, and well-curated secondhand shops. When you're done hunting for that perfect souvenir, stop in at any of the strip's plethora of restaurants and bars, explore the neighboring streets of historic bungalows and mini mansions, or head a few blocks to the beach. Young families flock to Bayshore Beach at the east end of the strip for the protected, flat waters of the marina, while those seeking the classic ocean beach experience make their way south to Belmont Shore's eponymous strand of sand. ⊠ *2nd St., Long Beach* ✛ *Between Livingston Dr. and Bay Shore Ave.*

Chapter 14

DISNEYLAND AND ORANGE COUNTY

14

Updated by
Jill Weinlein

👁 Sights	🍽 Restaurants	🛏 Hotels	🛍 Shopping	🍸 Nightlife
★★★★★	★★★★☆	★★★★★	★☆☆☆☆	★☆☆☆☆

WELCOME TO DISNEYLAND AND ORANGE COUNTY

TOP REASONS TO GO

★ **Disneyland:** Walking down Main Street, U.S.A., with Sleeping Beauty Castle straight ahead, you really will feel like you're in one of the happiest places on Earth.

★ **Beautiful beaches:** Surf, swim, kayak, paddleboard, or just relax on some of the state's most breathtaking stretches of coastline. Calm coves offer clear water for snorkeling and scuba diving.

★ **Santa Catalina Island:** Just 22 miles from the mainland, Santa Catalina Island is the only inhabited island of the Channel Islands chain. A fast and easy cruise away on a high-speed catamaran, once there you can explore the Mediterranean-inspired small town of Avalon, dive or snorkel through the state's first underwater park, or explore the unspoiled beauty of the island's wild interior.

★ **Family fun:** Ride roller coasters, eat ice cream and frozen chocolate-dipped bananas, bike on oceanfront paths, fish off ocean piers, or rent a Duffy boat and cruise around the calm harbors.

1 Disneyland Resort. Southern California's top draw is now a megaresort, with more attractions spilling over into Disney's California Adventure.

2 Knott's Berry Farm. Think: thrill rides, the *Peanuts* gang, and lots of fried chicken and boysenberry pie.

3 Huntington Beach. This resort destination is known as Surf City U.S.A.

4 Newport Beach. There's something for every taste here, from glamorous boutiques to simple snack huts.

5 Corona del Mar. No matter your preferred outdoor activity, you'll find it on one of the beaches here.

6 Laguna Beach. With 30 beaches and coves to explore, there's plenty to keep visitors busy.

7 San Juan Capistrano. Take a trip back in time exploring a historic Spanish Missions.

8 Catalina Island. Just off the Orange County coast is an island paradise with walkable streets filled with shops and restaurants in the charming town of Avalon. Beyond is a large land and underwater nature preserve to explore.

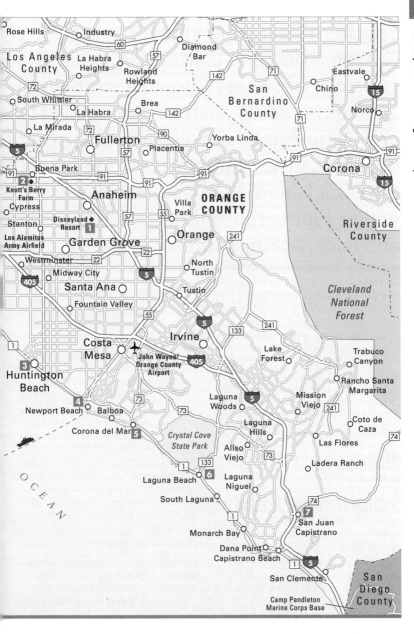

With its tropical flowers and palm trees, the stretch of coast between Seal Beach and San Clemente is often called the Southern California Riviera. Upscale Newport Beach and artsy Laguna are the stars, but lesser-known gems on the glistening coast—such as Corona del Mar and Dana Point—are also worth visiting. Offshore, meanwhile, lies picturesque Catalina Island, an unspoiled paradise and a favorite for tourists, boaters, divers, and backpacking campers alike.

Few of the citrus groves that gave Orange County its name remain. This region south and east of Los Angeles is now ruled by tourism and high-tech business rather than agriculture. Despite a building boom that began in the 1990s, the area is still a place to find wilderness trails, canyons, greenbelts, and natural environs. Just offshore is a deep-water wilderness that's possible to explore via daily whale-watching excursions.

Planning

Getting Here and Around

AIR
Orange County's main facility is John Wayne Airport Orange County (SNA), which is served by 12 airlines. Long Beach Airport (LGB) is served by four airlines and is 30 minutes by car to Anaheim.

The best way to get to your destination from one of the airports is logging into Lyft or Uber for door-to-door service.

BUS
The Orange County Transportation Authority will take you virtually any-where in the county, but it will take time; download the OC Bus app to plan, pay, and ride easily. Purchase a one day or more bus pass, find bus times and bus stop locations. OC buses go from Knott's Berry Farm and Disneyland to Newport Beach. Anaheim offers Anaheim Resort Transportation (ART) service that connects hotels to Disneyland Resort, downtown Anaheim, Buena Park, and the Metrolink train center. Download the A-Way WeGo app. One-way rides are $4 or $6 for a full-day pass.

CONTACTS Anaheim Resort Transportation (ART). ⊠ 2099 S. State College Blvd., Suite 600, Anaheim ☎ 714/563–5287 ⊕ rideart.org. **Orange County Transportation**

Authority. ✉ *550 S. Main St., Anaheim* ☎ *714/636–7433* ⊕ *www.octa.net.*

CAR

Driving is the most convenient option to explore Orange County. Download the Waze app to get the best directions to your destination. The San Diego Freeway (Interstate 405) is the coastal route, and the Santa Ana Freeway (Interstate 5) is more inland running north–south through Orange County. South of Laguna, Interstate 405 merges into Interstate 5 (called the San Diego Freeway south from this point). A toll road, Highway 73, runs 15 miles from Newport Beach to San Juan Capistrano; prices fluctuate on weekdays, weekends, and off-peak hours, and this option is usually less jammed than the regular freeways. Do your best to avoid all Orange County freeways during rush hours (6:30–9 am and 3:30–6:30 pm). Highway 55 leads to Newport Beach. The Pacific Coast Highway (Highway 1) allows easy access to beach communities and is the most scenic route but expect it to be crowded, especially on summer weekends and holidays.

FERRY

There are two ferries that service Catalina Island; Catalina Express runs multiple departures daily from San Pedro, Long Beach, and Dana Point. From each port, it takes about 70 minutes to reach the island. The Catalina Flyer runs from Newport Beach to Avalon in about 75 minutes. Reservations are strongly advised for summer months and weekends. During the winter months, ferry crossings are not as frequent.

TRAIN

Amtrak Pacific Surfliner makes five Orange County stops. The easiest stop without a car is the San Juan Capistrano station, which puts you within easy walking distance of lodging, restaurants, shopping, and the California Mission. Metrolink is a weekday commuter train that runs to and from Los Angeles and Orange County. On weekends the train offers a $10 Weekend Day Pass. Download the Metrolink app.

CONTACTS Amtrak. ✉ *2626 E. Katella Ave., Anaheim* ☎ *800/872–7245* ⊕ *www. amtrak.com.* **Metrolink.** ✉ *800 N. Alameda St., Los Angeles* ☎ *800/371–5465* ⊕ *www.metrolinktrains.com.*

Restaurants

Guests dining at restaurants in Orange County generally wear beach-casual or resort wear, although at top resorts and fine-dining venues, guests usually choose to dress up. Of course, there's also a swath of casual places along the beachfronts—seafood takeout, taquerias, burger joints—that won't mind if you wear shorts and flip-flops. Reservations are recommended for the nicest restaurants.

Hotels

Lodging prices tend to be high along the coast, and there are some remarkable luxury resorts and smaller boutique hotels. Splurge and stay at Laguna Beach's Montage resort to swim in the mosaic tile pool. For an exclusive California beach club experience, an overnight at the Waldorf Astoria Monarch Beach will give you a taste of the O.C. glam life. The Resort at Pelican Hill is an idyllic place to stay and enjoy lunch, brunch, or dinner at its Coliseum Grill overlooking the world's largest circular pool and the ocean beyond. For nautical scenery, stay overnight overlooking multimillion-dollar yachts in Newport harbor at the Balboa Bay Resort. If you're looking for value, consider a hotel that's inland along the Interstate 405 freeway corridor. In most cases, you can take advantage of some of the facilities of the high-end resorts, such as restaurants and spas, even if you aren't an overnight guest.

⇨ *Restaurant and hotel reviews have been shortened. For full information, visit Fodors.com. Prices in the restaurant reviews are the average cost of a main course at dinner or, if dinner is not served, at lunch. Prices in the hotel reviews are the lowest cost of a standard double room in high season.*

What It Costs in U.S. Dollars

$	$$	$$$	$$$$
RESTAURANTS			
under $20	$20–$30	$31–$40	over $40
HOTELS			
under $200	$200–$350	$351–$500	over $500

Visitor Information

Visit Anaheim is an excellent resource for both leisure and business travelers and can provide materials on transportation and special offers on many area attractions. Visit California has an Orange County section on their site that is helpful and informative.

CONTACTS Orange County Visitors Association. ⊕ *www.travelcostamesa. com/visittheoc.* **Visit Anaheim.** ✉ *2099 S. State College Blvd., Suite 600, Anaheim* ☎ *714/765–2800* ⊕ *www.visitanaheim. org.*

Disneyland Resort

26 miles southeast of Los Angeles, via I–5.

The snowcapped Matterhorn, the centerpiece of Disneyland, punctuates the skyline of Anaheim. Since 1955, when Walt Disney chose this once-quiet farming community for the site of his first amusement park, Disneyland has attracted more than 650 million visitors and tens of thousands of workers, and Anaheim has been their host. Today, there are more than 60 attractions and adventures in the park's nine themed lands: Fantasyland, Adventureland, Tomorrowland, Frontierland, Main Street U.S.A., New Orleans Square, Critter Country, Mickey's Toontown, and Star Wars: Galaxy's Edge.

The sprawling complex that includes Disney's two amusement parks (Disneyland and Disney's California Adventure); three hotels; and Downtown Disney, a shopping, dining, and entertainment promenade are celebrating 100 Years of Wonder.

GETTING THERE
Disney is about a 30-mile drive from either LAX or Downtown. From LAX, follow Sepulveda Boulevard south to the Interstate 105 freeway and drive east 16 miles to the Interstate 605 north exit. Exit at the Santa Ana Freeway (Interstate 5) and continue south for 12 miles to the Disneyland Drive exit. Follow signs to the resort. From Downtown, follow Interstate 5 south 28 miles and exit at Disneyland Drive.

SAVING TIME AND MONEY
If you plan to visit one of the parks, each guest is required to have a theme park reservation and ticket (as of January 2024, date-based tickets will not require reservations). For more than a day, you can save money by buying multiday Park Hopper tickets that grant same-day "hopping" privileges between Disneyland and Disney's California Adventure. Start at one park, and then enter the other park at a certain time and go between parks (based on availability).

Single-day and park hopper admission prices vary by date. A one-day Park Hopper pass usually costs approximately $154–$214 for anyone 10 or older, $149–$209 for kids ages three to nine. Admission to either park (but not both) is approximately $104–$179 for adults or $98–$169 for kids three to nine; kids two and under are free.

In addition to tickets, parking is $30 (unless your hotel has a shuttle or is within walking distance), and meals in the parks and at Downtown Disney range from $15 to $75 per person.

Disneyland

★ Disneyland

AMUSEMENT RIDE | FAMILY | Disneyland is the only place where guests visit nine imaginative lands, from a galaxy far, far away in the *Star Wars* land; to a world of pirates in search of Jack Sparrow from the *Pirates of the Caribbean* series; and a boat ride to Storybook Land, with its miniature replicas of animated Disney scenes from classics such as *Frozen* and *Alice in Wonderland*. Beloved Disney characters appear for autographs and photos throughout the day; times and places are posted at the entrances and on the Disneyland mobile app. Live shows, parades, strolling musicians, fireworks (on weekends and during the summer and holidays), and endless creative snack choices add to the carnival atmosphere. You can also meet some of the animated icons at one of the character meals served at the three Disney hotels (open to the public, but reservations are needed). Belongings can be stored in lockers just off Main Street while stroller rentals, wheelchairs, and Electric Conveyance Vehicles (ECV) are at the entrance gate as convenient options for families with mobility challenges. The park's popularity means there are always crowds, especially during the holidays and summer months, so take advantage of the Disney Genie+ and Lightning Lane to spend less time waiting in lines. Some rides offer Single Rider Lanes which are also much shorter. Also be sure to make dining reservations at least three weeks before your visit to guarantee a table without a wait. The park is expertly run, with perfectly maintained grounds and a helpful staff ("cast members" in the Disney lexicon). ✉ *Disneyland Park, 1313*

S. Disneyland Dr., between Ball Rd. and Katella Ave., Anaheim ☎ *714/781–4636 guest information* ⊕ *disneyland.disney. go.com* ✉ *From $97; parking $20.*

PARK NEIGHBORHOODS
MAIN STREET, U.S.A.
Walt's hometown of Marceline, Missouri, was the creative inspiration behind this romanticized small-town America, circa 1900. Celebrating 100 Years of Magic, Main Street and lampposts dazzle in royal blue and platinum banners. Find the platinum Mickey Mouse statue in the Town Square. The sidewalks are lined with a penny arcade, magic shop, and an endless supply of colorful confections in the candy store. Disney-themed clothing and a photo shop that offers souvenirs created via Disney's PhotoPass (on-site photographers capture memorable moments digitally—you can access them in person or online via the Disneyland app). Main Street opens half an hour before the rest of the park, so it's a good place to explore if you're getting an early start to beat the crowds (it's also open an hour after the other attractions close, so you may want to save your shopping for the end of the day).

Step into city hall to receive a complimentary button showcasing whatever you're celebrating (your first visit, a birthday, a marriage, or just Disney in general); throughout the day, Disney cast members will congratulate you with friendly smiles and well wishes. Main Street Cinema offers a cool respite from the crowds and six classic Disney animated shorts, including *Steamboat Willie*. There's rarely a wait to enter. Grab a cappuccino and fresh-made pastry at the Jolly Holiday bakery to jump-start your visit. Board the Disneyland Railroad, an authentic steam-powered train located at the entrance that makes stops in the park's different lands. The 20-minute scenic round-trip gives you unique behind-the-scene views of Star Wars: Galaxy's

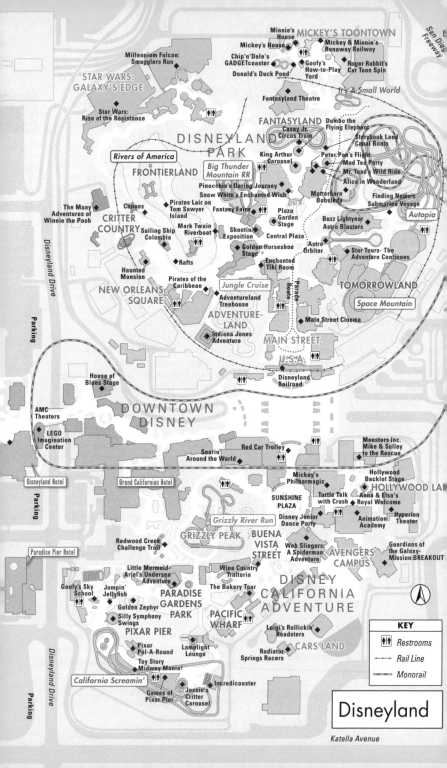

Disney's Top Attractions

■ **Star Wars: Galaxy's Edge:** Enter the planet of Batuu, the park's newest and largest immersive themed land, where you can join the Resistance and meet some of your favorite Star Wars characters. There are a variety of galactic snacks, food, and beverage options to try, many of which appeared in the movies.

■ **Haunted Mansion:** A "doombuggy" takes you through a dark and spooky old mansion filled with 999 happy spirits.

■ **Matterhorn Bobsleds:** At the center of the Magic Kingdom, this roller coaster simulates bobsleds.

■ **It's a Small World:** This Fantasyland boat ride takes guests around the world with more than 300 animatronics dressed in traditional cultural costumes.

■ New **Mickey's Toontown** is a kaleidoscope of color, sound, and sensation.

Edge, Autopia, the Grand Canyon, and Rivers of America.

Beyond Main Street, U.S.A., is Sleeping Beauty's Castle sparkling in platinum, gold, pink, and blue colors. Two new majestic water fountains create excitement in the moat.

NEW ORLEANS SQUARE

It's Mardi Gras every day at New Orleans Square French Quarter with larger-than-life masks and decorations providing a festive atmosphere. Stroll through the narrow streets and hidden courtyards to Tiana's Place. Walk into "Eudora's Chic Boutique" featuring Tiana's Gourmet Secrets. Inspired by the movie *The Princess and the Frog* is a new retail store that Tiana opened with her mother, Eudora. Later in 2024, Tiana's Bayou Adventure is a thrilling new theme attraction. Listen to live street performances near the Cajun-inspired Blue Bayou restaurant, set inside the Pirates of the Caribbean ride. While dining, watch visitors float on a weathered barge ride to discover Jack Sparrow and his band of pirates among enhanced special effects and battle scenes (complete with cannonball explosions). Be sure to stop for a pillowy Mickey beignet and refreshing nonalcoholic mint julep drink at the Mint Julep Bar. It's located next to Tiana's Place and the Disneyland Railroad Depot, and nearby Haunted Mansion. This popular attraction continues to spook guests with its stretching walls and "doombuggy" ride through a house of happy ghosts. Tim Burton's *Nightmare Before Christmas* holiday overlay is an annual tradition that starts in the fall and extends throughout the holidays to the end of January. Enjoy a Monte Cristo sandwich at Cafe Orleans. Food carts offer everything from just-popped popcorn to churros, fresh fruit, beverages, and Mickey Mouse–shaped ice cream chocolate bars.

FRONTIERLAND

Between Adventureland and next to New Orleans Square, Frontierland transports you to the wild, wild West with wood sidewalks and swinging door buildings, a shooting gallery, foot-stompin' The Golden Horseshoe dance hall, and a pretty Spanish-tile courtyard with a fountain. The marquee attraction, Big Thunder Mountain Railroad, is a relatively tame roller coaster ride (no steep descents) that takes the form of a runaway mine car as it rumbles and turns through desert canyons and an old mining town. Be sure to take a ride on the beautifully restored 19th-century Mark Twain Riverboat. The 14-minute paddleboat cruises around Pirates Lair and Tom Sawyer Island. Another boat ride is the Sailing Ship Columbia, a full-scale replica of a merchant ship that once sailed the globe (usually limited to weekends and select seasons only). Families enjoy taking a motorized raft over to Pirate's Lair on Tom Sawyer Island, where you can explore pirate-themed caves, go on a treasure hunt, and climb a fort. Dine outside at the River Belle Terrace for a variety of shrimp and catfish Cobb salad, fried chicken sandwich, or sweet and sticky pulled pork. This restaurant also offers three plant-based options that include BBQ tofu and meatballs with grits for lunch and dinner. Or take a seat on the festive Mexican terrace at the quick-service Rancho del Zocalo for a trio of street tacos, fire-grilled citrus-marinated chicken, plant-based cauliflower tacos, and cinnamon crisps for dessert. There is a Disney Kids menu.

CRITTER COUNTRY

Iconic Splash Mountain was the biggest draw to this down-home country-themed area, but the ride closed in 2023 to make way for Tiana's Bayou Adventure, scheduled to open in 2024. In the meantime, little ones love to take a peek through Winnie the Pooh's Hundred-Acre Wood, and families paddling along the Rivers of America on Davy Crockett's Explorer Canoes stop at Tom Sawyer Island to explore the interactive Pirate's Lair.

GALAXY'S EDGE

This 14-acre expansive land has guests step into the planet Batuu, designed from architectural locations in Morocco, Turkey, and Israel. Star Wars storytelling has expanded to include new tales and characters, including the legendary bounty hunter Boba Fett and mercenary Fennec Shand, as well as late-2023 additions, The Mandalorian and Grogu.

Ride *Star Wars: Rise of the Resistance* to accept a mission from the Resistance to fight against the First Order. You can also take a thrilling interactive ride in a six-person cockpit on **Millennium Falcon: Smugglers Run,** where you will be given the task of a pilot, gunner, or engineer, as you soar into hyperspace on a smuggling mission. Purchase a MagicPlus+ band to follow the lights and vibration down the right path to your bounty. The Droid Depot offers a build-your-own droid workshop stocked with colorful parts, chips, and tech items. Starting at $119.99, you will receive a basket and blueprint to build your droid. Another treasure to purchase and take home is a hand-built lightsaber at Savi's Workshop.

For dining, popular Oga's Cantina is good for coffee, all-day light snacks, and unique cocktails for grown-ups. Galactic food and drink options can be found at the Milk Stand, where guests can sample the blue and green beverages, similar to what Luke Skywalker drank in the movies. Docking Bay 7 Food and Cargo offers lunch and dinner fare starting at $14.99. Ronto Roasters has roasted meats and savory grilled sausages.

ADVENTURELAND

Modeled after the lands of Africa, Polynesia, and Arabia, this tiny tropical paradise is worth braving the crowds that flock here for the ambience and better-than-average food. Sing along with the animatronic birds and tiki gods in the Enchanted Tiki Room, sail the rivers of the world with joke-cracking skippers on Jungle Cruise, and climb the new Adventureland Treehouse, a tribute to the Walt Disney movie *Swiss Family Robinson* that Disney and his Imagineers built in the early 1960s. Follow the wood rope stairway up to the boughs of the tree to explore various rooms.

Cap off the visit with a wild jeep ride at the recently refurbished Indiana Jones Adventure. Some of the best fast-casual dining options include The Tropical Hideaway along the open-air dock overlooking the Jungle Cruise ride. Snacks include

Best Tips for Disneyland

Download the Disneyland mobile app on your smartphone. Buy entry tickets here in advance or at nearby Disney Good Neighbor hotels or through Disney's website. Get the complimentary Disney Genie service loaded with features to enhance your visit. This stores your tickets, and informs you about attraction wait times, character visits, and parade times. You can view restaurant menus and make dining reservations; preorder and pay for contactless pickup at both parks; and download and share Disney PhotoPass photos.

Best Days to Visit: Midweek. Weekends (especially during the summer, Halloween, and winter holidays) are often the busiest times to visit. A rainy winter weekday is often the least crowded time to check out the parks.

Plan your times to hit the most popular rides. Get to the park as early as possible, even before the gates open, and make a beeline for the top rides before the crowds reach a critical mass. Staying at one of the three Disneyland Hotels offers Early Entry Admission. Later in the evening the parks thin out and you can catch a special show or parade. Save the quieter attractions for midafternoon.

Purchase Disney Genie+ starting at $25 to move forward on your favorite rides and save time in line. Another purchase is the new Discover Magic Band+. Pair it to your smartphone and Disneyland app for additional enhancement experiences.

Avoid peak mealtime crowds. Outside food and beverages in nonglass containers are allowed inside the parks, but dining at one of the park's many theme restaurants can be an experience to remember. For any sit-down establishment, be sure to make dining reservations months in advance, especially for The Blue Bayou in Disneyland's New Orleans Square or Carthay Circle at Disney California Adventure. You can make a reservation up to 60 days in advance online or via the Disneyland app. If you just need a quick recharge, Disney carts offer creative snacks including popcorn in souvenir buckets, Mickey Mouse–shaped pretzels, cute cake pops, and a variety of ice cream. It's always a good idea to bring water, juice boxes, and snacks for little ones.

Check the daily events schedule online, on the Disneyland app, or at the park entrance. During parades, fireworks, and other special events, sections of the parks are filled with crowds. This distraction can work in your favor to take advantage of shorter lines at dining venues and rides. It also can work against you in maneuvering around a section of the park so plan ahead.

pineapple, mango, or strawberry Dole Whip, plus Dole Whip floats and Asian-style *bao* buns. Skewers and rice plates, plus a vegetarian hummus trio, are available at Bengal Barbecue. The Tiki Juice Bar has pineapple juice and pineapple Dole Whip.

FANTASYLAND

Sleeping Beauty Castle marks the entrance to Fantasyland where guests can climb steps and walk inside to explore the epic tale of Princess Aurora. There are sounds, three-dimensional displays, and exciting special effects. Beyond the castle is a visual wonderland of princesses, spinning teacups, flying elephants, and other classic storybook characters. Bibbidi Bobbidi Boutique offers princess makeovers for ages 3-12, with hair, makeup, nails, and even a princess dress for purchase. Fantasy Faire is a fairy-tale-style village where Disney princesses gather together for photos and autographs. Each has her own reception nook in the Royal Hall.

Restaurants in this area of the park include the fairy-tale Red Rose Taverne, inspired by Belle's provincial town in Beauty and the Beast. Families with tots love It's a Small World on the east end of Fantasyland with its dancing animatronic dolls from every country, cuckoo clock–covered walls, and variations of the song everyone knows in different languages. Other memorable rides include the King Arthur Carrousel with 68 hand-painted horses and fancy chariot. Look up to see to see nine hand-painted vignettes of Disney's animated Sleeping Beauty fairy tale. Ride Casey Jr. Circus Train to tour miniature scale sites from some of Disney's most popular movies from a higher vantage than on Storybook Land Canal Boats. This is also home to some of the first rides at Disneyland including Mr. Toad's Wild Ride, Peter Pan's Flight, Snow White's Enchanted Wish, and Pinocchio's Daring Journey. They are all classic movie-theater-dark rides that immerse riders in Disney fairy tales. Keep an eye out for the Abominable Snowman when he pops up on the Matterhorn Bobsleds, a fun roller coaster that twists and turns up and around on a made-to-scale model of the real Swiss mountain.

MICKEY'S TOONTOWN

Mickey's Toontown is reimagined with new experiences for families with small kids. CenTOONial Park is ideal for little ones to run around the grassy lawn. There is a pretty fountain featuring water tables for guests to have a sensory experience and a dreaming tree for children to crawl and explore the sculpted tree

roots. Inside the El CapiTOON Theater, is the new Mickey & Minnie's Runaway Railway. Engineer Goofy takes guests on a wacky ride filled with twists and turns through a fun adventure. The cartoonlike downtown is where Mickey, Donald, Goofy, and other classic Disney characters hang their hats. Over near Goofy's house, watch honey drip from a beehive into a chute that travels into his home. Step inside to help Goofy make treats with his new candy-making interactive contraption with silly appliance sounds. Outside is the new Goofy How-To-Play-Yard where kids can explore an elevated off-the-ground clubhouse. There is a whimsical sound garden to hear some funny noises. Over at Donald's Duck Pond little ones can get wet near the spinning water lilies, balance on beams and rocking toys, and see bubbles in the porthole windows on Donald's Boat. One of the most popular attractions is Roger Rabbit's Car Toon Spin—board Lenny the Cab for a twisting, turning cab ride through the Toontown of *Who Framed Roger Rabbit?* Head over to Chip 'n' Dale's GADGETcoaster for a low-key thrill ride. Little ones love to walk inside Mickey's and Minnie's homes to meet and be photographed with these famous mice.

For food, the new Cafe Daisy has Daisy Duck serve kid classic fare at her new sidewalk table eatery. Toontown offers fresh Farmers Market items at Good Boy!Grocer, a grab-and-go roadside stand offering treats and drinks.

TOMORROWLAND

This popular section of the park continues to tinker with its future, adding and enhancing rides regularly. Families find Nemo's Submarine Voyage allows guests to search for the beloved clown fish Nemo, and friends Dory, Marlin, and other characters from the Disney-Pixar film. *Star Wars*–themed attractions can't be missed, like the immersive, 3-D Star Tours-The Adventures Continue, where you can join the Rebellion in a galaxy far,

Did You Know?

The plain purple teacup in Disneyland's Mad Tea Party ride spins the fastest—though no one knows why.

far away. The interactive Buzz Lightyear Astro Blasters lets you zap laser beams and compete with others for the highest score. Hurtle through the cosmos at fast speeds in the dark on Space Mountain or check out mainstays like driving along a miniature motorway road trip on Autopia powered by Honda, with a working gas pedal and steering wheel to maneuver curves and inclines. Soar on futuristic Astro Orbiter rockets. Disneyland Monorail and Disneyland Railroad both have stations here.

Go to the Disneyland app to discover daily live-action shows; parades are always crowd-pleasers.

■TIP→ **Arrive early to secure a good view; if there are two shows scheduled for the day, the second one tends to be less crowded. A fireworks display lights up weekends and most summer evenings.**

Disney California Adventure

★ **Disney California Adventure**
AMUSEMENT PARK/CARNIVAL | FAMILY | The sprawling Disney California Adventure, adjacent to Disneyland (their entrances face each other), pays tribute to the Golden State with multiple theme areas. Take your park experience to the next level of fun with Play Disney Parks, a mobile app with entertaining games, activities, and trivia. Admire the vintage art-deco architectural shops and dining venues along Buena Vista Street. Learn about movie magic at Hollywood Land, and Avengers Campus is home for a new generation of superheroes, focusing on the characters of the Marvel Cinematic Universe. Ride on Web-Slingers: A Spider-man Adventure, where guests of all ages can help wrangle Spider-bots while wearing 3D glasses and accumulate points. Screams can be heard around the park from the free-falling Guardians of the Galaxy–Mission: BREAKOUT! See your favorite characters from several hit Pixar films when crossing over Pixar

Pier. Ride the superfast Incredicoaster, and collect points playing along the interactive Toy Story Midway Mania ride. Stop to win a prize playing games at the carnival area in Pixar Pier. The 12-acre Cars Land features Radiator Springs Racers, a speedy trip in six-passenger speedsters through scenes featured in the blockbuster hit. The Single Rider Lane saves time to experience the thrills quicker. At night the park takes on neon hues as glowing signs light up Route 66 in Cars Land and Pixar Pal-A-Round, a giant Ferris wheel. Cocktails, craft beers, and premium wines from California are available in the Pacific Wharf dining area. This area in the park is being reimagined into San Fransokyo from the movie *Big Hero 6,* where East meet West. There is a place to meet Baymax, plus new dining and shopping venues. Live nightly entertainment features a 1930s jazz troupe and seasonal entertainers throughout the year. The MagicBand+ is a new way to unlock Disney storytelling. This hands-free wearable on your wrist enhances your park experience in exciting new ways with color changing, haptic vibrations, and gesture recognition features. Certain rides have Lightning Lanes with Disney's Genie+ to save time in line. Be sure to stay for the World of Color-One, a light-and-sound show celebrating Walt Disney's 100 Years of Wonder storytelling. ⊠ *1313 S. Disneyland Dr., between Ball Rd. and Katella Ave., Anaheim* ☎ *714/781–4636* ⊕ *disneyland.disney. go.com* ✉ *From $114 during the week and $150 on weekends; parking $30.*

PARK NEIGHBORHOODS
BUENA VISTA STREET
California Adventure's grand entryway re-creates the 1920s Los Angeles that Walt Disney encountered when he moved to the Golden State. There's a Red Car trolley (modeled after Los Angeles's bygone streetcar line); hop on for the brief ride to Hollywood Land. Buena Vista Street is also home to a Starbucks outlet—within the Fiddler, Fifer and Practical

Café—and the upscale Carthay Circle Restaurant and Lounge, which serves modern craft food, cocktails, and beer. The comfy booths of the Carthay Circle restaurant on the second floor feel like a relaxing world away from the theme park outside. Keep an eye out for Officer Blue; he is known to give guests a citation to take home as a unique souvenir. The circle with a fountain in the middle has live entertainment throughout the day, ride times, and park information.

GRIZZLY PEAK

This woodsy land celebrates California's national parks and the great outdoors. Test your skills on the Redwood Creek Challenge Trail, a challenging trek across net ladders and suspension bridges. Grizzly River Run mimics the river rapids of the Sierra Nevada; be prepared to get soaked.

Soarin' Around the World is a spectacular simulated hang-gliding ride over internationally known landmarks like Switzerland's Matterhorn and India's Taj Mahal.

There is an entrance into Disney's Grand Californian Hotel & Spa from this area in Disney's California Adventure Park.

HOLLYWOOD LAND

Movie moments take place along a main street modeled after Hollywood Boulevard, with a fake sky backdrop, and real sound stages guests can step into—Monsteropolis on an exciting Monsters, Inc. Mike & Sulley To The Rescue ride to return Boo home. Sorcerer's Workshop is where Disney Animation gives you an insider's look at how animators create characters and what character is most like you. Turtle Talk with Crush lets kids have an unscripted chat with a computer-animated Crush, the sea turtle from *Finding Nemo*. Grab a bite at Award Weiners for gourmet hot dogs and fries. Delicious fruit smoothies are blended at Schmoozies! Grab-and-go snacks and drinks are available at Studio Catering Co.

CARS LAND

Amble down Route 66, the main thoroughfare of Cars Land, and discover a pitch-perfect re-creation of the vintage highway. Hop onto Mater's Junkyard Jamboree spinning ride and the Italian-theme Luigi's Rollickin' Roadsters. One of the most popular rides in Cars Land is Radiator Springs Racers. Strap into a nifty sports car and meet the characters of Pixar's *Cars* before a speedy auto race through a red rock canyon featuring a waterfall and desert in Radiator Springs. There is a Single Rider Lane and Lightning Lane for quicker wait times. Quick, creative eats are found at the Cozy Cone Motel (in an orange, tepee-shaped motor court) while Flo's V8 café serves hearty comfort food. Fresh fruit, vegetables, and drinks are available in the psychedelic Fillmore's Taste-In service station.

■ TIP→ **To bypass the line, there's a single-rider option for Radiator Springs Racers.**

PACIFIC WHARF

In the midst of the California Adventure you'll find multiple dining options, from light snacks to full-service restaurants at the new San Fransokyo. The San Francisco Bay theme and Tokyo Bay–inspired design is from Disney's *Big Hero 6* animated film. They kept many of guests' favorite food court options such as Lucky Fortune Cafe, Ghirardelli Soda Fountain and Chocolate Shop, and Pacific Wharf Cafe, with breads by Boudin, San Francisco's world-famous artisanal bakery. They sell loafs of Mickey Mouse–shaped sourdough bread.

PARADISE GARDENS PARK

The far corner of California Adventure is a mix of floating and flying rides. Soar via the Silly Symphony Swings; Goofy's Sky School rollicks and rolls through a cartoon-inspired landscape; and the sleek retro-style gondolas of the Golden Zephyr mimic 1920s movies and their sci-fi adventures. Journey through Ariel's colorful world on The Little Mermaid—Ariel's

Undersea Adventure. The best views of the nighttime music, water, and light show, World of Color, are from the paths along Paradise Bay. FastPass tickets are available. Or for a guaranteed spot, book dinner at the Wine Country Trattoria that includes a ticket to a viewing area to catch all the show's stunning visuals.

PIXAR PIER

The most popular ride in this area is Toy Story Midway Mania! This fun 4D shooting game usually has a wait. This is a re-creation of California's famous seaside piers, featuring Pixar films' beloved characters. Join the Incredibles family on the Incredicoaster, a fast-moving roller coaster that zooms from zero to 55 mph in about four seconds. Riders scream through tunnels, steeply angled drops, and a 360-degree loop. Pixar Pal-A-Round is a giant Ferris wheel with gondolas named after Disney and Pixar characters. Hop in one and soar 150 feet in the air. Some of the gondolas spin and sway for an extra thrill while overlooking the park. There are also carnival games to win prizes, an aquatic-themed carousel, and Inside Out Emotional Whirlwind ride. Dining options include soft-serve ice cream, turkey legs, popcorn, and churros for quick snacking. At the Lamplight Lounge adults can chill out and overlook the action while sipping on craft cocktails.

AVENGERS CAMPUS

Assemble with fellow superfans and prepare to spring into action at this training ground for superheroes of the Marvel Cinematic universe. Team up with your favorite Avenger while exploring the mysterious ancient sanctum to learn the secrets of Doctor Strange. Help Spider-Man wrangle rogue Spider-Bots while on the Web Slinger ride and join Rocket to rescue the Guardians of the Galaxy in an accelerated drop tower dark ride. Watch the mightiest heroes spring into action throughout the day at Avengers Headquarters and train with Black Panther's loyal bodyguards in Wakanda.

OTHER ATTRACTIONS

★ Downtown Disney District

PEDESTRIAN MALL | FAMILY | The exciting Downtown Disney District is a walking promenade filled with international dining, shopping, and lively entertainment that connects the resort's hotels and theme parks. More than a dozen new and reimagined establishments include the popular Asian restaurant Din Tai Fung, specializing in Taiwanese soup dumplings, and grab-and-go Earl of Sandwich along with the sit-down Earl of Sandwich Tavern. Jazz Kitchen Coastal Grill & Patio offers Southern-inspired food and live music on welcoming patios, verandas, and dining rooms. Be sure to try their signature seasonal flavor beignets that can be dipped, drizzled, and sprinkled. Southern California's iconic Porto's Bakery and Cafe offering Cuban-California–inspired pastries, desserts, and specialty items is set to open later in 2023. Enjoy a cold beer at Ballast Point Brewery and gourmet burger at Black Tap Craft Burgers. Save room for sweet treats at Salt and Straw for gourmet ice cream flavors such as honey lavender and oat milk and cookies, and Sprinkles for decadent frosted cupcakes.

Disney merchandise, souvenirs, and artwork are showcased at the brightly lit World of Disney store. At the megasize LEGO Store there are bigger-than-life LEGO creations, hands-on demonstrations, and space to play with the latest LEGO creations.

All visitors must pass through a security checkpoint and metal detectors before entering. ⊠ *1580 Disneyland Dr., Anaheim* ☎ *714/781–4565* ⊕ *disneyland. disney.go.com/downtown-disney* 🎟 *Free.*

 ## Restaurants

Anaheim White House

$$$ | ITALIAN | FAMILY | The owner and executive chef Bruno Serato is one of the most beloved and famous philanthropists in Anaheim, known as much for his mission to feed America's hungry children as for his fine-dining Italian restaurant where standout dishes include lobster ravioli, Italian gourmet pizza, and his signature steamed salmon "chocolat" served with Belgium white-chocolate mashed potatoes. Grilled hanger steak dazzles with a green chimichurri sauce, and the Angus beef filet mignon is served with a savory Italian porcini sauce. **Known for:** classic Mediterranean cuisine; celebratory fine-dining venue; celeb chef. [$] *Average main: $40* ✉ *887 S. Anaheim Blvd., Anaheim* ☎ *714/772–1381* 🌐 *www.anaheimwhitehouse.com* 🕒 *Closed Mon. and Tues.*

★ Napa Rose

$$$$ | **AMERICAN** | Done up in a handsome Craftsman style, the upscale dinner venue Napa Rose prepares rich seasonal cuisine paired with an extensive wine list. For a look into the open kitchen, sit at the counter and watch the chefs as they whip up signature dishes such as warm duck confit salad, sautéed diver scallops, and beef filet mignon. **Known for:** upscale food and wine; kid-friendly options; gorgeous dining room and lounge. [$] *Average main: $60* ✉ *Disney's Grand Californian Hotel, 1600 Disneyland Dr., Anaheim* ☎ *714/781-4636* 🌐 *disneyland.disney.go.com/grand-californian-hotel/napa-rose.*

Hotels

Anaheim Majestic Garden Hotel

$ | **HOTEL** | **FAMILY** | This sprawling replica of an English Tudor estate is a little prince or princess's dream hotel. **Pros:** large, attractive lobby; spacious rooms with comfortable beds; shuttle to the theme parks. **Cons:** confusing layout; hotel sits close to a busy freeway; decor is dated. [$] *Rooms from: $150* ✉ *900 S. Disneyland Dr., Anaheim* ☎ *714/778–1700, 844/227–8535* 🌐 *www.majesticgardenhotel.com* 🛏 *489 rooms* 🍴 *No Meals.*

★ Courtyard by Marriott Anaheim Theme Park Entrance

$$$ | **RESORT** | **FAMILY** | Near the entrance to both Disney Parks, and featuring a Surfside Waterpark with a fun splash zone, waterslides, and a heated swimming pool, this is not your typical Courtyard by Marriott. **Pros:** fun waterpark; family-friendly rooms; prime location by Disney Parks. **Cons:** no sit-down restaurant; valet parking only; water park requires reservations. [$] *Rooms from: $329* ✉ *1420 S. Harbor Blvd., Anaheim* ☎ *714/254–1442* 🌐 *www.marriott.com/en-us/hotels/snadt-courtyard-anaheim-theme-park-entrance* 🛏 *200 rooms* 🍴 *No Meals* ☞ *Valet Parking only $35 per day.*

★ Disneyland Hotel

$$$$ | **HOTEL** | **FAMILY** | Staying at one of "The Happiest Places on Earth" is almost as fun as visiting Disney's two parks. **Pros:** great location; early entrance into parks; pools, slides, and Disney characters. **Cons:** pool's crowded in the summer; this magic does not come cheap; restaurants require reservations. [$] *Rooms from: $650* ✉ *1150 Magic Way, Anaheim* ☎ *714/778–6600* 🌐 *disneyland.disney.go.com* 🛏 *970 including 71 suites* 🍴 *No Meals.*

★ Disney's Grand Californian Hotel and Spa

$$$$ | **RESORT** | **FAMILY** | The most opulent of Disneyland's three hotels, the Craftsman-style Grand Californian offers views of Disney California Adventure and Downtown Disney. **Pros:** early entrance into parks; family-friendly with three beautiful pools; direct access to California Adventure. **Cons:** expensive; valet parking is $65 a day; reserve dining in advance. [$] *Rooms from: $850* ✉ *1600 S. Disneyland Dr., Anaheim* ☎ *714/635–2300* 🌐 *disneyland.disney.go.com/grand-californian-hotel* 🛏 *1019 rooms* 🍴 *No Meals.*

Hilton Anaheim

$ | **HOTEL** | **FAMILY** | Attached to the Anaheim Convention Center, this busy Hilton is the largest hotel in Orange

County. **Pros:** good location; special hotel packages; large resort with amenities. **Cons:** dated decor; not a lot of green space; megasize parking lot maze. [$] *Rooms from: $175* ✉ *777 Convention Way, Anaheim* ☎ *714/750–4321* 🌐 *www.hiltonanaheimhotel.com* 🛏 *1572 rooms* 🍴 *No Meals.*

★ JW Marriott, Anaheim Resort

$$ | **RESORT** | **FAMILY** | This luxury four-diamond hotel is just blocks from Disneyland and the Anaheim Convention Center. **Pros:** Tocca Ferro Italian Chophouse; great fireworks views; luxury amenities. **Cons:** rooftop views from lower-level rooms; no Disneyland-themed rooms; pricey valet parking and added daily fees. [$] *Rooms from: $350* ✉ *1775 S. Clementine St., Anaheim* ☎ *714/294–7800* 🌐 *www.marriott.com* 🛏 *468 rooms* 🍴 *No Meals.*

Park Vue Inn

$$ | **HOTEL** | **FAMILY** | Watch the frequent fireworks from the rooftop sundeck at this bougainvillea-covered Spanish-style inn, one of the closest lodgings to the Disneyland Resort main gate. **Pros:** easy walk to Disneyland, Downtown Disney, and Disney California Adventure; free parking until midnight on checkout day; some rooms have bunk beds. **Cons:** all rooms face the parking lot; no breakfast on-site; inefficient room air-conditioners. [$] *Rooms from: $250* ✉ *1570 S. Harbor Blvd., Anaheim* ☎ *714/772–3691, 800/334–7021* 🌐 *www.parkvueinn.com* 🛏 *86 rooms* 🍴 *No Meals.*

★ The Viv Hotel

$$ | **HOTEL** | **FAMILY** | This family-friendly hotel offers spacious guest rooms and Disney magic throughout, from the blue fiberglass-and-resin life-size Star Wars Stormtroopers who greet guests arriving from the parking garage to the Fantasia-style hallway carpet and the views of Disneyland and Disney California Adventure Park from some rooms. **Pros:** heated family pool with fun water features; family-friendly, spacious rooms; rooftop restaurant, bar, and outdoor lounge. **Cons:** some freeway noise in rooms facing Disneyland; not a prime location; hard to enter driveway by car. [$] *Rooms from: $250* ✉ *1601 S. Anaheim Blvd., Anaheim* ☎ *714/408–2787* 🌐 *www.thevivhotelanaheim.com* 🛏 *326 rooms* 🍴 *No Meals.*

★ Westin Anaheim

$$$ | **RESORT** | Opened in 2021, and within walking distance of the parks, this convention-friendly hotel was designed by the same architect who designed the Mirage and WYNN Hotels in Las Vegas, and the ground-level heated swimming pool and hot whirlpool with fountain feature and cabanas definitely bring Las Vegas vibes. **Pros:** rooftop bar with views; ideal location for Disney parks and Convention Center; lots of dining options. **Cons:** valet parking is $45; lacks Disney vibes; pool can get crowded in prime season. [$] *Rooms from: $425* ✉ *1030 W. Katella Ave., Anaheim* ☎ *657/279–9786* 🌐 *www.westinanaheim.com* 🛏 *618 rooms* 🍴 *No Meals.*

Activities

Anaheim Ducks

HOCKEY | **FAMILY** | The National Hockey League's Anaheim Ducks, winners of the 2007 Stanley Cup, play at Honda Center. Concerts are also hosted here. ✉ *Honda Center, 2695 E. Katella Ave., Anaheim* ☎ *877/945–3946* 🌐 *nhl.com/ducks.*

Los Angeles Angels of Anaheim

BASEBALL & SOFTBALL | **FAMILY** | Professional baseball's Los Angeles Angels of Anaheim have called Anaheim and Angel Stadium home since 1966. An "Outfield Extravaganza" celebrates great plays on the field, with fireworks and a geyser exploding over a model evoking the California coast. ✉ *Angel Stadium, 2000 E. Gene Autry Way, Anaheim* ☎ *714/940–2000* 🌐 *www.mlb.com/angels/ballpark* [M] *Metrolink Angels Express.*

Knott's Berry Farm

25 miles south of Los Angeles, via I–5, in Buena Park.

The iconic Knott's Berry Farm theme park appeals to all ages. Explore the Ghost Town, ride some thrilling roller coasters, and save room for fried chicken and boysenberry treats.

Sights

Knott's Berry Farm

AMUSEMENT PARK/CARNIVAL | FAMILY | This lively amusement park is fun for all ages. Once a 160-acre boysenberry farm, it's now an entertainment complex with close to 40 rides, dozens of restaurants and shops, arcade games, live shows, and a brick-by-brick replica of Philadelphia's Independence Hall. Take a step back into the 1880s while walking through Knott's Old West Ghost Town. Ride on a horse-drawn stagecoach or board a steam engine to start your journey into the park; just keep your valuables close to you, as bandits might enter your train car and put on quite a show. Camp Snoopy has plenty of rides to keep small children occupied as they explore 15 kid-friendly attractions. There are awesome thrill rides in the Boardwalk area, including the zooming HangTime that pauses dramatically then drops nearly 15 stories, and the exhilarating steel moto-coaster Pony Express that goes from zero to 35 mph in less than three seconds.

Be sure to get a slice of boysenberry pie, as well as boysenberry soft-serve ice cream, jam, juice, you name it. There's even a Boysenberry Food Festival once a year. In the fall, part of the park is turned into Knott's Scary Farm, a popular activity for teens and adults. Buy adult tickets online for a discount. Buy a bundle for parking and food included with your ticket. FastLane wristbands give you quicker access to the most popular rides. Nearby Knott's Soak City is open during the summer for guests who want to float on the lazy river, go down waterslides, and swim in the wave pool.

Fun fact: In 1934, Cordelia Knott began serving chicken dinners on her wedding china to supplement her family's income. The dinners and her boysenberry pies proved more profitable than her husband Walter's berry farm, so the two moved first into the restaurant business and then into the entertainment business. ✉ *8039 Beach Blvd., Buena Park* ✛ *Between La Palma Ave. and Crescent St., 2 blocks south of Hwy. 91* ☎ *714/220–5200* ⊕ *www.knotts.com* 🎟 *$80* ♿ *Purchase online* ☞ *Parking is $25.*

Knott's Soak City

WATER SPORTS | FAMILY | Knott's Soak City Waterpark is directly across from Knott's Berry Farm on 15 acres offering speed tubes, family rafting, a lazy river, and body slides. Pacific Spin is an oversize waterslide that drops riders 75 feet into a catch pool. There's also a children's pool, a 750,000-gallon wave pool, and a fun house. Soak City's season runs mid-May to mid-September and is a separate admission ticket. ✉ *8200 Beach Blvd., Buena Park* ☎ *714/220–5200* ⊕ *www.knotts.com/soak-city* 🎟 *$49.99* 🕐 *Open mid-May through Sept.*

PARK NEIGHBORHOODS
THE BOARDWALK

Thrill rides and skill-based games dominate the scene at the Boardwalk. Roller coasters including Coast Rider, Surfside Glider, and Pacific Scrambler surround a pond that keeps things cooler on hot days. HangTime towers 150 feet above the Boardwalk as coaster cars hang, invert, and drop the equivalent of 15 stories. The Boardwalk is also home to a string of test-your-skill games that are fun to watch whether you're playing or not. Dining options include the all-American diner Johnny Rockets.

CAMP SNOOPY

Kids love this miniature High Sierra wonderland where the *Peanuts* gang hangs out. Tykes can push and pump their own mini-mining cars on Huff and Puff, soar around on Charlie Brown's Kite Flyer, and hop aboard Woodstock's Airmail, a kids' version of the park's Supreme Scream ride. Most of the rides here are geared toward kids only, leaving parents to cheer them on and take photos from the sidelines. Sierra Sidewinder, a roller coaster near the entrance of Camp Snoopy, is aimed at older children, with spinning saucer-type vehicles that go a maximum speed of 37 mph.

FIESTA VILLAGE

The renovated Fiesta Village has brand-new experiences, entertainment, shopping, dining, and thrills. Along vibrant Fiesta Mercado, inspired by Olvera Street in Downtown Los Angeles, shop for authentic and unique souvenirs, and wander among pretty fountains and magenta bougainvillea flowers. Order fresh Mexican fare with a *cerveza* or margarita at the full-service Casa California restaurant and Cantina Del Sur. The Fiesta Stage has been transformed, offering live-entertainment shows. Thrill seekers will want to ride the next chapter in Montezooma's Revenge—MonteZOOMa: The Forbidden Fortress.

GHOST TOWN

Stop and chat with a blacksmith, crack open a geode, and visit Sad-Eye Joe sitting in the town jail while you walk among authentic old buildings relocated from their original mining-town sites in this town. Step inside a circa-1879 one-room schoolhouse for another step-back-in-time experience, as well as riding on an original horse-pulled Butterfield stagecoach. Looming over the area is GhostRider, Orange County's first wooden roller coaster. Traveling up to 56 mph and reaching 118 feet at its highest point, it's one of the park's biggest attractions. On the Western-themed Silver Bullet, riders are sent to a height of 146 feet and then back down 109 feet. Riders spiral, corkscrew, fly into a cobra roll, and experience overbanked curves. The Calico Mine ride descends into a replica of a re-created working gold mine complete with 50 animatronic figures. The Timber Mountain Log Ride is a visitor favorite: the flume ride tours through pioneer scenes before splashing down. Also found here is the Pony Express, a roller coaster that lets riders saddle up on packs of "horses" tethered to a steel platform before taking off on a series of hairpin turns at speeds of 38 mph. Take a step inside the Western Trails Museum, a dusty old gem full of Old West memorabilia and rural Americana, plus menus from the original chicken restaurant and an impressive antique button collection. Calico Railroad departs regularly from Ghost Town station for a round-trip tour of the park (bandit holdups notwithstanding). You can order a boysenberry soft-serve ice-cream cone nearby afterward. This section is also home to Big Foot Rapids, a splash-fest of white-water river rafting over towering cliffs, cascading waterfalls, and wild rapids.

INDIAN TRAILS

Celebrate Native American traditions through interactive exhibits like tepees and daily dance and storytelling performances.

🍴 Restaurants

★ **Mrs. Knott's Chicken Dinner Restaurant**
$$ | AMERICAN | FAMILY | Cordelia Knott's fried chicken and boysenberry pies drew crowds so big in the 1930s, that Knott's Berry Farm built a park to keep the hungry customers occupied while they waited. The Western-theme restaurant serves crispy home-style fried chicken, along with handmade biscuits, mashed potatoes, gravy, and Mrs. Knott's signature chilled cherry-rhubarb compote. **Known for:** famous fried chicken; long waits especially

on weekends; pies and desserts.
Ⓢ *Average main: $22* ⊠ *Knott's Berry Farm Marketplace, 8039 Beach Blvd., Buena Park* ☎ *714/220–5200* ⊕ *www.knotts.com/california-marketplace/mrs-knott-s-chicken-dinner-restaurant.*

 Hotels

Knott's Berry Farm Hotel

$$ | **HOTEL** | **FAMILY** | This newly renovated hotel next to Knott's Berry Farm offers farm-theme-designed guest rooms with mini-refrigerators, two tennis courts, a basketball court, and swimming pool. **Pros:** easy access to Knott's Berry Farm; swimming pool; on-site dining. **Cons:** can be noisy; parking $15 a day; lower level has no view of park. Ⓢ *Rooms from: $230* ⊠ *7675 Crescent Ave., Buena Park* ☎ *714/995–1111, 866/752–2444* ⊕ *www.knotts.com/knotts-berry-farm-hotel* ⇲ *249 rooms* ⟊◯⟊ *No Meals* ⌇ *Bed and Breakfast package and Room and Knott's Berry Farm ticket packages are available.*

Huntington Beach

40 miles southeast of Los Angeles.

Huntington Beach is commonly referred to as Surf City U.S.A. This town offers a range of luxury and boutique hotels overlooking or just a block away from its broad white-sand beaches. Take a walk along the long wood pier to watch surfers glide across the surface on some-times-towering waves. At the beginning and end of the lively pier are a few restaurants. Other shops and restaurants can be discovered on Main Street. A draw for surf fans is the U.S. Open pro-fessional surf competition, which brings a festive atmosphere to town annually in late July. There's even a Surfing Walk of Fame, with plaques set in the sidewalk around the intersection of PCH and Main Street. Surf City Nights are every Tuesday with the first three blocks of Main Street

closed to cars for a weekly farmers' mar-ket, street fair, and kids activities.

ESSENTIALS

VISITOR INFORMATION Visit Huntington Beach. ⊠ *155 Fifth St., Suite 111, Huntington Beach* ☎ *714/969–3492, 800/729–6232* ⊕ *www.surfcityusa.com.*

 Sights

Bolsa Chica Ecological Reserve

WILDLIFE REFUGE | **FAMILY** | Wildlife lovers and bird-watchers flock to Bolsa Chica Ecological Reserve, which has over 1,300 acres of salty marshland home to 200 different bird species—including great blue herons, snowy and great egrets, and brown pelicans. Throughout the reserve are easy-to-walk trails for bird-watching along a 1½-mile loop. There are two entrances off the Pacific Coast Highway: one close to the Interpretive Center and a second 1 mile south on Warner Avenue, opposite Bolsa Chica State Beach. Each parking lot connects to 4 miles of walking and hiking trails with scenic overlooks. ⊠ *3842 Warner Ave., Huntington Beach* ☎ *714/846–1114* ⊕ *www.bolsachica.org* ⌷ *Free.*

Bolsa Chica State Beach

BEACH | **FAMILY** | In the northern section of the city, Bolsa Chica State Beach is usually less crowded than its southern neighbors. The sand is somewhat gritty and not the cleanest, but swells make it a hot surfing spot. The Huntington Beach bike trail runs along the edge of the sand for 7 miles north to the south of Hunting-ton Beach. Picnic sites can be reserved in advance. Firepits attract beachgoers most nights. **Amenities:** food and drink; lifeguards; parking; showers; toilets. **Best for:** sunset; surfing; swimming; walking. ⊠ *Pacific Coast Hwy., between Seapoint St. and Warner Ave., Huntington Beach* ☎ *714/377-5691* ⊕ *www.parks.ca.gov* ⌷ *$15 parking.*

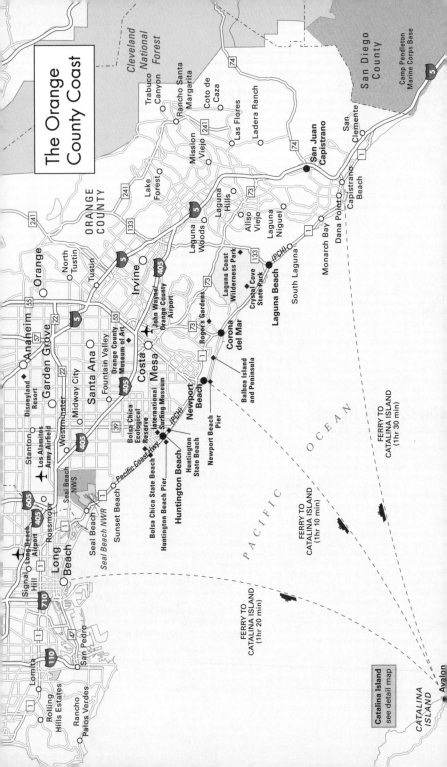

Huntington Beach Pier

MARINA/PIER | **FAMILY** | This municipal pier stretches 1,856 feet out to sea, past the powerful waves that gave Huntington Beach the title of "Surf City U.S.A." Well above the waves, it's a prime vantage point to watch the dozens of surfers in the water below. On the pier you'll find a snack shop and a shop where you can buy fishing rod rentals, tackle, and bait to fish off the pier. ✉ *Pacific Coast Hwy., Huntington Beach* 🌐 *www.surfcityusa.com.*

Huntington City Beach

BEACH | **FAMILY** | Stretching for 3½ miles from Bolsa Chica State Beach to Huntington State Beach, Huntington City Beach is most crowded around the pier where amateur and professional surfers brave the waves daily. There are 100 fire rings, numerous concession stands, bike paths, and well-raked white sand. Surfboard rental shops make this a popular beach year-round. **Amenities:** food and drink; lifeguards; parking; showers; toilets. **Best for:** sunset; surfing; swimming; walking. ✉ *Pacific Coast Hwy., from Beach Blvd. to Seapoint St., Huntington Beach* ☎ *714/536–5281, 714/536–9303 surf report* 🌐 *www.huntingtonbeachca.gov/residents/beach_info* 🎫 *Parking from $15.*

Huntington State Beach

BEACH | **FAMILY** | This peaceful state beach offers 121 sandy acres and 200 firepits, so it's popular during the day and evening. There are changing rooms, and two new concession stands—the Huntington Beach House and Sahara Sandbar. There are year-round surf lessons, lifeguards, Wi-Fi access, and ample parking. An 8½-mile bike path connects Huntington to Bolsa Chica State Beach. Picnic areas can be reserved in advance for a fee depending on location; otherwise it's first come, first served. On hot days, expect crowds at this broad, soft-sand beach. **Amenities:** food and drink; lifeguards; parking; showers; toilets. **Best for:** sunset; surfing; swimming; walking. ✉ *21601 E. Pacific Coast Hwy., from Beach Blvd. south to Santa Ana River, Huntington Beach* ☎ *714/536–1454* 🌐 *www.parks.ca.gov/?page_id=643* 🎫 *$15 parking.*

International Surfing Museum

HISTORY MUSEUM | **FAMILY** | Just up Main Street from Huntington Pier, in an iconic art-deco building, the International Surfing Museum pays tribute to the sport's greats with an impressive collection of surfboards and related memorabilia. Exhibits are designed to encourage families to learn about the history of surfing. Highlights include Duke Kahanamoku's surfboard and the "World's Largest Surfboard" measuring 42 feet long, 11 feet wide, 16 inches thick, and weighing 1,300 pounds. ✉ *411 Olive Ave., Huntington Beach* ☎ *714/960–3483* 🌐 *www.huntingtonbeachsurfingmuseum.org* 🎫 *$3* 🕒 *Closed Mon.*

🍴 Restaurants

Duke's

$$$$ | **SEAFOOD** | **FAMILY** | Freshly caught seafood reigns supreme at this homage to surfing legend Duke Kahanamoku; it's also a prime people-watching spot right at the beginning of Huntington Beach Pier. Choose from several fish-of-the-day selections—many topped with Hawaiian ingredients—and shellfish like lobster, king crab, and shrimp. **Known for:** Hawaiian-style decor; gorgeous sunset views; mai tai cocktails. [$] *Average main: $45* ✉ *317 Pacific Coast Hwy., Huntington Beach* ☎ *714/374–6446* 🌐 *www.dukeshuntington.com.*

Wahoo's Fish Taco

$ | **MEXICAN FUSION** | **FAMILY** | Proximity to the ocean makes this eatery's seafood-filled tacos and burritos taste even better. The healthy fast-food chain—tagged with dozens of surf stickers—brought Baja's fish tacos north of the border to quick success. **Known for:** organic

Lively Huntington Beach is a center for surfing on the coast.

ingredients; Hawaiian onion ring burrito; casual beachy ambience. [$] *Average main: $13* ✉ *120 Main St., Huntington Beach* ☎ *714/536–2050* 🌐 *www.wahoos.com.*

Hotels

Hyatt Regency Huntington Beach Resort and Spa

$$$ | **RESORT** | **FAMILY** | The Mediterranean design of this sprawling resort incorporates arched courtyards, beautiful tiled fountains, and firepits, all a nod to California's Mission period. **Pros:** close to beach with exclusive access; variety of pool areas; some rooms have private firepits. **Cons:** some partial ocean-view rooms; resort and daily valet fees; some rooms can hear the traffic on PCH. [$] *Rooms from: $400* ✉ *21500 Pacific Coast Hwy., Huntington Beach* ☎ *714/698–1234* 🌐 *www.hyatt.com* 🛏 *517 rooms* 🍴 *No Meals.*

★ Kimpton Shorebreak Resort

$$$ | **HOTEL** | **FAMILY** | This surfer-style Kimpton hotel is not only across the street from the beach, but it's the closest hotel to the Huntington Beach Pier and Main Street. **Pros:** proximity to beach and shops; free surfboard storage; quiet rooms despite central location. **Cons:** $35 valet parking fee; courtyard rooms have uninspiring alley views; additional resort fee to receive best perks. [$] *Rooms from: $450* ✉ *500 Pacific Coast Hwy., Huntington Beach* ☎ *714/861–4470, 877/212–8597* 🌐 *www.shorebreakhotel.com* 🛏 *157 rooms* 🍴 *No Meals.*

Pasea Hotel & Spa

$$$ | **RESORT** | **FAMILY** | Painted in shades of coastal blue, the contemporary-style Pasea is eight stories offering ocean views from almost every guest room, with balconies to take in the fresh breezes. **Pros:** excellent ocean views; pet friendly; supercomfortable beds. **Cons:** pool can get crowded; $40 valet parking fee; noise issues from nearby bars at Pacific City. [$] *Rooms from: $500*

✉ *21080 Pacific Coast Hwy., Huntington Beach* ☎ *866/478–9702* 🌐 *www.meritagecollection.com/pasea-hotel* 🛏 *250 rooms* 🍴 *No Meals.*

The Waterfront Beach Resort, a Hilton Hotel
$$$ | RESORT | FAMILY | This two-tower resort offers a variety of amenities for families, couples, and business travelers alike. **Pros:** quick walk to beach and pier; fun surf decor; oceanfront views from rooms. **Cons:** different towers have different vibes; overnight valet parking $48; crowded pool and deck during summer. [$] *Rooms from: $475* ✉ *21100 Pacific Coast Hwy., Huntington Beach* ☎ *714/845–8000,* 🌐 *www.waterfrontresort.com* 🛏 *290 rooms* 🍴 *No Meals.*

Shopping

Huntington Surf and Sport
SPORTING GOODS | FAMILY | The largest surf-gear source in town is Huntington Surf and Sport, right across from Huntington Pier. Staffed by true surf enthusiasts, it's also one of the only surf shops with a Java Point coffee counter inside. Surfboard rentals are $15 an hour or $50 all day, while soft-top boards are $10 per hour or $30 a day. They also rent wet suits for $15 a day. ✉ *300 Pacific Coast Hwy., Huntington Beach* ☎ *714/841–4000* 🌐 *www.hsssurf.com.*

Activities

SURFING

Corky Carroll's Surf School
SURFING | FAMILY | Learn the fundamentals of both longboard and shortboard surfing at Bolsa Chica State Beach. Run by the 1960s first professional surfer Corky Carroll, the surf school organizes beginning and more experienced surfing lessons, and provides hard- and soft-top boards and wet suits to rent during your lesson. ✉ *18581 E. Pacific Coast Hwy., Huntington Beach* ☎ *714/969–3959* 🌐 *www.surfschool.net.*

Surfing Walk of Fame

Many of the world's most famous surfers are represented on the Surfing Walk of Fame (along Main Street at 300 Pacific Coast Highway in Huntington Beach) including Robert August, the star of *Endless Summer*, Corky Carroll, a pioneer surfing promoter, and Mark Richard, winner of the most surfing championships. Super-surfers have been selected since 1994 by a committee representing the surfing industry worldwide. Inductions take place during the annual U.S. Open Surfing event held in the summer in Huntington Beach.

Dwight's Beach Concession
BIKING | FAMILY | You can rent surrey or cruiser bikes, wet suits, surfboards, bodyboards, umbrellas, and beach chairs at Dwight's, one block south of Huntington Pier. They also serve casual beach food, including their world-famous cheese strips. ✉ *201 Pacific Coast Hwy., Huntington Beach* ☎ *714/536–8083* 🌐 *www.dwightsbeachconcession.com.*

Zack's HB
LOCAL SPORTS | FAMILY | This go-to sport rental and quick food spot is steps from the pier and Main Street. Zack's rents beach equipment, surfboards, wet suits, and bicycles. There is a walk-up window to purchase a quick hamburger, corn dog, grilled fish sandwich, fries, slush puppy, and ice cream. Zack's also has a gift shop with sunglasses, hats, and shirts. ✉ *405 Pacific Coast Hwy., at Main St., Huntington Beach* ☎ *714/536–0215* 🌐 *www.zackssurfcity.com.*

Newport Beach

Just south of Huntington Beach, Newport Beach has evolved from a simple seaside village to a sophisticated coastal playground, featuring 10 distinctive neighborhoods. Newport Harbor is home to million-dollar yachts, adorable Duffy boats, kayaks, and stand-up paddleboarders enjoying the largest recreational harbor on the west coast. Biking and walking are popular along the serene coastal wetlands in the Back Bay, while Fashion Island is a premier shopping and dining destination. Some of the most luxurious and unique boutique hotels are located in each neighborhood, except the residential Balboa Island, a short car ferry ride from the historic Balboa Peninsula. The Balboa Island loop is just over a 2½-mile walk around two connected islands in the middle of Newport Harbor. Stroll the public sidewalk along the waterfront and visit some of the unique shops and restaurants while admiring the million-dollar homes and boats docked in their backyards. Maybe you can't live here but you can enjoy Balboa Island's frozen treats—a Balboa Bar (vanilla or chocolate ice cream on a stick rolled in sprinkles, nuts, or other toppings) and frozen bananas dipped in chocolate.

ESSENTIALS

VISITOR INFORMATION Visit Newport Beach Concierge. ⊠ *Atrium Ct. at Fashion Island, 1600 Newport Center Dr., Newport Beach* ☎ *949/719–6100* ⊕ *www. newportbeachandco.com.*

◉ Sights

★ Balboa Island
ISLAND | FAMILY | This sliver of terra firma in Newport Harbor boasts quaint streets tightly packed with impossibly charming multimillion-dollar cottages. The island's main drag, Marine Avenue, is lined with picturesque cafés, frozen chocolate banana shops, and apparel, decor, and souvenir stores. There are bicycle and walking paths encircling much of the island for an easy and scenic visit. Rent a bike or walk the 2½-mile bike path and boardwalk that encircles much of the island for an easy and scenic visit.

To get here, you can either park your car on the mainland side of the PCH in Newport Beach and walk or bike over the bridge onto Marine Avenue, or take the Balboa Island Ferry, the country's longest-running auto ferry. The one-way fare is $1.50 for an adult pedestrian; $1.75 for an adult with a bike; and $2.50 to take your car on board. ⊠ *Marine Ave., Newport Beach* ☎ *949/719–6100* ⊕ *www. visitnewportbeach.com.*

Balboa Peninsula
BEACH | FAMILY | Newport's best beaches are on a 3-mile stretch called Balboa Peninsula. The picturesque Newport Harbor is on one side, and sandy, broad beaches on the other. The most intense spot for bodysurfing in Orange County, and arguably on the West Coast, known as the Wedge, is at the south end of the peninsula. It was created by accident in the 1930s when the Federal Works Progress Administration built a jetty to protect Newport Harbor. ⚠ **Rip currents and punishing waves mean it's strictly for the pros—but it sure is fun to watch an experienced local ride it.** ⊠ *Newport Beach* ⊕ *www.visitnewportbeach.com/ beaches-and-parks/the-wedge.*

Newport Beach Pier
BEACH | FAMILY | Jutting out into the ocean near 21st Street, Newport Pier is a popular fishing spot. Below is 5 miles of sandy beach for sunbathing, surfing, and walking along the beach. Street parking is difficult, so grab the first space you find and be prepared to walk. Early on Wednesday–Sunday morning you're likely to encounter dory fishermen hawking their predawn catches, as they've done for generations. On weekends the area is alive with kids of all ages on in-line skates, skateboards, and bikes dodging

Newport Beach is another popular place in the O.C. to catch waves.

pedestrians and whizzing past fast-food joints and classic dive bars. Skate, bike, and surfboard rental shops are nearby. ✉ *70 Newport Pier, Newport Beach* ☎ *949/644–3309* ⊕ *www.visitnewport-beach.com.*

★ **Newport Harbor**
BODY OF WATER | **FAMILY** | Sheltering nearly 9,000 small boats, Newport Harbor may seduce even those who don't own a yacht. Spend an afternoon exploring the charming shops and restaurants along the boat slips. California's shortest auto ferry takes visitors across to Balboa Island, which is popular with pedestrians, joggers, and bicyclists. Several grassy areas on the primarily residential Lido Isle have views of the water. To truly experience the harbor, rent a kayak or an electric Duffy boat for a pleasant picnic cruise or try stand-up paddleboarding to explore the sheltered waters. ✉ *Pacific Coast Hwy., Newport Beach* ⊕ *www. balboaislandferry.com.*

Orange County Museum of Art
ART MUSEUM | **FAMILY** | Founded by 13 visionary women in 1962 and one of the earliest contemporary art museums in California, the OCMA opened in late 2022 in its new $94 million home at the Segerstrom Center for the Arts in Costa Mesa. Designed by Pritzker Prize–winning architect Thom Mayne, OCMA's striking 53,000-square-foot building has 25,000 square feet of free-flowing gallery space to house its extensive collection of over 4,500 works produced in the 20th and 21st centuries by artists with ties to California. Outside, a grand staircase provides amphitheater seating and serves as a community gathering point, inspired by the steps at the Metropolitan Museum of Art in New York. There is a bar, café, and sculpture terrace on Level 2. Programs include Art + Play for little ones and Art Happy Hour & Pop-Up Talks for adults. ✉ *3333 Ave. of the Arts, Costa Mesa* ☎ *71471/714/780–2130* ⊕ *www.ocma.art* 🎟 *Free* ☉ *Closed Mon.*

Sculpture Exhibition in Civic Center Park
PUBLIC ART | **FAMILY** | This outdoor "museum without walls" is a favorite walking spot for locals and visitors. Located in the Newport Beach Civic Center, there is a car-free walking path displaying meaningful and whimsical public art sculptures. Take a self-guided walking tour by downloading the MyNB app in advance of your visit. ✉ *1000 Avocado Ave., Newport Beach* ☎ *949/717–3802* 🌐 *www.newportbeachca.gov.*

🍴 Restaurants

Basilic Restaurant
$$$$ | **BRASSERIE** | This intimate French–Swiss bistro adds a touch of old-world elegance to Balboa Island with its white linen and flower-topped tables. Chef Bernard Althaus grows the herbs used in his classic French dishes. **Known for:** French classics; fine wine; old-school ambience. [$] *Average main: $50* ✉ *217 Marine Ave., Balboa Island* ☎ *949/673–0570* 🌐 *www.basilicrestaurant.com* 🕒 *Closed Sun. and Mon.*

★ **Bear Flag Fish Co.**
$ | **SEAFOOD** | **FAMILY** | Expect long lines in summer at this indoor–outdoor dining spot serving up the freshest local fish (swordfish, sea bass, halibut, and tuna) and a wide range of creative seafood dishes (the Hawaiian-style poke salad with ahi tuna is a local favorite). Order at the counter, which doubles as a seafood market, and sit inside or outside on a grand patio. **Known for:** fresh catches thanks to restaurant fishing boat; fish tacos with homemade hot sauce; craft beers. [$] *Average main: $15* ✉ *Newport Peninsula, 3421 Via Lido, Newport Beach* ☎ *949/673–3474* 🌐 *www.bearflagfishco.com.*

Bluewater Grill
$$$ | **SEAFOOD** | **FAMILY** | On the site of an old sportfishing dock, this popular spot offers a variety of seasonal seafood, shellfish, meat, and poultry. There's a tranquil bay view from either the dining room, which is adorned with early-1900s fishing photos, or the waterfront patio. **Known for:** boat and harbor views; happy hour specials; daily-changing menu of fresh fish. [$] *Average main: $35* ✉ *Lido Peninsula, 630 Lido Park Dr., Newport Beach* ☎ *949/675–3474* 🌐 *www.bluewatergrill.com.*

The Cannery
$$$ | **SEAFOOD** | This 1920s cannery building still teems with fish, but now they go into dishes on the eclectic seafood menu rather than being packed into crates. Many diners arrive by boat, as there's a convenient dock at the front entrance. **Known for:** waterfront views; seafood specialties; craft cocktails. [$] *Average main: $40* ✉ *3010 Lafayette Rd., Newport Beach* ☎ *949/566–0060* 🌐 *www.cannerynewport.com.*

Gulfstream
$$$ | **SEAFOOD** | **FAMILY** | Established in 1999, this trendy restaurant has an open kitchen, comfortable booths, and outdoor seating. The patio is a fantastic place to hang out to enjoy a shrimp cocktail and glass of wine. **Known for:** oysters on the half shell; local hangout; outdoor patio. [$] *Average main: $40* ✉ *850 Avocado Ave., Newport Beach* ☎ *949/718–0188* 🌐 *www.gulfstreamrestaurant.com.*

Sugar 'N Spice
$ | **ICE CREAM** | **FAMILY** | Stop by ice cream parlor Sugar 'N Spice for a Balboa Bar—a slab of vanilla ice cream dipped first in chocolate and then in a topping of your choice such as hard candy, chopped nuts, or Oreo crumbs. Other parlors serve the concoction, but Sugar 'N Spice claims to have invented it back in 1945. **Known for:** inventor of the Balboa Bar; frozen banana; local institution. [$] *Average main: $6* ✉ *310 Marine Ave., Balboa Island* ☎ *949/673–8907.*

Hotels

Balboa Bay Resort
$$$$ | RESORT | FAMILY | Once a private club that was a luxury hangout for Humphrey Bogart, Lauren Bacall, and Ronald Reagan, this esteemed waterfront resort now offers contemporary coastal elegance and one of the best harbor bay views, especially from the spacious bay-view guest rooms. **Pros:** exquisite bayfront views; comfortable beds; local-favorite restaurant. **Cons:** swimming pool in the middle of the resort has no views; $35 nightly hospitality fee; some rooms don't face the bay. [$] *Rooms from: $550* ✉ *1221 W. Coast Hwy., Newport Beach* ☎ *949/645–5000* 🌐 *www.balboabayresort.com* 🛏 *160 rooms* 🍴 *No Meals.*

Hyatt Regency Newport Beach
$$$ | RESORT | FAMILY | The best aspect of this beloved resort-style Newport hotel is its lushly landscaped acres: 26 of them, all overlooking the Back Bay. The casually elegant architecture, spread over the generous grounds, will appeal to travelers weary of high-rise hotels. **Pros:** good amenities and activities; centrally located for shopping; pet-friendly hotel. **Cons:** $36 self-parking is far from main property; 10-minute drive to beach; $40 daily resort fee. [$] *Rooms from: $379* ✉ *1107 Jamboree Rd., Newport Beach* ☎ *949/729–1234* 🌐 *www.hyatt.com* 🛏 *410 rooms* 🍴 *No Meals.*

★ **Lido House, Autograph Collection**
$$$$ | RESORT | FAMILY | This Marriott Autograph Collection resort is located at the gateway of the exclusive Lido Island and three blocks from the beach. **Pros:** large hot tub and pool deck; lively hotel pub-style bar; free bikes to cruise the nearby boardwalk. **Cons:** no beach or water view; $35 resort fee; $49 valet parking. [$] *Rooms from: $500* ✉ *3300 Newport Blvd., Balboa Island* ☎ *949/524–8500* 🌐 *www.lidohousehotel.com* 🛏 *130 rooms, 5 cottages* 🍴 *No Meals.*

Newport Beach Hotel
$$$ | B&B/INN | FAMILY | This charming historic home turned into a boutique hotel offers direct views of the Pacific Ocean and Catalina Island and is the closest lodging to the beach and Newport Beach pier. **Pros:** beach and ocean-view guest rooms; in a lively area near restaurants; steps to the pier and beach. **Cons:** some rooms are small; not all rooms have views; parking is $30 a day. [$] *Rooms from: $450* ✉ *2306 W. Oceanfront, Newport Beach* ☎ *949/673–7030* 🌐 *www.thenewportbeachhotel.com* 🛏 *20 rooms* 🍴 *Free Breakfast.*

★ **VEA Newport Beach Marriott Hotel and Spa**
$$$$ | RESORT | FAMILY | This centrally located, newly renovated property is across the street from the popular Fashion Island shopping-and-dining complex. **Pros:** spectacular views; gorgeous swimming pool, deck, and lounge; central location across from Fashion Island. **Cons:** sprawling floor plan; walk by conference rooms to get to Sky Suites; valet parking $55 a day. [$] *Rooms from: $500* ✉ *900 Newport Center Dr., Newport Beach* ☎ *949/640–4000* 🌐 *www.marriott.com* 🛏 *400 rooms* 🍴 *No Meals.*

Shopping

★ **Fashion Island**
STORE/MALL | The ritzy Fashion Island outdoor mall is designed with a cluster of archways and courtyards complete with koi pond, fountains, and a mix of high-end shopping and chain stores. Multiple dining venues include Fleming's Steak House, True Food Kitchen, and Sushi Roku. Well-known department store anchors include Macy's, Neiman Marcus, Nordstrom, and Bloomingdale's, plus boutiques like St. John, Brandy Melville, and See's Candies. ✉ *401 Newport Center Dr., between Jamboree and MacArthur Blvds., off PCH, Newport Beach* ☎ *949/721–2000* 🌐 *www.fashionisland.com* 🎟 *free.*

A whimbrel hunts for mussels at Crystal Cove State Park.

 Activities

BOAT RENTALS

★ Boat Rentals of America

BOATING | FAMILY | Pack a picnic with food and drinks to enjoy while touring the waterways surrounding Lido and Balboa Islands on either a power motorboat ($175 for two hours for up to six people), or an electric Duffy boat ($220 for two hours for up to eight people). ✉ *510 E. Edgewater Ave., Balboa Island* ☎ *949/673–7200* ⊕ *www.boats4rent. com.*

BOAT TOURS

Catalina Flyer

BOATING | FAMILY | The *Catalina Flyer,* the largest passenger-carrying catamaran on the West Coast, operates a 75-minute round-trip catamaran ferry passage daily to Catalina Island for $78. Reservations are required; check the schedule for times, as crossings may be rescheduled due to weather or annual maintenance. All-day parking is up to $30 a day in a nearby Newport Beach lot. Payment is made at self-serve pay stations. ✉ *400 Main St., Balboa Island* ☎ *949/673–5245* ⊕ *www.catalinainfo.com.*

★ City Experiences Cruises and Events

ENTERTAINMENT CRUISE | FAMILY | This operator books two-hour harbor cruises, Sunday brunch cruises, and weekend dinner cruises with dancing. The trips traverse the scenic waters of Newport Harbor with barking seals, million-dollar yachts, and water-view homes and restaurants. ✉ *2431 W. Coast Hwy., Newport Beach* ☎ *949/650–2412* ⊕ *www.cityexperiences.com.*

FISHING

Davey's Locker

FISHING | FAMILY | In addition to a complete tackle shop, Davey's Locker offers two-hour whale-watching cruises starting at $34, and half-day deep-sea fishing trips starting at $65. They also offer Duffy electric boats and skiff rentals. ✉ *Balboa Pavilion, 400 Main St., Balboa Island* ☎ *949/673–1434* ⊕ *www.daveyslocker. com.*

GOLF

Newport Beach Golf Course

GOLF | FAMILY | This 18-hole executive Newport Beach Golf Course is a walking course starting at $26 on Monday–Thursday, and $29 on Friday–Sunday and holidays. A pull cart is $5, and an electric cart is $24. They do offer a discount to junior and senior golfers. Reservations are accepted up to one week in advance, but walk-ins are accommodated when possible. Note: The front 9 holes are shorter and the back 9 holes are more challenging. ⊠ *3100 Irvine Ave., Newport Beach* ☎ *949/474–4424* ⊕ *www.new-portbeachgolfcoursellc.com* ⌚ *From $18* ⚑ *18 holes, 3180 yards, par 59.*

Corona del Mar

Coronal del Mar is often referred to as a small jewel on the Pacific Coast, but its name translated from Spanish is actually "The Crown of the Sea," which is fitting considering the area includes some of Orange County's most expensive residential areas surrounding a trendy seaside village. Corona del Mar is 2 miles south of Newport Beach and known for its exceptional beaches. One of the best sunset view spots is Little Corona Beach with its rocky cliffs and coastal vegetation.

◉ Sights

★ Corona del Mar State Beach

BEACH | FAMILY | This half-mile beach is actually made up of two beaches, Little Corona and Big Corona, separated by a cliff and rocky jetty. Both have soft, golden-hue sand to set up chairs and towels for the day. You can find a parking spot on the street on weekdays. **Amenities:** lifeguards; parking; showers; toilets. **Best for:** snorkeling; sunset; swimming. ⊠ *3100 Ocean Blvd., Corona del Mar* ☎ *949/718–1859* ⊕ *www.parks.ca.gov* ⌚ *Free.*

★ Crystal Cove State Park

BEACH | FAMILY | Midway between Corona del Mar and Laguna Beach is Crystal Cove State Park, a favorite of local beachgoers and wilderness trekkers. It encompasses a 3.2-mile stretch of unspoiled beach and has some of the best tide-pooling in Southern California. Here you can see starfish, crabs, and sea anemones near the rocks. The park's 2,400 acres of backcountry are ideal for hiking and mountain biking, but stay on the trails to preserve the beauty. The Moro Campground offers campsites with picnic tables, including spots designated for RVs and trailers. ⊠ *8471 N. Coast Hwy., Laguna Beach* ☎ *949/494–3539* ⊕ *www.parks.ca.gov/crystalcove* ⌚ *$15 parking.*

The Park Store at Crystal Cove Cottages

STORE/MALL | Located in Crystal Cove's Historic District, The Park Store carries fine art works by local plein air artists, as well as sea glass and ocean-themed jewelry, children's toys, snacks, and beach toys and apparel. ⊠ *State Park Historic District, Newport Coast* ☎ *949/376–6200* ⊕ *www.crystalcove.org/visit/things-to-do/store-gallery.*

Roger's Gardens

GARDEN | FAMILY | One of the largest retail gardens in Southern California, Roger's showcases some of the best garden ideas and holiday decorations during Easter, Halloween, and Christmas. The on-site Farmhouse at Roger's Gardens restaurant is popular with visitors and locals during lunchtime and dinner. The chefs prepare locally sourced menu items to enjoy while overlooking the bucolic gardens. ⊠ *2301 San Joaquin Hills Rd., Corona del Mar* ☎ *949/640–5800* ⊕ *www.rogersgardens.com* ⌚ *Free.*

Sherman Library and Gardens

GARDEN | FAMILY | This 2½-acre botanical garden and library specializes in the history of the Pacific Southwest. You can wander among cactus gardens, rose gardens, a cool fern garden, and a tropical conservatory. There's a good garden gift shop, and a restaurant named 698 Dahlia that serves lunch on Wednesday through Sunday from 11 am to 2 pm. ✉ *2647 E. Pacific Coast Hwy., Corona del Mar* ☎ *949/673–2261* 🌐 *www.thesherman.org* 🎟 *$5.*

🍴 Restaurants

The Beachcomber Cafe at Crystal Cove
$$ | **SEAFOOD** | Beach culture flourishes in this Crystal Cove Historic District's restaurant, thanks to its umbrella-laden deck just a few steps above the white sand. This is where you can sip a really good mai tai at the Bootlegger Bar, while waiting for your chance to sample ahi tacos, Maine lobster pasta, or blue crab–stuffed salmon. **Known for:** beachside cocktails; fresh seafood; big crowds and long waits. [$] *Average main: $30* ✉ *15 Crystal Cove, Corona del Mar* ☎ *949/376–6900* 🌐 *www.thebeachcombercafe.com.*

Shake Shack at Crystal Cove
$ | **DINER** | **FAMILY** | This Southern California landmark sitting on a bluff off the PCH is the perfect spot to get a quick breakfast burrito or pancake combo. During lunch and dinner they make tasty Cove burgers served with a side of French fries or coleslaw, fish-and-chips, and a seared ahi sandwich. **Known for:** over 30 different shake flavors; incredible ocean views; small parking lot with 30-minute limit. [$] *Average main: $15* ✉ *7703 E. Coast Hwy., Newport Coast* ☎ *949/464–0100* 🌐 *www.crystalcoveshakeshack.com.*

🛏 Hotels

Crystal Cove Historic District Cottages
$ | **HOUSE** | The Crystal Cove Historic District is home to a collection of unique and historic cottages decorated and furnished to reflect the 1935 to 1955 beach culture that flourished here. **Pros:** great views and location; beachfront; affordable for this location. **Cons:** not all cottages offer the same decor and outdoor space; in demand so reservations require advance planning; some cottages are dorm-style. [$] *Rooms from: $94* ✉ *35 Crystal Cove, Corona del Mar* ☎ *800/444–7275 reservations* 🌐 *www.reservecalifornia.com* 🛏 *24 cottages* 🍽 *No Meals.*

★ The Resort at Pelican Hill
$$$$ | **RESORT** | **FAMILY** | Built on a protected coastal enclave across the PCH and Crystal Cove State Park, this upscale Italian Renaissance–style resort is one of the most spectacular resorts in Orange County and features a dramatic domed rotunda and Tuscan columns and pilasters in the lobby. **Pros:** ocean-view paradise for golfers; spectacular swimming pool (the largest of its kind in the world); great spa and dining options. **Cons:** one of the most expensive resorts in Orange County; swimming pool can get very crowded during the holidays; pricey resort fee. [$] *Rooms from: $1000* ✉ *22701 Pelican Hill Rd. S, Newport Coast* ☎ *833/260–8926* 🌐 *www.pelicanhill.com* 🛏 *204 rooms, 128 villas* 🍽 *No Meals.*

🛍 Shopping

Crystal Cove Promenade
STORE/MALL | **FAMILY** | This Mediterranean-inspired upscale strip mall is across the street from Crystal Cove State Park, with the shimmering Pacific Ocean in plain view. Crystal Cove Promenade offers a mix of well-known storefronts such as Williams Sonoma and Trader Joe's, plus unique boutiques, and popular restaurants that include Javier's, Mastro's Ocean Club, and Bear Flag Fish Co. ✉ *7845–8085 E. Coast Hwy., Newport Beach* 🌐 *www.shopirvinecompany.com.*

Laguna Beach

10 miles south of Newport Beach on PCH, 60 miles south of Los Angeles, I–5 south to Hwy. 133, which turns into Laguna Canyon Rd.

Looking for shells on Laguna Beach, one of the nicest stretches of sand in Southern California.

Driving in along Laguna Canyon Road from the Interstate 405 freeway gives you the chance to cruise through one of the most gorgeous coastal communities with 30 unique coves and beaches to explore and some of the clearest water in Southern California. During the summer, there's a convenient and free trolley service that cruises from North Laguna to Main Beach and all the way to the picturesque Ritz Carlton Laguna Niguel.

Laguna's welcome mat is legendary. On the corner of Forest and Park Avenues is a gate proclaiming, "This gate hangs well and hinders none, refresh and rest, then travel on." Art galleries dot the village streets, and there's usually someone daubing en plein air on the bluff in Heisler Park. Along the Pacific Coast Highway you'll find dozens of clothing boutiques, jewelry stores, cafés, and seafood restaurants.

ESSENTIALS
VISITOR INFORMATION Visit Laguna Beach Visitors Center. ✉ *381 Forest Ave., Laguna Beach* ☎ *949/497–9229,* *800/877–1115* ⊕ *www.visitlagunabeach. com.*

 Sights

Festival of Arts and Pageant of the Masters
ARTS CENTER | An outdoor amphitheater near the mouth of the canyon hosts the annual Pageant of the Masters, Laguna's signature art event. Local participants arrange tableaux vivants, in which live models and carefully orchestrated backgrounds merge in striking mimicry of classical and contemporary paintings. The pageant is part of the Festival of Arts, held in July and August; tickets are in high demand, so plan ahead. ✉ *650 Laguna Canyon Rd., Laguna Beach* ☎ *800/489–3378* ⊕ *www.foapom.com* 🎟 *Tickets: $40–$110.*

Heisler Park
BEACH | FAMILY | One of the most picturesque parks in Laguna Beach, Heisler Park offers plenty of fun and relaxation. There is a picnic beach with tables overlooking palm trees and panoramic

ocean views. Take the stairs down to Diver's Cove for snorkeling, scuba diving, and tide-pool exploring. Take the paved walking path along the cliff all the way to Laguna's Main Beach. There are public restrooms and outdoor showers. This is also a popular area for plein air artists to set up an easel and chair and paint for hours. ✉ *400 Cliff Dr., Laguna Beach* 🌐 *www.visitlagunabeach.com* 🎫 *Free.*

Laguna Art Museum

ART MUSEUM | This museum displays work by California artists from all time periods, representing scenery in Laguna, and life and history of the Golden State in general. Special exhibits change quarterly. ✉ *307 Cliff Dr., Laguna Beach* ☎ *949/494–8971* 🌐 *www.lagunaartmuseum.org* 🎫 *$12* 🕒 *Closed Mon.*

Laguna Coast Wilderness Park

HIKING & WALKING | **FAMILY** | With easy, moderate, and difficult trails spread over 7,000 acres of canyon to coastal territory, Laguna Coast Wilderness Park is a hiker's paradise. The 40 miles of trails offer expansive views and are also popular with mountain bikers. Trails open daily at 7 am and stay open until sunset, weather permitting. No dogs are allowed in the park. ✉ *18751 Laguna Canyon Rd., Laguna Beach* ☎ *949/923–2235* 🌐 *www.ocparks.com/parks/lagunac* 🎫 *$3 parking.*

Beaches

★ Main Beach Park

BEACH | **FAMILY** | Centrally located in the main town of Laguna Beach near multiple dining venues, art galleries, and shops, Main Beach Park has a fitting name. Walk along this soft-sand beach to Bird Rock and explore nearby tide pools or just sit on one of the benches and watch people bodysurfing, play beach volleyball, or scramble around two half-basketball courts. The beach also has a children's play area with climbing equipment. Most of Laguna's hotels are within a short (but hilly) walk. **Amenities:** lifeguards; toilets; showers. **Best for:** sunrise, sunset; swimming. ✉ *Broadway at S. Coast Hwy., Laguna Beach* 🌐 *www.visitlagunabeach.com.*

1,000 Steps Beach

BEACH | **FAMILY** | Off South Coast Highway at 9th Street, 1,000 Steps Beach isn't too hard to find and actually only has 217 steps. It's one of the many coves in Laguna Beach offering a long stretch of soft sand, waves, and dramatic rock formations. Sea caves and tide pools enhance the already beautiful natural spot. Walking back up to your car, you will feel like you got a good workout. **Amenities:** showers. **Best for:** snorkeling; surfing; swimming. ✉ *S. Coast Hwy., at 9th St., Laguna Beach* 🌐 *www.visitlagunabeach.com.*

Wood's Cove

BEACH | **FAMILY** | Off South Coast Highway, Wood's Cove is especially quiet during the week. Big rock formations hide lurking crabs. This is a prime scuba-diving spot, and at high tide much of the beach is underwater. Climbing the steps to leave, you can see a Tudor-style mansion that was once home to Bette Davis. Street parking is free yet limited. **Amenities:** none. **Best for:** snorkeling; scuba diving; sunset. ✉ *Diamond St. and Ocean Way, Laguna Beach* 🌐 *www.visitlagunabeach.com.*

Restaurants

The Cliff

$$$ | **SEAFOOD** | **FAMILY** | Walk through the quaint Laguna Beach artist village to get to the Cliff and its 180-degree views of Main Beach and the Pacific coastline. The multilevel dining patios serve hearty breakfasts and coastal seafood favorites for lunch and dinner. **Known for:** some of Laguna Beach's best ocean-view dining; reservations necessary; splurge-worthy seafood towers. [$] *Average main: $40* ✉ *577 S. Coast Hwy., Laguna Beach*

☎ *949/494–1956* 🌐 *www.thecliffrestaurant.com.*

Gelato Paradiso
$ | **EUROPEAN** | **FAMILY** | Each morning this gelato shop makes fresh small batches of artisanal gelatos and dairy-free sorbettos in a variety of appealing flavors. Located in back of the charming Peppertree Lane shopping center, there is a small outdoor patio where people gather to enjoy the authentic Italian gelato after a day at the beach or to cap off an evening. **Known for:** authentic Italian gelato; fruit flavors; patio gathering spot. [$] *Average main: $6* ✉ *Peppertree La., 448 S. Coast Hwy., Laguna Beach* ☎ *949/464–9255* 🌐 *www.gelatoparadiso.com.*

★ **Las Brisas**
$$$$ | **MEXICAN FUSION** | **FAMILY** | Located in what used to be the Victor Hugo Inn, Las Brisas is now a Laguna Beach landmark restaurant. Sit on the expansive patio to take in the spectacular coastline views while enjoying signature margaritas and coastal Mexican cuisine with a California twist. **Known for:** fresh seafood; panoramic coastal views; reservations a must. [$] *Average main: $45* ✉ *361 Cliff Dr., Laguna Beach* ☎ *949/497–5434* 🌐 *www.lasbrisaslagunabeach.com.*

The Rooftop Lounge
$$$ | **INTERNATIONAL** | Another popular sunset view venue in South Laguna, The Rooftop Lounge at the top of Casa del Camino top floor is a hot seat for sunset cocktails, so plan ahead. Snag a table to enjoy a variety of different flavor mojitos or a pomegranate martini along with a cheese board, spicy fish-and-chips, or a veggie sandwich. **Known for:** spectacular sunset views; craft cocktails; burgers, pasta, salads, and sandwiches. [$] *Average main: $40* ✉ *1289 S. Coast Hwy., Laguna Beach* ☎ *949/497–2446* 🌐 *www.rooftoplagunabeach.com.*

Sapphire and The Pantry
$$ | **INTERNATIONAL** | **FAMILY** | This Laguna Beach establishment set in a historic Craftsman-style building is part gourmet pantry (a must-stop for your every picnic need) and part global dining adventure. Enjoy comfort cuisine from around the world paired with an eclectic wine and beer list. **Known for:** sapphire salad; weekend brunch; pet-friendly patio. [$] *Average main: $30* ✉ *The Old Pottery Place, 1200 S. Coast Hwy., Laguna Beach* ☎ *949/715–9888* 🌐 *www.sapphirelagunabeach.com.*

★ **Selanne Steak Tavern**
$$$$ | **STEAKHOUSE** | Located inside a historic 1934 home along Pacific Coast Highway, and named after one of the owners—Hockey Hall of Famer and six-time Olympian Teemu Selanne—Selanne Steak Tavern serves modern steak-house fare paired with stellar Napa Valley wines. There is a cozy Carrara-topped tavern-style bar where bartenders make artisanal cocktails and martinis, and a formal fine-dining experience upstairs. **Known for:** Monkey Bread dessert; variety of dining settings; prime cuts of meat. [$] *Average main: $70* ✉ *1464 S. Coast Hwy, Laguna Beach* 🌐 *www.selannesteaktavern.com.*

The Stand Natural Foods
$ | **VEGETARIAN** | **FAMILY** | Since 1975, this old-school, artsy eatery in Laguna provides healthy, organic vegan salads, bowls, burritos, tamales, veggie burgers, pita pocket sandwiches, fresh fruit soft serve, and smoothies. **Known for:** nut-milk shakes; 100% plant-based vegan food; brown rice burritos. [$] *Average main: $15* ✉ *238 Thalia St., Laguna Beach* ☎ *949/494–8101* 🌐 *www.thestandnaturalfoods.com.*

Taco Loco
$ | **MEXICAN** | **FAMILY** | This may look like a fast-food taco stand with salads, quesadillas, and nachos on the menu, but the quality of the food here equals that in many higher-price restaurants. Some Mexican standards get a seafood twist, like swordfish, calamari, and shrimp tacos. **Known for:** vegetarian and vegan tacos; sidewalk seating; surfer clientele.

§ *Average main: $16* ⊠ *640 S. Coast Hwy., Laguna Beach* ☎ *949/497–1635* ⊕ *www.lagunabeachmexicanfood.com.*

Urth Caffe

$$ | BAKERY | FAMILY | A local favorite in the morning and throughout the day for organic heirloom coffee and hand-blended fine organic teas, Urth also serves health-conscious food as well as pastries outside on the charming garden patio looking out at the Laguna Art Museum across the street. For lunch and dinner, they offer a variety of salads, soups, bowls, pizzas, and signature sandwiches. **Known for:** health-conscious cuisine; organic coffee and tea; long lines on the patio during peak hours and weekends. § *Average main: $20* ⊠ *308 N. Pacific Coast Hwy., Laguna Beach* ☎ *949/376–8888* ⊕ *www.urthcaffe.com.*

Zinc Café and Market

$$ | AMERICAN | FAMILY | It's always brunch time at his small Laguna Beach institution where—from 7 am to 4 pm—you will find reasonably priced breakfast-to-lunch (okay, brunch) items that include everything from signature quiches, poached eggs, and homemade granolas, to healthy salads, homemade soups, quesadillas, and pizza. All the sweets are homemade, including the megasize brownies. **Known for:** gourmet pastries, some gluten-free; coffee bar; busy outdoor patio. § *Average main: $20* ⊠ *350 Ocean Ave., Laguna Beach* ☎ *949/494–6302* ⊕ *www.zinccafe.com.*

 ## Hotels

★ Inn at Laguna Beach

$$$$ | HOTEL | FAMILY | This golden local landmark is stacked neatly on the hillside at the north end of Laguna's Main Beach and it's one of the few hotels in the area set almost on the sand. **Pros:** rooftop with fabulous ocean views; beach essentials provided; beachfront location. **Cons:** ocean-view rooms are pricey; tiny hot tub; nonrefundable $100 pet fee and

daily amenity fee. § *Rooms from: $650* ⊠ *211 N. Coast Hwy., Laguna Beach* ☎ *949/497–9722, 800/544–4479* ⊕ *www.innatlagunabeach.com* ⮑ *70 rooms* ⫟ *No Meals.*

La Casa del Camino

$$$ | HOTEL | The look is Old California at the 1929-built La Casa del Camino, with dark woods, arched doors, wrought iron, and a beautiful tiled fireplace in the recently refreshed lobby. **Pros:** breathtaking views from rooftop lounge; beach lovers will appreciate surf-theme rooms; steps to the beach. **Cons:** some rooms face the highway; no pool; $25 resort fee but it includes parking. § *Rooms from: $400* ⊠ *1289 S. Coast Hwy., Laguna Beach* ☎ *949/497–2446* ⊕ *www.lacasadelcamino.com* ⮑ *36 rooms* ⫟ *Free Breakfast.*

★ Montage Laguna Beach

$$$$ | RESORT | FAMILY | Built on a picturesque coastal bluff above the Pacific Ocean and Treasure Island Beach, this elegant Craftsmen-style resort features 30 acres of grassy lawns, soft sand beaches, and a stunning mosaic tile swimming pool. **Pros:** picturesque coastal location; stunning tiled mosaic swimming pool; residential style villas with sweeping ocean views. **Cons:** one of the area's priciest resorts, especially during holidays or summer weekends; $75 valet parking per night; $65 daily resort fee and $220 nonrefundable pet fee. § *Rooms from: $1100* ⊠ *30801 S. Coast Hwy., Laguna Beach* ☎ *949/715–6000, 866/271–6953* ⊕ *www.montagehotels.com/lagunabeach* ⮑ *258 rooms* ⫟ *No Meals.*

★ The Ranch at Laguna Beach

$$$$ | RESORT | Set in an incredible lush canyon landscape, just a short walk from a stunning stretch of coastline, the Ranch at Laguna Beach offers morning yoga by the heated pool, 9 holes of golf on a verdant course nestled between two canyons, and two-story contemporary beach cottages. **Pros:** incredible setting; immersive activities; sustainable hotel.

Cons: parking $25 a day; no ocean view; $46 daily resort fee. $ *Rooms from: $550* ✉ *31106 S. Coast Hwy, Laguna Beach* ☎ *888/316–0959* ⊕ *www.theranchlb.com* ⬩ *97 rooms* ⦿ *No Meals.*

★ Surf and Sand Resort

$$$$ | RESORT | FAMILY | One mile south of downtown, on an exquisite stretch of beach with sometimes thundering waves, this is a getaway for those who want a boutique hotel experience with surf and sand. **Pros:** easy sandy beach access; intimate boutique resort; good restaurant with wonderful views. **Cons:** pricey valet parking; surf can be loud; no air-conditioning (but overhead fans help). $ *Rooms from: $650* ✉ *1555 S. Coast Hwy., Laguna Beach* ☎ *877/579–8554* ⊕ *www.surfandsandresort.com* ⬩ *167 rooms* ⦿ *No Meals.*

Shopping

Candy Baron

CANDY | FAMILY | Get your sugar fix at the time-warped Candy Baron, filled with old-fashioned goodies like gumdrops, licorice, bull's-eyes, sugar-free candies, and more than 50 flavors of saltwater taffy. ✉ *231 Forest Ave., Laguna Beach* ☎ *877/798–2339* ⊕ *www.thecandybaron. com.*

San Juan Capistrano

5 miles north of Dana Point, 60 miles north of San Diego.

San Juan Capistrano is best known for its historic mission, where the swallows traditionally return each year, migrating from their winter haven in Argentina. The town offers charming antiques stores, fun restaurants, boutique hotels, and lively night venues.

GETTING HERE AND AROUND

If you arrive by train, which is far more romantic and restful than battling freeway traffic, you'll be dropped off across from the mission at the San Juan Capistrano depot. With its appealing brick café and preserved Santa Fe cars, the depot retains much of the magic of early American railroads. If driving, park near Ortega and Camino Capistrano, the city's main streets.

Sights

★ Los Rios Historic District

MUSEUM VILLAGE | FAMILY | Take a walk back in time on the oldest residential street in Southern California, where houses date to the 1790s. The Silvas Adobe is a typical example of the dozen or more one-room adobes in the area. It's located near Mission San Juan Capistrano, the first Californian mission to allow workers to live outside the mission grounds. On the street you'll also find the Historical Society Museum and the ZOOMARS petting zoo for families. Shopping and dining options line this lovely community on the National Register of Historic Places. ✉ *31831 Los Rios St., San Juan Capistrano* ☎ *949/493–8444* ⊕ *www. sanjuancapistrano.net* 🎫 *free.*

★ Mission San Juan Capistrano

HISTORIC SIGHT | FAMILY | Founded in 1776 by Father Junípero Serra (consecrated as St. Serra), Mission San Juan Capistrano was one of two Roman Catholic outposts between Los Angeles and San Diego. The Great Stone Church, begun in 1797, is the largest structure created by the Spanish in California. After extensive retrofitting, the golden-hued interiors are open to visitors who may feel they are touring among ruins in Italy rather than the O.C. Many of the mission's adobe buildings have been restored to illustrate mission life, with exhibits of an olive millstone, tallow ovens, tanning vats, metalworking furnaces, and the padres' living quarters. The beautiful gardens, with their fountains and koi pond, are a lovely spot in which to wander. The bougainvillea-covered Serra Chapel is believed to be the oldest church still standing in California

Mission San Juan Capistrano was founded in 1776.

and is the only building remaining in which St. Serra actually led Mass. Enter via a small gift shop in the gatehouse. *✉ 26801 Ortega Hwy., San Juan Capistrano ☎ 949/234–1300 🌐 www.missionsjc.com 🎟 $18 🕓 Closed Mon. ✍ Advanced online tickets are encouraged.*

🍴 Restaurants

Cedar Creek Inn
$$$ | AMERICAN | FAMILY | Just across the street from Mission San Juan Capistrano, this restaurant has a patio that's perfect for a late lunch or a romantic dinner. The menu is fairly straightforward, with dishes that are tasty and portions that are substantial—try the "Brown Derby" Cobb salad or Cedar Creek burger at lunch, or the prime rib for dinner. **Known for:** view of the historic Mission; coconut cake; comfortable seating and patio. *[$] Average main: $40 ✉ 26860 Ortega Hwy., San Juan Capistrano ☎ 949/240–2229 🌐 www.cedarcreekinn.com.*

L'Hirondelle
$$$ | FRENCH | Locals have romanced at cozy tables for decades at this delightful restaurant directly across from the San Juan Capistrano Mission. Such classic dishes as beef bourguignon and a New York strip in a black-peppercorn-and-brandy sauce are the hallmarks of this French and Belgian restaurant, whose name means "the little swallow." The extensive wine list is matched by an impressive selection of Belgian beers. **Known for:** popular Sunday brunch; traditional French and Belgian cuisine; good Belgian beer selection. *[$] Average main: $39 ✉ 31631 Camino Capistrano, San Juan Capistrano ☎ 949/661–0425 🌐 www.lhirondellesjc.com 🕓 Closed Mon.; brunch only on Sun.*

The Ramos House Cafe
$$$$ | AMERICAN | It may be worth hopping the Amtrak to San Juan Capistrano just for the chance to have breakfast or lunch at one of Orange County's most beloved restaurants, located in a historic board-and-batten home dating back to 1881. This café sits practically on the railroad

tracks across from the depot—nab a table on the patio and dig into a hearty breakfast featuring seasonal items, such as the smoked bacon scramble with wilted rocket and apple fried potatoes. **Known for:** Southern specialties; weekend brunch; historic setting. [$] *Average main: $45* ✉ *31752 Los Rios St., San Juan Capistrano* ☎ *949/443–1342* 🌐 *www.ramoshouse.com* 🕒 *Closed Wed. No dinner.*

Hotels

★ Inn at the Mission San Juan Capistrano

$$$$ | **HOTEL** | **FAMILY** | This family-friendly hacienda-style boutique hotel is located across the street from the famed San Juan Capistrano Mission. **Pros:** great location next to the mission; terrific culinary program; luxury rooms and suites. **Cons:** guests may hear freeway noise; beach is almost 3 miles away; daily amenity fee and expensive parking. [$] *Rooms from: $500* ✉ *26907 Old Mission Rd., San Juan Capistrano* ☎ *949/503–5700* 🌐 *www.marriott.com* 🛏 *135 rooms* 🍴 *No Meals.*

★ The Ritz-Carlton, Laguna Niguel

$$$$ | **RESORT** | **FAMILY** | Located on an oceanfront bluff with an unparalleled view of the Pacific Ocean, and offering the Ritz's signature top-tier service, you are in the lap of luxury at this resort. **Pros:** beautiful grounds and views; excellent dining options; sophisticated service. **Cons:** some rooms are small for the price; in-house dining prices are high; $60 daily resort fee. [$] *Rooms from: $1000* ✉ *1 Ritz-Carlton Dr., Dana Point* ☎ *949/240–2000, 800/542–8680* 🌐 *www.ritzcarlton.com/en/hotels/california/laguna-niguel* 🛏 *396 rooms* 🍴 *No Meals.*

Nightlife

Coach House

LIVE MUSIC | A roomy, premier entertainment venue, Coach House draws music crowds of varying ages for dinner and entertainment. Make a dinner reservation and receive priority seating to listen to the next hip new band, popular cover bands, and legacy musicians. The calendar of shows is online. ✉ *33157 Camino Capistrano, San Juan Capistrano* ☎ *949/496–8930* 🌐 *www.thecoachhouse.com.*

Swallow's Inn

BARS | Across the way from Mission San Juan Capistrano you may spot a line of Harleys in front of the down-home and downright funky Swallow's Inn. Despite a somewhat tough look, it attracts all kinds—bikers, surfers, modern-day cowboys, and grandparents—for a drink, a casual bite, and live entertainment. Happy hour is all day on Monday, and the rest of the week from 4 to 7 pm. ✉ *31786 Camino Capistrano, San Juan Capistrano* ☎ *949/493–3188* 🌐 *www.swallowsinn.com.*

Catalina Island

Just 22 miles across from Orange County and Long Beach, Catalina is a Mediterranean-looking and-feeling island offering unspoiled mountains, canyons, coves, and beaches.

Water sports are a big draw, as divers and snorkelers come for the exceptionally clear water surrounding the island. Kayakers are attracted to the calm cove waters and thrill seekers book the eco-themed zipline that traverses a deep canyon. The beach community of the main town of Avalon is where yachts and pleasure boats bob in the crescent bay. Wander beyond the pedestrian waterfront and find brightly painted little bungalows and million-dollar homes up in the hills. Bicycles and golf carts are the preferred mode of transportation.

In 1919, William Wrigley Jr., the chewing-gum magnate, purchased a controlling interest in the company developing Catalina Island, whose most famous landmark, the Casino, was built in 1929 under his orders. Because he owned the Chicago Cubs baseball team, Wrigley made

Catalina the team's spring training site, an arrangement that lasted until 1951.

In 1975, the Catalina Island Conservancy, a nonprofit foundation, acquired about 88% of the island to help preserve the area's natural flora and fauna, including the bald eagle and the Catalina Island fox. These days the conservancy is restoring the rugged interior country with plantings of native grasses and trees. The organization helps oversee the interior's 50 miles of bike trails and 165 miles of hiking trails and helps protect the island's 60 endemic species. Along the coast you might spot oddities like electric perch, saltwater goldfish, and flying fish.

GETTING HERE AND AROUND
FERRY TRAVEL
Set sail to Catalina Island with four convenient port locations. Two companies offer ferry service to Catalina Island—Catalina Express and Catalina Flyer. These boats have both indoor and outdoor seating and snack bars. There is an extra fee for bicycles and surfboards. The waters around Catalina can occasionally get a little rough, so if you're prone to seasickness, come prepared. During the summer there are more departures. Winter, holiday, and weekend schedules vary, so reservations are strongly recommended.

Catalina Express makes an hour-long run from Long Beach or San Pedro to Avalon and a 90-minute run to Two Harbors. It also has a boat that leaves from Dana Point to Avalon. Round-trip fares begin at $77, with discounts for seniors and kids. On busy days, a $40 upgrade to the Commodore Lounge, when available, is worth it. You also receive a complimentary snack and nonalcohol or alcoholic beverage. Service from Newport Beach to Avalon is available through the *Catalina Flyer*. The boat leaves from Balboa Pavilion at 9 am (in season), takes 75 minutes to reach the island, and costs $78 round-trip. Reservations are required for the

Catalina Flyer and recommended for all weekend and summer trips.

■ TIP→ **Keep an eye out for dolphins, which sometimes swim alongside the ferries.**

FERRY CONTACTS Catalina Express. ✉ *320 Golden Shore, Long Beach* ☎ *562/485–3200* ⊕ *www.catalinaexpress.com.* **Catalina Flyer.** ✉ *Balboa Pier, 400 Main St., Newport Beach* ☎ *949/673–5245* ⊕ *www.catalinainfo.com.*

GOLF CARTS
Golf carts constitute the island's main form of transportation other than walking or biking to sightsee in the area. Some parts of town are off-limits, as is the island's interior. Drivers 25 and over with valid driver's license can rent them along Avalon's Crescent Avenue and Pebbly Beach Road. Four passenger carts are $120 for two hours, with a $60 refundable deposit, payable via cash only. A few six-passenger carts are available on a first-come, first-served basis.

GOLF CART RENTALS Catalina Island Vacation Rentals. ✉ *212 Catalina Ave., Avalon* ☎ *855/631–5280* ⊕ *www.catalinavacations.com.*

TIMING
Although Catalina can be seen in one thrilling day, several inviting hotels make it worth extending your stay for one or more nights. A short itinerary might include breakfast at the hotel before a tour of the interior to see buffalo, or snorkeling at Casino Point. Finish the day at the Descanso Beach Club and take a zipline adventure before a toes-in-the-sand waterfront dinner in Avalon.

After late October, rooms are much easier to find on short notice, rates drop a little, and many hotels offer packages that include transportation from the mainland and/or sightseeing tours. January to March you have a good chance of spotting migrating gray whales on the ferry crossing.

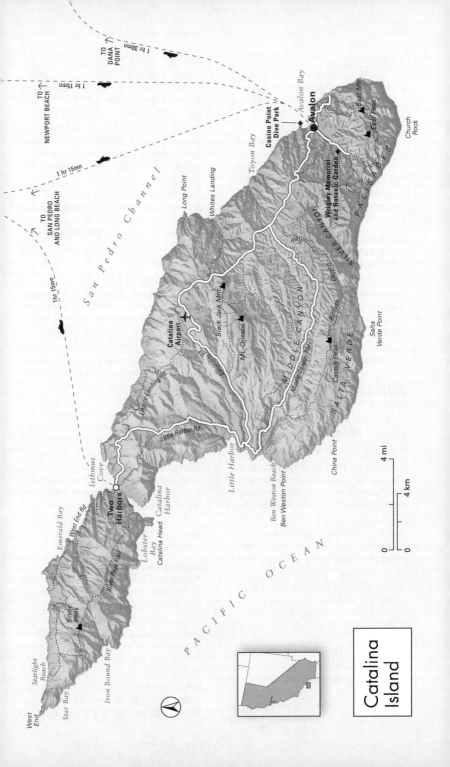

TOURS

Santa Catalina Island Company runs both land tours that include a Bison Expedition and Ridgetop Eco Adventure. Ocean tours include the *Flying Fish* boat trip (summer evenings only) and a glass-bottom boat. The eco-themed zipline tour traverses a scenic canyon; and a fast Cyclone boat tour takes you to the less populated center of the island, Two Harbors. Reservations are highly recommended for all tours. Tours range in cost $18 to $139.

CONTACTS Catalina Adventure Tours. ✉ *302 Pebbly Beach Rd., Avalon* ☎ *562/432–8828* ⊕ *www.catalinaadventuretours.com.* **Catalina Island Conservancy.** ✉ *708 Crescent Ave., Avalon* ☎ *310/510–2595* ⊕ *www.catalinaconservancy.org.* **Santa Catalina Island Company.** ✉ *150 Metropole Ave., Avalon* ☎ *310/510–2000* ⊕ *www.visitcatalinaisland.com.*

Avalon

A ferry ride from Long Beach, San Pedro, Newport Beach, or Dana Point.

Avalon, Catalina's only real town, extends from the shore of its natural harbor to the surrounding hillsides. Its resident population is about 3,800, but it swells with tourists on weekends and during the summer months. Most of the city's activity, however, is centered on the pedestrian mall on Crescent Avenue, and most sights are easily reached on foot. Rental golf carts and bicycles and electric bikes can be rented from shops along Crescent Avenue.

 Sights

★ Casino

NOTABLE BUILDING | Built in 1929, this iconic circular white structure is an architectural masterpiece. The entrance offers Spanish-inspired Catalina tile and painted murals in marine blue, sand, and sea foam green colors. This *casino* was named after the Italian word for "gathering place," not gambling. The circular ballroom with a soaring 50-foot dome ceiling once famously hosted 1940s big bands and is still used for jazz festivals and gala events. The Santa Catalina Island Company leads two different types of guided walking tours of the Casino. On the lower level is the historic Avalon Theatre with over 1,000 seats; first-run movies show here on the weekend. Look up to see one of the most beautiful art deco murals by John Gabriel Beckman. ✉ *1 Casino Way, Avalon* ☎ *310/510–0179* ⊕ *www.visitcatalinaisland.com.*

Casino Point Dive Park

WILDLIFE REFUGE | The crystal clear waters of the Casino Point Dive Park are home to protected marine life. This is where moray eels, bat rays, spiny lobsters, harbor seals, and brilliant orange garibaldi (California's state marine fish) cruise around kelp forests and along the sandy bottom. It's a terrific site for scuba diving, with some shallow areas suitable for snorkeling. Equipment can be rented on-site next to the world-famous Catalina Casino. Water temperature ranges in the low 70s during the summer, with September to mid-October being the warmest. Glass-bottom-boat tours and a submarine tour take guests to the shallow waters of Lover's Cove, across the harbor, another spot filled with marine life. ✉ *1 Casino Way, Avalon* ⊕ *www.divingcatalina.com.*

Catalina Island Museum

PUBLIC ART | **FAMILY** | Inside this local art and history interactive museum, visitors can learn about the island's native Chumash people, Catalina Island's owner and creative developer William Wrigley Jr., his baseball team, his Hollywood celebrity friends and and love for big band music. The exterior of the Catalina Island Museum is a beautiful Spanish Mission style with art deco enhancements. Upstairs the rooftop and gardens are a pretty

event space with native plants and colorful glass art. There is a gift shop worth exploring for Catalina-themed souvenirs and reproductions of the island's signature colorful Catalina pottery tiles. The first Friday of the month they sponsor a "Culture between Cocktails" event from 5 to 7 pm. ✉ *217 Metropole Ave., Avalon* ☎ *310/510–2414* ⊕ *www.catalinamuseum.org* ✉ *$18* ⊘ *Closed Mon.*

Green Pleasure Pier

MARINA/PIER | Head to the Green Pleasure Pier for a good vantage point of Avalon Harbor. On the pier you can find a visitor information office, fish-and-chip snack stands, a bait shop, a tour boat ticket stand and gathering spot, plus rental boat and water sport rentals. ✉ *1 Green Pleasure Pier, Avalon* ⊕ *www.lovecatalina.com.*

Wrigley Memorial and Botanic Garden

GARDEN | FAMILY | Two miles south of the bay is Wrigley Memorial and Botanic Garden, home to many plants native only to Southern California and the Channel Islands. Today there are five different sections where you can see Catalina ironwood, wild tomato, and rare Catalina mahogany. The Wrigley family commissioned the garden as well as the monument, which has a grand staircase and a Spanish-style mausoleum inlaid with colorful Catalina tile. Wrigley Jr. was once buried here but his remains were moved to Glendale, CA, during World War II. You'll find great views at the top. ✉ *Avalon Canyon Rd., Avalon* ☎ *310/510–2897* ⊕ *www.catalinaconservancy.org* ✉ *$12.*

🍴 Restaurants

Bluewater Grill

$$$ | SEAFOOD | FAMILY | Overlooking the entire harbor, this open-to-the-sea-air patio is the preferred spot to dine on freshly caught fish, savory chowders, and all manner of shellfish. Order a swordfish steak, the lobster roll, or the sand dabs if they are on the menu. **Known for:** fresh local fish; handcrafted cocktails;

Catalina's Bison

Zane Grey, the Western writer, spent a lot of time on Catalina, and his influence is still evident in a peculiar way. As the story goes, when the movie version of Grey's book *The Vanishing American* was filmed here in 1924, American bison were ferried across from the mainland to give the land that western plains look. After the crew packed up and left, the buffalo stayed, and a small herd of about 150 still remains. Tours are available for $89.95. ⊕ *www.visit-catalinaisland.com/things-to-do/land-tours/bison-expedition*

overwater harbor views. $ *Average main: $35* ✉ *306 Crescent Ave., Avalon* ☎ *310/510–3474* ⊕ *www.bluewatergrill.com.*

Catalina Coffee & Cookie Company

$ | AMERICAN | FAMILY | There is no Starbucks on the island, so the Catalina Coffee & Cookie Company is very popular in the morning. While you're grabbing your coffees, lattes, and mochas, you may want to kickstart the day with fresh-baked pastries, a hot breakfast burrito, or one of their custom made-to-order bagel sandwiches. **Known for:** dark chocolate pistachio bars; bagel sandwiches; popular breakfast spot. $ *Average main: $10* ✉ *205 Crescent Ave., Avalon* ☎ *310/510–2447* ⊕ *www.catcookieco.com* ☞ *Open daily 6 am to 4 pm.*

★ **Descanso Beach Club**

$$ | AMERICAN | FAMILY | Set on an expansive deck overlooking the water and a few boats, Descanso Beach Club serves a wide range of favorites: grilled burgers, street tacos, clam chowder, salads, and layered nachos, along with the island's

sweet signature cocktail, Buffalo Milk—a mix of fruit liqueurs, vodka, and whipped cream. Firepits and chic beach cabanas add to the scene, as does the sound of happy and terrified screams from the zipliners in the canyon above the beach. **Known for:** tropical beach vibe; scenic views; chic cabana rentals. $ *Average main: $20* ✉ *Descanso Beach, 1 Descanso Ave., Avalon* ☎ *310/510–7410* ⊕ *www.visitcatalinaisland.com.*

★ Eric's on the Pier

$$ | AMERICAN | Grab a stool at this little snack bar on the Green Pleasure Pier for people-watching while drinking a draft beer and munching on a burrito, fish-and-chips, or signature buffalo burger. **Known for:** comfort foods; quick eats; beachside location. $ *Average main: $20* ✉ *4 Green Pier, Avalon* ☎ *310/510–2550* ⊕ *www.lovecatalina.com/listing/erics-on-the-pier/23* ⊗ *No dinner.*

★ The Lobster Trap

$$$ | SEAFOOD | Seafood rules at the popular Lobster Trap, because the restaurant's owner has his own boat and fishes for the catch of the day and, in season, spiny lobster. Ceviche is a great starter, always fresh and brightly flavored. **Known for:** locally caught seafood; convivial atmosphere; local hangout. $ *Average main: $35* ✉ *128 Catalina St., Avalon* ☎ *310/510–8585* ⊕ *catalinalobstertrap.com.*

Steve's Steakhouse and Seafood

$$$ | STEAKHOUSE | FAMILY | A hop, skip, and a jump from the bay, this popular second-floor restaurant keeps regulars happy with sizzling steaks and locally caught swordfish and shrimp. The sultry black-and-blue decor and old-fashioned supper club feel creates a romantic atmosphere set off with stunning harbor views. **Known for:** friendly staff; water views; steak and seafood dinners. $ *Average main: $40* ✉ *417 Crescent Ave., Avalon* ☎ *310/510–0333* ⊕ *www.stevessteakhouse.com.*

Hotels

Aurora Hotel

$$$ | HOTEL | In a town dominated by historic properties, the Aurora is refreshingly contemporary, with a hip attitude and sleek furnishings. **Pros:** comfortable rooms; quiet location off main drag; close to restaurants. **Cons:** standard rooms are small; no elevator; two-night minimum stay required. $ *Rooms from: $350* ✉ *137 Marilla Ave., Avalon* ☎ *310/510–0454* ⊕ *www.auroracatalina.com* ⇌ *18 rooms* ⊚| *Free Breakfast.*

The Avalon Hotel

$$$$ | B&B/INN | This charming boutique hotel one block from the beach, decorated with photos and artifacts of Avalon, has clean and well-maintained rooms and a showstopper rooftop lounge area to luxuriate in Avalon Bay views and breezes. **Pros:** unique and quaint; good location; rooftop lounge overlooking Avalon Bay. **Cons:** rooms are small; some rooms are noisy; no elevator. $ *Rooms from: $500* ✉ *124 Whittley Ave., No. 706, Avalon* ☎ *310/510–7070* ⊕ *www.theavalonhotel.com* ⇌ *15 rooms* ⊚| *Free Breakfast.*

Bellanca Hotel

$$ | HOTEL | One of the closest boutique hotels to the Catalina Casino and the beach, this sea theme hotel also offers a communal rooftop lounge area where guests can enjoy a cup of coffee and take in the 180-degree views of Avalon. **Pros:** romantic setting; close to beach; expansive sundeck with comfortable lounge furniture. **Cons:** ground-floor rooms can hear golf carts drive by; some rooms are on the small side; no elevator. $ *Rooms from: $299* ✉ *111 Crescent Ave., Avalon* ☎ *310/510–0555, 888/510–0555* ⊕ *www.bellancahotel.com* ⇌ *35 rooms* ⊚| *No Meals.*

★ Hotel Atwater

$$$ | HOTEL | FAMILY | Located one block from the beach in the heart of Avalon, Hotel Atwater originally opened in 1920 and was recently redesigned in 2019, to honor Helen Atwater Wrigley (daugher-in-law of famed local William Wrigley). **Pros:** elegant hotel featuring historical decor; central location; nice amenities. **Cons:** some rooms have street noise; $40 daily destination fee; not on the beach. [$] *Rooms from: $400* ✉ *125 Sumner Ave., Avalon* ☎ *877/778–8322, 310/510–1673* 🌐 *www.visitcatalinaisland.com* 🛏 *95 rooms* 🍴 *No Meals.*

Hotel Metropole and Market Place

$$$$ | **HOTEL** | Set over a bustling maze of shops, this boutique hotel offers beach decor in a quaint setting. **Pros:** complimentary breakfast; outdoor-view hot tub and sundeck; convenient location. **Cons:** some rooms on small side; soundproofing issues; no hotel shuttle to dock. [$] *Rooms from: $500* ✉ *205 Crescent Ave., Avalon* ☎ *310/510–1884, 800/541–8528* 🌐 *www.hotel-metropole.com* 🛏 *52 rooms* 🍴 *Free Breakfast.*

Hotel Vista del Mar

$$$ | **HOTEL** | **FAMILY** | On the bay-facing Crescent Avenue, this third-floor property is steps from the beach, so complimentary towels, chairs, and umbrellas await guests as do rooms with balconies, views, and fireplaces. **Pros:** comfortable and luxurious; central location; rooms have fireplaces. **Cons:** no restaurant or spa facilities; few rooms with ocean views; no elevator. [$] *Rooms from: $450* ✉ *417 Crescent Ave., Avalon* ☎ *310/510–1452, 800/601–3836* 🌐 *www.hotel-vistadelmar.com* 🛏 *14 rooms* 🍴 *Free Breakfast.*

★ **Mt. Ada**

$$$$ | **B&B/INN** | A stay in the 1921 mansion that William Wrigley Jr. built, includes breakfast, lunch, beverages, an evening wine and charcuterie plate, gelato, house-made cookies, and snacks—all the comforts of a millionaire's home. **Pros:** timeless charm; all-inclusive services, including complimentary shuttle from ferry dock; incredible canyon, bay, and ocean views. **Cons:** some rooms and bathrooms are small; a far walk into town; pricey for the amenities available. [$] *Rooms from: $600* ✉ *398 Wrigley Rd., Avalon* ☎ *877/778–8322* 🌐 *www.visitcatalinaisland.com* 🛏 *6 rooms* 🍴 *All-Inclusive.*

★ **Pavilion Hotel**

$$$ | **HOTEL** | This mid-century modern hotel is steps from the sand and water. **Pros:** steps to the beach and harbor; lower level rooms have semiprivate patios; shabby-chic decor. **Cons:** no pool; $40 daily destination fee; no elevator. [$] *Rooms from: $450* ✉ *513 Crescent Ave., Avalon* ☎ *877/778–8322, 310/510–1788* 🌐 *www.visitcatalinaisland.com* 🛏 *71 rooms* 🍴 *No Meals.*

Snug Harbor Inn

$$$ | **B&B/INN** | Calm, comfort, and charm await at this adults-only escape where you will find picturesque mountain, harbor, or ocean views from Cape Cod–chic rooms. **Pros:** breakfast brought to your room; wine and hors d'oeuvres each evening; great location. **Cons:** small and reserves quickly; some rooms are quite snug; some rooms showing wear. [$] *Rooms from: $495* ✉ *108 Sumner Ave., Avalon* ☎ *310/510–8400* 🌐 *snugharbor-inn.com* 🛏 *6 rooms* 🍴 *Free Breakfast.*

★ **Zane Grey Pueblo Hotel**

$$$ | **HOTEL** | Best-selling Western novelist Zane Grey built his home as a retreat to take in the views of Avalon while writing over 100 books; his home was turned into this quaint boutique hotel with suites named after Zane Grey book titles. **Pros:** breathtaking views; complimentary continental breakfast; the only ocean-view hotel with a swimming pool. **Cons:** older rooms are dark; a hike up a hill from town; bell tower chimes can be loud for some people. [$] *Rooms from:*

$400 ⌧ 199 Chimes Tower Rd., Avalon ☎ 310/510–0966 ⊕ www.zanegreyhotel. com ⇋ 16 rooms ⦾ Free Breakfast.

Activities

BICYCLING

Brown's Bikes

BIKING | FAMILY | Look for Brown's Bike rentals near the Catalina Express boat pier on Pebbly Beach Road. Beach cruisers start at $30 per day, mountain bikes are $40 per day, and electric bikes are $65 for a day rental, and a good choice to explore Catalina's steep hills. They also rent tandem bikes, strollers, and wheelchairs. ⌧ *107 Pebbly Beach Rd., Avalon* ☎ *310/510–0986* ⊕ *www.catalinabiking. com.*

DIVING AND SNORKELING

Catalina Divers Supply

SCUBA DIVING | Head to Catalina Divers Supply to rent equipment, sign up for guided scuba and snorkel tours, and attend certification classes. It also has an outpost at the Dive Park at Casino Point and one on the Green Pleasure Pier. Both offer gear rental and tank air fills. ⌧ *1 Casino Way, Avalon* ☎ *310/510–0330* ⊕ *www.catalinadiverssupply.com.*

HIKING

The Trailhead

HIKING & WALKING | FAMILY | Permits from the Catalina Island Conservancy are required for hiking into Santa Catalina Island's rugged interior, where there are more than 165 miles of trails of all levels to explore. If you plan to backpack overnight, you'll need a camping reservation. The interior is dry and desertlike; bring plenty of water, sunblock, a hat, and all necessary supplies. The permits are free or you can make a donation to the Conservancy. It's also possible to hike between Avalon and Two Harbors, starting at the Hogsback Gate, above Avalon, but the 28-mile journey has an

elevation gain of 3,000 feet and is not for the weak. A popular hike is the three- to five-day, 38.5 mile Trans-Catalina Trail for which you will need a permit. You don't need a permit for shorter hikes, such as the 20-minute one from Avalon to the Wrigley Botanical Garden. There is a great restaurant, Toyon Grill, up on the second floor overlooking the Green Pleasure Pier, Harbor and Casino. Bluewater Avalon teamed up with the Catalina Island Conservancy to offer a casual, sit-down spot with a full bar. Try the Island's own Rusack Vineyard wines by Wrigley and Geoff Rusack. The vineyards are located at Middle Ranch (Wrigley's family horse ranch) in the island's interior. ■ **TIP→ For a pleasant 4-mile hike out of Avalon, take Avalon Canyon Road to the Wrigley Botanical Garden and follow the trail to Lone Pine. At the top there's an amazing view of the Palisades cliffs and, beyond them, the sea.** ⌧ *708 Crescent Ave., Avalon* ☎ *310/510–2595* ⊕ *www.catalinaconservancy.org.*

PARASAILING

Catalina Parasailing

PARASAILING | FAMILY | Sail up, up, and away in a brightly colored parasail from Catalina Tours, until you are suspended up to 800 feet above the clear blue Pacific Ocean taking in the dolphins and bobbing boats in the harbor blow. Get fitted in a harness and vest for a solo, tandem, or three-at-a-time ride. If floating is not your thing, you can also pay $25 to just ride in the boat and enjoy the view. Sails take about one hour and 15 minutes and depart from Green Pleasure Pier. ⌧ *20 Pleasure Pier, Avalon* ☎ *310/510–9280* ⊕ *islandwatercharters.com* ⌧ *$69.*

Index

Photo Credits

Front Cover: Wirestock/iStockPhoto [Description: A vertical aerial view of the beautiful Echo Park Lake near the downtown Los Angeles skyline]. **Back cover, from left to right:** TierneyMJ/Shutterstock. Boarding1Now/iStockPhoto. Cameron Venti/Shutterstock. **Spine:** JingleBeeZ Photo Gallery/Shutterstock. **Interior, from left to right:** 4nadia/iStockphoto (1). Choness/iStockphoto (2-3). Valeria Reza/iStockphoto (5). **Chapter 1: Experience Los Angeles:** Chones/Shutterstock (6-7). Vern Evans Photo/Courtesy of Walt Disney Concert Hall (8-9). Marco Rubino (9). Visit Santa Monica (9). Hamilton Pytluk/Universal Studios Hollywood (10). Courtesy of Los Angeles County Museum of Art (10). Matt Marriott/Courtesy of Los Angeles Tourism (10). Walter Cicchetti/Shutterstock (10). Lux Blue/Shutterstock (11). Mike Kelley/Courtesy The Broad (11). Gabriele Maltinti/Shutterstock (12). Julia-Bogdanova/ Shutterstock (12). Carl Yu/Sunset Boulevard (12). Courtesy of Los Angeles Tourism (12). Ershov_Maks/iStockphoto (13). Egdigital/iStockphoto (14). Courtesy of Los Angeles Tourism (14). Briana Edwards/Paramount Studios (14). Kevinleestudio7/Dreamstime (14). Olos/shutterstock (15). Courtesy of Griffith Observatory (15). Nicholas Roberts (22). Suzanne Pratt/Shutterstock (23). Jon Bilous/Dreamstime (24). Rosana Scapinello/Dreamstime (24). Kim.jihoon/Shutterstock (24). DavidMSchrader/Dreamstime (24). Lucky-photographer/ Shutterstock (25). F11photo/iStockphoto (26). Don Riddle/Donald Riddle Images (26). Divanov/Shutterstock (26). Lisa Bronitt/Shutterstock (26). Sean Pavone/Shutterstock (27). The Hollywood Roosevelt (28). Nicholas Roberts/LA Restaurant (28). The Grove (28). Pinz Bowling Center (28). Henry Hargreaves (29). Catch Hospitality Group (29). Rob Stark (29). Chateau Mormont (29). Tina Whatcott (30). Courtesy of Cole's French Dip (31). Jill Krueger/The Last Bookstore (32). Mitchblatt/Dreamstime (33). **Chapter 3: Malibu:** Nick Fox/Shutterstock (59). Andy Konieczny/Shutterstock (64). Benny Marty/Shutterstock (66). **Chapter 4: Santa Monica with Pacific Palisades and Brentwood:** Appalachianviews/Dreamstime (69). Ingus Kruklitis/iStockphoto (74). Asterixvs/Dreamstime (81). Mark Roger Bailey/Shutterstock (83). Wolterk/Dreamstime (87). Biker x days/Shutterstock (88). **Chapter 5: Westside,Venice, Marina del Rey, Sawtelle Japantown, and Culver City:** Brunocoelhopt/iStockphoto (91). ViewApart/iStockphoto (96). Engel Ching/Shutterstock (98). Merkuri2/iStockphoto (99). Wolterk/Dreamstime (99). Valeria Reza/iStockphoto (99). Arkantostock/Dreamstime (102). Wolterk/iStockphoto (105). **Chapter 6: Beverly Hills:** Kitleong/Dreamstime (107). Michaelvi/Dreamstime (112). Pastorscott/iStockphoto (114-115). **Chapter 7: West Hollywood, Fairfax, and Mid-Wilshire:** Michael Gordon/Shutterstock (121). Felix Mizioznikov/iStockphoto (128-129). Anne Czichos/Shutterstock (129). Michael Gordon/Shutterstock (129). IK's World Trip/Flickr (130). Stepan Mazurov/Flickr (131). Whaleseye/Shutterstock (131). Hyatt (131). Natalia Macheda/Shutterstock (132). Julian E./Flickr (132). 4kclips/Shutterstock (136). Justin Higuchi (138). ChrisGoldNY/Flickr (142). Steve Cukrov/Shutterstock (145). **Chapter 8: Hollywood:** Sepavo/Dreamstime (147). Chicco7/Dreamstime (154). Gary Bembridge/Flickr (156). Davel5957/iStockphoto (158). **Chapter 9: The Valley, Burbank, Studio City, North Hollywood, and Universal City:** Trekandshoot/Dreamstime (167). TMP - An Instant of Time/Shutterstock (170). David Sprague (177). **Chapter 10: Downtown and Koreatown:** Eddie Hernandez Photography/iStockphoto (179). Biansho/Dreamstime (182). Merkuri2/Dreamstime (187). Lilyling1982/Dreamstime (193). F11photo/Shutterstock (195). Jakob N. Layman/Wexlers Deli (196).Christian Haugen/Flickr (203). Mega Pixel/Shutterstock (203). Tam/Flickr (204). Tannaz/Flickr (204). Elise Thompson/thelosangelesbeat (204). Atomazul/Dreamstime (204). Thomas Hawk/Flickr (205). Melanie Wynne/Flickr (205). Vidalia/Filckr (205). Sardonical/Dreamstime (205). Public Domain (206). Leslie Kalohi/Flickr (206). Scott Beale/Flickr (206). Bengt1955/Flickr (206). Arnold|Inuyaki/Flickr (206). Public Domain (206). Usataro/Dreamstime (207). **Chapter 11: Los Feliz, Silver Lake, and the Eastside:** Yhelfman/Shutterstock (213). Livingpix/iStockphoto (214). Clinton Steeds/Flickr (215). Wolfsavard/Flickr (215). Meinzahn/iStockphoto (219). Arsija/Dreamstime (229). **Chapter 12: Pasadena:** Kit Leong/Shutterstock (239). James Casil/Shutterstock (245). Madonna and Child/Wikimedia Commons (246). Kit Leong/Shutterstock (249). **Chapter 13: The Beaches:** Harun Ozmen/Shutterstock (251). Kirk Wester/Shutterstock (258-259). Rigucci/Shutterstock (262). **Chapter 14: Disneyland and Orange County:** Jon Bilous/Shutterstock (265). Eric Castro/Flickr (277). Ashley Hadzopoulos/Shutterstock (288). KKfotostock/Dreamstime (291). Blickwinkel/Alamy Stock Photo (294). Aleen Simms/Brett Shoaf/Artistic Visuals Photography (297). Alessandro Campagnolo/Shutterstock (302). BackyardProduction/iStockphoto (307). **About Our Writers:** All photos are courtesy of the writers except for the following: Candice Yacono, courtesy of Christopher Cargo.

Every effort has been made to trace the copyright holders, and we apologize in advance for any accidental errors. We would be happy to apply the corrections in the following edition of this publication.

Fodor's LOS ANGELES

Publisher: Stephen Horowitz, *General Manager*

Editorial: Douglas Stallings, *Editorial Director;* Jill Fergus, Amanda Sadlowski, *Senior Editors;* Brian Eschrich, Alexis Kelly, *Editors;* Angelique Kennedy-Chavannes, *Assistant Editor;* Yoojin Shin, *Associate Editor*

Design: Tina Malaney, *Director of Design and Production;* Jessica Gonzalez, *Senior Designer;* Jaimee Sconziano, *Graphic Design Associate*

Production: Jennifer DePrima, *Editorial Production Manager;* Elyse Rozelle, *Senior Production Editor;* Monica White, *Production Editor*

Maps: Rebecca Baer, *Senior Map Editor;* David Lindroth, Mark Stroud (Moon Street Cartography), *Cartographers*

Photography: Viviane Teles, *Senior Photo Editor;* Namrata Aggarwal, Neha Gupta, Payal Gupta, Ashok Kumar, *Photo Editors;* Eddie Aldrete, *Photo Production Intern;* Kadeem McPherson, *Photo Production Associate Intern*

Business and Operations: Chuck Hoover, *Chief Marketing Officer;* Robert Ames, *Group General Manager*

Public Relations and Marketing: Joe Ewaskiw, *Senior Director of Communications and Public Relations*

Fodors.com: Jeremy Tarr, *Editorial Director;* Rachael Levitt, *Managing Editor*

Technology: Jon Atkinson, *Director of Technology;* Rudresh Teotia, *Associate Director of Technology;* Alison Lieu, *Project Manager*

Writers: Paul Feinstein, Michelle Rae Uy, Jill Weinlein, Candice Yacono

Editor: Jacinta O'Halloran

Production Editor: Elyse Rozelle

30th Edition

ISBN 978-1-64097-634-4

ISSN 1095-3914

All details in this book are based on information supplied to us at press time. Always confirm information when it matters, especially if you're making a detour to visit a specific place. Fodor's expressly disclaims any liability, loss, or risk, personal or otherwise, that is incurred as a consequence of the use of any of the contents of this book.

SPECIAL SALES
This book is available at special discounts for bulk purchases for sales promotions or premiums. For more information, e-mail SpecialMarkets@fodors.com.

PRINTED IN CANADA

10 9 8 7 6 5 4 3 2 1

About Our Writers

 Paul Feinstein is an international travel writer based in Los Angeles. He has written countless guides, reviews, and articles in cities around the world, including Bangkok, Barcelona, Florence, Stockholm, the French countryside, and Tokyo. An avid traveler, Paul has been to nearly 60 countries, lived in Israel, and is particularly obsessed with Italy and Japan. This edition, he updated the Experience, Travel Smart, Beverly Hills, West Hollywood, Mid-Wilshire and Koreatown, and Downtown Los Angeles chapters.

 Michelle Rae Uy loves travel, adores photography, and is obsessed with animals. When she isn't off on a new adventure, she is seen at home cuddling with her cats and devouring films, often with a snack or two on hand. Michelle is a travel and tech writer based in Los Angeles. She updated Hollywood and the Studios and Los Feliz and the Eastside chapters this edition.

 Los Angeles-based freelance writer **Jill Weinlein** writes a weekly restaurant news and reviews column in the *Beverly Press and Park LaBrea News*. Her travel reviews are also featured in *JustLuxe* and *Luxe Beat* Travel. In addition, she has a monthly travel column in *Not Born Yesterday* and maintains her own "Dine and Travel" blog. While updating the Disneyland and Orange County chapter, she discovered some new hotels, restaurants, gardens, and outdoor activities that are featured in this book.

 California native **Candice Yacono** is an English and Journalism professor as well as a writer, editor, and designer for clients worldwide. She never learned to ride a bike, so she overcompensates today with cars, trains, and planes. When she's traveling, you can usually find her traipsing through ruins, digging into dusty archives, or volunteering on archaeological digs. Candice updated the Santa Monica, Pacific Palisades, and Brentwood; Malibu; Westside; Pasadena, and the Beaches chapters.